Critical Theory, Politics and Society:
An Introduction

Peter M.R. Stirk

PINTER

London and New York

Pinter
A Cassell Imprint
Wellington House, 125 Strand, London WC2R 0BB
370 Lexington Avenue, New York, NY 10017–6550

First published 2000

British Library Cataloguing in Publication Data
A catalogue record for this book is available from the British Library.

ISBN 1–85567–558–7 (hardback)
    1–85567–559–5 (paperback)

Library of Congress Cataloging-in-Publication Data
Stirk, Peter M. R., 1954–
    Critical theory, politics, and society: an introduction/Peter
M. R. Stirk.
        p.   cm.
    Includes bibliographical references and index.
    ISBN 1–85567–558–7 (hb.). — ISBN 1–85567–559–5 (pb.)
    1. Frankfurt school of sociology.   2. Critical theory.
3. Political sociology.   I. Title.
HM467.S75   1999
301—dc21   99–16470
                                                                              CIP

Typeset by York House Typographic Ltd, London
Printed and bound in Great Britain by Biddles Ltd, Guildford & King's Lynn

This book is dedicated to Sue

Contents

	Acknowledgements and Notes on References	vi
	Biographical Notes	vii
	Introduction	1
1	The Frankfurt School	14
2	A Preliminary Outline of Critical Theory	31
3	The Failure of Metaphysics	46
4	The Critique of Positivism	62
5	The Attractions and Limits of Psychology	76
6	The Analysis of Bourgeois Society	93
7	Paradoxes of Reason	111
8	The Contours of Critical Theory	127
9	The Authoritarian and the Democratic State	142
10	Morality and Interests	159
11	Individual and Collective Identity	175
	Conclusion	188
	Notes	192
	Select Bibliography	232
	Index	243

Acknowledgements and Notes on References

I am grateful to Dr Julia Stapleton for comments on drafts of this book, which have helped to improve the clarity of the argument. I, of course, remain responsible for any remaining opacities.

In the notes, where the date of first publication, or occasionally the date of writing, of works by members of the Frankfurt School differs from the date of publication of the text cited, the former is given in square brackets for the first reference to that item in each chapter. The abbreviations GS for *Gesammelte Schriften* and ZfS for *Zeitschrift für Sozialforshung* have been used throughout.

Biographical Notes

Theodor Wiesengrund-Adorno (1900–69). According to the pioneering historian of the Frankfurt School, Martin Jay, he adopted the name Theodor W. Adorno at the request of Pollock in order to reduce the prominence of Jewish-sounding names at the Institute. Adorno was a philosopher, sociologist and musicologist. He was originally better known in the United States as one of the authors of the influential work *The Authoritarian Personality* (1950). His major works include a strong attack on Heidegger and his followers, *The Jargon of Authenticity* (1964) and a complex text titled *Negative Dialectics* (1966). Contemporary critical theorists critical of Habermas's reformulation of critical theory often turn to Adorno's aesthetics, especially his posthumously published *Aesthetic Theory* (1970). His *Minima Moralia* (1951), which bears the subtitle *Reflections from Damaged Life*, is a revealing and relatively accessible work.

Erich Fromm (1900–80). After his doctorate on *Jewish Law: A Contribution to the Sociology of the Jewish Diaspora* he taught in the Free Jewish School before turning to psychoanalysis in the mid-1920s. He was a member of the Frankfurt Institute of Psychoanalysis, established in 1929, and joined the Institute of Social Research in 1930. Although his contributions to the Institute's journal were central to its interdisciplinary research programme, he left the Institute in 1939 amidst some bitterness. He was a prolific and popular author as well as a practising psychoanalyst and was Professor in Mexico (1950–65). In the post-war period there were several very critical exchanges between Fromm on the one hand and Adorno and Marcuse on the other hand.

Jürgen Habermas (b.1929) published a highly critical review in 1953 of the publication of Heidegger's lectures from 1935. Like Marcuse, he was shocked by Heidegger's lack of remorse about his complicity with the Nazi regime. Habermas was later a research assistant in the Institute for Social Research (1956–9). Horkheimer was highly critical of the radicalness of his early work. His *Habilitationsschrift, The Structural Transformation of the Public Sphere. An Inquiry into a Category of Bourgeois Society* (1962) was supervised by Wolfgang Abendroth at Marburg. He later held chairs at Heidelberg and Frankfurt and was Director of the Max Planck Institute in Starnberg. He has been a prominent public critic in the Federal Republic of Germany as well as producing major theoretical works, including *Knowledge and Human Interests* (1968), *The Theory of Communicative Action* (1981) and *Between Facts and Norms. Contributions to a Discourse Theory of Law and Democracy* (1992).

Max Horkheimer (1895–1973). Director of the Institute of Social Research from 1930, he was responsible for the main methodological essays in the Institute's journal during the 1930s. He was the co-author, with Adorno, of *Dialectic of Enlightenment* (1947), a central reference point for many people (the French postmodernist Michel Foucault said that if he had read it earlier it would have saved him a lot of time). Horkheimer was Rector of Frankfurt University for two years from 1951. His reservations about post-war Germany were evident in posthumously published notes, which reveal, as Habermas put it, a man living on unopened suitcases.

Otto Kirchheimer (1905–65) wrote a doctorate on *Constitutional Theory in Socialism and Bolshevism* under the supervision of Carl Schmitt, though he sought to give some of Schmitt's ideas a radical socialist twist. He moved first to Paris in 1933, and became a research associate of the Institute in the following year, and then to New York in 1938. Initially he worked on *Punishment and Social Structure*, a work begun but left uncompleted by George Rusche. His contributions to the Institute's journal covered the comparative analysis of the party system and, more specifically, the development of the Nazi legal system. Kirchheimer joined the Office of Strategic Services in 1944 and subsequently the State Department, where he remained until 1955. He then returned to academia and moved to Columbia University in 1962, the year after he published *Political Justice*.

Leo Löwenthal (1900–93). Originally a philosopher, he became a sociologist of literature and was proud of having predicted the fascist sympathies of the Norwegian novelist Knut Hamsen. He also worked on right-wing political movements in the United States. He was employed in the American Office of War Information in 1943 and by Voice of America in 1949. He became Professor of Sociology in Berkeley in 1956, without, as he noted, having had an orthodox academic career.

Herbert Marcuse (1898–1979) was a pupil of Heidegger before joining the Institute. He was the author of two major books on Hegel as well as contributing to the Institute's journal. He was employed by the Office of Strategic Services in 1942 and remained in the service of the American government until 1951. He subsequently held various research and academic posts, including Professor of Philosophy at California (1965–70). He was famous for *Eros and Civilization* (1955) – a radical reinterpretation of Freud – and *One Dimensional Man* (1964) – a critique of the consumer society. He was popular with radical students in the 1960s and his support for them led to threats on his life. He was the most utopian of the older generation.

Franz Leopold Neumann (1900–54) was a lawyer who acted for German trade unions before emigrating. He retrained in London, doing a Ph.D. on the rule of law under the supervision of Harold Laski. He was taken on by the Institute initially to work on legal and administrative matters. He was the author of a major study of the Third Reich, *Behemoth*, which is still held in high regard by many historians despite being first published in 1942. He worked in the Office of Strategic Services with Marcuse and then in the State Department from 1942. In 1947 he became Professor at Columbia University, the same university which had offered the Institute refuge in 1934. Neumann died in a car accident in Switzerland.

Friedrich Pollock (1894–1970) was a close friend of Horkheimer. His own theoretical work suffered from the amount of time he devoted to the Institute's affairs and to supporting Horkheimer. Nevertheless he was the author of an early study of the Soviet economy and of articles on the nature of the Nazi economic system, which divided the Institute's members, as well as other works.

Introduction

According to Theodor Adorno 'philosophical terminology gains a decisive significance where firm philosophical schools form'.[1] This is true of the idea of 'critical theory' which is intimately associated with the 'Frankfurt School', one of whose most prominent members was that same Theodor Adorno. As so often, however, the link between terminology and the philosophical school was not straightforward and has been contested in various ways. In the case of critical theory and the Frankfurt School it was the terminology which came first. Critical theory was the philosophical banner raised in two essays published in 1937. The first, 'Traditional and critical theory' was written by Max Horkheimer. The second, 'Philosophy and critical theory' was written by Herbert Marcuse.[2] The source of publication, the *Zeitschrift für Sozialforschung* (*Journal of Social Research*), was important both to the coherence of the school and the later success of the terminology. The *Zeitschrift* was the house journal of the Institute for Social Research, of which Max Horkheimer was Director. The Institute provided financial autonomy for the three men and their colleagues whilst the journal provided a platform from which they could formulate their critical theory. In intent, at least, the coherence of their position was reinforced by strict editorial policy and careful consideration of each article.

The label, the Frankfurt School, came later and was initially used by others as a convenient shorthand to identify the advocates of critical theory. The choice of term arose from the association of the Institute of Social Research with the University of Frankfurt. This is not without some irony. For during most of the years in which the Institute's journal was published, that is 1932 to 1941, the Institute was based in New York. Since its members were not only Marxists, albeit mostly of an unorthodox variety, but also Jews, they were doubly suspect in the eyes of the Nazi regime. It was, however, their communism which the Gestapo invoked when it closed down

1

the Institute for 'activities hostile to the state'.[3] When the Institute returned to Frankfurt after the end of the Second World War, several of the critical theorists chose to remain in the United States. Although the diverse range of their interests makes many of them difficult to categorize in terms of traditional academic disciplines, only two of what might be called the Institute's philosophers returned to Germany, namely Horkheimer and Adorno. The third, Marcuse, remained in America. So too did the sociologist of literature, Leo Löwenthal, Franz Neumann and Otto Kirchheimer, both lawyers and political scientists, and the psychologist Erich Fromm. Indeed, of the core members only Horkheimer's close friend, the economist Friedrich Pollock, joined the two philosophers. It was after their return that the past and present members of the Institute began to be referred to as the Frankfurt School.

The label, the Frankfurt School, has been extended beyond the members of the original Institute to include Jürgan Habermas. Habermas, born a generation later than Horkheimer and his colleagues, also differed in not coming from a Jewish background. By his own account such biographical differences are of some significance in accounting for the tension between his advocacy of critical theory and the older generation. One characteristic he does share with the older generation is that diversity of interests which makes him difficult to pin down in disciplinary terms. Indeed one survey of political science in Germany described him as a philosopher and sociologist only to promptly note that he is regarded by German political scientists as a leading political theorist.[4]

Given the diverse interests between the individual members of the Frankfurt School, it is not surprising that critical theory has been taken up by a host of theorists on both sides of the Atlantic who have taken up different positions. The very success of critical theory has inevitably led to even greater difficulty in discerning the common features that define it. Indeed, one survey concluded that 'the question What is the meaning and significance of Critical Theory today? has to be answered in local terms. The response in Germany will differ from that in the United States.'[5] The growth of interest in the Frankfurt School and critical theory has led to another problem with the use of these terms. After the pioneering work of Martin Jay, *The Dialectical Imagination. A History of the Frankfurt School and the Institute of Social Research, 1923–1950*, commentators began to explore the contributions of individual members.[6] Again it is not surprising that such studies often discerned omissions in the broader accounts, including Jay's, and, more importantly, were impressed by the differences between individual members of the Institute or by alliances hitherto unnoticed or insufficiently emphasized.[7] Similarly, while Marcuse and Adorno received the most scholarly attention, other commentators have sought to rescue the comparatively neglected members of the Institute from their relative obscurity.[8] That has also led to emphasis on individual virtues, and vices, which makes the unity conveyed by the terms Frankfurt School and critical theory seem questionable. The emphasis on diversity at the expense of unity has been aided by the fact that the critical theorists themselves became critical of each other in varying degrees. Thus Fromm split from the Institute in 1939 amidst considerable acrimony and was later attacked by Adorno and Marcuse over his interpretation of Freud. There had always been some tension between Adorno and Marcuse and their response to the student radicalism of the 1960s differed substantially. Adorno, however, was supportive of the young Habermas whereas Horkheimer was damning. Habermas in turn was later highly critical of Horkheimer and Adorno, though more so of the latter.

In the light of all this emphasis upon divergence, is it then still helpful to write about the Frankfurt School and critical theory? There is a strong prima-facie case that it is, namely that all of the putative members of the School, for some part of their career at the very least, adopted some form of collective label and clearly believed that they were engaged in a common enterprise. As part and parcel of that common enterprise, they identified common opponents whom they attacked in often highly polemical fashion. They differed over the adequacy with which each expressed their common endeavour and over the prospects of success, some, especially Horkheimer, succumbing to a deep pessimism, which had accompanied him to some degree throughout his life, others, especially Marcuse, retaining an optimistic streak despite the pessimism of some of his works.

The problem of unity versus diversity is naturally greatest when comparing the ideas of Habermas with those of the older generation, if for no other reason than the difference in biography associated with their dates of birth and background. The older generation were all born around the turn of the century. Horkheimer, born in 1895, and Pollock, born in 1894, were slightly older than the others. The youngest, Kirchheimer, was born in 1905. Although some were conscripted towards the end of the war, none belonged to the front generation whose life was marked by the trenches of the First World War. For the critical theorists, the beginning of their adult experience coincided more or less with the opening of the Weimar Republic amidst revolution, especially the defeat and suppression of those who wanted to go beyond the compromises of the Weimar Republic.

The frustration of revolutionary ambition was one common element of the Weimar experience for those on the left. Yet Leo Löwenthal also recalled a certain optimism. He noted:

> that what was extraordinarily characteristic of the time after the First World War was, let me say, a kind of readiness to take up everything that was different. That was, first of all, of course, the socialist, if not actually communist motif. But that coupled itself at the same time with a rejection of everything that seemed bourgeois, including the bourgeois organization of science and bourgeois philosophy.[9]

Insofar as Löwenthal and his future colleagues exhibited such openness, they were met halfway by Weimar society. In all kinds of ways Weimar marked what the historian Detlev Peukert has characterized as 'the crisis of classical modernity'.[10] According to Peukert, Weimar meant on the one hand conflict between the generations, attempts to create a new more rational economic order, social policies which foreshadowed the modern welfare state, the breakdown of traditional social melieux, the transition to mass culture and mass consumption and the development of ' "modern" *life-styles'*.[11] On the other hand, Weimar witnessed a reversion to more conflictual policies in industrial relations, the reversal of concessions to the working class under the pressure of economic crisis and the demands of obdurate industrialists, the emergence of mass manipulation and mass mobilization by extreme political movements and the denunciation of modern lifestyles as symbolic of the Americanization of life.

In intellectual terms this was a world in which the unorthodox Marxists, Georg Lukacs, Karl Korsch and Ernst Bloch opened up new perspectives linking Marxism with philosophy and utopian thought. Freud's psycho-analysis offered yet another novel perspective and attracted Löwenthal, Fromm and Horkheimer. Even the more reserved Adorno sought to incor-porate Freud into his unsuccessful *Habilitationsschrift* on *The Concept of the Unconscious in the Transcendental Doctrine of the Soul*.[12] It was also a world in which, when Adorno met Lukacs in 1925, he was shocked to find that Lukacs was already retracting precisely what Adorno found fascinating in the attempt to restore his reputation with Communist Party authorities.[13] Others also found that putative intellectual mentors could prove unreliable. In varying degrees Neumann and Kirchheimer looked to the jurist and political scientist Carl Schmitt, while Marcuse started his *Habilitations-schrift* under Martin Heidegger. The attraction of both Schmitt and Heidegger was that, albeit in quite different ways, they seemed to deal directly with contemporary experience. As Marcuse later recalled, 'Philoso-phy was at that time totally empty, the academic scene was dominated by neo-Kantianism, neo-Hegelianism, and then suddenly [Heidegger's] *Being and Time* appeared as a truly concrete philosophy. There, there was talk of "Being-there" [*Dasein*], of "existence", of "man", of "death", of "care". That seemed to concern us.'[14] Insight into the paralysis of a sterile parlia-mentarianism, into the dissipation of individual identity amidst pressure to conform, crude utilitarianism and a naïve faith in technological progress, was what seemed to be offered by critics like Schmitt and Heidegger. Yet both Heidegger and Schmitt promptly lined up to praise the Nazi regime.

The openness and radicalism of the Weimar intellectual agenda, even if sometimes ambivalent and deceptive, contrasted sharply with the 1950s, the decade in which Habermas, who was born in 1929, embarked upon his academic career. The Federal Republic of Germany in these years was animated by an anti-communist ethos. The small Communist Party was banned in 1956 and Marxism was marginalized in German Universities. Few professors would even openly acknowledge being socialist.[15] The Institute of Social Research, now re-established in Germany, sought to conceal the radical past of its leading figures, not always successfully. Habermas recalled that 'from the academic standpoint, I grew up in a provincial German context, in the world of German philosophy, in the form of a declining Neo-Kantianism, of the German Historical School, of phenomenology, and also philosophical anthropology'.[16] Like others who gravitated to the left, he had to reappropriate the texts of radical Marxism stage by stage, including the earlier works of Adorno and Horkheimer.[17] Likewise he progressively incorporated realms of Anglo-Saxon theory into ever more complex theoretical structures. His trajectory is well summarized by Max Pensky:

> The irony is that Habermas has become *the* intellectual of the Federal Republic by consistently championing precisely those universalistic democratic political ideals that seek to oust Germany's long-held and calamitous fascination with characteristically German forms of collective identity. Insofar as it takes its bearing from the particular historical and cultural *situation* of postwar Germany, Habermas's political and theoretical work is highly particular. And yet ... the dynamic that it derives from its own particular context has impelled Habermas's thought towards a thoroughgoing political universalism.[18]

To that extent the suggestion that the meaning and significance of critical theory has to be answered in local terms is both true and false. It is true in the sense that any attempt to appropriate a body of theory takes place against the background of culturally specific sets of assumptions, interests and sensitivities. From this perspective the notion that 'the response in Germany will differ from that in the United States' is both inevitable and unobjectionable. Yet it is also false. For the meaning and significance of critical theory only become apparent when the culturally specific sets of assumptions, interests and sensitivities of its authors are taken into account. As Pensky implicitly argues, that need not issue in any form of relativism. Indeed the culturally specific may itself drive theory beyond the contexts in which it originates. Part of the abiding fascination of the Frankfurt School consists precisely in that dynamic.

Another reason for this fascination lies in the interdisciplinary ambitions of the critical theorists. There is some dispute about how far the older generation held to the original programme of interdisciplinary research and indeed about whether it was ever viable at all.[19] There is, however, a general sense in which the critical theorists sought to break through disciplinary barriers. Within all of the social sciences, or to be more precise, within dominant schools within the individual social sciences, there is a tendency not only to focus on diverse institutionally determined aspects of human behaviour, but also a tendency to privilege specific modes of rationality and motivation. That, in turn, also leads to attempts to overcome these delimitations and typically to attempts to put back the whole man in place of the abstraction created with the promise of greater analytic rigour.

Although the image of the 'whole man' exerted some attraction upon the early Marcuse, the critical theorists were generally more discriminating. By seeking to link approaches to the capacities and competencies of individuals – and the deformations of individual capacities and competencies – with approaches to the public actions of individuals – and their unintended consequences – they not only transcended the disciplinary boundaries of their day, but also sought to break through the antithesis of agency and structure without sacrificing the distinction between the two. In that sense they belong with theorists like Anthony Giddens who have sought to refine Marx's insight that 'Men make history but not in circumstances of their own choosing.'[20]

Much of course depends upon how much significance one ascribes to the weight of circumstance. The older generation of critical theorists have often been criticized for construing the weight of society as so oppressive that the scope of agency shrinks to a vanishing point. In some formulations that criticism is justified. There is, however, another side to that coin. This other side is a sensitivity to the self-defeating illusion that the individual is some safe point of refuge. According to the older generation, this notion took the shape of the cult of inwardness, that is, one of those traits favoured by those disposed towards the idea of a distinctive German political culture. Habermas has been much more assertive of the possibilities of human agency, but he too has warned against excessive expectations about individual capacities. It is arguable that such caution, though it can be criticized in detail, is relevant today. Amidst the growing literature on globalization and the increase in the risks associated with modern life, there is also an emphasis upon the ability and necessity of greater reflexiveness in the modern world. The ability to choose, to treat one's identity as a project which can be purposefully constructed, is exalted. So far has this gone that Giddens can argue that 'in some circumstances of poverty, the hold of tradition has perhaps become even more thoroughly disintegrated than elsewhere. Consequently, the creative construction of lifestyle may become a particular characteristic feature of such situations.'[21] As is suggested below, Habermas may have gone too far in emphasizing the constraints on identity formation, yet his caution may turn out to be preferable to the exaltation of the possibilities open to those who live in poverty. Indeed, the latter sounds suspiciously like the old cult of inwardness turned inside out. Where the cult of inwardness discerned some realm for personal development cut off from the wider world, the new imagery presents the world as a screen on which the individual can project himself, having chosen from the endless possibilities of a globalized world.

As is suggested in the conclusion to this book, there are other ways in which critical theory, and not only the most recent formulations of critical theory, are relevant to the contemporary agenda. Indeed, the difficulty is less in discerning that it is relevant than in choosing between the multiple claims for its relevance in so many areas. A similar difficulty lies in putting together a survey of this nature. Attempts at bibliographic stocktaking of works on Herbert Marcuse and Theodor Adorno produced lists in excess of four hundred items.[22] The publication of the collected works of several critical theorists, the 'rediscovery' of the importance of members of the Institute who had been relatively neglected in the initial waves of research, and the continuing vitality of the work of Jürgen Habermas, have all added to the voluminous literature on critical theory.

The sheer extent of the literature has meant that attempts to provide an overview of critical theory have become increasingly difficult. It is notable that since Martin Jay's pioneering and still invaluable *Dialectical Imagination. A History of the Frankfurt School and the Institute of Social Research, 1923–1950*, surveys have tended to grow longer. David Held's *Introduction to Critical Theory* exceeded five hundred pages. The last major survey, *The Frankfurt School* by Rolf Wiggershaus, weighed in at over seven hundred pages in both the German and English editions, and this was published before Habermas's major work on democracy and the rule of law.[23] If one took an even broader approach to critical theory, and this is certainly legitimate, one would need several volumes of such length.[24] However, instead of producing an even longer book, I have tried to provide a shorter but well illuminated access route through the critical theory of the Institute and Habermas. That has meant making choices about what to include and what to exclude. Even a well illuminated access route does not necessarily allow one to peer down every side street and some major roads may also remain in the dark. In this case Adorno's aesthetic theory and work on music have been passed over, as has the work of Walter Benjamin, despite his importance to Adorno.[25] Karl Wittfogell has also been ignored.[26] Such omissions are not intended as judgements on the quality or intrinsic merits of what has been left out of this account. Considerations of space and the coherence of the argument in the individual chapters have determined the choice of material to be included. In contrast, the political context and significance of critical theory, issues of rationality, morality and identity have been emphasized, as has the idea of critical theory as a form of reflection upon the vicissitudes of bourgeois society. Readers already familiar with critical theory will readily detect the influence of Habermas in this choice of perspective, though it is a perspective that, I argue, allows us to make sense of much of the work of the older generation. I do not claim that other access routes lack their own virtues, though short of a much larger work each is bound to leave something in the dark. I have sought to combine a reasonably comprehensive and up-to-date treatment of the topics that I have selected while conveying some sense of the nature of the arguments advanced by the critical theorists.

The account which follows has been structured with the intent of allowing those unfamiliar with the critical theory of the Frankfurt School to approach it in stages. Hence, Chapter 1, 'The Frankfurt School', begins with an account of the formation of the Institute of Social Research and introduces the critical theorists and their major works. Emphasis is placed upon the subsequent development of the Institute and on the political background against which the critical theorists wrote. A central idea here is their role as critics in the public sphere. Despite the sometimes difficult style in which some of them wrote, most notably, though in quite different ways, Adorno and Habermas, the critical theorists have been prominent public critics. In part that was a product of their unanticipated renown. That in turn was related to the fact that the Institute had intentionally preserved an aspect of German culture which the Nazi regime had sought to extirpate. As is explained below, Horkheimer and Adorno were selective in how much of that culture they put back into the public domain. Consideration of the political background induced a certain amount of what might be called self-censorship. Neither Marcuse nor Habermas seems to have felt such strong constraints, though Marcuse was clearly walking a tightrope in his support for student radicalism, being both encouraging yet warning against an enthusiasm which tipped over into self-indulgence.[27]

Chapter 2, 'A Preliminary Outline of Critical Theory', draws on the work of the Frankfurt School's 'philosophers' in order to provide a broad framework for understanding critical theory. The first characteristic of critical theory identified in this chapter is, as Habermas put it, recognition of the 'embedding of theoretical accomplishments in the practical contexts of their genesis and employment'.[28] This should not be understood in a reductionist sense or be seen as implying relativism. It is directed against conceptions of philosophy, whether epistemological or moral, which have disdained entanglement in the contingency of the empirical world in favour of some supposedly higher reality. It is compatible with a fairly wide array of more specific strategies, with, for example, Adorno's persistent, and problematic, attempts to reveal the social origins of even the most abstract concepts of the philosophy of Søren Kierkegaard and Edmund Husserl. It is also compatible with Marx's famous assertion that 'You cannot transcend philosophy without realizing it.'[29] Insistence upon the importance of the genesis and employment of ideas is, they argued, compatible with notions of truth and obligation, though they differed in how the validity of those notions was to be determined. The second broad characteristic concerns the relationship between human agency and social structures. The claim was that society had to be construed as the product of human agency yet as something that had escaped human control and confronted individual human agents as if it were comparable to natural processes. Although both the older generation and

Habermas agreed on the importance of the general dilemma, the older generation construed it in a more pessimistic and more utopian manner. That is, they placed more emphasis on the obduracy and opacity of social processes while holding out the prospect of a revolutionary transformation that would make them fully transparent and controllable. The weaker their faith in the possibility of this utopian transformation became, the more pessimistic they became. Habermas rejected the image of a fully transparent society while at the same time he argued that there is more scope for human agency than the older generation allowed. Despite this considerable difference in emphasis, the general point, that there are some social processes whose autonomy *vis-à-vis* human agents is neither necessary nor desirable, defines the scope of the critique. The final broad characteristic picked out in Chapter 2 is the interdisciplinary ambition of critical theory referred to earlier. Several issues are at stake here. One is that the complexity of the relation between agency and structure in the modern world cannot be dealt with from the perspective of any single discipline. But this is less important than another issue, namely the assumptions about human agency, including the cognitive and moral components of human agency, that are bound up with disputes within and between the different disciplines. Again, Habermas has been more cautious and arguably more discriminating than the older generation.

Chapters 3 and 4 serve the dual function of providing some illustration for the outline of critical theory and setting the critical theory of the Frankfurt School in the context of competing theories. It is true, and not entirely trivial, that any theory is more intelligible when placed in the context of what its author takes to be competing theories. With the Frankfurt School, however, there is an additional reason for this focus. Both their contemporary opponents and commentators have sometimes been surprised by the vehemence of the critical theorists. This is true even in the case of Habermas, who has more often shown a striking willingness to incorporate the insights of competing theories. Again choices have had to be made about which competing theories to include. The first group, dealt with in Chapter 3 under the heading 'The Failure of Metaphysics', might appear somewhat strange. For it includes those who sought to reassert the validity of metaphysics, notably Martin Heidegger, and the self-avowed postmodernists who have condemned the Western philosophical tradition precisely for its pursuit of grand metaphysical visions. Nevertheless, Habermas discerned some continuity between the two. The important issue here is that the critical theorists saw themselves as defenders of the Enlightenment. This is true of the older generation despite their own trenchant criticism of the Enlightenment project, most notably in Horkheimer's and Adorno's *Dialectic of Enlightenment*.[30] It is their hostility to the Enlightenment that unites the opponents of critical theory, a hostility that the critical theorists saw as theoretically and practically injurious to viable conceptions of human agency.

Opposition to these opponents and to the positivists considered in Chapter 4 has also been a strong factor in the self-avowed unity of the Frankfurt School, despite their differences. As Habermas put it, 'The dual confrontation of the old Frankfurt School, against positivism on the one side and *Lebensphilosophie* and general metaphysical obscurantism on the other side, has sadly become contemporary again.'[31] Strictly speaking, this was not entirely accurate. While *Lebensphilosophie* and obscurantism may have resurfaced in another guise, militant positivism as a philosophy of the natural and social sciences has faded away, as Habermas noted. Yet the encounter with positivism was a defining experience for the older generation and confrontation with positivist doctrines played a crucial role in Habermas's early work.

Chapter 5, 'The Attractions and Limits of Psychology', deals, as the title suggests, not with competing theories in a strict sense, though there is an element of that in the reaction of the older generation. Predominately, however, psychological theories, especially Freud's, were one of those innovations that Löwenthal noted. They also played an important role in the internal dynamics amongst the older generation. The early importance of Erich Fromm arose from his attempts to integrate Freudian theory into the Institute's interdisciplinary project, yet his interpretation of Freud and others also became the occasion of acrimonious dispute between Fromm on the one hand and Adorno and Marcuse on the other. At the same time Marcuse sought to develop a utopian vision on the basis of a reworking of Freud, a vision which made an important impression on Habermas in the mid-1950s. Yet Habermas did not attempt to pursue Marcuse's strategy. Instead, he integrated Freud into his criticism of positivism, using Freud to provide a model of critical theory. Although he never renounced his interpretation of Freud, he did not pursue this strategy either, turning instead to other psychologists. These disputes and fluctuations point to the difficulty which the Frankfurt School has had in integrating psychological theories. The difficulty is significant for two reasons. First, the promise of psychology was that it would help to explain the mediation between structure and agency, social processes and the individual. Second, psychological theories deal directly with motives, and motives, as is suggested in the conclusion, are a strong candidate for the future development of critical theory.

While the first four chapters are skewed towards an emphasis upon the broad context of critical theory, subsequent chapters have a more thematic character. Chapter 6, 'The Analysis of Bourgeois Society', argues for the centrality of this concept, despite what some regard as its archaic connotations. For the older generation the prominence of the idea of the decline of the bourgeoisie is warrant enough for this emphasis. Yet there is another reason, namely their concern for what Löwenthal called 'the increasing fragility of the bourgeois individual'.[32] For all their revolt against 'everything that seemed bourgeois, including the bourgeois organization of science and bourgeois philosophy', they did not want to cast out the virtues of the bourgeoisie along with its vices. That such virtues existed for Habermas too was evident in his criticism of the 'cynicism of bourgeois consciousness [which] has progressed to the point that the neo-conservative heirs to the bourgeois emancipation mistrust the latter's own achievements and entreat us not, please, to take too literally its acknowledged ideals'.[33] Although it is no longer fashionable to say so, these ideals were the product of a specific social class in a specific part of the world. To vary Pensky's argument about context and political universalism in Habermas's thought, the fact that these ideals had a specific origin has in no way restricted their universal validity.

Chapter 7, 'Paradoxes of Reason', focuses upon a specific aspect of bourgeois ambition as understood by the critical theorists, namely the claim to shape the world in accordance with the dictates of reason. The starting point for both the older generation and Habermas was the Hegelian version of this ambition. Of the older generation Marcuse clung most firmly to Hegel, though he conceded that the Hegelian system was flawed. Horkheimer and Adorno, though greatly influenced by Hegel in other respects, ruthlessly pursued the earthly origins of rationalist thought, linking it tightly to imperatives of self-preservation. Indeed so tightly did they construe this link that they found it increasingly difficult to keep in sight the possibility of using reason to check that imperative. It is argued, however, that one can accept much of their argument without drawing the conclusions that they did. Indeed, alternatives are easily discerned within their own work. The fact that they did not take up these alternatives is to be explained primarily by the historical context, that is, by the paralysing image of the Third Reich and by specific features of their account of bourgeois society. Habermas's alternative is not reliant upon the Hegelian edifice and offers a highly persuasive and nuanced strategy. Yet it does have one troubling aspect, that is the difficulty in linking reason and motivation.

One of the reasons contributing to the pessimistic logic of Adorno and Horkheimer was their methodological commitment to the principle of immanent critique. Such methodological considerations form the focus of Chapter 8, 'The Contours of Critical Theory'. The choice of title here, 'contours' not methodology, is deliberate. Though it is perfectly legitimate to treat the work of the Frankfurt School within the framework of 'methodologies', there is a risk that their explicit reservations on this issue are neglected. Again Löwenthal serves as a good guide. He denied that methodology had been their prime concern and insisted instead upon the relationship of theory to practice.[34] In fact their hopes in this respect were constantly frustrated. By contrast, Habermas adopted more modest ambitions for the role of theories, but precisely in order to create more room for a conception of political practice that was attainable by contemporary citizens and protected from the tutelage of privileged insight, which has so often plagued discussion of the relationship between theory and practice in the Marxist tradition. Habermas took apart what the older generation bundled together in another sense. In quasi-Hegelian fashion the older generation construed immanent critique not just as an intellectual activity but as a kind of logical development of society and culture. Applied in the context of the paradoxes of reason, this contributed to the difficulty of taking up the alternatives to a fateful dialectic of enlightenment. By drawing distinctions between different types of critique and by insisting upon a normative foundation for critical theory, independent of the contingencies of history, Habermas has sought to avoid the difficulties that confronted the older generation.

During the decisive years for the older generation, that is from the 1920s to the 1940s, the prospects for meaningful activity by ordinary citizens were not auspicious. It was inevitable that they would focus upon the politics of authoritarian states. As discussed in Chapter 9, 'The Authoritarian and the Democratic State', that in turn meant a sensitivity to the arbitrary use of political power and the fragility of the rule of law when faced with powerful sectional interests and organized violence. The conception of politics primarily as naked power, the historical roots of the state in the use of force, are, however, aspects of only one conception of politics, albeit a conception for which it is all too easy to find illustration. One of Habermas's aims has been to break through the dichotomy between the idea of political integration by means of law on the one hand and political integration by means of power on the other. The twin aim has been to rescue the rule of law from its apparent impotence and, equally important, to circumvent the celebration of the executive force of the state associated with the ideas of Carl Schmitt. For citizens of democratic states, Habermas's normative argument is potentially attractive. Yet, despite an excessive tendency to discern the incipient return of the past in post-war democratic states, the older generation's concern with the dynamics of power in the authoritarian state is not without its merits.

One of the advantages of law according to Habermas's conception of the rule of law is that it provides a substitute for deficient moral motivation. Although the law should be consistent with morally motivated action, it is sufficient if the citizen obeys the law for purely instrumental reasons. This sets his theory apart from those that place a higher priority upon the existence of civic virtue as the basis of the polity. The issue of motivation is central to Chapter 10 on 'Morality and Interests'. The older generation usually exhibited more skepticism than Habermas about the validity of universal moral norms. Yet they were not dismissive of morality, which they saw as one of those phenomena of bourgeois society that reflected both its virtues and vices. The virtue lay, they argued, not in the universal norms but in the moral sentiments and interests that underlay them. This had the advantage of identifying strong sources of motivation. But it also had disadvantages. If recourse is made to interests, then it is not long before the need for a distinction between justifiable and unjustifiable interests emerges, or, from the perspective of a critically orientated revolutionary ambition, the distinction between true and false interests. Similarly, sentiments are not always especially discriminating. Worse still, is the possibility that the desired sentiment is simply not present. It is argued in Chapter 10 that the older generation did not have any convincing answers to these dilemmas, dilemmas of which they were aware. Yet Habermas escapes from such dilemmas only by deliberately restricting the scope of moral norms and severing the link with sentiment and interest.

Although Habermas has warned against excessive expectations of the capacities of the individual, his conception of individual identity ascribes greater resources to the individual. It is argued in Chapter 11, 'Individual and Collective Identity', that Habermas provides a better solution to the criticism of the supposed self-sufficiency of the individual that motivated the older generation. Again the historical context explains their heavy emphasis upon the diminishing scope for the individual. The real contrast, however, emerges in the speculative account of identity formation in *Dialectic of Enlightenment*. There, the formation of individual identity is associated with deception and self-denial in the context of a moral vacuum. The analogous account offered by Habermas is associated with mutual understanding and role-playing in a normatively laden context. Divergent biographies also lie behind the different responses to collective identity. For the older generation the emergence of national fervour was associated with manipulative strategies. This is a potentially useful corrective to the naïve assumption of naturalness of national identity. However, it leaves little space for anything between the individual and full-blown cosmopolitanism. Habermas, who has also been highly sensitive to the dangers of national fervour, allows for a constitutional patriotism that makes weaker claims upon the individual.

It is probably already clear that on most issues I find Habermas's argument more persuasive than that of the older generation. Yet the older generation, stamped as they inevitably were by a darker period of history, can, by virtue of that fact, still offer useful insights into the dynamics of power. It is also probably clear that I am broadly sympathetic to the enterprise of critical theory. The chapters that follow are an attempt to make accessible what are sometimes complex and daunting texts. I have not hesitated to offer assessments of the arguments advanced by the critical theorists, but hope that I have not allowed these to become too obtrusive.

CHAPTER 1

The Frankfurt School

The circumstances and intellectual climate surrounding the foundation of the Institute for Social Research in 1923 were prophetic in more ways than one.[1] The main force behind the Institute was the young Felix Weil, the son of a wealthy Jewish businessman who had made his fortune in the grain trade in Argentina. There was, as many later noted, some irony in the fact that a capitalist funded the creation of the first Marxist research institute to be attached to a German University. In part this paradox can be explained by the fact that Felix concealed the full extent of his ambitions from his father, emphasizing the history of the labour movement and anti-Semitism instead of Marxism.

The immediate background to Felix's initiative was the First Marxist Work Week that took place in 1922. In reality this was a discussion group consisting mainly of young Marxists, many of whom would later acquire great fame, including Georg Lukacs and Karl Korsch. It had no official connection with any political party. The topics included socialization, which had been on the political agenda of the recently established Weimar Republic and on which Weil had written his doctorate. Another theme was the relationship between Marxism and philosophy on which Korsch was working. The intention had been that this would be the first of several such discussions, but this idea sank into the background as Felix Weil turned his attention to the foundation of an Institute.

Persuading his father to provide the substantial sums of money required was only the first hurdle. Felix also had to negotiate with the Ministry of Culture and the University of Frankfurt. The former proved easier. The Ministry was dominated by social democrats though Felix's negotiating partner, Carl Heinrich Becker, was not a social democrat. He was, however, committed to reform of German Universities and especially to breaking down their high level of specialization. With this aim in mind, Becker looked favourably upon sociology, which he understood in very broad terms as a synthetic discipline incorporating political science and contemporary history. In 1929 Felix Weil claimed that in his negotiations with the Ministry he had made no secret of the fact that the Institute would be devoted to scientific Marxism. By his own account, Felix Weil proceeded more cautiously in his negotiations with the University. The University authorities were initially enthusiastic but soon became worried by the degree of autonomy that Felix Weil sought for the Institute. At the end of protracted negotiations, Felix secured most of what he wanted. By the time they were concluded, the man envisaged as Director of the Institute, Kurt Albert Gerlach, had died at the early age of 36 from diabetes.

Gerlach's successor was Karl Grünberg. Grünberg had started as a lawyer and political economist and founded the *Archiv für die Geschichte des Sozialismus und der Arbeiterbewegung* (Archive for the History of Socialism and the Labour Movement) in 1910. In his inaugural speech he counterposed 'pessimists' and 'optimists'. The former, he said, claimed that the world was in ruins, but what really lay in ruins, was not the world as a whole but their world. He meant the world of the bourgeoisie. Grünberg placed himself in the camp of the optimists who held that they were in the middle of a 'transition from capitalism to socialism'.[2] Yet he was not a dogmatic Marxist and did not even believe in the formation of 'schools' of thought. Under his Directorship the focus of the Institute's work followed the *Archiv für die Geschichte des Sozialismus und der Arbeiterbewegung*, and some of the Institute's members published substantial works on related themes, namely Henryk Grossmann, *Das Akkumulations- und Zusammenbruchgesetz des kapitalistischen Systems* (The Law of Accumulation and Collapse in the Capitalist System) and Friedrich Pollock, *Die planwirtschaftliche Versuche in der Sowjetunion 1917–1927* (Experiments in Economic Planning in the Soviet Union 1917–1927).[3] The only substantial exception was Leo Löwenthal who joined the Institute in 1925/6 to work on the sociology of literature.

Both Grossmannn and Pollock had by then attracted unwelcome attention. Grossmann had been under suspicion from the outset because of his temporary membership of the Polish Communist Party. As a Polish citizen he was particularly exposed and dependent on the sanction of the authorities for his residence in Germany. This was obtained only after Grünberg guaranteed that Grossmann 'will abstain from any political activity and will devote himself exclusively to scientific work'.[4] Grossmann had to refer back to this guarantee when the Institute in general came under suspicion. The cause of this suspicion was the announcement of the plan to establish a publishing enterprise bearing the name of Marx–Engels within the Institute's building. The application, made by Pollock, as business manager, and Weil, created a furore that culminated in a police investigation of the backgrounds of the Institute's members. The outcome was that the police concluded that

Weil and Pollock were undoubtedly communists. Though they could not find evidence of involvement in the Communist Party, Pollock came in for special criticism on the grounds of his activities during the Munich Soviet of 1919.

Despite the protests of the University authorities, the Institute did proceed with its publishing venture in the following year. Yet when this came to light there was little response. In the meantime the true nature of the enterprise had also become apparent. The University authorities had feared that an academic establishment was going to be used as a cover for party-political activity. In reality, the publishing venture formed part of the attempt to produce the first critical edition of the collected works of Marx and Engels, with the Institute acting as a mediator between the Moscow-based Marx–Engels Institute and the (anti-communist) German Socialist Party which controlled part of the archives of Marx and Engels. This, it seems, reassured the academic establishment, temporarily.

The suspicions and acrimony flared up again in 1930 when Professor Fritz Schmidt, an economist, wrote to the Ministry of Culture denouncing Weil as a communist, adding that 'The Ministry will not be able to remain indifferent to this at a time when in the state of Prussia the revolutionary communist movement is persecuted as an enemy of the state.'⁵ Schmidt's intervention was induced by the dispute over Grünberg's successor. Grünberg had been seriously ill since the beginning of 1928 and it took some time to agree upon his successor, Max Horkheimer. Horkheimer was not the most obvious candidate. He was young, had published little, lacked the appropriate academic status of Ordinarius and had not even played a prominent role in the Institute's early years.

Horkheimer was, however, a close friend of Pollock. Both were the sons of Jewish businessmen and had formed a close friendship in 1911. That friendship was quite extraordinary, defined and redefined over the years in memoranda. It had a passing resemblance to the relationship between Marx and Engels. Horkheimer was not financially dependent upon Pollock, as Marx had been upon Engels. But Pollock did consciously sacrifice his own intellectual career, though it was still not without substance, by taking on administrative tasks in an attempt to give his friend more freedom to think and write. Horkheimer also had the support of Paul Tillich, a theologian and religious socialist, who had joined the University in 1928. Tillich was a member of a discussion group which included Horkheimer and Löwenthal as well as the sociologist Karl Mannheim and Kurt Riezler, Rector of the University. More important, Horkheimer was not politically suspect. When the police had checked the backgrounds of the Institute's members, they had failed to notice that Horkheimer had been in Munich with Pollock. Horkheimer was also regarded as a gifted and popular teacher by the Faculty. The result was that he was appointed as a Professor of Social Philosophy and Director of the Institute of Social Research in July 1930.

From the outset, the members of the Institute had been very much critics in the public sphere, caught between the desire to extend the criticism of bourgeois society and the periodic need to conceal or play down the radical character of their criticism.[6] It was a dilemma which would haunt some of them to the end. The political and cultural climate in 1930 was ominous. One attempt, by the cultural historian Gustav Schivelbusch, to summarize the climate in Frankfurt in this year pits the sociologists, amongst whom could be counted Horkheimer, Tillich and Mannheim, against the circle around the poet Stefan George. According to Schivelbusch, whereas the focus of the sociologists was the criticism of ideology, that of the George's circle was myth. Against the concept of society George's circle invoked the idea of an élite and against rational concepts in general they invoked 'inner vision'.[7] The authoritarianism inherent in the George circle fitted the political trend better than the rationalism of the sociologists.

In Frankfurt that trend was evident in the changing tone of the once liberal *Frankfurter Allgemeine Zeitung*. A former editor recalled the speculation around 1930 about the need to revise the 'old "pure doctrine"' and to rally around a new conception of *Bürgerlichkeit*.[8] On the broader political front, the attempt to do precisely that, by forming a new political movement to rally the centre ground and draw in elements of the youth movements which proliferated in Germany, failed abjectly. One of the beneficiaries of this disarray in the bourgeois camp was the National Socialist Party. Its electoral breakthrough, obtaining 18 per cent of the vote, occurred in September 1930. According to Löwenthal, the day after the election, he, Horkheimer, Weil and Pollock decided to prepare for emigration. For this purpose they set up a subsidiary branch in Geneva and began to transfer the Institute's financial assets out of Germany.

As the Institute prepared for emigration, it was taking on a different complexion from the one it had in the days of Grünberg's directorship. As Director, Horkheimer's interests were evidently important in this change. Horkheimer had received a broad education and had originally intended to submit a dissertation in Gestalt psychology, but eventually he settled on a study of Kant's philosophy. His teaching at the University during the 1920s was primarily in the history of philosophy. But Horkheimer had a wider agenda for the Institute. As he specified in his inaugural lecture, the future lay in the development of an interdisciplinary research programme. Amongst enterprises he mentioned were 'sociological and psychological investigations of the press and of fiction' and 'survey research'.[9] He also alluded to the branch in Geneva, without of course indicating its real purpose. These various allusions all had a bearing upon present, and future, members of the Institute, who would contribute towards its distinctive character in the 1930s.

The reference to fiction fitted in with Löwenthal's research. Löwenthal had originally turned to Judaism and worked in the Freie Judische Lehrhaus, which sought to revive fading aspects of Jewish culture and bridge the gap between 'Western' and 'Eastern' Jews. Not long before joining the Institute, he had gone to Heidelberg to take part in the psycho-therapeutic practice of Frieda Reichmann. From 1926 he was employed part-time by the Institute but became a full-time employee when Horkheimer became Director. Erich Fromm made the same transition from the Freie Judische Lehrhaus to psychoanalysis, but more thoroughly, becoming a trained analyst himself. The connection with Löwenthal facilitated the establishment of a Frankfurt Psychoanalytic Institute, of which Fromm was a member, which was provided with space in the Institute's building. The connection with Fromm was consolidated when he was appointed by the Institute to work on socio-psychological issues and especially a questionnaire-based study of workers and white-collar employees.

Löwenthal also played a role, albeit a smaller one, in the recruitment of Herbert Marcuse. Marcuse shared Löwenthal's interest in literature and had written a doctorate on a genre of novel. Some time after, he became a pupil of Heidegger's. The transition from Heidegger pupil to member of a Marxist institute was a substantial one, but it was not the only occasion on which the Institute was to recruit people who had been influenced by its philosophical opponents. Marcuse had tried, with increasing difficulty, to reconcile Heidegger and Marxism. As the cracks in this edifice began to show, his relationship with Heidegger deteriorated and Kurt Riezler interceded in an attempt to find a new home for Marcuse. At this point Löwenthal was commissioned to interview Marcuse, who was accepted, and promptly dispatched to Geneva.

The alacrity with which Marcuse was sent to Geneva was warranted. On 13 March 1933 the Institute's building was searched and then closed by the police. In July Horkheimer was formally informed by the Gestapo that the Institute's assets in Frankfurt had been seized. The preparations for emigration had proved their worth. Plans to salvage the Institute's substantial library failed, but the financial assets were secure, as were most of the Institute's members. One early member of the Institute, Karl Wittfogel, made the mistake of returning from Switzerland in March and was promptly thrown into a concentration camp. It took until November 1933 to secure his release. A man with looser connections to the Institute, Theodor Wiesengrund Adorno remained in Germany until 1934.

Adorno had met Horkheimer in 1922 when they were both doctoral students of the neo-Kantian Hans Cornelius. Adorno had several occasions in the 1920s to acknowledge his thanks for Horkheimer's help and influence but was not involved in the Institute's affairs. Interested in both philosophy and music, he spent three years in Vienna studying music before returning to Frankfurt and philosophy in 1928. Since he was not a member of the Institute or politically active, Horkheimer judged that he was not at immediate risk in March 1933, as was in fact the case. Indeed, Adorno hoped to remain in Germany and even published a favourable review of a song book including material from the Nazi youth leader Baldur von Schirach. As late as July 1934 he expected the army to take over in Germany during the winter. Desperate to stay in Germany, it was only as one opportunity after another was closed down that he accepted that he would have to leave.[10] It is indicative of the tensions of the time, and personal sensitivities, that Adorno and Horkheimer did not communicate directly until October 1934. The ice was broken by a sharp letter from Horkheimer, which elicited counter-accusations from Adorno that he had been abandoned. Several long letters followed before both agreed that the problem was misunderstanding rather than indifference.

The Institute had been ruthlessly expelled from its home and the public realm in which it had begun to make its voice heard. But it did have a platform, the *Zeitschrift für Sozialforshung*. Volume one appeared in 1932. Each issue contained a series of essays, mostly by members of the Institute, plus an extensive review section. In the first issue the reviews were grouped under the headings of 'philosophy', 'general sociology', that is sociological theory, 'psychology', 'social movements and social policy', 'special sociology' which included what would now be called political science and anthropology, 'economics' and 'literature'. 'History' was soon added and 'literature' dropped. The broad pattern indicates the range of interests the *Zeitschrift* sought to cover in its pursuit of what Horkheimer called in the first issue a 'theory of contemporary society as a whole'.[11] With issue 3 of Volume 8, published in 1940, the review section was drastically curtailed and subheadings were no longer useful. More importantly, that issue appeared in English under the title *Studies in Philosophy and Social Science*. Given that the Institute had been based in New York since 1934, the delay in publishing in English was striking. The Institute had in fact long been encouraged to publish in English in order to raise its profile, and the accessibility of its work, in what was an English-speaking environment. Reluctance to do so was not primarily a product of the difficulty of writing in another language. It was rather a deliberate attempt to preserve, in German, a cultural heritage which was rejected and defamed by Germany's Nazi rulers.

It was a heritage to which the institute adopted a critical, but not dismissive, attitude. Alongside this theme the Institute devoted considerable energy to the collective work *Studien über Autorität und Familie* (Studies on Authority and the Family) which drew upon the empirical studies on attitudes to authority which the Institute had begun in the Weimar Republic.[12] It was intended to publish the empirical material itself, but this did not happen until long after the war and indeed after the death of most of the original members. By the end of the 1930s the only other substantial publications which the Institute could book to its credit was *Punishment and Social Structure* by Georg Rusche and Otto Kirchheimer, published in 1939.[13] The book was begun by Rusche but completed and revised by Kirchheimer.

Otto Kirchheimer was a student of Carl Schmitt's but had adopted an independent stance critical of Schmitt's celebration of authoritarian politics. Kirchheimer had joined the Institute's Paris branch in 1934 before moving to New York. Another legal expert, also influenced by Schmitt, Franz Neumann joined two years later, in 1936. Neumann had acted as a lawyer for German trade unions and was a pupil of the labour lawyer Hugo Sinzheimer. Ironically, although he was not a pupil of Schmitt's, he was less discriminating than Kirchheimer at the start, partly because he shared the faith in the legal system which dominated the trade unions and socialists.[14] That changed after 1933. Neumann first went to England to retrain as a political scientist under the English socialist H.J. Laski. The result was *The Rule of Law*, a study of its degeneration into an *arcanum dominationes*.[15] Neumann came to the Institute indirectly. When Laski asked Horkheimer to help find a position for Neumann, Horkheimer, not knowing Neumann, turned to Löwenthal who recalled him from his student days. The addition of Kirchheimer and Neumann greatly strengthened the political and legal scope of the Institute, though later critics complain that it was not fully exploited. There were certainly difficulties in integrating Neumann's work. His first article for the *Zeitschrift* required extensive discussion before it was agreed that it had the appropriate form.[16]

Neumann's first article for the *Zeitschrift* may have required unusually long discussion, but the general principle of internal discussion of prospective articles was standard. Several motives were at work here. In part the aim was to ensure that pieces properly represented the Institute's stance. There was a very strong sense at the time of a need to form a common front, to defend their critical theory against opponents. Another important reason was the fear of falling foul of the American authorities. Quite how marked this was is evident in comments on a memorandum of 1938 outlining the Institute's programme. The author of the comments, Julian Gumperz, wrote to Horkheimer warning that the 'Institute will live by its work, but it might die by its declarations of faith'. In a lengthy elaboration, he suggested that the programme might form the basis of a lecture to selected friends. They might then be given an abstract 'that could not be misconstrued and used to the detriment of the Institute'.[17] Gumperz had no need to worry. That had been Horkheimer's intention all along. As Marxists, Jews and aliens in a capitalist land in which anti-Semitism was widespread, that fear was understandable. It was also a fear which had a significant effect on the work of the Institute's members. Their relationship to the public realm was always ambiguous and often distorted by the perceived need to gloss over their true beliefs.

Theoretical unity led to one of the more bitter internal disputes and to the departure of Erich Fromm. Adorno had long been critical of Fromm, but by April 1937 Horkheimer was agreeing that there was a certain danger that Fromm would slide into a revisionist stance. By the end of 1939 this danger had become a reality and Fromm left amidst a bitter wrangle over money.[18]

The financial dispute pointed to a general problem for the Institute. Its assets suffered badly in 1937 and there was a continual drain on resources as it struggled to assist fellow refugees.

Financial constraints led to a determined effort to secure external funding for the Institute. These efforts distracted Horkheimer from his long-standing desire to write a dialectical logic. This project, intended as his masterpiece, never came to fruition in its intended form. According to the original conception it would have dealt with concepts traditionally found in works on logic, including 'reality' and 'cause', but also concepts like 'culture', 'family' and 'authority'. The latter three were dealt with in Horkheimer's contribution to the *Studien über Autorität und Familie* and much of Horkheimer's work in the 1930s and 1940s can be seen as fragmented elements of the intended 'logic'.[19]

In 1940, however, attention was focused on external funding. The Institute had two projects in mind. The first was eventually submitted under the title 'Cultural Aspects of National Socialism', though earlier titles included 'German Economy, Politics and Culture, 1900–1933' and 'The Collapse of German Democracy and the Expansion of National Socialism'. Here a variety of long-established themes were at work, an attempt to understand the rise of authoritarian states and the cultural conditions which made this possible as well as an attempt 'to "save", through documentation and theoretical interpretation, what we consider fertile in this period', that is in the period 1900–33.[20] The project was stillborn through lack of funding. Nevertheless, fragments of these ideas appeared in the *Zeitschrift*, in a collection of essays which was distributed to a restricted circle, and in Neumann's monumental work, *Behemoth*.[21]

The contrasts between these pieces, in terms of size, style, argument and impact, were marked. Horkheimer's brief essay with its apocalyptic tone remained almost an internal discussion document. Neumann's *Behemoth*, long and empirically detailed, had a major impact, influencing thinking in government circles as well as becoming a standard reference point in the historiography of the Third Reich. The theoretical differences were sharpest between Neumann and Pollock, whose essay on 'State Capitalism' claimed that the economic laws of the free market had been set aside by the authoritarian state.[22] Neumann denied this.

The second project was a study of anti-Semitism. As outlined in the *Zeitschrift*, this was an ambitious plan for a systematic study stretching from 'current theories about anti-Semitism' and 'anti-Semitism and mass movements' to the 'foundations of national socialist anti-Semitism' and an 'experimental section'. The latter was to consist of responses to a specially made film designed to reveal covert anti-Semitic sentiments.[23] This was sensitive territory. The predominant, official, view was that anti-Semitism was both undemocratic and un-American. Yet some of the Institute's members believed that social anti-Semitism, that is discrimination in the form of exclusion from resorts and certain clubs, was even more prevalent in America than it had been in Weimar Germany.[24]

At first the prospects of the anti-Semitism project looked bleak. Not until early in 1943 did the Institute finally acquire the funds to launch the project. It began with a dual focus. One group based on the east coast was to work on types of anti-Semite and authoritarian. Another group based in California was to work on the psychological dimension. The project continued for several years, with the results not beginning to appear in published form until 1950. In the intervening period the project had involved numerous people from outside the Institute and Horkheimer had lost control of the project. It had become a project in which the Institute was involved rather than the Institute's project. Nevertheless the resulting volumes were an important contribution to Studies in Prejudice as the series was called. Probably the most influential was The Authoritarian Personality, of which Adorno was one of the authors.[25]

By the time the Institute received funds for the anti-Semitism project it had already begun to disintegrate. First Neumann then Marcuse and Kirchheimer, under increasing pressure to find alternative sources of employment and payment, had sought financial refuge with the United States government. To use the colourful language of one historian, the Frankfurt School had gone to war.[26] To be more precise, Neumann, Marcuse and Kirchheimer had joined the Research and Analysis Branch of the Office for Strategic Services. Their task was to collate and analyse information about national socialist Germany. Like much of the other research carried on within American government agencies, including the State Department, impact on policy was minimal. They did, however, play some part in policy relating to the occupation and de-Nazification of Germany. Marcuse, for instance, was involved in drafting the order which dissolved the Nazi party.[27] More importantly, they all played a part in preparing material for use at the war crimes trials.

As the end of the war approached, these men had ambiguous expectations. On the one hand there was some hope that the end of the war would be accompanied by 'something new', but there were also fears that the de-Nazification process would be half-hearted. The skepticism was quickly confirmed. In October 1946 Neumann wrote to Horkheimer that the position was even worse than in 1945. The remaining years of the 1940s did little to improve his assessment of the situation. In a work on Germany and the Future of Europe published in 1951, to which Neumann, along with Marcuse, Kirchheimer and others contributed, he expressed 'grave doubts that, first German society is stable and, second, that the political power centres in German society are committed to democracy'.[28]

Although Neumann and Kirchheimer were more reconciled to the postwar West European order than some of their colleagues, both harboured doubts about the stability and quality of the democratic order. The Federal

Republic of Germany soon followed the United States in its pursuit of growth, mass consumption and virulent anti-communism. But Neumann was not persuaded of its stability. In a lecture of 1954 Neumann argued that lurking behind the façade of success was a persistent anxiety which contradicted President Roosevelt's promise, in 1941, of freedom of speech and religion and freedom from want and fear.[29] Not long after he delivered this lecture Franz Neumann died in a car accident.

Kirchheimer's worries were somewhat different, but scarcely more optimistic. He found the proclamation of the end of a class-divided society to be premature and where others saw confident, if not over-assertive, citizens, sure of their own competence, Kirchheimer saw 'industrial jungle-dwellers and one-dimensional privates in the consumers' army'.[30] He was also worried by the style of the new 'militant democracy'. The idea of militant democracy had arisen in response to the collapse of democratic order in the inter-war Europe.[31] Democracies, it was argued, could not remain neutral and indifferent when faced with internal critics who aimed not just at a change of government but at the destruction of the democratic order. Kirchheimer, however, feared that behind this rhetoric of the defence of democracy lay a tendency to proceed against critics on the basis of vague and indeterminate principles like hostility to the constitution. Opposition, he feared, was being criminalized. Such were the themes of his major work, *Political Justice*, of 1961.[32]

While Neumann and Kirchheimer made academic careers for themselves in the United States, as did Löwenthal, Horkheimer and Adorno returned to Germany. The decision was not easily or quickly taken. The two had grown closer together as a result of their work on Horkheimer's dialectical logic. The end product was not the envisaged one, but *Dialectic of Enlightenment*. This was a curious work. An introductory essay on the concept of enlightenment was followed by two excursuses, another essay on the culture industry and then two groups of shorter pieces, one under the heading 'elements of anti Semitism', the other simply 'notes and drafts'. Beneath this fragmentary purpose lay a consistent question and a consistent answer. The question was 'why mankind, instead of entering into a truly human condition, is sinking into a new kind of barbarism'.[33] The answer was that the historical process of enlightenment had been flawed from the outset.

When *Dialectic of Enlightenment* was finished, in 1944, it circulated, in German, in a limited number of copies. Not until 1947 was it published in Amsterdam, with modifications. The reasons for the modifications varied, but one striking feature was the dilution of overtly Marxist categories. Where the 1944 text referred to the capitalist, the proletarian and exploitation the revised text referred to the entrepreneur, the worker and suffering. In part this reflected a desire to avoid controversy and the continuing fear that too direct professions of faith might mean the death of the Institute.

Horkheimer and Adorno were uncertain what their next step should be, either in terms of the continuation of the project to which *Dialectic of Enlightenment* was seen as a beginning or in terms of the future of the Institute. As far as *Dialectic of Enlightenment* was concerned, they simply could not agree. Horkheimer wanted to 'save' the Enlightenment and suggested that they turn to the contemporary political agenda and political economy but Adorno would not agree.[34] An offer to re-establish the Institute in Frankfurt came as early as 1946, from members of the academic establishment who were implicated in the persecution of the Institute in the 1930s. Horkheimer, however, did not visit Frankfurt until 1948. He did then begin to seek to re-establish the Institute, which was officially reopened in 1951. Money had come from the University, the City and the American High Commission.

The Germany to which Horkheimer, Adorno and Pollock returned was an uneasy amalgam of continuities and changes compounded by the desire to suppress memory of the recent past. The continuities were revealed by the Institute's first major project, the so-called *Gruppenexperimente*. In reality this was a study of political attitudes, which revealed a lack of enthusiasm for democracy and a reluctance to display any guilt about the events which occurred in the Third Reich. Nor were such attitudes revealed only by research. One of the reasons which Horkheimer gave for seeking early retirement in 1956 was the anti-Semitism of a colleague.

Yet Horkheimer also played a prominent public role. He was elected Rector of Frankfurt University in 1951 and was the first Jew to occupy such a position in Germany after the war. He was honoured by the City of Frankfurt, frequently addressed important conferences and gave talks over the radio. The Institute itself carried out research contracts for the Mannesmann corporation, whose chairman, Wilhelm Zangen, had been a leading official of the Nazi war economy, as well as the German trade unions. Especially in his public speeches, Horkheimer adopted a moderate tone which stood in sharp contrast to his privately expressed thought. With only slight exaggeration Jürgen Habermas later said that Horkheimer

> was a merciless observer and perceptive analyst of those false continuities which were so characteristic of the Adenauer period; but the fear in which he lived (and not only a need for recognition) made him keep up a facade, behind which he lived as if he were sitting on unopened suitcases.[35]

One of the continuities to which Habermas referred was significant for his own development. Habermas, born in 1929, had grown up during the Third Reich. The early philosophical influences were provided by Heidegger and Gehlen. By his own account, however, it took Habermas considerable effort to find out what these and other leading intellectuals had believed only fifteen years earlier. One revelation was provided by Heidegger himself when he republished a lecture first given in 1935, a lecture in which he had spoken of the 'inner truth and greatness' of the 'movement', by which was meant the Nazi movement.[36] Outraged by the fact that Heidegger had republished this lecture without any apology whatsoever, Habermas denounced Heidegger in the *Frankfurter Allgemeine Zeitung*. Ironically, Habermas knew little until later of Adorno's hostility to Heidegger. That became fully apparent only with the publication of *The Jargon of Authenticity* in 1964.[37]

Habermas had read *Dialectic of Enlightenment* and he was impressed by a lecture given by Marcuse on Freud. Marcuse's work on Freud overlapped with his preparation of a book on *Soviet Marxism*.[38] This was the first publication by a key member of the Frankfurt School on the Soviet Union since Pollock's book on Soviet planning. Despite being well aware of what was happening in Stalin's Soviet Union, they had remained deliberately silent, for fear of contributing to the criticism of what they saw as the main enemy of Nazi Germany. Earlier there had been hopes, rather fragile ones, that a more humane socialism might emerge. Privately, Horkheimer still occasionally expressed such hopes even after the war, but the predominant image was one of a barbaric totalitarianism which threatened to engulf the West.

The lecture which so impressed Habermas was part of a series on 'Freud in the Present'. Habermas recalled that the simple assertion of the contemporary relevance of Freud was striking enough, at least in the context of German university life. Even more striking was Marcuse's radical, utopian streak.[39] That utopianism was embodied in Marcuse's *Eros and Civilization* which had appeared, in English, before he delivered the lecture.[40] *Eros and Civilization* was in part a continuation of the dispute with Fromm and the appendix contained a polemical criticism of the revisionists. It was also an indictment of the consumer society from a radical, left-wing perspective.

Adorno, and even more so Horkheimer, had been impressed by the book and had wanted, first, to have it appear under the Institute's imprint and then to publish a German translation. It was sadly indicative of the distance between Marcuse and the others, as well as of the baleful influence of Adorno's sensitivities, that this did not happen. Marcuse had been one of the most enthusiastic supporters of the idea of re-launching the *Zeitschrift*. That too never occurred. Horkheimer toyed with the idea for years but was plagued by doubts about his own ability to write anything of substance and by the lack of personnel committed to a common viewpoint, which he held to be necessary to a revival of the *Zeitschrift*. All that remained of these plans was a series of books, the *Frankfurt Contributions to Sociology*. Horkheimer's productive years were indeed behind him. In the posthumously published notes recorded by his friend Pollock and in the occasional pieces he published, Horkheimer saw himself as standing at the end of a bourgeois era whose early promise was being abandoned.[41] Adorno on the other hand entered into a highly productive phase. His book on Husserl, *Against Epistemology*, on which he had been working since the 1930s, finally appeared in 1956.[42] Throughout the 1950s a series of books and other pieces covered sociology, literature, music and philosophy.

It was Adorno who supported his assistant, Habermas. Horkheimer was hostile. What bothered Horkheimer was Habermas's radicalism. In a survey of student attitudes, Habermas put forward a conception of participatory democracy which he contrasted with a state which fostered political apathy and reserved political power to the bureaucracy and interest groups. Habermas did have hopes for the protest movement against NATO's decision to equip German forces with nuclear weapons, which flourished from 1957 to 1959. But this failed to develop the potential he saw in it. Horkheimer, however, asked, in a letter to Adorno,

> How is a people which is 'being held in the shackles of bourgeois society by a liberal constitution' to change into the so-called political society for which, according to H. [Habermas], it is 'more than ripe', other than by violence? It is simply not possible to have admissions of this sort in the research report of an Institute that exists on the public funds of this shackling society.[43]

The accusation that Habermas's goals could only be achieved by violence reflected the narrowing of Horkheimer's vision more than anything else. Habermas, as his major study *The Structural Transformation of the Public Sphere* made clear, looked not to revolutionary violence but to debate within public spheres from which privilege, authority and force were excluded. Horkheimer's hostility ensured that this was not submitted in Frankfurt. Instead Habermas took his work to Wolfgang Abendroth, who had been a pupil of Sinzheimer. The idea of the public sphere had, he claimed, been a specifically bourgeois concept. Habermas could, however, find few remnants of this public sphere in his own day. All that was left was 'public spheres internal to parties and special-interest associations'.[44] His own experience of such forums was not a very happy one. When Habermas and others founded an association to support the German Socialist Students League, the SPD, in November 1961, promptly declared that membership of both the association and the League was incompatible with membership of the SPD.

On the academic front Habermas's target was what he called the scientization of politics, that is advocacy of a technocratic model of society in which there was no scope for either participatory democracy or public spheres in Habermas's sense. In this Adorno sided with Habermas. The two also stood on the same side of the fence in the so-called 'positivist dispute', which was sparked off at the German Sociological Congress of 1961. The positivist dispute, though, was less of a direct conflict than a series of passing shots fired on one side by Adorno and Horkheimer and on the other by Karl Popper, who denied that he was a positivist though he did exhibit the old Weberian desire to separate out science and rational discussion of values.

The disputes induced by growing student radicalism were less sedate. Both

Marcuse and Habermas figured prominently in these debates. Marcuse's own radicalism had not abated as both *One Dimensional Man* (1964) and a highly provocative essay 'On repressive tolerance' (1965) showed.[45] The references in the latter to an educational dictatorship and the sanctioning of violence were carelessly formulated and Marcuse was soon to sound a different tone. His radicalism did make him popular with the German Socialist Students League. He spoke at a conference organized by it in 1966, after which there was a massive demonstration against the Vietnam War. The following year tension escalated. Fearful that student activism would provoke a violent backlash, Habermas urged caution and when the latter seemed to be ignored he accused the more radical students of 'left wing fascism'. Marcuse remained more sympathetic, and ambiguous. But he too ultimately disappointed the radicals, for much the same reason. Where they wanted concrete guidance, Marcuse provided only utopian speculation along with warnings about revolutionary posturing. Relations between Adorno and the students were even worse.

The tension faded as the German government decided to 'risk' more democracy and promised reform. By then Adorno had died. Of the two major works on which he had been working in his later years, he had managed to complete only one, *Negative Dialectics* published in 1966. The other, *Aesthetic Theory*, was published posthumously.[46] In 1983 when a conference on Adorno was held in Frankfurt only Leo Löwenthal remained to offer his recollections. Horkheimer had died in 1973 and Marcuse in 1979.

In the same year as the Adorno conference, Habermas published an essay on 'Zivil Ungehorsam – Testfall für den demokratischen Rechtsstaat' (Civil Disobedience – Test Case for the Rechtsstaat) in which he lamented the supposition, spread by government ministers and elements of the press, that 'peaceful protest is violence'.[47] He wrote in the same spirit as Kirchheimer when he too worried that radical opposition risked being criminalized. Habermas was not seeking an indiscriminate legitimation of civil protest, but reacting to a political mood which, on an earlier occasion, Chancellor Helmut Schmidt described as a 'hysteria for order'. Schmidt was commenting on the atmosphere in 1977, a true test case for the Rechtsstaat. The climate was dominated by terrorist acts, especially the brutal murder of a leading German businessmen. In this climate Alfred Dregger, a regional Christian Democratic leader, declared on television that the Frankfurt School was one of the causes of terrorism. The sentiment had been expressed earlier by academics and was repeated again later on.

Comments of that ilk induced Habermas to identify with the older generation of critical theorists, though he was moving further away from them in other respects. He was helped in this by a greater openness to alternative philosophies and social theories, including pragmatist philosophers and advocates of linguistic analysis whom the older generation had regarded with great suspicion. He was also willing to learn from people from a more conservative camp, especially Hans-Georg Gadamer, a pupil of Heidegger's, and the technocratically inclined Niklas Luhmann. These and other influences combined with an early critical stance towards Marx. This was already evident in the early works but became prominent in *Knowledge and Human Interests*, first published in 1968.[48]

Knowledge and Human Interests was a direct attempt to provide a new justification for a critical theory. It also attracted considerable attention. Habermas conceded that some of the criticism was valid. More importantly, the basic strategy proved to be one with which Habermas became dissatisfied. *Knowledge and Human Interests* still operated within the framework of an epistemologically orientated philosophy. It was this that Habermas turned his back on as he drew on linguistic analysis more and more. His new strategy was formulated in numerous articles and culminated in a new major work in 1981, the two-volume *The Theory of Communicative Action*.[49] *En route* Habermas added his own contribution to the literature on the crisis of the welfare state, *Legitimation Crisis*. There was more to the book than just that, though. It had a broader scope than most of that literature and formed part of Habermas's reworking of Marx. The same was true of *Zur Rekonstruktion des historischen Materialismus* (1976).[50]

The Theory of Communicative Action was, amongst other things, an ambitious attempt to rescue the ideas of the Enlightenment from the *cul de sac* to which Horkheimer and Adorno's *Dialectic of Enlightenment* had consigned it. It was also a reconstruction of Max Weber's theory of modernization which offered a less dismal outcome. Even before this was published, Habermas was turning to deal with the postmodernist challenge. The result, *The Philosophical Discourse of Modernity*, included a new and more radical criticism of *Dialectic of Enlightenment*.[51] The differences between the older generation and Habermas now seemed so marked that, in his words, 'Today it is only possible to take up again the same theoretical motifs across a divide which cannot be closed by an act of will.'[52] It was Habermas's belief in a viable conception of reason that would not abandon us to Weber's competing gods and demons that led him to this conclusion. It was, then, ironic that in the same interview in which he referred to this divide he reported accusations that his own work contributed to the suspicion of reason. With some justice he protested that 'It is not the glaring falsity of the assertion which disturbs me, but the deliberate propagation of such untruths.'[53]

The contention surrounding Habermas's role as critic in the public sphere did not abate. The next major furore resulted from a combination of events. There was a trend amongst certain historians, supported by the German government, to reassert Germany's status as a 'normal' nation. For Michael Stürmer historians have a special role to play in this process. Stürmer argued that West Germans were suffering from a 'loss of orientation' and it was the historian's task to provide orientation, and more specifically a patriotic orientation. Stürmer set this in a broader context in which national identity and patriotism were the only viable substitutes for the sense of meaning which religion had once provided.[54] The way in which the return to normalcy and a sense of orientation were provided provoked a response from Habermas. One was the visit of President Reagan to a cemetery at Bitburg where members of the German army killed during the war were buried. So too, it transpired, were members of the Waffen-SS. The other was a newspaper article by the historian Ernst Nolte, in which he asked 'Was not the "class murder" of the Bolsheviks the logical and factual *prius* of the "race murder" of the National Socialists.'[55] Habermas's response sparked off an acrimonious debate that lasted several years.

This debate concerned the apologetic tendencies which Habermas discerned in the work of Nolte, Stürmer and others, but also more general issues about collective identity and the Enlightenment. Towards the end of *The Philosophical Discourse of Modernity*, Habermas had suggested that the only successful framework for uniting these had been the 'democratic constitutional nation state' which had emerged from the French Revolution.[56] It was this form of state which was the focus of his last major work, *Between Norm and Fact*. In it he sought to steer a course between the liberal and communitarian visions, though he clearly leaned towards the former. It was a work which returned to the themes of *The Structural Transformation of the Public Sphere* and sought to provide a political theory which made the idea of autonomy within the 'democratic constitutional nation state' plausible.

The Institute for Social Research had been created in an unstable political climate in which its founders felt it necessary to conceal their true motives and ambitions. No sooner had it begun to take on the characteristics which would later make it famous, under the Directorship of Horkheimer, than the prospect of emigration loomed. The new, American, environment paradoxically provided the refuge in which they sought to preserve a certain tradition of German social and political philosophy, addressing, as it were, an absent public realm. Yet there were contacts and collaborative projects with American researchers as well as government service for some members of the Institute. Those experiences were, however, not always reassuring. There were too may traces of the prejudices from which they had fled and they had little faith in the commitment of the Allied governments to the ideals which they formally espoused. Those who returned to Germany lived, as Habermas noted, under the shadow of Auschwitz. Their role was a complex one. They were committed to democratization and educational reform and played in this regard a prominent public role, yet they hesitated to republish their earlier work and did not even disseminate it amongst their own students. They hated what they saw as the arthritic grip of a capitalist system, yet feared that political radicalism would lead to disaster. Something of these ambiguities, of a tension between private convictions and the public realm, was evident in the Preface to Adorno's *Negative Dialectics*: 'The author is prepared for the attacks to which *Negative Dialectics* will expose him. He feels no rancor and does not begrudge the joy of those in either camp who will proclaim that they knew it all the time and now he was confessing.'[57] Those who remained in America finally made the transition. As Löwenthal noted in 1979, 'Marcuse and I are, if you will, integrated members of the American educational system and the American intelligentsia', though he added, 'without having given up what's German for it.'[58] That did not necessarily mean a lessening of radicalism. Indeed Marcuse found a new audience, on both sides of the Atlantic, amidst the radicalism of the late 1960s. It was Marcuse's own radicalism that had attracted Habermas in the mid-1950s. Habermas has exhibited a confidence as a critic in the public realm more characteristic of Marcuse than the equivocation of Horkheimer and Adorno and has found an even wider audience, on both sides of the Atlantic. That is evident in the commentary of a leading German newspaper which announced that ' "the German philosopher who enjoys a world renown as no other" has "intervened not least because others are silent" '.[59] The occasion for such praise was a discussion with the socialist candidate for the Chancellorship on the contemporary political agenda. As Habermas has often noted, the differences between his biographical background and those of the older generation – younger, German but not Jewish – help to explain differences in what he and they considered to be viable political, and philosophical, options. Yet Habermas too has lived under the shadow of Auschwitz and he too has had frequent occasion to express alarm at the fragility of the public sphere and the institutions which support it.

CHAPTER 2

A Preliminary Outline
of Critical Theory

The advocates of critical theory were, to varying degrees, Marxists. Most were also trained in philosophy, whose culminating point they identified in the figures of Immanuel Kant and George W.F. Hegel. The exceptions to this were the two legal experts, Kirchheimer and Neumann, and the psychologist Fromm, whose early interests also lay in law. Yet, even for them the prevailing neo-Kantianism was inescapable. Both of these reference points, Marxism and German idealism, are important in locating critical theory.

This location has been forcefully specified by Habermas, according to whom 'we remain contemporaries of the Young Hegelians'.[1] But agreement on the importance of this location, the transition point between idealism and Marxism, does not guarantee agreement on the consequences of it. In some respects Habermas and Adorno draw diametrically opposed conclusions. For Habermas, the conclusion is that this transition signified a break with the philosophical tradition sufficient to warrant speaking of the end of philosophy. Adorno, at the beginning of his *Negative Dialectics*, proclaimed that 'Philosophy, which once seemed obsolete, lives on because the moment to realize it was missed.'[2] In other respects both qualify their apparently clear-cut statements and are closer to each other than at first appears.

Habermas meant an end to a specific conception of philosophy, albeit arguably the conception that had dominated philosophical thought from Plato through to Hegel. This conception, variously identified as metaphysics or idealism, was characterized by the claim that there was a rational order to the world. Further, this order was held to be complete and hence unchanging. Connected with this is the claim that, in Habermas's words, philosophy 'is also "pure" in the sense of having been purged cathartically of all traces of its earthly origins'.[3] It was precisely this conception of philosophy that is the object of sustained criticism in Adorno's *Negative Dialectics*. The ultimate difference between Habermas and Adorno is simply that Adorno believed

31

there was no alternative to working through this philosophical tradition, consistently exposing its inadequacy, whereas Habermas offers an alternative.

Where they agree again is on the position of theory after the failure of idealism. In the first place, it can offer no eternal truths. Knowledge, even in the natural sciences, has proved to be provisional, subject to constant revision in the light of new experiences and methods of inquiry. Second, theoretical insight of whatever kind was very much marked by its 'earthly origins'. According to Habermas this involves recognition of the 'embedding of theoretical accomplishments in the practical contexts of their genesis and employment'.[4] This would be true regardless of whether the 'theoretical accomplishment' is a theory about the sub-atomic nature of the world or a moral injunction.

The suggestion of consensus between Habermas and the older generation does, however, gloss over an important difference, in addition to the one already mentioned. Both could sympathize with Marx's assertion that 'You cannot transcend philosophy without realizing it.'[5] This idea of realizing philosophy was a common theme amongst the older generation. Horkheimer and Marcuse in particular frequently resorted to it. What they meant by the realization of philosophy was quite straightforward. They meant the realization of the bourgeois virtues of freedom, equality and justice by means of a revolution. For Habermas this was no longer a plausible solution. Hence, his gloss on Marx's famous clarion call was that:

> Marx's saying about the realization of philosophy can also be understood in this way: what has, following the disintegration of metaphysical and religious worldviews, been divided up on the level of cultural systems under various aspects of validity, can now be put together – and also put right – only in the experiential context of lifeworld practices.[6]

The 'experiential context of lifeworld practices' is not the revolutionary practice whose absence Adorno cited in order to justify the continuation of 'obsolete' philosophy.

The assertion of the primacy of practice was not just a call to action, let alone a call for uninformed activism at the expense of deliberation and insight. The latter, the critical theorists agreed, had been the error of the student radicals in the 1960s. It did mean that what Habermas called 'theoretical accomplishments' had to be seen in 'the practical contexts of their genesis and employment'. Both elements are important: the genesis and the employment. Neither was construed in a reductionist manner. A good way of provisionally formulating the intent is provided by Toulmin's reference to 'functional responses to the changing problematics of the different sciences in different social milieux'.[7]

According to the advocates of critical theory, the primacy of practice was itself a product of the development of idealist thought, though the two key figures, Kant and Hegel, had limited or curtailed the role and nature of practice. Kant's complex architectonic of reason included a *Critique of Practical Reason*, where practical reason meant moral action. Kant, however, resolutely refused to embed morality in the practical contexts of its genesis. Practical reason, he insisted, must not be guided by the interests and desires of moral agents. To that extent it provides a prime example of Habermas's complaint about a pure doctrine 'purged cathartically of all traces of its earthly origins'.

The severance of practical reason from the context of motivation created difficulties in understanding how this reason was to be effective in the world. It was this that led to Hegel's complaint that practical reason, as construed by Kant, was impotent. His response was to emphasize contexts of genesis and employment in a radical way. He applied this strategy to both epistemology and moral reasoning, setting both in an ambitious historical survey of forms of consciousness. In terms of epistemology Hegel saw this strategy as a solution to the vacillation between emphasis upon the cognitive subject and emphasis upon the external world. His *Phenomenology of Spirit* purported to show the genesis of each and of the vacillation between the two. Morality was incorporated into the same story of development of forms of consciousness. The story was driven forward by the inconsistencies and inadequacies of the forms of consciousness. This immanent critique allowed, he claimed, each form to condemn itself in the light of its own criteria and prepare the way for the next. But Hegel was an idealist. He could not allow the story to end in inconsistency and contradiction. Hence, the purported reconciliation of the divergent views had to come.

Part of the reconciliation came in the form of an attempt to circumvent the supposed deficiencies of Kant's practical reason and related forms of consciousness. This entailed emphasis upon the ethical community of a particular people or nation as the starting point of Hegel's history of spirit. The story unfolds as Hegel exhibited the demise of this community at the hands of external forces or internal solvents. He recorded attempts to find individual solutions to the ensuing dilemmas, but each of these is found to be inadequate. Of one, he complained that 'It does well to preserve itself in its purity, for it *does not act*; it is the hypocrisy which wants its judgements to be taken for an *actual* deed, and instead of proving its rectitude by actions, does so by uttering fine sentiments.'[8] Put more prosaically, Hegel insisted that this hesitant moralist, if he takes his own sense of duty seriously, has to enter the public arena. That the moral could not be protected from the political was accepted by the critical theorists, with overt reference to Hegel. As Adorno wrote in an essay published in 1969: 'To the extent that Hegel expanded the concept of morality into the concept of politics, he dissolved it. Since then apolitical reflections on praxis are unconvincing.'[9]

Hegel's insistence upon the importance of the ethical community and the

33

political realm were important components of the transition from idealism to Marxism. Marx, however, like the other Young Hegelians was equally struck by the idealist elements of Hegel and by the way in which he seemed to believe that history had run its course. If, as Hegel argued, the forms of consciousness had run their course, then history could not bring forth anything fundamentally new. This was no more acceptable to Marx than the vision of a world transparent to reason. Marx and the Young Hegelians, like the younger Hegel himself, saw a world characterized by division and delusion.

They too would have to prove the rectitude of their insights by their deeds. They had to do so in the context of a conception of history that had not been curtailed by an idealist heritage. That meant that the rectitude of their insights, for Marx, the revolution, was in question. The critical theorists, whether envisaging revolution or not, were in the same position. Indeed this position can serve as a first provisional definition of critical theory. By insisting upon the 'embedding of theoretical accomplishments in the practical contexts of their genesis and employment', they sacrificed the claim to certainty which had characterized idealism. But if the certitude of idealism has to be dispensed with, does that mean they were committed to relativism? Their answer was no, though combining the practical and historical contexts of knowledge with a non-relativist stance did not prove easy. Horkheimer's attempt to do so in 'Traditional and Critical Theory' both inspired and worried a younger member of the Institute, Hans Mayer. Mayer wrote, asking 'And how should I understand your sentence, that it is impossible "to speak, in a genuine sense, of changes to a correct theory"? Logically that is naturally right, – but how and by what means does one know the unchangeable "correctness" of the theory?'[10]

The rejection of idealism in favour of the primacy of practice, joined with the attempt to avoid relativism, is common to the critical theorists. But there are important differences of emphasis and interpretation. Amongst the older generation, both their more radical Marxism, at least in the 1930s, and their reaction to the denigration of reason in favour of more primeval forces, induced language reminiscent of Hegel's invocation of reason and spirit. This was especially true, as Mayer already noted, of Marcuse.[11] Much more important are the differences between Habermas and the older generation concerning the meaning of practice. The older generation, as Habermas complains, followed Marx in his emphasis upon labour and production as the key to the reproduction of societies. This is evident when Adorno recalled that:

> Marx received the thesis of the primacy of practical reason from Kant and the German idealists, and he sharpened it into a challenge to change the world instead of merely interpreting it ... The *telos* of due practice, according to him, was the abolition of the primacy of practice in the form that had prevailed in bourgeois society.[12]

Habermas argued that another dimension of societal reproduction, namely communicative interaction, had been recognized by Hegel in his *Jena Philosophy of Mind* before it was submerged by the dictates of his mature systems of thought. It was also evident in Marx, though he suppressed it in favour of the image of productive labour alone as the key. The importance of communicative interaction to Habermas is enormous. He did not seek to systematically test the relative significance of the two, labour and interaction, in the development and stability of modern societies. But he suggested that interaction has greater analytic importance in several ways. First, he argues that interaction, not labour, distinguishes specifically human forms of social reproduction. The latter was said to be distinct by virtue of 'a system of norms that presupposed language'.[13] Second, Habermas argued that major civilizational transitions cannot be construed as the product of the development of production. The latter followed, rather than preceded, civilizational transitions.[14] Equally striking is the contrast between Adorno and Habermas. Adorno drew the obvious conclusion from his comments on Marx's refashioning of the concept of practice: 'The possible reduction of labor to a minimum could not but have a radical effect on the concept of practice.'[15] According to Habermas, however, '*Liberation from hunger and misery* does not necessarily converge with *liberation from servitude and degradation*, for there is no automatic developmental relation between labor and interaction.'[16]

These differences clearly signify divergent understandings of society, but there are equally important similarities that serve as a second provisional definition of critical theory. Here, the starting point is the apparently trivial one that society is the product of the activities of its members. This is only apparently trivial, for idealist constructions of history have portrayed various spiritual agencies as the determining force. It was this kind of suggestion, as embodied in Hegel's work, that Marx spent much of his time attacking. More important, although society is the product of the activity of its members, it has, the argument continues, outstripped their grasp and comprehension. In Horkheimer's words:

> The two-sided character of the social totality in its present form becomes, for men who adopt the critical attitude, a conscious opposition. In recognizing the present form of economy and the whole culture which it generates to be the product of human work as well as the organization which mankind was capable of and has provided for itself in the present era, these men identify themselves with this totality and conceive it as will and reason. It is their own world. At the same time, however, they experience the fact that society is comparable to nonhuman natural processes ... [17]

That there are limits, and possibly severe ones, to men's ability to determine their own fate, is not the preserve of critical theory. Helmut Schelsky's assertion of 'objective exigencies of scientific-technical civilization' which cannot be understood in terms of choices or convictions is a clear example of that.[18] Where Horkheimer differs from Schelsky is in his claim that there is an alternative, that society can be reordered such that it does fall within the comprehension and grasp of its members.

To varying degrees all of the critical theorists subscribed to this claim. Even Habermas, who has considerable reservations, to say the least, concluded his *Legitimation Crisis* with a call for a defence of 'the struggle against the stabilization of a nature-like social system *over* the heads of its citizens'.[19] For Adorno, the inability of men to determine their own fate seemed so overwhelming that he claimed men had been reduced to the status of objects. Indeed, he came close to Schelsky's position, differing more in his protest against the situation than in his ability to point to an alternative.[20]

One of the striking features of the older generation was the way in which they sought to explore this process from the viewpoint of the individuals affected by it. It was here that the social psychology, first developed by Fromm, played a key role. The argument was that it was not sufficient to analyse the mechanics of the 'nature-like social system'. It was necessary to explain how individuals adapted to their roles within this social system. Horkheimer stressed that it was how *individuals* adapted that mattered. He carefully distanced himself from any postulation of a 'mass soul' or a mass consciousness'.[21] This focus served to strengthen the image of the impotence of individuals in the face of the social process unfolding over their heads. Adorno, for example, claimed to discern this impotence in the detail of contemporary life, even down to the content of the *Los Angeles Times* astrology column. The social psychology favoured by Adorno, let alone its nuances, did not find favour with all of the older generation. Franz Neumann's work shows little trace of it, until near the end of his life. But in 'Anxiety and Politics' he picked up the same themes in an attempt to explain why Franklin D. Roosevelt's promise of a post-war world free from fear had not been fulfilled.[22]

The general supposition of a 'struggle against the stabilization of a nature-like social system *over* the heads of its citizens' places critical theory firmly within the Marxist approach. It was central to Marx's argument that in pre-capitalist modes of production 'relations of personal dependence' were transparent. The slave and the serf were in no doubt that they laboured for the benefit of the owner or lord. In the capitalist mode of production, however, where men were formally independent and free, dependency was hidden behind a veil. That veil was the commodity form in which social wealth, and hence relations between men, appeared.[23] In place of directly political subordination of the pre-capitalist modes of production stepped the anonymous world of the market in which the labour power of the proletarians appeared as just another commodity for sale.

For the critical theorists, and indeed many other Marxists, including

Lukacs, the commodity form played a major role in their analysis of capitalism. Initially the emphasis was placed upon the distortion created by what Marx called 'the whole mystery of commodities, all the magic and necromancy that surrounds the products of labour on the basis of commodity production'.[24] This model, however, came to seem increasingly tenuous to the older generation. The implication of domination exercised through the anonymous operation of a market, of domination as an economic rather than a directly political relationship, ran counter to the trends of the 1930s. At that time state intervention in the economy and the overt assertion of totalitarian politics, notably in the fascist states but not only there, suggested a refeudalization of society.

That trend was evident in Marcuse's lapidary comment, the 'anarchy of the market is abolished, labour becomes compulsory service'.[25] That was an oversimplification, even of the fascist states. It was, of course, the authoritarian and totalitarian states of the 1930s and 1940s that pushed the critical theorists in this direction. Their reassessment, however, was not abandoned with the restoration of democracy, at least in the West. It was, rather, consolidated and extended. In part this can be accounted for by the failure to return to the limited state of the nineteenth century and the growth of the welfare state in the post-war world. Only in part, for more direct political domination now seemed a more pervasive characteristic of the liberal state. According to Neumann this had always been evident to political reactionaries. His conclusion was that 'The primacy of politics was always a fact, which was at times glossed over, at times openly recognized.'[26] Max Horkheimer developed the same theme in more polemical fashion, describing political and economic power as a form of racket. These rackets consisted of seizing onto socially necessary functions, like protection from external threats, monopolizing them and extorting payment in return. Although Horkheimer and Neumann often emphasized the continuity of this primacy of politics, they also utilized a contrast between the liberal state and market on the one hand, and the post-liberal state and market on the other hand, without coming to any clear conclusion about the relative merits of these two models.

Again Habermas has followed the general trend, but drawn significantly less pessimistic conclusions. Continuity is evident in his early work, *The Structural Transformation of the Public Sphere*, where he wrote of the 'refeudalization' of society. This rested upon the idea of a transition from the liberal order in which there was a distinction, not unequivocal but clear enough, between the public and the private, the political and the societal. That distinction, he claimed, had been undermined with the emergence of the welfare state. Habermas also wrote of the refeudalization of society in a slightly different, but related, context, namely the public sphere. In the contemporary world, he complained, 'Publicity work is aimed at strengthening the prestige of one's own position without making the matter on which a compromise is to be achieved itself a topic of *public discussion*.'[27] The liberal ideal, at least, had involved the formation of a public opinion by means of a public debate of issues, and that debate was supposed to endow the opinion with legitimacy. But all this, Habermas argued, was irrelevant to modern organizations, for which publicity is the display of status and reputation. It was this emphasis upon public display rather than public debate, which conjured up feudal models of the public realm.

This idea of a refeudalization of society became less important for Habermas than two other, related, trends. The first was the scientization of politics, which can be grouped under the heading of direct political subordination, rather than subordination to the anonymous process of economic markets. The second was what Habermas called the 'colonization of the lifeworld'. This covers both direct political subordination and subordination to the anonymous process of economic markets. By the scientization of politics Habermas referred to a technocratic understanding of politics. Here politics is essentially a matter of choices that can be made on the basis of knowledge 'whose certainty obviates public discussion'.[28] This kind of technocracy, represented in the work of Schelsky, is incompatible with what Habermas described as the 'experiential context of lifeworld practices'. The latter lacks the certainty claimed by the technocratic approach, is related to the earthly experiences and interests of members of society and can only be justified in the light of public discussion. The technocratic approach, in addition to its claim to certainty, eschews public discussion and seeks its justification in the supposedly 'objective exigencies of scientific-technical civilization'.[29]

The colonization of the lifeworld also has, Habermas argues, a debilitating effect upon the 'experiential context of lifeworld practices'. In part this colonization merely refers to the subordination of men to the dictates of market processes. Here it is the restriction of self-determination by heteronomously defined occupation roles and the reduction of the citizen to the role of a consumer that is the focus. In part it refers to the effects of increasing intervention by agencies of the state in areas of life previously considered to constitute part of the private sphere. Although intended to protect individuals against the vagaries of market processes, these interventions tend to restrict individual self-determination by defining the individual as a 'client' of the state agencies. It is this role of the client that particularly worries Habermas. He argues that it lacks even the element of choice found in the consumer. Indeed the role itself is 'first constituted by legal fiat' and individuals in that role are subject to control by various experts ranging from the courts to therapists and social workers.[30] That in turn, he claims, has been facilitated by the emergence of a 'fragmented consciousness', that is, an inability to bring together the diverse elements of modern culture and society in a coherent and meaningful whole.[31] This obviously has serious implications for Habermas, since he continues to believe that 'what has, following the disintegration of metaphysical and religious worldviews, been divided up on the level of cultural systems under various aspects of validity, can now be put together – and also put right – only in the experiential context of lifeworld practices'.[32] If the 'fragmented consciousness' is as typical as he claims, it is difficult to see how it can be put together.

For Habermas the suggestion that it could be put together would, in any event, have to be qualified. Given the complexity of modern societies, praxis philosophy had erred in believing that the diverse social processes which unfolded 'over the heads of its citizens', 'can be brought into the horizon of the lifeworld'.[33] The supposition that it could had been an essential element of Marx's thought from the outset. It did, as Habermas complained, also play a dominant part in the thought of the older generation of critical theorists. The image of a society that would be transparent to its members acquired a distinctive hue in Horkheimer's work. When he wrote of the 'two sided character of the social totality' he explained that the appearance of society as analogous to 'nonhuman natural processes' arose 'because cultural forms ... are not the creation of a unified self-conscious will'.[34] This idea of a 'unified self-conscious will' is problematic to say the least. In other formulations the older generation compounded the problem. Adorno insisted on the importance of the 'potential of society as a subject' in a context where 'subject' meant not 'subject-matter' but the cognitive subject of traditional epistemology.[35]

The potential ascription of subjectivity to society readily sounds like the idealism which Horkheimer and Adorno denounced. Neither consciousness nor will can be ascribed to anything other than individuals, save by analogy or as shorthand. Yet it is clear that Horkheimer and Adorno intended more than this. Horkheimer wrote that 'in the transition from the present form of society to a future one mankind will for the first time constitute itself as a conscious subject'.[36] The objections raised to this kind of statement include, of course, those already noted. They also include the accusation that it presumes, illegitimately, that there is a unified history of mankind in the first place. That accusation can draw upon Horkheimer's own criticism of any metaphysics of history.[37]

Habermas exercises more caution. The idea of a society as a subject, let alone of mankind constituting itself as a subject through history, he dismisses as a fiction. Yet he insists that it is legitimate to look for some order, and even progress, in history, so long as this order is not ascribed to any agent which might be construed as consciously or unconsciously creating that order. In the same spirit he finds that the idea of the 'self producing subject of history' is not entirely meaningless. The underlying intention to tie social development to models of self-determination is plausible, albeit not in the elevated, and exaggerated, sense sometimes suggested by Horkheimer and Adorno.[38]

Issues like the fragmentation of consciousness and the extent to which history can be construed as ordered and progressive, point to a third provisional definition of critical theory. The critical theorists agreed that the Hegelian construction of a unified and ultimately rational science of the appearance and development of the forms of consciousness was no longer plausible. But they were dissatisfied with the contemporary fragmentation of sciences. Critical theory is, in part, defined by the attempt to come to terms with, or overcome, that fragmentation.

The critical theorists were concerned by two interconnected groups of problems here. The first was the fragmentation of the sciences in the sense of the various academic disciplines. Related to this were questions about the status and role of philosophy and the extent of specialization within the various disciplines, especially within the discipline of sociology. The second group was defined largely by the structure of Kant's philosophy, that is by its division into the three critiques, of pure reason, of practical reason, and of judgement. That in turn rested upon the traditional trinity of the true, the good and the beautiful, to which philosophy was supposed to be devoted.[39] Of these three it was the pair of the true and the good that enjoyed pre-eminence. In the Kantian construction the respective forms of knowledge, defined by the critiques of pure and practical reason, generated a dualistic approach to science and men. From the perspective of the critique of pure reason man was a piece of nature, explicable in terms of laws of causality and empirical observation. From the perspective of the critique of practical reason, man appeared as a moral being, possessed of free will and the ability to act in accordance with the dictates of universally valid moral laws. This basic dualism was passed down in the nineteenth century and refined into a dualism constituted by the division between the natural sciences and the cultural sciences (*Geisteswissenschaften*).

That dualism, and protests against it, still dominated the agenda faced by the older generation of critical theorists, and was still significant enough to Habermas to form the starting point of his *On the Logic of the Social Sciences*. It appeared at the end of Horkheimer's *Habilitationsschrift* on Kant, where he called for clarification of the doctrine underlying modern culture as a whole, namely 'the bifurcation of the rational person as a juxtaposition of will and reason'.[40] At the end of the day Horkheimer wanted not so much to clarify this bifurcation as to circumvent it. Essentially he followed Hegel's criticism of Kant in pursuit of a reformulated Marxism. The outcome was a definition of critical theory in terms of its commitment to radical change. The warrant for that commitment was the assumption that 'the objective realities given in perception are conceived as products which in principle should be under human control and, in the future at least, will in fact come under it'.[41] In other words it presumed the validity of the first two provisional definitions of critical theory given above, and presumed their validity in their more radical form.

This solution of the Kantian dualism, if solution it was, was of little help in dealing with the fragmentation of the sciences. For the latter, Horkheimer prescribed an interdisciplinary research programme. The purpose of this programme was to answer 'the question of the connection between the economic life of society, the psychical development of individuals and the changes in the realm of culture in the narrower sense'.[42] It has been suggested that philosophy was to play a privileged role within this interdisciplinary framework, identifying the problems that were to be addressed by those working within the other disciplines. There is some truth in this insofar as Horkheimer wrote of the 'animating impulses' which philosophy could provide. At this stage, however, Horkheimer also ascribed an interest in 'larger philosophical questions' to all 'true researchers', regardless of their discipline.[43] This was consistent with his general insistence at the time that there were no fundamental, methodological differences between the various disciplines, not even between the natural sciences and the cultural sciences.[44]

What agitated Horkheimer was evident in an essay on 'On Bergson's metaphysics of time'. There he complained of two things. First, he noted that the separation of the individual scientific disciplines from philosophy was accelerating and that philosophy seemed to be in danger of having no role left. But this was not the main concern. The real problem was that these individual sciences had lost any connection with 'the interests of society as a whole'.[45] He did not mean to deny that these sciences were not embedded 'in the practical contexts of their genesis and employment'. His complaint was that they had a restricted horizon. Second, he complained of what one might call a loss of sight of 'larger philosophical questions' by both the individual sciences and the philosophy, positivism, which claimed to justify them. The former fled to the mere accumulation of data, the latter to empty abstractions.

Over twenty years later, in a survey of German sociology, Adorno raised similar complaints. His general point was that contemporary German sociology lacked any perspective of society as a whole. He implied that this deficiency could be attributed to sociology's distance from philosophy, for 'the perspective of the totality is necessarily philosophical'.[46] That claim is patently false unless philosophy is taken to be what Hegel and Adorno himself said it was. Adorno was on sounder ground when he took exception to the division between political economy and sociology. By consigning economic issues to the former, contemporary sociology was pushed to 'fetishize "inter-human relations"', from which relations generated by the mode of production had been excluded.[47] A similar criticism of industrial sociology led to a more general point, namely that the demarcation lines between disciplines were being mistaken for definitions of an 'ontological order'.[48]

The danger of mistaking disciplinary perspectives for distinctions between different realms of society is real enough. Adorno's complaint that the pursuit of disciplinary identity can involve an undesirable neglect of certain issues, is confirmed by the long-term development of the various disciplines, which are periodically marked by attempts to remedy precisely those deficiencies. On the other hand, Horkheimer's call for an interdisciplinary research programme was based on recognition of the fact that the diversity of the various disciplines, to say nothing of the substantive material accumulated by each of them, had escaped the grasp of any one individual. Horkheimer's solution, as expressed in a review of the Institute's activities in 1938, was that each member of the Institute should continue to work within his discipline. Coherence was to be sought by the common questions they asked. Even so, he had to admit to some difficulty in integrating psychology into the fold. As he noted, they were helped by the fact that they could draw on a common philosophical tradition, but he ignored the frequently expressed differences, both of substantive interpretation and of the presentation of their ideas.[49]

Habermas has retained a concern with 'society as a whole', as called for by Adorno, though ironically he identified sociology as the discipline where that perspective had been best maintained. There are also echoes of Horkheimer's original project in Habermas's justification of his choice of sociology: 'Sociology arose as the theory of bourgeois society; to it fell the task of explaining the course of the capitalist modernization of traditional societies and its anomic side effects.'[50] Yet Habermas even more than the older generation has repeatedly asserted that the Hegelian enterprise is no longer plausible. In his *Between Facts and Norms* he explains the frequency of references to Kant and comparative neglect of Hegel by his 'aversion' to the Hegelian model and its over-ambitious goals. He also admits to a 'pluralistic approach', drawing on 'moral theory, social theory, legal theory, and the sociology and history of law'.[51] In reality that list could be expanded without causing undue surprise to any of the relevant disciplines.

Habermas asks, what then is left to philosophy if the Hegelian, and even the Kantian enterprise is judged to be over-ambitious? His answer is that philosophy is left with the roles of a 'stand-in' and an interpreter. By the former he suggested that philosophy has no privileged domain, nor can it play the role of arbiter as Hegel and even Kant had assumed. Philosophy here can do no more than provide 'reconstructive hypotheses for use in empirical settings'.[52] An example of such hypotheses would be his own 'Toward a Reconstruction of Historical Materialism'. The role of interpreter at first seems simple: philosophy is to interpret the specialized languages of experts for the benefit of laymen. Given the complexity of Habermas's own language, this involves a certain irony. More importantly, it is not the theme on which Habermas concludes his justification of 'Philosophy as stand-in and Interpreter'. His concluding point is a confession of his own commitment to philosophy as 'the guardian of rationality'.[53]

The status of Habermas's reconstructive hypotheses is linked with his doubts about the underlying philosophy of history that he ascribed to the older generation. That, in turn, is linked to his understanding of the relationship between history and the social sciences. In an attempt to rigorously exclude the temptation to repeat something like Hegel's *Phenomenology of Spirit* he argues that:

> If we separate the logic from the dynamics of development – that is, the rationally reconstructible *pattern* of a hierarchy of more and more comprehensive structures from the *processes* through which the empirical substrates develop – then we need require of history neither unilinearity nor necessity, neither continuity nor irreversibility.[54]

The suggestion is that we can, retrospectively, discern different civilizational principles in history and we can even see these as marking some kind of progress or advance. But we must not construe this progress as willed or intended. Equally important, there is no guarantee that any particular society will cross the boundary marking the retrospectively discerned civilizational principle. Even if it does, it may lapse behind it again. For much the same reason, he insists that the writing of history takes on a narrative form which must not be confused with the presentation of evolutionary theories.[55]

Habermas is inclined to accept a differentiation of academic disciplines for other reasons. The distillation of separate disciplines of political science and economics appears as neither contingent nor unjustified. They correspond to real historical developments, insofar as their objects, the market economy and the state, have become 'sub-systems' of society with distinct processes and languages. This does not mean that Habermas is arguing for a division of labour and a defence of demarcation lines. The breadth of his own work is clearly incompatible with that and his public forays have occasionally led to the retort that the layman should pay more attention to such boundaries.[56]

Habermas's acceptance of the consequences of modernization, part of which is constituted by the development of those sub-systems, has a broader significance. Although Habermas has used different formulations, three main principles stand out. First, modernity excludes any recourse to tradition as a guide. He explains how this principle first broke through in the dispute between the 'ancients' and the 'moderns' over aesthetic judgements. The moderns rejected the models of the classical world, arguing instead for an approach to beauty which accepted the historical contingency and relativity of aesthetic judgement. Aesthetic judgement has concerned Habermas less than moral judgement. But the principle is the same. There are no binding traditions that can guide moral judgement. It was this dilemma which Hegel was the first to confront and which, according to Habermas, makes us contemporaries of the Young Hegelians.

Second, modernity involves the formation of those sub-systems, including the market economy and the state, each of which has developed specialized discourses and rules. This too forms part of the transition from tradition-governed systems. Thus in the case of law, which Habermas sees as a key indicator of this process:

> Modern compulsory law is uncoupled from ethical motives; it functions as means for demarcating areas of legitimate choice for private legal persons and scopes of legal competence for officeholders ... In these spheres of action, legal norms replace the prelegal substratum of traditional morals to which previously ... legal norms had reference.[57]

Third, modernity involves a differentiation of the spheres of the true, the good and the beautiful. In this sense modernity involves a radicalization of Kant's division of philosophy into the critiques of pure reason, practical reason and judgement. In part this differentiation is a quasi-institutional process, in which experts in the relevant area develop a specialized language and criteria. It is the latter which is especially important to Habermas. The questions that are raised, questions of truth, questions of justice and questions of taste, admit of different answers. The precise criteria applied differ in each field. But, Habermas argues, all of them are answerable. All of them raise claims to warrant the assent of others.

The triadic structure of truth, morality and beauty was not the only one deployed by Habermas. In *Knowledge and Human Interests* he distinguished between three cognitive interests: the technical, the practical and the emancipatory. Later, dissatisfied with the attempt to elaborate cognitive interests, he distinguished between types of communicative action: teleological or strategic, normatively regulated action and dramaturgical action. Again these forms of action can be judged, by reference to their truth, rightness and truthfulness.[58]

At this stage of provisional definitions the precise formulation used by Habermas is less important than the contrast of all of them with the theories of the older generation. Habermas has sought to build up a more differentiated model of society, of types of social action and types of knowledge. Similarly, he has ascribed different functions to different disciplines, insisting, in a Kantian manner, that one should not trespass on the terrain proper to another. Although Horkheimer, Adorno and Marcuse gave more credit to Kant towards the end of their lives, they all retained a greater sense of the validity of Hegel's criticisms of Kant. The outcome was an inclination to look for principles that cut across the types of distinction drawn by Habermas. Or put in more accurate chronological order, Habermas has produced more differentiated models in order to avoid some of the embarrassments he believes the older generation found themselves confronted with.

The older generation remained committed to asserting their theories' connection with 'the interests of society as a whole' and accepted Hegel's principle that those interests were historical ones. In agreement with the Young Hegelians they rejected Hegel's own attempt to avoid the contingency of that commitment to history. That would not have mattered so much, had they not construed those 'interests of society as a whole' so radically. It was the extent of their commitment to the ideals of bourgeois society combined with the Young Hegelian belief that such ideals had to prove themselves in practice, that raised the stakes to be decided by the actual historical trends.

CHAPTER 3

The Failure of Metaphysics

The reference point for the failure of metaphysics is the rationalist systems of the German idealists, and especially that of Hegel. Hegel's ambition has been succinctly summarized by the historian of German philosophy, Herbert Schnädelbach. According to Schnädelbach Hegel's Absolute Idealism consisted of three theses: '(1) the unity of being and thought in the Absolute; (2) the unity of the true, the good, and the beautiful in the Absolute; (3) the science of the Absolute as the philosophical system'.[1] The 'Absolute' is nothing more than this unity grasped within a rational and systematic philosophy. It is what Habermas called the 'emphatic' concept of reason, a concept that he no longer found persuasive.[2]

Nor did the older generation of critical theorists who were confronted with attempts to revive or find a substitute for the certainties offered by traditional metaphysical systems. This 'new metaphysics', as Horkheimer designated it, was formulated in a different intellectual climate from that dominant in the days of Hegel. The changed mood, and the difference from Hegel, was expressed by Wilhelm Dilthey: Hegel, he complained, 'constructed communities on the basis of the general rational will. Today, we have to start from the reality of life ... And present-day analysis of human existence fills us all with the feeling of frailty, of the power of dark instincts, of the passion for darkness and illusion.'[3] However, Dilthey's concern, the 'feeling of frailty', was not shared by all who invoked 'the power of dark instincts'. What they espoused was not metaphysics in the sense that that term could be applied to Hegel, but some unifying and invigorating force which was often counterposed to reason. That contrast can even be discerned in a mere title. Whereas Hegel's major work was called *Phänomenologie des Geistes* (Phenomenology of Spirit), Ludwig Klages titled his work, published over the years 1929 to 1933, *Der Geist als Widersacher der Seele* (Spirit as the Opponent of the Soul).[4]

More important than Klages was Martin Heidegger. Strictly speaking Heidegger was a self-avowed critic of traditional metaphysics, which he claimed to have 'overcome' or 'destroyed'. Traditional metaphysics, he claimed, was dominated by a distinction between essence and existence which merely obscured the important question. The important question was announced in the heading to the first paragraph of *Being and Time*: 'The Necessity for Explicitly Restating the Question of Being.'[5] Merely reformulating the question was a protracted business, but Heidegger gave a preliminary answer quite quickly: 'the question of Being is nothing other than the radicalization of an essential tendency-of-Being which belongs to Dasein itself'.[6] Quite what the central category of Dasein, literally 'being-there', means is far from clear or agreed. What is clear is that it was intended to provide an alternative to the traditional epistemological enterprise and its basic concepts.

Heidegger's importance to the critical theorists arose not just from his metaphysical theories but also from his influence on Marcuse and Habermas and, even more so, from his public role. Above all it was his role during the Third Reich, his very public support for Adolf Hitler, that raised questions about the relationship between his philosophy and this political commitment and about the public role and responsibilities of philosophers. Those questions were inevitably important to Heidegger's French admirers, including the self-avowed postmodernists Jean-François Lyotard and Jacques Derrida. Their defence of Heidegger was less important to Habermas than their continuation of Heidegger's project of the 'destruction' of traditional metaphysics.[7] In their version this radical criticism, stylized under the label of postmodernism, has issued in the celebration of 'difference' and 'diversity' in place of the unity favoured by Hegel, and a radical dismissal of 'metanarratives', under which label Hegel's philosophical system would undoubtedly fall. Although their language is scarcely more accessible than Heidegger's, Lyotard provides a relatively clear indication of their outlook in his claim that 'There is no politics of reason, neither in the sense of a totalizing reason nor in that of the concept. And so we must do with a politics of opinion.'[8]

What unites the critical theorists is their conviction that while the comprehensive certitude offered by Hegel is no longer plausible, attempts to find a substitute, be it in the primeval forces of Klages's *Der Geist als Widersacher der Seele* or Heidegger's Dasein, are philosophically unsound and politically dangerous. Nor does acceptance of the failure of metaphysics need to lead to the relativism of the postmodernists. The consistency of their opposition to these strategies varied, most notably in the case of Herbert Marcuse. Marcuse was the first of the critical theorists to deal at length with Heidegger. It was, indeed, Heidegger's *Being and Time* which induced Marcuse to return to the study of philosophy. It is worth asking what the attraction of Heidegger's book was? The answer is quite simple: the attraction lay in its challenge to the predominant dualistic philosophy of the day, which set subject against object, transcendental ego against empirical ego, theoretical reason against practical reason and so on. Even when the charm of Heidegger began to fade the same motive was at work in Marcuse's estimation of other philosophers. Thus Marcuse praised Dilthey for reviving the Hegelian and Marxist insight into 'the historical unity of man and world, consciousness and being', adding that 'The flattening of this living relationship to an epistemological "relation", to the abstract subject–object relation which had thereafter established itself again, is led back anew by Dilthey into the ontological unity.'[9]

Marcuse sought to reconcile Heidegger's ontology with a praxis orientated Marxism which stressed will and action. So enthusiastic was his commitment to this stance at the beginning of the 1930s that he praised Hans Freyer's *Soziologie als Wirklichkeitswissenschaft* as the most radical contemporary reflection upon sociology. Amongst its supposed virtues was its definition of sociology's basic attitude as ethical, volitional and resolute as opposed to logical and epistemological.[10] Heidegger too wrote about resolve and Marcuse sought to fuse Heidegger's rhetoric with a Marxism that blamed the failure of revolution on the absence of will. Hence Heidegger's weakness was supposed to be that he ascribed the requisite resolution to the individual, whereas, Marcuse insisted, it should properly be ascribed to a class, the proletariat. The proletariat, like Heidegger's Dasein, was called upon to act. Within the Heideggerian context Marcuse wrote that Dasein's 'freedom lies only in the acceptance of its heritage – for which one is ready to die – and in the self-chosen fulfillment of necessity'.[11] In the slightly more prosaic language of his Marxism, Marcuse had already noted the historical destiny of the proletariat, that is revolution. In effect Marcuse was asserting that the general characteristics of Dasein were those which could only be fulfilled by the proletariat. Part of those characteristics involved 'the acceptance of its heritage – for which one is ready to die'. Again returning to the more prosaic language of Marxism this might be taken to mean simply accepting the risk of death which revolutionary action entailed. But Heidegger was no Marxist. In the same paragraph from which Marcuse quoted Heidegger's invocation of 'resoluteness' and 'heritage', Heidegger spelled out what this meant: 'in anticipating death ... [Dasein] ... understands itself unambiguously in terms of its own most distinctive possibility ... Only by the anticipation of death is every accidental and "provisional" possibility driven out ... Dasein *hands* itself *down* to itself, free for death, in a possibility which it has inherited and yet has chosen.'[12]

Marcuse had turned to Heidegger as a philosophical alternative to the epistemology of the prevailing neo-Kantianism. He had hoped to find a fuller grasp of 'the reality of life' to which Dilthey appealed and yet to retain the order and certainties offered by a 'fundamental ontology'. All that in turn was to be deployed in the service of a revolutionary Marxism. The strain of trying to hold all this together was too much. Marcuse had to gloss over the incompatibility of Heidegger with Marxism and he was left with little more than a philosophy of radical action, which was so abstract that it was difficult, to say the least, to connect it with historical reality. Even before he joined the Institute for Social Research he had begun to draw more heavily on Hegel, but he still found it difficult to shake off Heidegger's influence.[13] But by 1934 he was assimilating Heidegger to a new anthropology and asking: 'What manner of "historicity" is meant, what form of political action and of practice is intended? What kind of action is it, then, that the new anthropology enjoins as the "authentic" practice of man?'[14]

Max Horkheimer was not tempted by the new metaphysics in any of its guises. In part this was because of a simple suspicion. He did not know, he wrote, if there was some metaphysics that was right, but he was sure that metaphysicians were not usually concerned by what tormented men.[15] Similarly to Marcuse, Horkheimer referred to 'philosophical anthropology' as well as metaphysics or the 'new metaphysics', without necessarily referring to different authors. Nicolai Hartmann and Max Scheler were dealt with under more than one of these labels, as was Martin Heidegger. The common themes underlying the various commentaries were the social function played by these doctrines, their inherent dogmatism and the disparagement of human volition and reason that Horkheimer claimed they entailed.

In terms of social function Horkheimer claimed that they all responded to the need for a sense of order and direction in the wake of the modernization of society. To that extent the 'new metaphysics' or 'modern philosophical anthropology' was no different from idealism. The attempt, however, was misguided. It was misguided in the first place because it could never succeed. The excessive ambition was evident in Max Scheler's claim to prove that 'all the specific achievements and works of man – language, conscience, tools, weapons, ideas of right and wrong, the state, leadership, the representational function of art, myths, religion, science, history and social life – arise from the basic structure of human existence'.[16] It was misguided in the second place because problems related to the distribution of goods, occupational roles, and even international relations were rooted in conflicts of interest and 'social contradictions'. Any attempt to explain these problems in terms of an invariant 'basic structure of human existence' entailed hiding the real conflicts beneath a veil of some 'deeper meaning'. Thus, when Scheler conceded that no such meaning could be discerned, Horkheimer promptly claimed that he thereby 'repudiated the strongest impulse to metaphysics'.[17]

It is fairly evident that in attacking metaphysics Horkheimer was primarily concerned with its supposed normative implications. He argued that deriving norms from ontologies only really made sense where the metaphysics included a theology, for only a God could make normative demands upon men, issue commands, make judgements about sin and so forth. Metaphysicians, he continued, tried to maintain the same normative implications even in the absence of an explicit theology. Here, they glossed over the absence of a personal being capable of these actions, by writing of 'fittingness, genuineness, authenticity, or, more generally, philosophical wisdom'.[18]

In counterposing his own materialism to metaphysics Horkheimer sought to guard against any supposition that this materialism was itself a metaphysics. In a trivial sense, of course, it was a metaphysics insofar as it made some general assumptions about the nature of reality. But Horkheimer insisted that these assumptions were 'minimal in content' and totally devoid of normative status.[19] Horkheimer was too conscious of the impact of the natural sciences upon our understanding of the nature of reality to believe that it was possible to set up any invariant account of it. Even Kant's attempt to provide a philosophical justification for the natural sciences was dismissed as 'extraordinarily narrow', as neglectful of the specific investigations of the natural sciences and restricted to little more than a 'few general principles'.[20] Horkheimer's general attitude is evident in his praise of Ernst Mach against his more materialist critic, Max Planck, for emphasizing the way in which concepts are formed. The idea of science as involving 'models' or 'hypotheses' was more congenial to Horkheimer than proclamations about the ultimate reality of the world.[21]

The inherent dogmatism and the disparagement of reason and volition were closely bound up in Horkheimer's account of the new metaphysics. Here he focused on Max Scheler and especially the ethics of Nicolai Hartmann. Horkheimer's objections to Hartmann were numerous. Again the starting point was the dissolution of tradition-bound society and the efforts of philosophers to establish some sure basis for moral action to fill the gap. Hartmann was, to that extent, merely a recent representative of bourgeois philosophy. What was novel about Hartmann and Scheler was that they asserted the existence of a realm of ethical values which existed independently of judgements made by men. The peculiarity of their position is well summarized by Herbert Schnädelbach: 'according to Scheler values are, exist, and do not merely have validity ... The values which exist in-themselves, independently of any subject, can be grasped and exhibited, because they "appear" in that which is valuable.'[22] For Horkheimer this was objectionable in the first place because there were no such invariant values. He also noted that Hartmann wanted to distance his ethics from any involvement in the social conflicts of the day, and hence refused to provide any ethical code. Yet while Hartmann emphasized the element of volition in ethics, he crippled it in advance by ascribing to values an inherent obligation. The same point emerges more strongly when Marcuse quoted Scheler in 1936. Scheler claimed that values crystallized around certain 'personal prototypes'. Of these he said that 'We do not choose them, for they possess and attract us before we can choose.'[23] Although neither Horkheimer nor Marcuse referred to it, it is probably Hartmann's account of 'ethical revolution' which best brings out the mysticism of this doctrine. According to this, 'ethical leaders' play an important role. But they are not 'inventors' of values. They could not be, given Hartmann's belief that values simply exist and cannot be invented. The leader, Hartmann continues, 'can only discover what lives darkly in the valuational sentiment of the crowd, and presses forward to expression'.[24]

Horkheimer was not wholly dismissive of the new metaphysics, at least in the form of *Lebensphilosophie*. He understood the attraction of doctrines which turned against a primarily epistemological conception of philosophy as too restrictive and narrow and which took the broader concept of 'life' in which other factors played a role. It was precisely that dimension which had attracted Marcuse. More important for Horkheimer's own views was his sympathy for an essentially epistemological argument advanced by the advocates of *Lebensphilosophie*, especially Bergson. The argument was that traditional rationalist epistemology was wrong to present perception as the perception of chaotic sensory data into which the epistemological subject, reason, introduced order and meaning. What we perceive, the argument continues, is already ordered and structured. The dualism maintained by the traditional school is bogus. Horkheimer, influenced as he was by Gestalt psychology, agreed. But the advocates of *Lebensphilosophie* were not content, he noted, to add this necessary corrective. They went on to denigrate reason as a whole, elevating direct intuition into a self-sufficient means of cognition.[25]

Part of the problem with *Lebensphilosophie*, and the associated revolt against what was seen as a cold and superficial reason, was that it was changing so fast. What had, in Horkheimer's eyes, begun as a legitimate protest against excessive rationalism and a legitimate protest against the havoc wreaked by capitalism, had rapidly turned into a dismissal of rationalism and a celebration of impotence. It had become 'practically as well as theoretically debilitating'.[26] Horkheimer and his colleagues pursued the origins of this trend back into the nineteenth century. In the field of literature Leo Löwenthal even claimed to be able to date its appearance to a precise year – 1890, the year in which the Norwegian novelist Knut Hamsun published *Hunger*.[27] Similarly Adorno explored the role of myth and the celebration of death and the overpowering force of nature in Richard Wagner.[28] Both emphasized the extent to which such cults denied men the capacity to determine their own fate. Both implicitly adopted Horkheimer's standard and condemned the doctrines they dealt with as practically and theoretically debilitating.

One variant which Horkheimer dealt with briefly was the invocation of technology by writers like Oswald Spengler, Ernst Jünger and Edgar Dacqué. According to the latter, technology offered 'a glimpse and realization of an eternal idea, if we view this activity as the physical realization of a primal image through an act of the mind'.[29] The ambiguity in Dacqué's paean to technology is evident: on the one hand technology involves the application of reason, on the other hand it is, according to Dacqué, the 'realization of a primal image'. The attempt to fuse myth and reason was one which many German technocrats and engineers were obliged to adopt under the ideological regime of the Third Reich. Yet the fusion of myth and reason was not a case of an unwilling adaptation to circumstances. It was a long-standing attempt to reconcile the imperatives of modern society, especially insofar as these fed into the military potential of nations, and archaic and nationalist values. Ironically, as many commentators have noted, there are similarities between the vision of technology in the work of writers like Jünger and that later adopted by some of the older generation of critical theorists, though the latter never took up the affirmative stance of Jünger.[30]

Marcuse proved to be especially susceptible to the charms of metaphysics, writing, mainly negatively but not solely so, about ontology in both of his major post-war works: *Eros and Civilization* and *One Dimensional Man*. He did so, however, with some equivocation. It is evident in the latter work where Marcuse sought 'To avoid a misunderstanding: I do not believe that the *Frage nach dem Sein* [the question of being] and similar questions are or ought to be an existential concern ... The history of mankind has given definite answers to the "question of Being" and has given them in very concrete terms, which have proved their efficacy. The technological universe is one of them.'[31] This could mean one of two things. It could mean that the technological approach to the world, characterized by calculation and manipulation, is *the* way in which human beings must relate to the world. Alternatively, it could mean that it is the predominant way in which they have related to the world, but neither the only way nor even the necessarily predominant way in which they can relate to the world. Often it is clear that Marcuse favoured the latter option.[32] But elsewhere Marcuse gave the contrary impression. He also invoked the 'metaphysics of liberation' in *One Dimensional Man* and references to ontologies of one kind or another abound in *Eros and Civilization*. He did not systematically seek to demonstrate that any of these ontologies was in fact valid and exhibited more interest in their social function than their truth or falsity. That question, however, cannot be avoided if ontologies are to be marshalled as part of the vocabulary of a critical theory.

Earlier, under Horkheimer's influence in the 1930s and 1940s, Marcuse had either avoided that vocabulary or, in the case of Hegel, tried to show that the vocabulary of ontology contained, and glossed over, an understanding of the 'embedding of theoretical accomplishments in the practical contexts of their genesis and employment'. He had also followed Horkheimer in insisting that there was a viable alternative to metaphysical speculation as a source of guidance, namely reference to the practical needs and interests of men.[33] It was this which was said to have been the great service of the German idealists: that they had sought not to sacrifice the interests of individuals and had held out the image of a reconciliation of the interests of the members of society with the interests of society as a whole. It was the same sentiment that underlay Horkheimer's definition of the unifying element in the concept of justice – a concept that he said was older than that of morality. Having noted diverse conceptions of justice, conceptions based on equality, merit and need, he continued 'All of them make reference to the point that happiness ... is not to be determined by fortuitous, capricious factors which are external to the individual – in other words, that the degree of inequality of the life conditions of individuals at least be no greater than that dictated by the maintenance of the total social supply of goods at the given level.'[34]

Whereas Marcuse later ignored the question about the truth of ontology, Adorno's post-war work frequently returned to that theme, and came up with a consistent answer: Heidegger's claim to have escaped from the traditional epistemological dualism was false. Adorno's hostility to Heidegger's 'fundamental ontology' has been traced back to an early work on the concept of the unconscious.[35] Adorno soon abandoned the relatively orthodox rationalism of that work, but there is one notable feature of it that characterized his criticism of Heidegger, namely the accusation that Heidegger was merely repeating errors already identified by Kant. Adorno was not satisfied with mobilizing Kant's epistemology against Heidegger. He was an incisive critic of the jargon deployed by Heidegger and his followers, hence the title *Jargon of Authenticity*. In his lectures Adorno held up to ridicule Heidegger's radio broadcast 'Why we remain in the provinces'. The target was an easy one. Heidegger's assertion that 'The philosophical work does not take its course like the aloof studies of some eccentric. It belongs right here in the midst of the peasant's work' met with the retort that there was more honesty in admitting to the eccentricity of philosophy than in the pretence of being a 'craftsman or simple man of the people'.[36]

Of more significance was his attack on Heidegger's concept of authenticity. Adorno noted that 'authentic' was originally used to distinguish what was essential from what was contingent or secondary. But what, he asked, is it that Heidegger refers to when he invokes authenticity. Adorno's answer was that Heidegger failed to specify what it was.[37] Nor was Adorno convinced by the central role ascribed to death in the account of Dasein. He argued that 'once thought recurs ... to the absolutely isolated individuality, then there remains nothing tangible for it except mortality: everything else derives only from the world, which for Heidegger, as for the idealists, is secondary'.[38] In other words, Heidegger had to strip the individual of every conceivable characteristic and social relationship in order to define it by its mere mortality.

Adorno's main criticism concerned Heidegger's claim to have broken away from the traditional epistemological dualism. Heidegger wanted to construe his Dasein as something which was both a part of the world and a vantage point from which the things in the world could be revealed. Adorno argued that the vantage point brought with it the specific conceptual framework through which we view the world and that there was no getting behind some such framework. Putting it in more traditional epistemological language, the subject had to be construed on the one hand as a conceptual framework which shapes the way in which we perceive the world, and, on the other hand, as a part of that world, but as such can only be grasped through the conceptual filter of subjectivity in the first sense. There remained, Adorno insisted, a difference between the two. They could not be flatly equated. But, he continued, this is precisely what Heidegger did, or rather he wanted to claim the characteristics of each, the shaping of the world and being a piece of the world, for some third entity which was supposedly unknown to traditional epistemology: Dasein. In doing so he merely fell foul of the amphiboles and paralogisms of reason which Kant had warned against.[39]

Adorno, here following Kant, insisted that our knowledge of the world is dependent upon the conceptual frameworks that we impose upon it; to that extent our knowledge is a relative one. But it is also dependent upon the data given to us through our senses. Without the check of the latter we would be unable to distinguish between the conjectures of our fantasy and the real world. Without the former there would be no order to our knowledge of the world. For Adorno the task of philosophy was to indict any attempt to circumvent that dual dependence. Heidegger's Dasein was precisely that: a doomed attempt to circumvent the dependence.[40] Adorno insisted upon these points with such persistence and vigour because he believed that any attempt to evade them impoverished experience.

Adorno's objection to Heidegger was not merely that his philosophy was unsound. He regarded it as politically dangerous: 'Heidegger's incorporation into Hitler's Führer state was no act of opportunism, but followed from a philosophy which identified Being and Führer.'[41] More generally, Adorno complained that Heidegger and the jargon of the post-war cult that surrounded him encouraged a resigned passivity. Its endowment of selected words with an aura of authority distorted communication and thought. Its injunction of humility aped that reverence once associated with man's relation to God, without believing in the traditional concept of God. The outcome was that the sense of impotence once justified by comparison with a God was celebrated for its own sake.[42] Such abstract advocacy of humility, impotence and self-sacrifice, was, to put it mildly, not conducive to a critical stance towards whatever political authority happened to exist.

Part of Adorno's criticism of Heidegger was also directed at the broader target of metaphysics in general, which included Hegel. Although Adorno frequently praised Hegel for maintaining the dialectical relationship between subject and object, concept and sense data, spirit and being, he also denounced him for building into his philosophical system the ultimate identity of these pairs. According to Adorno this was evident in the very structure of his works. His choice of 'Being' as the starting point of his works on logic already presupposed that there would, at the end of the day, be nothing that could not be grasped conceptually. There was still a difference between Hegel and Heidegger even at this level of abstraction for 'Heidegger repeats the Hegelian slight-of-hand maneuver, except that Hegel's is practiced openly while Heidegger, not wanting to be an idealist, shrouds and beclouds the ontologization of the ontical.'[43] That is, while Hegel openly proclaimed the transparency of the world to reason and subsumed the contingency of existence in the concept, Heidegger transfigured the contingency of existence into a metaphysical concept in its own right.

Whereas Adorno condemned the entirety of Heidegger's work, Habermas sought to discriminate between the Heidegger of *Being and Time*, which he holds to be 'the most profound turning point in German philosophy since Hegel',[44] from the later Heidegger. One of the attractions of Heidegger's *Being and Time* is that it promised to open up another perspective, an alternative to what Marcuse had called 'The flattening of this living relationship to an epistemological "relation", to the abstract subject-object relation.'[45] Even in *Being and Time*, however, Habermas argues that Heidegger was unable to make good this promise, in part because he disparaged the mundane practices of everyday life as something inauthentic.[46] Habermas is critical of the early Heidegger for other reasons. He accuses him of disparaging history in favour of an ontological concept of 'historicity', of a perverse approach to the idea of truth, and of an indifference to issues of moral obligation, all of which were theoretically enervating. However, it was, Habermas continues, only later, from 1929, that Heidegger adopted postures analogous to those of Schmitt, Klages and Jünger. It was later still that Heidegger made the further step towards identification with National Socialism. Decisive here is 'the nationalistic privileging of the *German* fate, the conflation of the collectivistically interpreted category of "Dasein" with the Dasein of the German people'.[47] Habermas distinguishes a third phase, after 1934, during which Heidegger constructed a history of Being in which a misguided metaphysics, transfigured into a technological imperative, is supposed to culminate in some kind of apocalypse. In this phase Heidegger's philosophy presents itself as a 'shepherd' of Being, fearful and attentive to this Being.

Despite Habermas's greater attention to the development of Heidegger's philosophy, his final judgement is close to that of Adorno. First, he repeats Adorno's claim that Heidegger had failed to escape from the traditional dualism of traditional epistemology. Second, he concludes that while the 'language of *Being and Time* had suggested the decisionism of empty resoluteness; the later philosophy suggests the submissiveness of an equally empty readiness for subjugation'.[48] In other words, whether Heidegger exalted an activist, vitalist stance or one of submission to an opaque fate, he offered no clear criteria for what kind of decision should be taken or what one was supposed to submit to. Habermas was no more sympathetic to the rhetoric and posturing which accompanied this advocacy.

Ironically, for all his agreement with Adorno's criticism of Heidegger, Habermas also discerned certain similarities between Adorno and Heidegger too. Both had indulged in a radical criticism of the Enlightenment that seemed to gloss over the complexity of modern societies in their eagerness to root out the connection between 'enlightenment and manipulation'.[49] Yet Habermas also objected to the bracketing together of Adorno and Heidegger, claiming that he 'would not mention Adorno and Heidegger in the same breath'.[50] The reason for this inconsistency is that Habermas was worried by the impact in Germany of French postmodernist ideas that were serving as a screen for the revival of indigenous streams of anti-modernist thought, including that of Heidegger. It was this which led to the observation that 'The dual confrontation of the old Frankfurt School, against positivism on the one side and *Lebensphilosophie* and general metaphysical obscuranticism on the other side, has sadly become contemporary again.'[51]

It is this which leads Habermas to insist that Adorno, for all his criticism of the dialectic of the Enlightenment, never abandoned the notion that the only solution to the vicissitudes of the Enlightenment was enlightenment itself. Similarly he claimed that Adorno was 'immune to any flat criticism of progress' and that he never succumbed to the temptation to present the archaic or mythical as if it could provide salvation from the dilemmas of modernitiy.[52] He clearly sympathized with Adorno's argument that contemporary criticsm of reason in favour of more primeval forces was hypocritical insofar as it made use of the reason it affected to disparage.[53]

Habermas's reassertion of his connection with the older generation went hand in hand with the polarization of debate between defenders of the Enlightenment project and its critics. Yet as for the older generation, the critics of reason and modernity exhibited more diversity than the label '*Lebensphilosophie* and general metaphysics' suggests. Indeed, from the outset, in his 'Modernity: An unfinished project', Habermas distinguished several strands of anti-modernism and these distinctions recurred in his later comments. Habermas introduced these distinctions under the heading of 'Three Conservatisms': young conservatism, old conservatism and new conservatism. He defined the first by its antipathy to modernity and specifially by its advocacy of 'spontaneous forces of imagination and self-experience, of affective life in general, in what is most distant and archaic'.[54] It is this characteristic which Adorno had criticized in earlier attacks on modernity, a criticism which Habermas recalled and employed. Habermas grouped the Frenchmen, Bataille, Foucault and Derrida, under the subheading of young conservatism. The second sub-group, the old conservatives, he defined by their advocacy of 'a return to positions *prior* to modernity' and included here the German philoosphers Hans Jonas and Robert Spaeman and further identified neo-Aristotelianism as the general strategy of the old conservatives.[55] Whereas the first group, the young conservatives, claimed to have followed through the dissolution of traditional social bonds and philosophical attempts to find a substitute for them, the old conservatives insisted upon the vitality of more traditional structures. The third group, the new conservatives, 'welcome the development of modern science so long as it only oversteps its own sphere in order to promote technological advance, capitalist growth and a rational form of administration'.[56] This meant that they were critical of what they saw as the corrosive effect of cultural modernism, of the celebration of individual freedom from traditional bonds and responsibilities. Elsewhere Habermas illustrated the mood of this sub-group with a quotation from one of their number, Peter Steinfels, according to whom 'The current crisis is primarily a cultural crisis ... The problem is that our convictions have gone slack, our morals loose, our manners corrupt.'[57]

Habermas acknowledged that this rough typology was of limited use, that the different strands could draw on each other, that the overlap between them was stronger in some national cultures than others, that dissatisfaction with the limits of one strand could induce enthusiasm for another. Young conservatism, he argued, had an especially strong resonance in Germany where it had flowered in the inter-war period, and had a lingering effect on post-war new conservatism. It is this background, he continued, which explains the different nuances of American and German new conservatism. In Germany the 'survivors and heirs' of pre-war young conservatism 'reconciled themselves to the progress of civilization, but they maintained their critique of culture. It is this compromise, this half-hearted accceptance of modernitiy, that distinguishes the German from the American, the formerly Young-Conservative from the formerly liberal neoconservatives.'[58] In America the neo-conservative agenda was dominated by former self-avowed liberals who now feared that liberalism had gone too far, issuing in an inflation of expectations which threatened to overburden the state and a celebration of a diversity of lifestyles which turned into the cultural crisis feared by Steinfels. In Germany there was no need to reinvent the criticism of cultural modernity for it had never disappeared. Again this context seems to have strengthened Habermas's appreciation of Adorno for, following Albrecht Wellmer, he praised Adorno as the 'rare case of a philosopher who both belonged wholly to modernity *and* to the German tradition'.[59]

Habermas effectively employed Adorno's approach in his attack on the French young conservatives who, he argued, were reinventing the stratgey of Nietzsche. Having construed, on the one hand, the enlightenment as a stripping away of myth, and on the other hand, modern philosophy as a cult of inwardness, and the modern social sciences as issuing in a 'paralysing relativism', Nietzsche looked back to some primal experience before these enervating developments took hold. He found it, Habermas continues, in the figure of Dionysus. Yet his invocation of Dionysus was plausible only because the associated elevation of aesthetic taste coincided with highly modernist approaches to aesthetics. In Habermas's words 'Nietzsche enthrones taste, "the Yes and the No of the palate", as the organ of a knowledge beyond true and false, beyond good and evil', confounding in the process modern aesthetics and the archaic, irrational, figure of Dionysus.[60]

According to Habermas this basic strategy is repeated by both Heidegger and Bataille. Whereas Heidegger indicts modern science and the associated philosophies, Bataille indicts modern capitalism with its reduction of everything to calculable utility and profit. For both, modernity, which they saw as characterized precisely by these traits, is self-destructive. Redemption can come only by returning to a point before the fateful development set in, which means returning to some archaic expereince, to, respectively, 'Being' and 'sovereignty' where ' "Being" is defined as that which has *withdrawn* itself from the totality of beings that can be grasped and known as something in the objective world; "sovereignty" as that which has been *excluded* from the world of the useful and calculable.'[61]

It is notable that when Habermas turns to criticize Adorno and Horkheimer in *The Philosphical Discourse of Modernity* the accusation is somewhat different. He does argue that they owe much to Nietzsche, that they follow Nietzsche in discerning the assertion of control, power, behind the ideals of Western civilization. Habermas's complaint is that they carry this so far that they lose sight of any standard which would justify their own critical stance towards the entwining of reason and power. It is this paradox, the persistence of the critical stance despite the exposure of each and every reason for adopting it, which characterizes their position. Nietzsche on the other hand 'suppressed that paradoxical structure and explained the complete assimilation of reason to power with a *theory of power* that was remythologised out of arbitary pieces'.[62]

Both types of criticism recur in Habermas's treatment of Derrida and Foucault, the other main figures amongst the French young conservatives. In the case of Derrida the emphasis is upon the first type of criticism, though others are also evident, including the charge that Adorno raised against Heidegger: that the asserted escape from the concepts of traditional epistemology is bogus.[63] Habermas's style of criticism is similar to Adorno's criticism of Heidegger in other ways. Derrida, he claims, installs not 'Being' but an 'archewriting' as a nebulous authority, autonomous from ordinary mortals.[64] Yet Habermas concedes that there is a significant difference between Heidegger and Derrida for the latter 'comes to the aid of a different, rather more subversive orientation. Derrida stands closer to the anarchist wish to explode the continuum of history than to the authoritarian admonition to bend before destiny.'[65] This is a significant concession which affects Habermas's evaluation of the French postmodernists as 'young conservatives' in general. For, although there are strong analogies between them and the inter-war radical conservatives, including the dismissal of reason, the emphasis upon unpredictability and the indictment of modernity, the inter-war German radical conservatives clearly supported authoritarian forms of politics while this cannot be said of the French postmodernists. As one commentator concluded, 'uncritical receptions of Foucault, Baudrillard, etc. can result in a more receptive attitude to radical conservatism than would critical receptions'.[66] That may be so, but it nevertheless leaves a difference between the open avowel of authoritarianism of Heidegger and their political stance.

Foucault presents a similar problem but in more acute form. For Foucault, albeit late in the day, presented himself as an heir to the tradition which led from Kant through to Adorno and Horkheimer.[67] Even leaving aside this problematic claim, Habermas criticizes Foucault primarily for the lack of any normative base from which to criticize the centralization of power. In Habermas's words, 'Foucault undertsands himself as a dissident who offers resistance to modern thought and humanistically disguised disciplinary power.'[68] Yet, Habermas complains, Foucault offers no reason for his resistance. Habermas condemns Foucault, not for invoking some primal experience in the manner of Heidegger or Derrida, but for leading us into a dead end.[69]

It has been objected by James Schmidt that Foucault is not so inconsistent as Habermas claims. Foucault could in fact offer a host of reasons for why we should resist the centralization of power, for along with a set of discourses justifying the centralization of power Foucault argues that a set of counter discourses developed in reaction to the centralization of power. Put succinctly the answer to the question 'how to govern?' was accompanied by answers to the question 'how not to be governed?'[70] Schmidt notes, however, that Foucault can offer no justification for choosing some of these reasons rather than others. Nor, he continues, can Foucault provide an answer to someone who asks 'why fight at all?'[71] Ultimately Foucault's position seems to be only marginally better than Derrida's position. According to the latter 'I try where I can to act politically while recognizing that such action remains incommensurate with my intellectual project of deconstruction.'[72]

Fixated by their antipathy to the Enlightenment, their conviction that reason is either nothing more than a veil thinly concealing the pursuit of power or a distraction from an archaic experience of one sort or another, the postmodernists follow Heidegger in enjoining either passivity or a more or less explicitly irrational decisionism. From this perspective it matters little whether, with Habermas, one sees Derrida's thought as issuing in 'an empty, formulalike avowal of some indeterminate authority', or emphasizes Derrida's own assertion that 'The instant of the decision is madness'.[73] Both are theoretically and practically enervating and it was precisely this that both the older generation of critical theorists and Habermas took exception to. It was this too which unites them, despite their differences. Those differences are significant. Habermas has argued that Adorno and Horkheimer came too close themselves to an indiscriminate reduction of reason to the pursuit of power, the reduction of reason to a mere instrument of calculation. But it is notable that faced with the challenge of postmodernism, and fears of its impact within Germany, Habermas has asserted that Adorno at least clung to the Enlightenment project.[74]

The critical theorists are united by the conviction that the metaphysical systems which had dominated much of the history of Western philosophy were no longer tenable. They were highly suspicious of what they saw as more or less covert attempts to reinvent them. Equally important they were dismissive of a relativism which exulted in the obsolescence of metaphysics, whether it appeared in the form of the sociology of Mannheim or the postmodernism of Derrida and Foucault.

But balancing the two convictions, the criticism of metaphysics and of relativism, was not always easy. Marcuse was tempted into trying to bolster his post-war utopian radicalism by the vocabulary of metaphysics whilst Horkheimer's despair led him into a lament for the lost certainties of metaphysics and even into construing belief in God as an inevitable, if undemonstrable, product of human longing. Adorno was more circumspect but came to a similar conclusion.[75] Precisely these sentiments have been put forward by Peter Dews as a counter to Habermas's criticism of metaphysics.[76]

Yet although Habermas insists that since the time of Hegel 'there has been no alternative to postmetaphysical thinking', he is not dismissive of religious vocabulary at least.[77] That does not mean that Habermas concedes any place to metaphysics within modern philosophy. The latter must do without the notion that it can discern some ultimate basis of our world, be it God or a less personal foundation. It must do without the notion that there is a 'unifying order' in the world which is guaranteed by some kind of conceptual template, it must do without the notion that self-reflection can lead to certainty of universal truths, it must do without the privileging of philosophy itself as a mode of life or road to salvation. In short, it must do without all of the traits which, Habermas claims, have characterized metaphysics.[78] Central to Habermas's position here is the idea that metaphysics was an attempt to salvage the certainties of religion, to link the notions of order in the world with the meaning and purpose of the life of the individual. This, he claims, is no longer plausible. Whatever order modern science discerns it 'no longer throws light upon the individual's position in the cosmos'.[79]

It is, however, precisely this same argument which induces Habermas to make a place for religion alongside modern philosophy: 'Philosophy, even in its postmetaphysical form, will be able neither to replace nor to repress religion as long as religious language is the bearer of a semantic content that is inspiring and indispensable, for this content eludes (for the time being?) the explanatory force of philosphical language.'[80] Despite his question, which seems to hold out the possibility of some reconciliation between the language of religion and the language of modern philosophy, elsewhere he insists that the two are irreconcilable insofar as the former presupposes a religious experience which the latter cannot appropriate.[81]

Despite the evident differences between the various critical theorists, to say nothing of the differences between phases in the careers of each of them, the underlying conviction of the failure of the grand metaphysical systems remained the same. So too did the principle that abandoning the certainties of these systems need not issue in unbridled relativism. This stance was given a sharper focus by three other common elements. First, it was sharpened by what they took to be the political implications of the ideas they criticized. Second, it was sharpened by the specific features of German history. Here, Adorno and even more so Horkheimer, were stamped by the experience of National Socialism and the Holocaust. Habermas too, although sharing a different generational perspective, has been highly sensitive to the resonances of those experiences. Third, it was sharpened by the tendency to deal with the arguments from the perspective of a history of philosophy which construes patterns of thought in epochal terms.[82] In this they followed Hegel and the first generation of his critics. In that sense too they were, as Habermas claimed, contemporaries of the Young Hegelians.

CHAPTER 4

The Critique of Positivism

Positivism as a doctrine was first formulated by Auguste Comte, whose philosophy was presented by Marcuse as a reaction to the 'negative' or 'critical' philosophy associated with Hegel in Germany and a wider stream of rationalist thought in his native France.[1] In doing so Marcuse explicitly presented Comte as a defender of the *status quo* against the critical spirit contained within Hegel's system and carried forward by the Young Hegelians and above all Karl Marx. As Marcuse acknowledged, however, Comte and later self-avowed positivists were linked by their opposition to 'metaphysical apriorism'.[2] This involved giving precedence to clarity and rational demonstration. It also involved the supposition that metaphysics not only obfuscated cognition but was also a social and political evil. It was in this spirit that A.J. Ayer wrote of the Logical Positivists gathered in inter-war Vienna, 'The war of ideas which they were waging against the Catholic church had its part in the perennial Viennese conflict between the socialists and clerical reaction.'[3]

There was then no evident political reason for the frequently polemical clash between the critical theorists and the positivists, at least not in the same sense that there was with the clash between the critical theorists and those who sought to revive metaphysics or who sought a substitute in the promotion of irrationalism. Comte's turn towards a religious order to buttress the hegemony of his new positive philosophy, his consistent search for sources of order and the strong technocratic traits of his work, provide ample reasons for Marcuse's hostility to Comte, reasons which do not evidently apply to the contemporaries of the older generation of critical theorists, let alone those of Habermas. Indeed, during the 1930s representatives of the positivists had sought to collaborate with the Institute for Social Research. Prominent here was Otto Neurath. Politically committed to the left, Neurath had even been a Commissioner for Socialization in the short-lived Munich Council Republic and Horkheimer had consented to the publication of his 'Inventory of the Standard of Living' in the Institute's journal.[4] When faced with Horkheimer's harsh published criticism of positivism, Neurath reacted with some surprise and suggested that the two groups meet in order to clear up their 'misunderstandings'. Horkheimer, without initially rejecting a meeting, did not accept that their differences amounted to 'misunderstandings'.[5] Privately, Horkheimer made scathing comments about the Logical Positivists. He also refused to open up the pages of the Institute's journal for a debate, insisting that the *Zeitschrift für Sozialforschung* was not intended as a platform for debate.[6] In part the strength of Horkheimer's hostility was due to the apparent popularity of the Logical Positivists. Writing to a fellow member of the Institute, Henryk Grossmann, in 1936, he noted that 'One can scarcely exaggerate the triumphal procession of this tendency amongst all scientifically interested circles, above all in the Anglo-Saxon world.'[7] The very fact that they were vigorous critics of metaphysics made them even more dangerous in Horkheimer's eyes, for it was this anti-metaphysical stance which made them attractive to opponents of fascism who were looking for intellectual ammunition to use against the romantic and metaphysical ballast of fascism's sympathizers.[8]

The prime reason for Horkheimer's hostility was that he believed that they were false friends to fascism's opponents. Their veneration of the natural sciences as the model of knowledge and consequent dismissal of everything else as metaphysical or meaningless was practically and theoretically debilitating. This did not mean that Horkheimer was hostile to the natural sciences *per se*. To the contrary he noted that 'it is true that any position which is manifestly irreconcilable with definite scientific views must be considered false'.[9] Indeed, earlier Horkheimer had argued that there were no fundamental differences between the natural sciences and philosophy, that the rigid counterposition of these forms of knowledge was a historically specific product that was beginning, albeit only beginning, to loosen.[10] Nor did his criticisms entail any antipathy to empirical research, though that is a frequent charge still erroneously levelled at the critical theorists.[11] Nor did his criticism entail any disparagement of the role of perception in cognition. To the contrary he aligned himself with earlier empiricists, amongst whom he quoted Locke and Hume, who, he claimed, argued that the sciences were merely refined products of the same kinds of perceptual and mental processes that individuals employed in their daily lives. But this assumption, that discriminating judgement and perception were the basis of science, had been abandoned by the Logical Positivists. They had given up their initial militant insistence that concepts had to be cashed out in terms of immediate perception and argued that science dealt with 'protocol sentences', about whose genesis they disagreed.[12]

For all his sympathy for the earlier empiricists, Horkheimer was too indebted to German idealism to accept perception as unproblematic. He invoked Kant in order to claim that the world we perceive 'is partially the result of the work of our understanding' and the contemporary philosopher Ernst Cassirer in order to argue for the role of language in affecting what we perceive. Even they, however, did not go far enough for Horkheimer. It was not only through their mental and linguistic behaviour that men shaped what they perceived but even more so through wider social processes, by which he understood primarily economic processes. What he meant by this is best explained by reference to Marx's observation that nature in its pristine form, that is untouched by the hand of man, existed, if at all, only on a few Pacific islands.[13] In his enthusiasm for emphasizing the active role of men, against what he saw as the passivity enjoined by Logical Positivism, Horkheimer only occasionally paused to reassert the limits to this transformative activity, the autonomy of the natural world from the human and social. Some such limit was evident in his acknowledgement that it is 'inadmissible to run counter to the tested results of science' but this point was not developed.[14] His energy was devoted instead to mobilizing every available argument against the Logical Positivists' veneration of natural science.

Of greatest importance to Horkheimer was the potentially debilitating impact of their doctrines upon political practice. This is evident in his complaint that 'Decision and praxis are held to be something opposed to thought – they are "value judgements", private caprices and uncontrollable feelings.'[15] Although some at least of the Logical Positivists conceded that these judgements were not entirely meaningless, the central issue which worried Horkheimer was the assertion that they were not amenable to any kind of rational deliberation. Thus, Moritz Schlick acknowledged that value judgements could have one kind of meaning: 'the moral valuations of modes of behaviour and characters are nothing but the emotional reactions with which human society responds to the pleasant and sorrowful consequences that, according to average experience, proceed from those modes of behaviour and characters'.[16] Schlick then would allow, for example, a survey to determine what was pleasurable or painful according to average experience. But Horkheimer dismissed this as irrelevant to the really important issues of justice, the development of society, the nature of the economic system and so on. Such issues could only be assessed by complex theories that might well confound existing expectations. Moreover, in such theories formal logic, which the Logical Positivists claimed distinguished their position from previous empiricism, was of little use.[17] Such theories required substantive propositions, often involving extensive elaboration, whose validity could be decided neither by the rules of formal logic nor by appeal to existing expectations.

This led to another major objection. For Horkheimer the political stance adopted by a social theorist ought to be derived from the theory which he held. If it was not, then it was arbitrary. It was precisely for this reason that Neurath's indignant appeal to his own personal courage in the cause of the left made no impression upon Horkheimer. What mattered was not only that people acted in the right way but that they had good reasons for doing so. In the case of the social theorist the reasons, he argued, should be embedded in his theory.[18] It is not difficult to discern the underlying assumptions here. As a Marxist and a refugee from Nazi Germany, he wanted to have good reasons, which also meant sophisticated theories about the nature of capitalism and the Nazi state, to justify his hostility to both.

Similar concerns animated Herbert Marcuse. More strongly influenced by Hegel than Horkheimer, Marcuse focused on the Logical Positivists' attack on Hegel and on the distinction drawn by him between essence and appearance. The attack was direct and unequivocal: 'There is only *one reality*, which is always *essence* and cannot be decomposed into essence and appearance. There are, to be sure, many sorts of real objects, perhaps infinitely many, but there is only one sort of reality, and all of them partake of it equally.'[19] Although heavily reliant upon Hegel, Marcuse invoked philosophers from Plato onwards in support of his contention that the distinction did in fact matter. However, he gave few indications of how this distinction might operate in a theory of society, save for the reference to Marxism. Thus he cited the idea of imperialism, arguing that if the specific historical situation could be accounted for 'both in its individual phases as well as in terms of the tendencies effective in it' then it made sense to talk about 'imperialism' as the essence of this situation.[20]

There are ambiguities in Marcuse's position, which are only partially clarified later, in *Reason and Revolution*. There he claimed that 'The social facts that Marx analyzed (for example, the alienation of labour, the fetishism of the commodity world, surplus value, exploitation) are not akin to sociological facts, such as divorces, crimes, shifts in population, and business cycles.'[21] It is far from clear in what sense the former are facts and even the latter are problematic, for divorces and even more so crimes are evidently categories open to social interpretation and definition in a variety of ways.[22] Nevertheless, the main point of contention is clear. Marcuse like Horkheimer defended complex theories that involved concepts that could not be accounted for by reference to formal logic and sense experience. He defended such theories because without them he could not explain the processes – the development of capitalism or of the Nazi regime – which evidently required some explanation. In a similar manner to Horkheimer he protested that what the Logical Positivists wanted to sweep aside as private caprices, that is ideas of 'reason, freedom, happiness and tolerance', were precisely the ideas pursued by the classic Enlightenment of eighteenth-century France whose heirs the Logical Positivists erroneously claimed to be.[23]

Although Horkheimer, Marcuse and Adorno were united by their polemical hostility to Logical Positivism, there were significant differences in their positions, differences which widened after the 1930s. The gap between Horkheimer and Adorno was evident in an internal discussion in 1939.

There Horkheimer set out from the position that the 'facts' to which the positivists on the one hand and the critical theorists on the other hand appealed, were simply different. This is not far removed from Marcuse's attempts to distinguish different kinds of facts. However, as Adorno argued for the idea that facts were always mediated by some kind of theory, even in the natural sciences, Horkheimer, probably suspicious of the relativistic implications of Adorno's position, insisted upon the autonomy of 'facts', without which there would be no criterion for what made sense and what did not. As Adorno reiterated his position Horkheimer replied 'What do you mean by theory? A theory is still a tension between itself and reality . . . ' and then 'If one is unjustly imprisoned one must still recognize the fact.'[24]

Such reservations did not initially mitigate the strength of Horkheimer's criticism of pragmatism. The motive for his hostility to pragmatism is not immediately evident, for the pragmatists accepted that theories of whatever kind were embedded in society, guided by interests and ultimately justified by the extent to which they served those interests. Horkheimer himself emphasized this, quoting John Dewey: '*If* ideas, meanings, conceptions, notions, theories, systems are instrumental to an active reorganization of the given environment, to a removal of some specific trouble and perplexity, then the test of their validity and value lies in accomplishing this work.'[25] Yet, Horkheimer objected that the pragmatists also venerated the natural sciences, modelling their concepts of truth and verification upon them. Their weakness lay in their failure to grasp these concepts more widely. He argued that it was typical of the era that philosophers and scientists developed a high degree of expertise in one area but were swayed by crude prejudice or even mysticism in other areas. As examples he cited William James, who, he claimed, turned to mysticism and belief in mediums and Hans Driesch's spiritualism.[26] Such developments reflected the faltering belief in the capacity of men to shape their world by means of rational action.

A second criticism, one that he also made against the Logical Positivists, was that 'the pragmatic concept of truth in its exclusive form . . . corresponds to limitless truth in the existing world'.[27] In part this can be understood as a general criticism. If truth is the successful 'reorganization of the given environment' then the truth about the environment is dependent upon the existence of an interest in thus reorganizing it, in the deployment of the requisite resources to make possible this accomplishment. The notion that some potential truths or discoveries are blocked by lack of interest or lack of resources or because such 'truths' are opposed by vested interests is hardly peculiar to Horkheimer's time. But, writing in the age of Hitler and Mussolini, and of the wholesale destruction and waste of resources entailed by the economic depression, such possibilities inevitably took on sharper focus. Horkheimer also had something more specific in mind. As a Marxist, one of the hypothetical truths which he had in mind was that capitalism would prove to be a transient social order. There was, he acknowledged, no guarantee that this prediction would finally be proved true. Yet he was reluctant to accept that historical developments thus far had refuted the Marxist prediction. Indeed, he claimed that 'the possibility of a more rational form of human association has been sufficiently demonstrated to be obvious', but promptly added 'its full demonstration requires universal success'.[28] The discrepancy between the two statements is clear. It arose from Horkheimer's own highly limited trust in the world and his attempt to avoid what he saw as the pragmatist's naiveté without sacrificing a complex theory, in this case Marxism, in the face of contingent failures.[29]

In the last two years of the 1930s Horkheimer's equivocal confidence began to collapse and his faith in the persuasiveness of ideas of 'freedom, justice and truth' began to wane.[30] The pragmatist doctrine seemed to be triumphant, opposed only by calls for a reassertion of dogmatic religious belief. Faced with this scenario, the emphasis in Horkheimer's criticism of positivism and pragmatism changed. This change was notable in his attitude to Kant. Whereas in 'On the problem of truth' he had presented Kant as a forerunner of the mixture of skepticism and dogmatism which he ascribed to James and Driesch, in *Eclipse of Reason* he wrote that Kant 'did not liquidate truth by identifying it with the practical actions of verification, nor by teaching that meaning and effect are identical. He tried ultimately to establish the absolute validity of certain ideas *per se*, for their own sake.'[31] His defence of Kant here was rooted in his fear of the consequences of the consensual theory of truth held by the pragmatists. Again the historical background is easy to detect. The totalitarian regimes of the day, and indeed the culture of American capitalism, seemed able to imprint their beliefs upon the masses with ease: what then were the prospects of ideas of autonomy and justice that did not mesh with these visions? Despite the change in emphasis Horkheimer still espoused a third way between dogmatism and relativism, although this time he cited Kant in support of this strategy.[32] He still insisted upon the need for complex social theories integrating the 'basic categories and relations of society, nature and history', although his conviction that a reformulated Marxism was that theory was clearly faltering.[33]

Horkheimer's fragmented post-war comments on positivism exhibited a mixture of resignation and militancy, reflecting his belief in positivism's triumphal procession on the one hand and remnants of his conviction that positivism was fundamentally wrong on the other.[34] Both traits were evident in his contribution to the Fourteenth German Sociologists Conference in 1959. Here many of his criticisms of positivism reappeared in a condemnation of the current state of sociology in Germany. He reverted to the idea of a fundamental difference between the natural and social sciences, namely that the former were properly orientated to the manipulation of nature and were not obliged to reflect upon the extra-scientific factors determining the use of scientific theories.[35] Sociology enjoyed no such exemption. So far as sociologists remained satisfied with middle-range theories they denied their true vocation, for 'sociology refers to the correct association of men'.[36] Its contemporary relevance lay in its ability to grasp the 'threatening stultification of the subjective qualities that form the presupposition of a more rational condition'.[37] Although Horkheimer laid at least equal stress on the impotence of the individual in complex modern societies, the significance of these comments lays in his insistence that sociology concern itself with the capacity of men to make non-arbitrary decisions about 'the correct association of men'. Horkheimer did not hesitate to state that failure to do this meant no less than failure to oppose totalitarianism. It was a reproach to which advocates of a less ambitious role for sociology replied in like vein.[38]

The vitriolic undertone was not far from the surface as Adorno and Habermas took up the cudgels in what became known as the positivist dispute; Horkheimer held aloof from this, disavowing familiarity with the critical theorists's opponents.[39] The dispute itself opened in 1961 with addresses by Karl Popper and Adorno and was continued over most of the decade with periodic contributions and replies by other participants. At the end Popper was left complaining that the whole affair was a misnomer, that he and his allies had never been 'positivists'. With equal vigour he regretted his failure to denounce what he saw as the irrationalism of the critical theorists and dismissed their ideas as trivial where they were not dangerous.[40] The critical theorists for their part accused the 'positivists' of a systematic refusal to understand, of 'pretending to be stupid'.[41]

Adorno did in fact spend much of his time attacking propositions which Popper rejected, though it is clear that what Adorno held to be important Popper also rejected in quite dismissive terms. In part Adorno rehearsed long-standing arguments seeking to expose the ambiguities of positivism. Typical of this was his citation of Wittgenstein's assertion that 'The world is everything that is the case'. Of this Adorno claimed that:

> Its apparent incontestability and its ambiguity are surely inextricably linked ... To be 'the case' can mean the same as to exist in factual terms, in the sense of what exists ... but it can also mean to have logical validity: that two times two is four is 'the case'. The positivists' basic principle conceals the conflict between empiricism and logistics, which the positivists have never settled.[42]

Habermas made the same accusation though he drew different conclusions from it.[43] For Adorno the positivists distorted both elements of the dichotomy, the empirical and the logical, constricting both so tightly that they blocked knowledge of the relationship between society and the individual. Adorno sought to elaborate this point from several different angles. Reflecting upon his encounter with American social science in the 1930s, he wrote that 'the full, unregulated breadth of "experience" is more restricted by the empiricist rules than is implied in the concept of experience itself. A sort of restitution of experience from its empiricist ill-treatment would not be the worst characterization of what concerned me thereafter.'[44] At its simplest what he had in mind was the experience of the tension between some moral intuition, conception of self-identity or conception of a new social order, on the one hand, and the behaviour or role forced upon someone by the existing social order.[45]

There is an evident risk here of venerating an unregulated experience that pits prejudice, delusion and perverse social utopias against an existing social order. But Adorno was far removed from the veneration of experience whatever its content. Indeed it is more typically argued that Adorno disparaged existing beliefs and aspirations in favour of those formulated from the stance of his critical theory. His empirical work, which was extensive, had taught him to be distrustful of the immediate data gathered by questionnaires or interviews. There was, however, a more general point behind this distrust, namely, that:

> Interpretation is the opposite of the subjective meaning endowment on the part of the knowing subject or of the social actor. The concept of such meaning endowment leads to an affirmative fallacy that the social process and social order are reconciled with the subject and justified as something intelligible by the subject or belonging to the subject.[46]

Adorno was so convinced that the capitalist social order was incompatible with the life-plans and moral intuitions of individuals that he held that to seek to interpret society from the perspective of such plans and intuitions was mere ideology. This conviction depended, of course, upon the validity of Marxism as a theory of the capitalist order. It was this that also lay behind his assertion that 'Society is a system in the sense of a synthesis of an atomized plurality, in the sense of a real yet abstract assemblage of what is in no way immediately or "organically" united.'[47] Society then is no community organized according to the morality and life-plans of its members. For Adorno the implication is that society cannot be understood in terms of the behaviour of its members alone. It is rather 'real yet abstract': explicable only in terms of the operation of the law of value as formulated by Marx.[48]

There was a second reason why Adorno did not succumb to the veneration of unregulated experience, which had more to do with his reading of Hegel. Again put at its simplest it could be said to be animated by Horkheimer's insistence that 'theory is still a tension between itself and reality'. From this perspective positivism appeared as an attempt to set logic, theory, concepts on one side and perception, the empirical, the given, on the other. For Adorno all such efforts must fail. He argued, at the level of epistemology, methodology and substantive theory of society, that perception, the empirical and the given were never free from taint of theory and concept. Yet he was also aware of the danger that this argument could lead to the evaporation of the perceived, the empirical and the given into mere constructs of theory. Adorno's response was to uphold what he saw as Hegel's strategy of pushing an argument to the point at which it becomes evident that it is reliant upon presuppositions its protagonists had disavowed. Thus, he took Husserl's assertion that 'Logic seeks to search into what pertains to genuine, valid science as such, what constitutes the idea of science, so as to be able to use the latter to measure the empirically given sciences' and argued that Husserl's logic already presupposed the validity of those 'empirically given sciences'.[49]

Adorno's involvement in the dispute over positivism in the 1960s served to consolidate his earlier criticism of it, his commitment to Marxism as a theory of society, and the ambiguities in his own thought. Habermas, however, ranged more widely in his attempt to counter the 'positivists'. In part, he did repeat the standard objections of the critical theorists, quoting Adorno's concept of society, berating the positivists for their indifference to the problematic relationship between the logical and the empirical which their theories bequeathed and, above all, denouncing their decisionism in matters of morality and even the basic commitment to rationality in scientific procedures.[50] With regard to the latter Habermas argued that:

> According to him [Popper], the rationalistic attitude consists in the willingness to decide upon the acceptance of theories on the basis of experiences and arguments. It cannot, however, be grounded either through arguments or through experiences. Certainly it cannot be justified in the sense of a deductive proof but it can in the form of a supporting argumentation.[51]

Ironically, this meant in one sense at least that Habermas displayed greater conviction in the rationality of natural science than Popper.

Yet Habermas was as hostile as the older generation of critical theorists to the elevation of science as the only possible form of knowledge. He even agreed that such veneration of science entailed a regression 'behind the level of reflection represented by Kant'.[52] He also shared their concern with the nature and role of technology in modern societies, though he differed from both their diagnosis of the problem and their purported solution. Of the older generation it was Marcuse who advanced the most radical criticism, and offered the most radical solution, in the 1960s. Drawing especially on Husserl's *Crisis of the European Sciences*, which he had reviewed in the 1930s, and Horkheimer's and Adorno's *Dialectic of Enlightenment*, Marcuse concluded that 'The science of nature develops under the *technological a priori* which projects nature as potential instrumentality, stuff of control and organization.'[53] He went further by claiming that this science was a 'specific societal project'.[54] This can be seen simply as the extension of the general principle underlying critical theory, namely that theories be understood in the 'practical contexts of their genesis and employment'. It was, however, a radical extension with a relativistic twist. For Marcuse sought to open up the possibility that this view of nature was not the only possible one.

He did so with some hesitancy but he went on to speculate upon '*a qualitatively new mode of "seeing"* and qualitatively new relations between men and between man and nature.'[55] In one sense, which Marcuse did not fail to exploit, there is nothing objectionable, and nothing radical, in his argument. Nature can be viewed as an aesthetic object as well as the object of science. But Marcuse wanted to suggest more than this, suggesting the possibility of a new kind of science and technology.[56] This was not just a matter of different applications of technology but of a fundamental change in basic concepts. Marcuse was aware that such a suggestion would meet with accusations of idealism and anthropomorphism and downright mysticism. In subsequent works he adopted a more equivocal stance, withdrawing from the more extravagant claims only to reintroduce them once again.[57]

Marcuse's equivocation, even in *One Dimensional Man*, was evident to Habermas who did not hesitate in placing the more extravagant claims in the context of mystical traditions. If, he continued, technology was a 'project' it was a project of the 'human species *as a whole*', and not one that could be historically surpassed.[58] What worried Habermas was not technology *per se* but the view that there was only one form of knowledge, that embodied in the scientific-technological project. Here Habermas was concerned both about positivist philosophies and about arguments that took the triumph of technology in the modern world as a basis for diminishing the range of human action. Central to the latter was the argument of Helmut Schelsky that:

> Political norms and laws are replaced by objective exigencies of scientific-technical civilization, which are not posited as political decisions and cannot be understood as norms of conviction or Weltanschauung. Hence the idea of democracy loses its classical substance, so to speak. In place of the political will of the people emerges an objective exigency, which man produces as science and labor.[59]

This rigid counterposition of 'objective exigencies' to human will and action was incompatible with the basic assumptions of the critical theorists.[60] Yet this thesis of the 'scientization of politics' was widespread at the time. Throughout the 1950s and 1960s the neo-conservatism of Schelsky, Arnold Gehlen and Hans Freyer enjoyed a wider public than the works of the critical theorists. Habermas left little doubt about the potential political implications of their ideas, namely a reversion to something akin to the politics of the authoritarian ideologues that foreshadowed Hitler.[61] In part Habermas's fears were fuelled by the acknowledgement that there was an element of truth in the neo-conservative argument. Decision-making about technological development, especially in the military field, was highly centralized and was guarded from public scrutiny and debate. The position was made worse by his belief that the public realm had been reduced to one of 'spectacles and acclamation'.[62]

Habermas countered their arguments at various levels. First, he pointed out that they were simply wrong. Technological development was not directed by 'objective exigencies' but by specific institutions, especially defence ministries, and by the private economic interests which profited from defence procurement. Moreover, even with respect to relatively narrow issues scientists frequently disputed the best means of solving particular problems.[63] Second, he dismissed such consolation as they offered, which was typically some form of 'spiritual compensation' or cult of 'inwardness'.[64] Third, and most importantly, he incorporated their adoption of standard positivist assumptions about the nature of science into his general assault upon positivism. That in turn was located within a review of the state of the social sciences that sought to counteract the 'mutually indifferent, albeit more hostile than peaceful coexistence' of the natural sciences on the one hand and the cultural sciences on the other, if only because 'the social sciences must bear the tension of divergent approaches under one roof'.[65]

It was the review of the social sciences that came first. In *On the Logic of the Social Sciences* Habermas repeatedly argued that across diverse fields the positivist attempt to escape reliance upon the interpretation of meanings held by social actors failed. Whether in the explanation of historical events, the attempt to account for the acquisition of linguistic competence or the attempt to develop functionalist sociological theories, reference to the meaning of events or processes could not be excluded.[66] The fact that the social scientist necessarily had to take into account the meanings bestowed by social actors blocked the positivist project of a social science modelled on the natural sciences. Habermas took care not to fall into the opposite trap of assuming that interpretation of meanings alone was sufficient. Societies were not reducible to the meanings of their citizens, for there are natural and social constraints that are not reducible to such meanings.[67]

Habermas's second strategy consisted of a 'historically oriented attempt to reconstruct the prehistory of modern positivism'.[68] Although it was a prehistory it is clear that Habermas held that modern positivism was guilty of much the same sins as its predecessors. Prime amongst these was the relapse into the very metaphysics that the positivists claimed to have disavowed. This is evident in Habermas's reference to Schlick: 'According to Moritz Schlick ... there is only one reality, "and it is always essence." In the positivist concept of fact the existence of the immediately given is asserted as the essential.'[69] Positivism's metaphysics is precisely this, that the world consists of facts. Yet, Habermas argues, there are no scientific 'facts' which are not subject, in principle, to revision. He found a more persuasive answer to this problem in the work of the pragmatist Charles Sanders Peirce. For Peirce the task was to explain how the progress of scientific knowledge could be reconciled with the principle that all individual scientific statements were, in principle, revisable. He discerned a solution in the process of scientific enquiry itself. In Habermas's words 'the logic of inquiry develops a methodological concept of truth. It explicates the rules according to which true statements about reality are obtained'.[70] In this model scientific truth is what those involved in scientific enquiry can agree is the truth. There are, moreover, no elements of this truth that can be immunized from doubt. Any of them might turn out to have been misguided beliefs, to have been the product of some form of deception or erroneous theory. There was, however, a risk in this approach, for it suggested a consensual theory of truth and the possibility that what we hold to be facts are nothing more than the product of consensus. For both Peirce and Habermas this relativistic outcome was unacceptable. In Habermas's words 'We cannot meaningfully conceive of anything like uninterpreted facts. Yet the facts cannot be exhaustively reduced to our interpretations.'[71] Habermas did not find Peirce's own attempt to deal with this problem convincing. Nor, in retrospect, was he content with his own account in *Knowledge and Human Interests*.[72]

In *Knowledge and Human Interests* Habermas was not only concerned with the empirical-analytic sciences but also with the cultural sciences. Here too he discerned the influence of positivism: 'Much as the cultural sciences may comprehend their facts through understanding and little though they may be concerned with discovering general laws, they nevertheless share with the empirical-analytic sciences the methodological consciousness of describing a structured reality within the horizon of the theoretical attitude.'[73] Dilthey, whom Habermas took as the correlate of Peirce in the cultural sciences, succumbed to the dominance of positivism and hence had to curtail his own insights, both into the implications of his theory of hermeneutics and his account of the origins and development of the cultural sciences. These two pointed, Habermas argued, to a direct relation to social practice, that is to the maintenance of self-identities and a level of mutual understanding within societies which make co-ordinated action possible without the resort to coercion. Central to his argument is the view that 'The cultural sciences' practical relation to life, which determines both their *historical genesis* as well as the *factual context of their application*, is not merely appended externally to hermeneutic procedure.'[74] Dilthey, however, suppressed this fact for fear that such entanglement would impair the scientific status of his theory.

That fear was misguided, for science too was guided by an entanglement in life and necessarily so. This is what Habermas meant by the '*knowledge-constitutive interest in possible technical control*' which underlay the sciences.[75] The point of seeking to demonstrate such an interest was in part to correct what Habermas saw as the errors of positivism as a doctrine, but it also had a more direct political purpose. In distinguishing the 'knowledge-constitutive interest' of the cultural science from the empirical analytic sciences and in distinguishing their respective object domains he was seeking to rule out the application of one type of knowledge in the object domain proper to the other. The purpose of that was to delegitimate an understanding of theory which long pre-dated positivism as a formal doctrine but which is easily recognized as a scientistic understanding of theory. Its characteristics were:

> First, the claim of scientifically grounded social philosophy aims at establishing once and for all the conditions of the correct order of the state and society as such ... Second, the realization or application of knowledge is a technical problem ... Third, human behaviour is therefore to be now considered only as material for science. The engineers of the correct order can disregard the categories of ethical social intercourse and confine themselves to the construction of conditions under which human beings will behave in a calculable manner.[76]

Habermas's aim was to defend this 'ethical social intercourse' as the basis for identity formation and a level of understanding that would permit the non-coercive co-ordination of action. It had to be defended against a scientization of political theory that would pre-empt and delegitimate it. It also had to be defended against the disparagement of ethical social intercourse as a realm of 'value judgements, private caprices and uncontrollable feelings'. The opponent in both cases was the same: positivism.

Not long after *Knowledge and Human Interests*, positivism began to fade from Habermas's agenda. The reasons for this were, first, that science and technology no longer seemed to play a prominent ideological role.[77] Second, with a few exceptions, the positions Habermas had attacked were no longer being defended. The predominant climate had become one of a 'post-empiricist' philosophy of science. Indeed the danger now was less of the assertion of a unified science in the manner of the logical positivists than of the relativism associated with the self-avowed postmodernists.[78] Third, Habermas came to 'the conclusion that it was of secondary importance to defend or establish critical social theory in epistemological terms'.[79] Yet the confrontation with positivism did much to define the goals of his later work, not least in the shape of what he called the 'intuitive conception' of discursive rationality.[80] Elaborating that conception of rationality, albeit within a different theoretical framework, was central to his subsequent work.

The clash with positivism, especially in its more polemical phases, united the advocates of critical theory. Yet positivism also had a different significance for each of them. Ironically, it turned out to pose the greatest challenge to Horkheimer who had mounted the first substantial attack upon positivism. Marcuse's Hegelianism and Adorno's metacritique of epistemology provided more enduring defences against positivism, even if this meant that they focused upon a militant form of positivism, associated with the Vienna circle, which itself found fewer adherents as the years passed. The declining influence of positivism, both in its methodological form and in its Comtean, technocratic form, meant that Habermas could treat it with greater equanimity. Equally important, though, was his greater discrimination, his recognition that the pragmatist tradition had more to offer than the older generation had been willing to concede.

CHAPTER 5

The Attractions and Limits of Psychology

Psychological theories, especially those of a Freudian provenance, do not stand in the same relation to critical theory as metaphysical and positivistic theories. To the contrary, the attempt to merge Freud and Marx has often been seen as a distinctive feature, or even the distinctive feature, of critical theory. Horkheimer and the Institute had been instrumental in securing the association of the Psychoanalytic Institute, headed by his friend Karl Landauer, to the University of Frankfurt in 1929. In the following year the Institute helped to persuade the city of Frankfurt to endow Freud with the Goethe prize. As Leo Löwenthal recalled, this was quite an achievement for what was then regarded as a 'despised and outlawed science'.[1] Much later Horkheimer affirmed that the Institute had incorporated psychoanalysis into its work and specified that it was psychoanalysis in its 'strictly Freudian shape'.[2] This abiding interest was also evident when, towards the end of his life, he was asked what focus an Institute should have. The answer was 'the transformation of the psychology of men in connection with the objective transformation of society'.[3]

The fact that Horkheimer still held out as a desideratum a strategy which had characterized the Institute under his directorship from the outset suggests that it had not been unproblematic. There are indeed tensions between his critical theory and psychological approaches, tensions that were aggravated by more specific differences of interpretation within the Institute, notably over the status of Freud's theory. From a different perspective Habermas, too, was attracted to psychological theories of a Freudian shape, albeit not strictly Freudian, and even after he had distanced himself from Freud something of that attraction still survived, and more generally, the relevance of psychological theories to the validity of his own critical theory was still evident.[4]

One of the consequences of the links with the Psychoanalytic Institute was the incorporation of Erich Fromm into its work. Initially, Fromm's influence was central to the Institute's self-perception. The importance of psychology to the Institute's project was evident in the first issue of the *Zeitschrift für Sozialforschung*, which included two articles on the subject, one by Fromm, 'The method and function of an analytic social psychology' and one by Horkheimer, 'History and psychology'. The same issue carried a review of Fromm's *Die Entwicklung des Christusdogmas* that praised it as the first concrete effort to unite Marxism and Freudian psychoanalysis.[5]

In 'The method and function of an analytic social psychology' Fromm argued that psychoanalysis and 'historical materialism' were united insofar as they 'do not start from "ideas" but from earthly life and needs'.[6] He sought to further reduce the distance between the two by insisting that Freud always dealt with man as a social phenomenon, though he promptly qualified this by accusing Freud of having neglected the social relativity of particular phenomena, namely the Oedipus complex, and absolutizing them as characteristics of mankind in general. Fromm had some difficulty clarifying where the line had to be drawn, for he accepted that 'in certain respects, the instinctual apparatus itself is biologically given'.[7] Subsequent reassertion of the social relativity of this biological substrate did little to solve the underlying ambiguity. Indeed Fromm's project circled around this dilemma. The basis of his analytic social psychology was the assumption that 'the phenomena of social psychology are to be understood as processes involving the active and passive adaptation of the instinctual apparatus to the socio-economic situation'.[8] Fromm gave little indication of exactly how this occurred other than to specify that the family was the prime agency of socialization, though he clearly was aware that this was insufficient for he referred, albeit briefly, to broader cultural processes. Despite this concession Fromm presented basically a two-dimensional structure, with the economy on one side and the instinctual apparatus on the other, with the family providing the prime instrument for transforming the latter in the light of the requirements of the former.

Fromm sought to expand this approach in 'Psychoanalytic characterology and its relevance for social psychology'. This set out in fairly orthodox terms the Freudian approach to the development of character and then, independently, a sketch of the character traits typical of bourgeois society – traits drawn not from the work of Freud and his followers but from prominent sociologists, especially Werner Sombart. Finding an analogy between the anal character type described by Freud and the bourgeois character type, Fromm promised that a thorough study of the issue would reveal 'how and to what extent these traits have developed as an adaptation to the requirements of the capitalist economic structure and to what extent, on the other hand, the underlying anal eroticism itself served as a productive force in the development of the capitalist economy'.[9] At this point, however, he could do no more than suggest that these traits were more conducive to success in a capitalist economy. A problem he did not avoid was why the same character traits were found across different social groups. It was not self-evident that they should be, for what was conducive to the success of the capitalist entrepreneur might not be conducive to the success of the proletarian, to say nothing of the difference between the employed and unemployed and intermediate social strata. Here Fromm had to fall back upon some autonomous influence of the family structure that was presumed to be less responsive to the changing requirements of the economy.

Many of these problems and ambiguities haunted Horkheimer's attempts to deal with the role of psychology. There were also differences between the two, despite their conviction that they were working towards the same goal with much the same arguments. First, Horkheimer gave greater prominence to the influence of a cultural sphere alongside the economy and the instinctual apparatus.[10] That was evident in his outline of the tasks of the Institute, namely to deal with the

> question of the connection between the economic life of society, the psychical development of individuals, and the changes in the realm of culture in the narrower sense (to which belong not only the so-called intellectual elements, such as science, art and religion, but also law, customs, fashion, public opinion, sports, leisure activities, lifestyle, etc.).[11]

Horkheimer returned to this cultural realm, which was not really narrow at all, in 'Authority and the family'. There he ascribed to it a variable historical significance, but a potentially large one. Indeed, he claimed that with the exception of brief periods of crisis it typically exerted great influence even amongst those who in other respects were systematically disadvantaged by a particular culture. Moreover he rejected any reduction of cultural practices to simple deception or to material interests.

Second, Horkheimer approached psychological theories as much as competing theories as potential complements to his version of Marxism. Thus in 'History and psychology' he rejected psychological theories of history, insisted upon the centrality of economic concepts and concluded that 'rather than a foundational science, psychology becomes instead an auxiliary science for history. Its content is influenced by this transformation of function. In the context of this theory, its object loses its unitary character. Psychology no longer has to do with human beings as such.'[12] In one sense this amounted to no more than Fromm's objections to the postulation of invariant psychological traits. The tone, however, is quite different. Horkheimer did not approach psychology as a trained psychoanalyst but as a social theorist highly suspicious of the temptation to have resort to arguments about human nature. In one of his more pointed formulations he observed that psychology was a useful complement to historical materialism but the latter was valuable in its own right. In terms of understanding history, psychological theories by themselves could contribute nothing.

Yet Horkheimer never succumbed to the dogmatic dismissal of psychological theories. Psychological theories were of varying value depending upon the historical situation. In Horkheimer's words, 'The more the historical action of human beings and groups is motivated by insight, the less the historian needs to revert to psychological explanations.'[13] This illustrates how radically he subordinated psychological theories to his broader vision of critical theory. It also illustrates the tension between his approach and that of a trained psychoanalyst. The logical consequence of Horkheimer's position is that where human action is guided by knowledge and insight, psychological theories have no relevance to critical theory. While it is true that Freudian psychoanalysis operates with some conception of normal, undisturbed behaviour, superficially analogous to Horkheimer's postulation of action guided by insight, Freud certainly did not believe that such behaviour could become so much the norm that psychological theories would, so to speak, loose their rationale.

While Horkheimer was, in principle, committed to such a possibility, the contemporary situation suggested to him that there was in fact a great need for psychological theories, given that action guided by insight and knowledge was not in evidence. In reality what this meant was revolutionary action. Even when Horkheimer had really abandoned any hope of revolution, he still clung to the same underlying assumption: that there were identifiable rational interests, that where men failed to follow such interests it was necessary to have resort to psychological explanations. Thus in a report on the series *Studies in Prejudice*, of which Horkheimer was co-editor, he wrote that 'The studies show the unconscious psychological conditions under which the masses can be won over to a politics which is contrary to their own rational interests.'[14] Further he claimed that one of the virtues of the series was that 'the existence of group hatred is not accepted as self-evident and necessary'.[15]

In view of Horkheimer's nuanced approach to psychological theories there is some irony in the fact that he broke with Fromm over Fromm's increasingly critical attitude to Freud. Fromm had played a central role in the Institute's early work, not only through his theoretical contributions to the Institute's journal but also in the empirical study of the attitudes of German workers, a study which remained unpublished until 1980.[16] Adorno, however, seems to have been suspicious of Fromm's ideas from the start and persistently emphasized the theoretical differences. One of his sharpest outbursts came in reaction to Fromm's criticism of Freud's strictures on the role of the analyst in therapy. Fromm was highly critical of Freud's authoritarian style and recommended a more affirmative attitude towards the patient.[17] Writing to Horkheimer, Adorno complained that Fromm has 'put me in the paradoxical situation of defending Freud'. He dismissed Fromm's article as 'sentimental and false' and wrote that 'I cannot keep from you the fact that I see this work as a real threat to the line of the journal'.[18] Even allowing for the less than charitable attitude which Adorno displayed towards other members of the Institute, the strength of these comments is striking. Underlying his antipathy was a fundamentally different view of the role of psychoanalytic theory. For Adorno the point was to force men to face up to their plight, 'to take away from them the illusory pleasures by means of which the loathsome order keeps itself alive'.[19] More rigorously than Freud himself, Adorno held apart the demand for instinctual gratification and the demand of society. Freud, he complained, could never make up his mind whether to indict culture as repressive of instincts or to praise the renunciation of instinct as the foundation of culture. Adorno stood firmly on the side of the demands of the instincts: 'He alone who could situate utopia in blind somatic pleasure, which, satisfying the ultimate intention, is intentionless, has a stable and valid idea of truth.'[20] The difficulty, of course, is that Adorno locates gratification in utopia, leaving the individual here and now confronted only with the confrontation between his demand for happiness and society. Worse still, Adorno wanted to sweep away those 'illusory pleasures' which might mitigate the tension. This was a stance that was hardly compatible with the very idea of psychotherapy, that is, with Fromm's chosen profession.[21]

Disagreement with Horkheimer was slower to develop, though by April 1937 he responded to Adorno's continued criticism with the observation that he and others were also concerned that Fromm might be sliding into the revisionist camp.[22] In part Horkheimer's concern about revisionism was that it undermined the critical dimension of Freudian theory, that psychotherapy too readily abandoned this in favour of teaching men how to adapt to the existing conditions of society. The demand for gratification stood at the centre of his defence of Freudian orthodoxy. In this he was encouraged by his friend Karl Landauer's harsh line towards the revisionism of Karen Horney, who, for a while, was closely associated with Fromm.[23] It was this that also led him to criticize Freud's later speculation upon the existence of a death instinct. Here Horkheimer was contemptuous: 'Like the devil in the Middle Ages, the eternal destruction drive is to be blamed for all evil. Freud, moreover, considers himself especially daring with this view.'[24] There was a certain underlying optimism in Horkheimer's attitude. Just as he was to reject the existence of group hatred as self-evident or natural, so too he rejected the postulation of some destructive instinct. Destructive urges, so far as they were to be explained psychologically, were to be traced back to the vicissitudes of the instinct for gratification, not to some eternal destructive instinct.

Horkheimer had a second objection to Freud here. Freud, he claimed, slid into a simplistic philosophy of history which repeated the old clichés about the need for élites, the inherent limits to the improvement of the life of the mass of the population and the ever-present threat of disorder.[25] Yet such simplifications were not merely the product of Freud's later psychology. For Horkheimer any attempt to give psychological explanations of complex social phenomena was likely to succumb to such vices. Moreover, in criticism of the philosopher Wihelm Dilthey Horkheimer insisted that 'He failed, however, to see that individual or social life cannot possibly be reconstructed by means of a psychology alone, whatever the school of psychology.'[26] Here Horkheimer has extended his criticism. It is not only complex social phenomena that cannot be explained by recourse to psychology but the individual too. On this point Horkheimer argued first that there was considerable similarity between Dilthey and Freud, and second, that where they differed Dilthey was the more sophisticated. Both agreed, he said, in setting out from the ideas that each individual life was a coherent whole, in terms of which distinct elements and experiences found their meaning. Broader explanatory potential was gained by extrapolating certain 'types' of experience common to different individuals and ages. Dilthey's theory, however, showed greater awareness of the role of 'the inner laws of the cultural spheres, etc.' in explaining the behaviour of individuals.[27] Despite the vagueness of Horkheimer's claim, glossed over by the 'etc.', the basic point is clear enough. Whereas psychological theories, whatever the school of psychology, set out from the coherence of the individual life, finding the meaning of each type of experience or phenomenon within that context, Horkheimer held that the meaning of each type of experience or phenomenon, could only be explained by also being put in the context of broader social trends, 'the inner laws of the cultural spheres', which could not be derived from psychology. What Horkheimer had in mind here can be illustrated by his and Pollock's response to a book proposal, provisionally entitled *Rebels*, drafted by Ludwig Marcuse.[28] Though sympathetic to the idea, they criticized what they saw as a tendency to interpret historical events by reference to psychological character types. They insisted that 'Bourgeois freedom movements do not take their typical course because the leaders are only rebels and not revolutionaries, but (schematically expressed) because under the specific conditions only men with these characteristic dispositions can have more than momentary success.'[29] It was the role fulfilled by the leader rather than the psychological characteristics that should stand at the centre of the explanation.

Again it should be emphasized that this did not mean that psychological theories were dispensable. To the contrary, in his contribution to *Anti-Semitism: A Social Disease* published in 1946, Horkheimer claimed that psychoanalytic studies were the only plausible starting point for understanding the phenomenon. But he concluded with the standard warning that purely psychological explanations were naïve. This view was consolidated by the fact that the Institute's members had found patterns of anti-Semitism and authoritarianism in the United States not so different from those in their native Germany. They had also undertaken detailed studies of the rhetoric of agitators whose style was strikingly similar to the fascist demagogues in Europe.[30] The underlying sentiments and psychological patterns were common. Horkheimer concluded that 'Socio-political issues determine whether or not they become manifest.'[31]

The explanations, however, had to make sense in terms of the psychology of individuals. Thus when Adorno, in a collaborative project on the authoritarian personality, sought to develop a typology he wrote that:

> we regard those types as being scientifically most productive which integrate traits, otherwise dispersed, into meaningful continuities and bring to the fore the interconnection of elements which belong together according to their inherent 'logic', in terms of psychological understanding of underlying dynamics.[32]

The types themselves are not, he continued, the product of autonomous psychological processes. They are, rather, the product of predominantly social processes. In a manner similar to Horkheimer, Adorno was trying to maintain a balance between the need to explain how these social processes or patterns of demagogic rhetoric could affect individuals and the need to avoid a reductionist account that relied upon invariant psychological processes.

Adorno had a second reason for exercising caution. He was suspicious of the enthusiasm generated by fascist propaganda. Paradoxically he claimed that 'cynical soberness is probably more characteristic of the fascist mentality than psychological intoxication'.[33] The same observation was prominent in a report by Marcuse that was circulated in the US Office of War Information. He wrote repeatedly of a 'cynical matter-of-factness', which pervaded 'The new German mentality' and was actually promoted by the Nazi ideology.[34] The implications of this for the role of psychology were evident when Adorno wrote of the response of the audience to fascist orators: 'To be sure, we may call this act of identification a phenomenon of collective retrogression. It is not simply a reversion to older, primitive emotions but rather the reversion toward a ritualistic attitude in which the expression of emotions is sanctioned by an agency of social control.'[35] For Adorno this had far-reaching implications for psychology. Psychology, Freud's especially, was based, he claimed, on the tension between individual autonomy and consciousness, on the one hand, and the pressures of the unconscious on the other hand. The former was abandoned in the ritualistic venting of emotions associated with fascist spectacles and oratory. Extrapolating far beyond the confines of his overt topic, Adorno evidently held this to be part of a broader trend in the twentieth century. The conclusion was that psychology had 'lost its substance'.[36] Much the same point was made by Horkheimer when he speculated that there seemed to be a 'kind of plurality personality structure' where the individual adopted a 'set of masks' rather than having a 'coherent, integrated personality'.[37]

Despite these reservations Horkheimer and Adorno continued to defend Freud against the revisionists. Adorno led the attack in 1946, focusing on Karen Horney though Fromm was also the implicit target. Adorno offered three main defences of Freud. First, Freud's libido theory and the associated account of the conflict between instinctual gratification and the demands of civilization was a better reflection of the course of history than the 'hasty' references to the influence of the social milieu of the revisionists. Second, and this Adorno counted as one of Freud's greatest achievements, he had undermined the unquestioning assumption of the integrity of personal character. Third, Freud's treatment of individuals as isolated monads was truer to social reality than the attempt to build a social dimension directly into the concept of character. Underlying this point was the idea that contemporary society was better described by the theories of Hobbes, Mandeville and de Sade, than by Horney's more affirmative vision.[38]

The comparison with Hobbes, Mandeville and de Sade was significant in two ways. It placed Freud within a long-standing philosophical tradition and it suggested the kind of distinction Horkheimer and Adorno drew between the thought of the early empiricists and their successors. Horkheimer made the same kind of distinction when he referred to 'the heroic period of psychoanalysis when it was struggling against the prejudices of official science' and the more equivocal contemporary situation where psychoanalysis seemed to be losing its critical edge and serving more for the successful adaptation of men to the prevailing society than as an indictment of it.[39] Yet Adorno and Horkheimer were highly critical of Freud in other respects. While Adorno praised Freud for his quasi-Hobbesian view of society, he condemned him for presupposing that precisely that form of society was the only one conceivable. In the same vein Adorno praised his insistence upon man's 'unfreedom' and then promptly added that under Freud's 'deadly medical gaze unfreedom becomes petrified into an anthropological constant'.[40] It was from the same standpoint that Horkheimer wrote to Marcuse: 'I don't have to tell you that I don't believe in psychology as a means to solve a problem of such seriousness [anti-Semitism] ... Also the term psychology as I use it in the project [the *Studies in Prejudice*] stands for anthropology and anthropology for the theory of man as he has developed under the conditions of antagonistic society.'[41]

Despite continuing to affirm the importance of Freud and psychoanalytic theory, both Horkheimer and Adorno became more critical in the post-war decades. Underlying Horkheimer's attitude was an alignment of Freud with the sceptical tradition out of which positivism had also emerged. From this perspective Freud appears as a late representative of a line of thinkers who had progressively stripped away whatever had served to endow men with unconditional dignity or had served as unconditional values.[42] Horkheimer was consistent enough to refuse all suggestions that such unconditional values could be salvaged; to have argued otherwise would have been to argue for a revival of metaphysics. Yet his antipathy to existing society combined with his lack of any vision of a radical alternative made his comments seem more like a lament. Freud's theories were less and less contrasted with, and subordinated to, a revised form of historical materialism. Instead they were seen as representative of the contemporary trend towards moral relativism, indeed towards a condition in which moral considerations were being displaced by mere adaptation to the pressures of society. Although Adorno expressed similar sentiments, he persisted with his earlier objections. Thus he warned his students that when the psychoanalyst sought to dig down through the layers of consciousness all he found was 'the amorphous unspecified libido'. Insight into this 'archaic and primitive' level, he claimed, offered little in its own right, precisely because this level was 'undifferentiated' and 'unhistorical'.[43] Behind such observation lay Adorno's criticism of the fundamental ontology, that is, of the supposition that an archaic, primeval origin was in some sense more genuine or significant than the derivative and the historical.

What Adorno disparaged, Marcuse sought to turn into the basis of a utopian project. The context for this consisted of the continuing dispute with Fromm. Fromm's post-war work was not as uncritical as his former colleagues claimed. Contrary to the supposition that the revisionists all subscribed to working for the adjustment of men to the existing form of society, Fromm explicitly asserted that 'mental health cannot be defined in terms of the "adjustment" of the individual to his society'.[44] To the contrary, he argued that the health of society had to be measured against a conception of human nature. It is less easy, however, to defend Fromm against the charge that his account of human nature too readily slid into a set of platitudes.[45] Marcuse's vision certainly did not issue in platitudes, but it was beset by other problems. His *Eros and Civilization* is the most ambitious attempt to integrate Freud's psychology into critical theory. The outcome in fact is to turn critical theory itself into a psychological theory.

The task was not an easy one, as Marcuse acknowledged at the beginning of his book. The obstacle was 'Freud's proposition that civilization is based on the permanent subjugation of the human instincts'.[46] Yet Marcuse claimed to discern in Freud's later, more speculative, works ideas which pointed in a different direction. Alongside Freud's counterposition of instinct and civilization lay another version of Eros, according to which the instinct, Eros, was more conducive to civilization. He quoted Freud's comments on Eros's proclivity 'to combine organic substances into ever larger unities'.[47] This image of Eros as a culture-builder fitted well with the idea that Freud's theory was already sociological and was not in need of any supplement of sociological and cultural factors as the revisionists claimed. Marcuse could also insert Freud's theory into a long, if suppressed, tradition of political thought that emphasized the erotic dimension of human community.[48] There were, however, problems with this strategy. In part Marcuse had to gloss over the fact that Freud frequently set strict limits to the speculations upon which Marcuse relied. Not untypical was Marcuse's attempt to circumvent the harsh contrast between the ego and the outside world. Freud, Marcuse argued, had also referred to a more expansive relationship, to an oceanic feeling. He had, indeed, but only to add that he had never experienced such feelings himself.[49] Marcuse also followed Freud where the latter was ambiguous. If the instinct, Eros, was a creative force then there would be no need to insist, as Freud had done, that instinct had to be sublimated in order to make civilization possible. As soon as Eros is construed as the culture-builder sublimation becomes redundant. Yet both Freud and Marcuse continued to talk about sublimation.[50] There was also a more serious problem. If, as Marcuse claimed, Eros was a culture-builder, would it not mean that the very societies of which Marcuse was critical would be strengthened by this erotic bond? Marcuse conceded that this was in fact the case in his 'Political preface 1966': 'the established society too has its eros'.[51]

Some at least of these difficulties were evident at the beginning of his book when Marcuse noted that his concern was 'not with a corrected or improved interpretation of Freudian concepts but with their philosophical and sociological implications'.[52] This led him to some speculations that exposed him to damning criticism. Prominent amongst these was his attempt to redeem sexual perversions. Arguing that they represented an earlier phase of psychic development, he concluded that they preserved the immediate demand for gratification. Fromm had little difficulty in exposing Marcuse's weakness. What Marcuse was recommending amounted to little more than 'infantile regression' and to the sanctification of the 'morbidity of a society he [Marcuse] wants to change'.[53] Marcuse's enterprise faced an even more insurmountable barrier. He wanted to establish the plausibility of an alternative reality principle and turned to Freud's comments on narcissism and the mythic figure of that name in order to elaborate this vision. But he concluded this part of his book with the observation that 'these images refer to the *aesthetic dimension* as the one in which their reality principle must be sought and validated'.[54] That amounted to an admission that Freud's psychology could not carry him all the way. He had to turn to the aesthetic theories of Kant and Schiller in order to make plausible what his interpretation of Freud alone could not.[55]

Whereas Marcuse was attracted to Freud's later, metapsychological, work, Habermas was drawn to his earlier work, especially the accounts of the technique of analysis and the interpretation of dreams. There is some irony in this, for it was precisely the therapeutic aspect of Freud's theory, and even more so its subsequent expansion and elaboration, of which the older generation were the most suspicious. Where they saw the injunction to adapt to the given society, Habermas discerned an 'example' of critical theory.[56] Indeed it is arguable that it was more than just an 'example' and served as a model for critical theory. Identifying the virtues of psychoanalysis involved

85

separating out Freud's critical insights from what Habermas saw as his positivistic and scientistic self-misunderstanding.

Equally important, Habermas has a specific approach to the status of the unconscious mind in Freud's theory, one that is rooted in Freud's own ambiguity.[57] Following through Freud's account of the analysis of dreams, Habermas came to the conclusion that 'Through the mechanism of repression, conscious motivations present in the public use of language are transformed into unconscious, as it were delinguisticized motives.'[58] In its strongest formulation the precedence given to the 'public use of language' and the interpretation of the unconscious as a kind of pathological distortion of that language, led to a severe relegation of the role of instincts. More generally, however, what Habermas took exception to was much the same as what Adorno took exception to: the notion that historically invariant instincts, independent of cultural formation, could play a significant explanatory role. For Habermas as for Adorno culturally undifferentiated instinct is largely amorphous.[59]

However, there are important differences between Adorno and Habermas about how these amorphous instincts are culturally differentiated. Habermas sets out from the priority of language in two senses. First he puts dreams in the context of the distortion of the public sphere of speech, a distortion in which language is 'privatized' by being linked to a set of repressed desires which cannot normally be expressed within the public realm. The language, or to be precise, *'the model of the language game of communicative action'*, in turn defines what counts as abnormal behaviour requiring psychoanalytic treatment.[60] Second, as already indicated, Habermas construes the unconscious itself as a form of distorted communication. This is essential to him since he cannot understand how psychoanalysis, that is a form of linguistic analysis, could be effective were the cause of the symptoms not somehow rooted in linguistic communication. Hence, he brushed aside Freud's distinction between images associated with language and non-linguistic images, though whether this is plausible has been questioned.[61]

The precise way in which psychoanalysis is effective is important to Habermas. The basis of it is the adoption by the analyst of the role of an 'interactive partner'. It works, claims Habermas, insofar as the patient is able at the end to accept the analyst's interpretation of the patient's life histories, including the patient's authorship of wishes that he had disavowed or repressed. It works, that is, insofar as it is able to, ' "restore" to the patient a portion of lost life history: that is it must be able to elicit a self-reflection'.[62] It was this quality of psychoanalysis that suggested its relevance to social theory more generally. So impressed was Habermas by this that he claimed that it opened up a dimension which Marx had not been able to discern. What Freud had grasped but 'Marx was not able to see [was] that power and ideology are distorted communication'.[63]

There was one important limit to Habermas's radical translation of psychoanalytic theory into a theory of language and its distortions, and it was also vital to his attempt to draw out the broader significance of psychoanalysis for social theory. The patient is motivated to undergo analysis by the distress which he experiences. It is this that gives him an 'interest' in the process of self-reflection.[64] As the title of *Knowledge and Human Interest* indicates, this connection is central to Habermas's argument. His criticism of positivism had revealed the 'interests' underlying the empirical-analytic and cultural sciences. Freud's psychoanalytic theory pointed to the interest underlying the processes of self-reflection and, hence, of critical theory. According to Habermas 'just as in the clinical situation, so in society, pathological compulsion itself is accompanied by the interest in its abolition ... for the social system, too, the interest inherent in the pressure of suffering is also immediately an interest in enlightenment'.[65] The flaw in this argument was soon identified even by those sympathetic to him. By rooting the interest in enlightenment in the experience of suffering Habermas threatened to exclude groups which did not exhibit this symptom from the need for enlightenment.[66] This problem was not so different from one that had induced Marcuse to turn to Freud. Despairing of more traditional motives for revolt, Marcuse took up Freud's idea of civilization as a repressive process which left behind it the scars of the renunciation of instinctual desires. The latter in turn were invoked to serve as the critic of existing society and the potential motive for revolt. But Marcuse had to concede that contemporary society, the society of the 1950s and even more so the 1960s, was more liberal than that of preceding decades. In that case the repression and the motive for rebellion would be smaller. Marcuse himself struggled against this conclusion, ultimately unsuccessfully. Both Marcuse and Habermas had made the motive for revolt/enlightenment dependent upon the existence of some strong form of dissatisfaction, either directly rooted in psychological processes (Marcuse) or analogous in effect to psychological processes (Habermas). Both are condemned to failure when social groups fail to exhibit the requisite 'pathological compulsion'.

There were other problems with Habermas's interpretation of Freud and his use of psychoanalysis as a model. Freud, it was argued, had argued for the existence of a realm of the psyche that was immune from the consciousness.[67] It would, so to speak, continue operating in the background according to its own logic, regardless of therapy or explanation. Habermas's response to such objections has been to question the status of assumptions about drives:

> It is evident by now, and it has been evident at any time, that there is no sufficient operationalisation of this concept of drive and energy. So that all hypotheses which Freud calls 'economic' hypotheses, are in a way in the open air and nobody knows how to relate them to empirical data except in the situation of the analyst and patient. And if you enter the latter situation, then of course the frame of reference is quite different;

there you cannot look at drives or energy potentials or changes of energy and so on, but what you have is *verbal* material.[68]

A second objection was Habermas's instance that the validity of the analyst's interpretation is only confirmed when the patient accepts that it is in fact an accurate account of his own experience and suffering. If this be so, the objection runs, what are we to make of the cases where the patient never accepts the analyst's interpretation? Does that mean that complexes which Freud had postulated as inevitable stages of ontogenesis, the Oedipus complex for example, exist in some cases, where the patient accepts the interpretation, but not in others, where the patient does not accept the interpretation?[69] Habermas was not in fact committed to this position and had allowed for the validity of hypotheses that had received sufficient confirmation, to be exempted from the hermeneutic circle requiring their confirmation by each and every patient. There was, however, a residual tension between the status of such hypotheses and the process of analysis.[70] The latter, Habermas continued to insist, required that the patient confirm the story told about him by the analyst.

Habermas was evidently more worried by another set of objections which related to the analogy between psychoanalysis and social developments. The psychoanalytic model, it was argued, contains an authoritarian asymmetry between the analyst and the patient, one that the patient voluntarily accepts in the interests of being cured. Neither was the case in social conflicts where, more typically, the authority of one side was disputed and where there was no consensus about the goal of the conflict. There were also reservations about the authoritarian dimension of the psychoanalytic model carried over into the political realm. Habermas readily concurred and sought to clarify his own position, emphasizing precisely these limitations. Thereby, of course, the analogy lost much of its attraction.[71]

Habermas did not renounce his interpretation of Freud.[72] Moreover his subsequent use of psychological theories exhibited significant continuity with his original interpretation of Freud. But non-Freudian psychological theories clearly gained in importance. Habermas drew on the ego psychology which had attracted Fromm away from Freud, and upon the cognitive developmental psychology of Jean Piaget and Lawrence Kohlberg and sought to link these with certain sociologies of action, especially that of Mead.[73] The latter link was especially important since it formed part of Habermas's continuing criticism of Freud. Freud had built into his psychological theory a structural barrier between ego-psychology and social psychology. Freud, he complained, 'conceived the development of the ego as the process of adaptation of an organism in the tension between natural instinct, physical surroundings and social environment – certainly not as a socialization process'.[74] Habermas's purpose in seeking to reintegrate this lost dimension was to generate a model of ego identity with normative implications. This in turn was intended to rescue what he took to be the underlying assumptions of the older generation of critical theorists from the consequences of their social analysis. For all their pessimism, embodied in Adorno's speculation that psychology had 'lost its substance', that is, that the albeit precarious autonomy of the ego had been undermined by the development of contemporary society, the older critical theorists had implicitly assumed the existence of strong ego identities.[75] It is worth recalling here that in the inter-war period especially, the appearance of modern forms of mass social movement, psychological theories of collective behaviour, both Freudian and non-Freudian, modern forms of advertising and propaganda had all combined to cast doubt upon the autonomy and integrity of the ego. The individual ego was seen less as the locus of moral autonomy and personal integrity and more as the object of manipulation subject to the play of unconscious forces beyond the control of the ego.

Habermas sought to redeem his defence of the possibility of strong ego identity through two broad strategies: a model of socialization which emphasized the importance of linguistic communication and an even more ambitious model of ego development which linked stages of ego development to stages of societal evolution. The model of socialization served primarily to indicate how and when the process is disturbed or distorted, issuing in weak ego identities. In 'Überlegungen zur Kommunikationspathologie' (Considerations on communicative pathology) he used literature on disturbed families to argue that these typically exhibited the repression of conflicts under the guise of familial consensus.[76] Central to his account of how this happens is the idea that distortions in the 'external organization of speech' are cashed out in distortions in 'the internal organization of speech'. Within the family at least a certain flexibility in interactions and role structures is required if it is to be a supportive environment of the formation of ego identities and familial solidarity. Disturbances occur where this external organization of speech is skewed by the power structure within the family. According to Habermas, 'The pressure of identity conflicts is passed on to the internal organization of speech and stabilized without being resolved.'[77] That is, family members seek to defend their identities, which are threatened by the skewed power relationship, by resorting to a strategic and manipulative use of language which preserves the façade, but no more than the façade, of family unity. Socialization which is dependent upon linguistic communication is thus disrupted. At this point, however, Habermas conceded that there is a problem, namely exactly how the pressure of identity conflicts is 'passed on': 'We can only understand this process if we follow its intrapsychic traces and become clear how the mechanism of the unconscious defence against conflict works and reaches into communicative action.'[78] That, however, points back to some general theory about the operation of unconscious psychic processes and Habermas himself did not offer such a general theory, whether Freudian in nature or not.

Habermas's observations on when socialization crises are likely to occur were not extensive. He set out from the normal pattern of family development which, he claimed, has become more liberal, egalitarian and supportive of the kinds of communication, the flexibility of interaction and role structure, conducive to the development of strong egos. This was no guarantee against socialization crises but, Habermas claimed, it was more consistent with the patterns of mental illness with which psychoanalysts are confronted. In brief, forms of hysteria and compulsion neurosis have given way to narcissistic disturbances. The Oedipal complex has become less and less useful as adolescent crises have become more predominant. Habermas concluded that these developments support his model of socialization: 'Instead of an instinct theory that represents the relation of ego to inner nature ... we have a theory of socialization that ... gives structures of intersubjectivity their due, and replaces hypotheses about instinctual vicissitudes with assumptions about identity formation.'[79]

While Habermas had found some support for his emphasis on socialization processes mediated by linguistic communication, there is some tension in his account between this emphasis and the reference to unconscious psychological processes which would explain how distortion of the external organization of speech issues in distortion of the internal organization of speech. The model of ego development and even more so the attempt to link this to stages of social evolution proved even more problematic. The idea of drawing a parallel between ontogenetic development and phylogenetic development was hardly new. It has a long, if dubious, pedigree. It had been used by Freud in a highly speculative manner and taken up by Marcuse in *Eros and Civilization*. Habermas turned not to Freud but to Jean Piaget and especially Lawrence Kohlberg for the basic pattern of development. At its most basic this involved a three-stage evolution: 'the preconventional level, on which only the consequences of action are judged, the conventional level, on which the orientation to norms and the intentional violation of them are already judged, and finally the postconventional level, on which norms themselves are judged in the light of principles'.[80] Both individuals and societies were said to proceed through these stages, with subsequent stages being judged to be superior to the earlier ones. Habermas had shown some hesitation in putting forward this idea of parallel development and had repeatedly warned against 'drawing hasty parallels'.[81] Nevertheless, he did claim that there were 'homologies' between the two processes. Criticism of this ambitious scheme was not long in coming. The most obvious one was that it was not compatible with the sophisticated competencies evidenced by even the most primitive societies. There were also objections to the normative judgement of evolutionary processes and the mechanisms by which societies were supposed to move from one stage to another. Moreover, both Kohlberg and Klaus Eder, whom Habermas had relied upon for empirical support for the pattern of societal evolution, revised their views.[82] On the side of psychology Habermas's starting point, the preconventional level, was questioned. The conclusion of Gertrud Nunner-Winkkler was simply that 'There is no universal amoral ("preconventional") stage for either cognitive or motivational moral learning. When children acquire norms, they learn them as intrinsically moral norms'.[83] The model had come under attack in terms of its claims about societal evolution, its claim about developmental psychology and the parallel between the two.

Once again Habermas responded to his critics by adopting a more cautious approach. He conceded that while some cultures were more conducive to reflection upon the validity of their customary norms, all contained the capacity for such critical reflection. Moreover, he conceded that 'Socialization and formation processes are person dependent learning processes. From these we must distinguish supra-subjective learning effects which manifest themselves as cultural and social innovations and are sedimented in the productive forces or structures of moral consciousness.'[84] Another distinction was of equal significance. Habermas objected to Kohlberg's claim that a philosophical account of the superiority of a later stage of development and a psychological theory of why a child progresses from one stage to another were merely different facets of the same theory. He argued that the philosophical account would in principle be the same account as that which would be offered by someone who had reached the higher stage; the ability to offer such an account being evidence of the attainment of the higher stage. The psychological account, while taking cognizance of the competencies possessed at the higher stage, would, however, claim to be true independently of any account offered by the subject who moved to the higher stage. In Habermas's words the psychologist's 'reflections can be assessed only in terms of their claim to propositional truth'.[85] This is clearly far removed from the model of Freudian psychoanalysis in which the analyst figures as a partner in discourse with the patient, albeit in an asymmetrical relationship.

While philosophical accounts and psychological accounts could not be elided they were, however, mutually relevant. They had to be consistent. From the perspective of moral philosophy, the perspective from which Habermas was writing, this meant that the kinds of competencies which the moral philosopher holds to be justifiably desirable must be ones which people are capable of exercising. The moral philosopher must not demand the psychologically impossible.[86] This is a much more modest view of the relationship between philosophy and psychological theories than that embodied either in Habermas's account of Freud, where Freudian psychoanalysis served as a model for critical theory, or his attempt to link ego development and societal evolution, where psychological theories provided the basic model for the supposed homology between the two processes. Yet there were also elements of continuity in Habermas's concerns. The potential discrepancy between the morally preferable and the psychologically possible was not far removed from the real discrepancy between competence and performance, between the ability to formulate specific moral judgements and the question of whether or not someone acted in accordance with those judgements. This had concerned Habermas from the outset.[87] Moreover, it opened up another field where psychological accounts were still necessary. Psychological theories not only served as an indirect test of moral judgements in general, but also served to explain why particular individuals did not act in accordance with their own moral judgements or capacities.[88]

The treatment of psychological theories by the critical theorists has been an important test of their desire to develop an interdisciplinary theory – a test with rather mixed results. In part the difficulty has arisen from the fact that psychology like other disciplines has developed according to its own internal and highly specialized logic. The difficulty has been greatest when the critical theorists tried to break down the barriers in a radical way and especially when they tried to solve problems of social theory by direct resort to psychological models, whether in the interpretation of Freud by Marcuse and Habermas, or Habermas's resort to developmental psychology. The attraction and limits of psychological theories for the refinement of a critical theory of society have been evident in both the older generation and in Habermas.

CHAPTER 6

The Analysis of Bourgeois Society

The choice of the concept of bourgeois society as a framework for the presentation of critical theory is not a self-evident one. For Marxists the more obvious candidate is the concept of capitalism. It is true, as has already been noted, that Horkheimer and Adorno had purged the original text of *Dialectic of Enlightenment* of explicitly Marxist terminology, but this did not signify an abandonment of the concept of capitalism. Indeed as late as 1968 Adorno responded to the debate over the relative merits of the categories of 'industrial society' and 'late-capitalism' with a staunch defence of the latter. He conceded that the category of 'industrial society' had its uses, but the concession was made within a Marxist model: 'society is an industrial society entirely according to the state of its productive *forces*' but it is 'capitalism in its *relations* of production'.[1] The latter were, if anything, more entrenched and more pervasive than in Marx's day. They had, as Adorno put it, become 'second nature'.[2] Adorno's point here is not so different from contemporary defences of the continuing validity of Marx, after the collapse of the eastern bloc. In this defence Marx appears as a prophet of globalization:

> Constant revolutionizing of production, uninterrupted disturbance of social conditions, everlasting uncertainty and agitation distinguish the bourgeois epoch from all earlier ones. All fixed, fast-frozen relations, with their train of ancient and venerable prejudices and opinions are swept away, all new forms become antiquated before they can ossify. All that is solid melts into air ... [3]

Faced with charges of the obsolescence of Marxism, the older generation leapt to the defence of Marx's theories, and hence to the defence of the concept of capitalism.

Despite Marx's own invocation of the 'bourgeois epoch', there are other reasons for doubting the utility of the concept of bourgeois society. The historian Jürgen Kocka, for example, argues that there is much in the terms 'bourgeois' and 'bourgeois society' which is archaic. The concept of the bourgeois conjures up, he continues, a division between the aristocratic and the bourgeois which is no longer relevant. Even the division between bourgeois and proletarian is contentious. Nor do matters improve if we turn to the idea of bourgeois society, for that conjures up the free market and the limited state which, despite advocates of the new right, seem equally obsolete. Even the bourgeois family is a thing of the past. Kocka concludes that we would be better advised to confine these terms to the period before the First World War.[4]

There are, however, reasons for resisting the temptation to cast aside the concept of the bourgeois. Most obviously because it plays such a prominent part in the vocabulary of the older generation of critical theorists. All of them wrote in similar terms here. Leo Löwenthal responded to a query about the focus of his own work by saying that:

> If you ask what was really the common denominator of the people at the Institute, the answer would probably be the shared concern for the fate of the individual. Horkheimer's 'Egoism and the freedom movement' or Marcuse's 'Affirmative culture', some works by Fromm, and my own literary studies are variations on the theme of the increasing fragility of the bourgeois individual.[5]

In the case of Habermas there are other candidates for an interpretive framework. Habermas himself writes of modernity and seeks to defend this against postmodernist approaches. What is at stake here is the notion of rational ideas and values, which have universal validity. Perhaps the concepts of modernity and postmodernity, less tied to the socio-economic vocabulary of history, might provide a better framework? There are certainly no inherent objections to such a choice. Yet Habermas too was worried about much the same kind of 'fragile autonomy' that the older generation saw as endangered. Moreover the subtitle of his first book, *The Structural Transformation of the Public Sphere*, was 'An Inquiry into a Category of Bourgeois Society'. The continuing relevance of ideas which Habermas specifically identified as 'bourgeois' are defended in his sarcastic dismissal of the 'cynicism of bourgeois consciousness [which] has progressed to the point that the neo-conservative heirs to the bourgeois emancipation mistrust the latter's own achievements and entreat us not, please, to take too literally its acknowledged ideals'.[6] Habermas does take these ideals literally, as did the older generation.

Concern with the fate of bourgeois ideals and the bourgeoisie itself was scarcely the preserve of critical theory. It was rather an acute and widespread phenomenon at the beginning of the twentieth century, above all in Germany where the political compromises made by liberals in the interests of political unity, the growth of the socialist party, the largest most coherent and intellectually sophisticated of the day, and the emergence of a new dema-gogic politics, all contributed to the search for political leaders who would be *'responsive* to the presumed needs of the populace, but not *responsible* directly to it'.[7] It was this which lay behind the development of Max Weber's political thought. He had begun by castigating the members of his own class for their cowardice, seeking to drive them to assert the leadership to which he believed their economic status entitled them. Although not losing sight of the need for a social basis for leadership, the strained relationship between the leader and his followers grew as the search for an ideal of political leadership became more pressing.[8]

In part the analysis of bourgeois society by the older generation consisted of an account of the vicissitudes of this relationship. It took on diverse nuances according to the relative specialisms of the members of the Institute. Löwenthal approached the problem through the literature of Conrad Ferdi-nand Meyer, seeking to set Meyer's 'heroic conception of history' in the context of the ambivalent position of late nineteenth-century German liber-alism.[9] A more indirect approach was adopted by Horkheimer in one of the essays which Löwenthal had chosen to illustrate their common concern: 'Egoism and the freedom movement', which bore the subtitle 'On the anthropology of the bourgeois era'. This took as its examples Cola di Rienzo, Gerolamo Savonarola and Maximilien Robespierre. Stretching from the fourteenth to the eighteenth centuries the revolts and revolutions in which these men were involved were presented by Horkheimer as a prehistory of the contemporary crisis in political leadership. Central to his argument was the inconsistency between the class-based interests of the political leader and the interests of those they sought to mobilize. In all three cases the tension finally condemned the political entrepreneur to failure. It was not the fact of failure, which Horkheimer regarded as prophetic of contemporary trends, but the manner in which the leader sought to manage the tensions:

> The less the policy of the bourgeois leader coincides with the immediate interests of the masses, the more exclusively his greatness must fill the public consciousness, and the more his character must be magnified into a 'personality'. Formal greatness, greatness regardless of its con-tent, is in general the fetish of the modern concept of history. The pathos of justice accompanied by ascetic severity, the demand for general happiness along with hostility to carefree pleasure, justice embracing rich and poor with the same love, vacillation between partisanship for the upper and the lower class, rhetorical spite against the benefactors of his own party and real blows against the masses that are to help him to victory – all these peculiarities of the leader follow from his historical function in the bourgeois world.[10]

In many respects this was, as it was meant to be, a highly perceptive portrayal of the ambiguities of the fascist and national socialist regimes, though, especially in relation to the latter, it underestimated the radicalism of Adolf Hitler.

Horkheimer's reference to 'formal greatness, greatness regardless of its content' is indicative of a common theme amongst the Institute's members, namely the celebration of authority in the abstract and the abnegation of political judgement. Again this was a common theme of the times. It had been picked up, for example, by the Viennese critic Karl Kraus, as Walter Benjamin noted.[11] In Horkheimer's hands it became a characterization of the trajectory of a class, from confidence in reason and criticism of tradition to 'the deification of naked authority as such'.[12] The same trend was followed through by Marcuse again with the intent of discerning earlier indications of what he saw as the current betrayal of reason. He found it, amongst other places, in the political theory of Friedrich Stahl. There, Marcuse wrote, 'the pure irrationality of the state-authority emerges again and again through the layer of ethical and organicist concepts which conceals it; this kind of authority can only demand obedience but cannot give a reason for it.'[13]

Parallel to the deification of naked authority and of the 'formal greatness' of political leaders went a cult of inwardness which was criticized by Adorno and Marcuse especially. Even before he was integrated into the Institute, Adorno had followed through this theme in his book *Kierkegaard*. Kierkegaard, claimed Adorno, had sought to escape from what he saw as the trivial contingencies of life and the false abstractions of philosophy by a retreat to the concept of the individual. Yet this 'individual' proved to be itself entirely abstract, stripped of all social relation and life.[14] Marcuse identified a related kind of escape from the social and historical world in his essay on 'Affirmative culture'. By this he meant 'that culture of the bourgeois epoch which led … to the segregation from civilization of the mental and spiritual world as an independent realm of value that is also considered superior to civilization'.[15] Central to this culture was the idea that it was within the grasp of each individual, but that the relation between the individual and this idealized realm had no bearing upon the other aspects of his life. This distinction between the public and the private was not without its virtues. It did designate a realm of culture and ethics, which were, in principle at least, exempt from social control. So far as the individual concerned himself with the cultivation of his own personality or soul he had little to fear. There was, however, a price to pay for this and this price, Marcuse implied, had increased. It had increased in the first place because the 'entire aura and rapture of inner plenitude' was bogus.[16] That was one of the main points of Adorno's criticism of Kierkegaard. It had increased in the second place because the cult of inwardness placed ever more demands upon the isolated individual, demands which he could not meet. As Marcuse put it, the 'rule of the soul has become more exacting inwardly and more modest outwardly'.[17] For all the differences in the style of their argument, and they were substantial, Adorno and Marcuse were making a similar point. The retreat into inwardness reflected the growing sense of the impotence of the individual, a sense of impotence which they saw as characteristic of the trajectory of the bourgeoisie.

This is undoubtedly one of the main strengths of the older generation of critical theorists. Adorno and Marcuse had followed the general strategy of, to use Habermas's formulation, setting 'theoretical accomplishments' firmly in their 'earthly origins'. In this case that meant showing how those theoretical accomplishments reflected the structure of the society upon which they were based. They were not averse to suggesting that these theories or forms of culture served certain interests, but that was not the main point. The central claim was that these theories and forms of culture reflected, consciously or not, the fact that society was a product of its members yet seemed alien to them, the fact that this bourgeois society developed the capacities of its members while at the same time isolating them from each other, the fact that this in turn created a tension between those capacities and the opportunities to deploy them.

In doing so, however, there was a risk which was revealed most clearly in Horkheimer's programmatic essay on 'Traditional and critical theory'. There Horkheimer wrote that:

> The bourgeois type of economy, despite all the ingenuity of the competing individuals within it, is not governed by any plan; it is not consciously directed to a general goal; the life of society as a whole proceeds from this economy only at the cost of excessive friction, in a stunted form, and almost, as it were, accidentally.[18]

In other words the bourgeois men met each other as commodity owners on the market, a market whose outcomes were uncertain, sometimes rewarding the individual with success, which he could then book to his genius, sometimes condemning him to frustration and ruin. Yet, Horkheimer argued, this contingency was purely a product of the isolation of these individuals from each other. Extrapolating from this he concluded that 'The individual sees himself as passive and dependent, but society, though made up of individuals, is an active subject, even if a nonconscious one and, to that extent a subject only in the improper sense.'[19] Horkheimer had been carried beyond the point of arguing that there was a common social interest, beyond the point of arguing that a planned socialist economy would do away with the contingency and waste of capitalist economies. He was tempted into his extravagant speculation on society as a subject in large part by a model of bourgeois society consisting solely of competing, isolated, commodity owners. Fixated by the impotence of the individual which he and his colleagues found littered across the intellectual landscape, convinced that this impotence was rooted in the peculiarities of bourgeois society, a society in which not the intentions of isolated men but the law of value described by Marx determined the outcomes of the market, he had concluded that doing away with the isolation of men would have radical consequences, consequences warranting the idea of society as a conscious subject. This was evident even where he emphasized the current impotence of the individual: 'Since the development of a higher spontaneity hinges on the creation of a rational community, it is impossible for the individual simply to decree it.'[20]

Although such speculations can be traced back to Marx's early work and the notion of man as a 'species being', the way in which Horkheimer constructed his argument was in some respects a curious one for a self-avowed Marxist. It was left to the most orthodox of the Institute's members Henryk Grossmann to point this out. Referring to Horkheimer's comments on a higher spontaneity, he expressed his approval of this in an article critical of the Logical Positivists: 'Against *these* people this emphasis was eminently necessary.' But Grossmann was also perplexed: 'in a class-divided society there is no general subject, [no] social subject; there are merely classes and class interests, which influence decisions'.[21] Grossmann's point is perhaps clearer if directed to Horkheimer's comment on 'society as an active subject, even if a nonconscious one and, to that extent a subject only in the improper sense'. Such a subject, with the attendant connotations of a unified interest and purpose, is not compatible with the idea of a class-divided society. It is also notable, though Grossmann did not make this point, that the model, which lies behind Horkheimer's speculation, consists only of commodity owners and their interaction. The proletariat is missing.[22]

There is some irony in the fact that Horkheimer employed an albeit truncated model of a liberal capitalist economy in order to extrapolate his utopian alternative to it, for that liberal economy was increasingly a thing of the past. Along with many other intellectuals of the time, the older generation saw themselves confronted with what appeared to be a Manichaean divide between Soviet communism on the one hand and fascism on the other. As late as 1947 Marcuse still held to this vision: 'the world is dividing into a neo-fascist and a Soviet camp. What still remains of democratic-liberal forms will be crushed between the two camps or absorbed by them.'[23] That the liberal-democratic order, that is, bourgeois society, was doomed, was in accord with the Institute's Marxism. Marcuse responded to this trend, however, by emphasizing elements of continuity between the bourgeois order and the emergent fascism. At the heart of both, he claimed, was the defence of private property. The fascist regimes only attacked those aspects of the organization of production, which were historically obsolete anyway.[24] There were other continuities as well, which Marcuse emphasized in a later work. For all their rhetoric, the fascist regimes did not renounce the pursuit of self-interest. They were rather the 'consummation of competitive individualism'. Their mass formations lacked any genuine common interest beyond the mere desire for survival. 'Atomization and isolation' were the order of the day.[25]

Horkheimer wrote in a similar vein. Parodying Wittgenstein's conclusion to his *Tractatus Logico-Philosophicus*, he wrote that 'whoever is not willing to talk about capitalism should also keep quiet about fascism'.[26] Yet although Horkheimer stressed the origins of fascism in capitalism, he drew different conclusions about the extent of the transformation which it signified. In this he was much influenced by Pollock's ideas, which were finally published in 'State capitalism' in 1941. There Pollock set out an 'ideal type' drawing mainly on the evidence of developments in Nazi Germany. One of the few assumptions he claimed to make was, however, a broader one, namely that the era of 'free trade and free enterprise' was giving way to the era of state capitalism. He conceded that the trend was so little advanced in non-totalitarian states that it was not even possible to outline a model for a democratic variant of state capitalism.[27] Even Nazi Germany only approached this model. Horkheimer, despite his support of Pollock against his detractors in the Institute, above all Franz Neumann, privately admitted that Germany was 'not even approximately' state capitalist.[28]

It was of great importance for Horkheimer's analysis of the trajectory of bourgeois society that he adhered to Pollock's model notwithstanding its problematic status. Always inclined to think in terms of epochal trends, he wrote that 'The transformation of the downtrodden job-seeker from the nineteenth century into the diligent member of a fascist organization recalls in its historical significance the transformation of the medieval master craftsman into the Protestant burger through the Reformation, or of the English village pauper into the modern industrial worker.'[29] He repeatedly extrapolated from the experience of Nazi Germany in order to make such far-reaching assertions about trends affecting bourgeois society in general. This even extended to his comments on the persecution of the Jews. Their economic function, as agents of the 'sphere of circulation', was obsolete. Such tasks had been taken over directly by the government. The Jews were redundant and, he implied, the expropriation of their property inevitable.[30] Here the weakness of Horkheimer's strategy becomes quite apparent. His history of bourgeois society involved a lack of historical discrimination. Taking exception to the title of Horkheimer's essay, 'The Jews and Europe', Gershom Scholem protested that it actually said little about either Europe or the Jews: 'He does not ask *for the Jews*: what will they be like when they are deprived of this soil, after terrible demoralisations and strategies of annihilation ... Nor does he ask *for Europe* what would a Europe actually look like after the elimination of the Jews?'[31]

After some initial hesitation Adorno also followed Pollock in emphasizing the significance of the transition represented by developments in Nazi Germany.[32] The divisions within the Institute as well as the equivocation and hesitation of some of its members arose partly from their proximity to the events at issue. The Nazi regime was not even a decade old and its policies were unfolding under the pressure of the exigencies of war. Yet even with the benefit of hindsight and several decades of research the issues which divided the Institute still remain highly disputed.[33] It is clear, though, that the ascription of an epoch-forming significance to the developments in Nazi Germany was misguided and that this error was not due purely to the fact that the Institute's members were contemporary witnesses of an uncertain and volatile development. Horkheimer's assertion that the 'fact that fascism was initially supported by bankrupt industries concerns its specific develop-ment, not its suitability as a universal principle'[34] was not only empirically dubious but also reflected a general weakness, that is the neglect of the historical contingency of the events at issue.[35]

The intractability of the Nazi phenomenon and its problematic relation to the society from which it emerged was evident even where Horkheimer emphasized the continuity between the two: 'Fascism solidifies the extreme class differences which the law of surplus value ultimately produced.'[36] The link between class formation and Marx's doctrine of surplus value ought to have been treated with more caution by Horkheimer. As early as 1936 discussions of the problems presented by Marx's theory of surplus value and also his doctrine of the tendency of the rate of profit to fall had proven quite inconclusive. Horkheimer did resist the more critical assessments of Pollock and Gumperz, but he had not been able to mount any effective defence of the utility of Marx's concepts in accounting for the specific economic trends of the day.[37] Adorno also made the connection between Marx's theory of surplus value and class but sought to take account of the changes which had occurred. Thereby he also confirmed the difficulty which some at least of the Institute's members were having in dealing with the concept of class. According to Adorno, 'In the market economy the untruth in the concept of class was latent: under monopoly [capitalism] it has become as evident [sichtbar] as its truth, the survival of classes, has become opaque [unsichtbar].'[38] The untruth of the concept of class was the presumption of the unity of each class. Even amongst the bourgeoisie that unity had always been a fiction. The equality between the bourgeoisie themselves was dis-torted by the disparate mass of capital at the disposal of each, the social power each could mobilize, alliances with feudal remnants, with adventurers and military élites. Moreover the bourgeoisie was indifferent to those of its members 'damned by the "objective tendency"', that is, those condemned to bankruptcy.[39]

This emphasis upon the internecine warfare within the bourgeoisie had always been evident in Horkheimer's work and it grew in Adorno's work in the post-war years. So too did his concessions to Marx's criticism. He made this with some reluctance, complaining that modern theories of social conflict 'conjured away' the question of 'their mediation by the class struc-ture'.[40] Yet he himself found it increasingly difficult to answer that question. The reason, he acknowledged, was the impossibility of 'objectively ground-ing the formation of classes without a theory of surplus value' and such a theory was irreconcilable with contemporary economic phenomena.[41]

Other members of the institute who responded to the Nazi economy with an emphasis upon continuity with the capitalist economy had less overt difficulty with the concept of class. In the same issue in which Pollock's 'State capitalism' appeared, Gurland denied that the emergence of economic managers apparently lacking significant ownership of capital made any difference. Their income, he wrote, 'is drawn from profits and depends on total profit, whether dividends are distributed or not'.[42] In the post-war world maintaining a relatively orthodox stance became increasingly difficult. Marcuse, who had been equivocal during the war, swung from acknowledging the same difficulties as Adorno to writing as if the old concepts of value, surplus value and the falling rate of profit, were unproblematic.[43] In principle, however, he emphasized that the rhetorical reiteration of the vocabulary of Marx without taking account of the intervening changes in the social structure of capitalism was futile.[44]

In different ways the confrontation with National Socialism predictably heightened the sensitivities of the critical theorists about the fragility of the bourgeois ego and also strengthened the suspicion of scepticism. Scepticism, Horkheimer argued, had once been a progressive trait. It had signified a refusal to join in the persecution associated with conflicts of religious faith. At that time, he wrote, the sceptic's conclusion 'is to retreat from any kind of unconditionality to a moderate self-interest'.[45] This clearly still had some attraction since it formed an alternative to the unalloyed revival of traditional values and faith, which Horkheimer found both implausible and futile.[46] For all the conformity implicit in Montaigne's stance, Horkheimer's reference, for example to Montaigne as ' the very paragon of the cultivated man throughout the bourgeois epoch', also betrays his admiration for the sixteenth-century sceptic.[47] Yet the sceptical attitude was itself no longer plausible to Horkheimer. Cultivation of one's personality and political conformity no longer guaranteed security. Now,

> If the individual falls into the clutches of the powers that be, he can not only be destroyed but twisted and turned upside down, according to the degree to which chemical and psychological techniques have advanced. This exposes the delusion of scepticism which, despite everything, regards the ego as a safe place of flight.[48]

The long reach of the totalitarian state as well as the techniques of modern science were clearly behind such fears. Even in more politically stable times Neumann drew a similar conclusion. It was possible, he speculated, that the modern intellectual might be so rich and famous or so utterly insignificant that the authorities would either not dare to touch him or would simply not notice him. But this was unlikely. Moreover, the totalitarian states had demonstrated that not even the rich and the insignificant were beyond the grasp of the state.[49]

The ambivalence towards the fragile bourgeois individual became even more marked as the post-war decades rolled by. According to Alfons Söllner, 'Even in Marcuse's sharpest criticism of the present ... there is neither indifference toward, nor contempt for the achievements of bourgeois democracy ... in his last book ... Marcuse took a turn, which, if the phrase were not so easily misunderstood in these neo-conservative times, might be described as a return to bourgeois conservatism.'[50] This assessment underestimates Marcuse's sometimes equivocal attitude towards democratic institutions, his periodic sympathy for a Leninist *avant garde* party as the only way to break through the integration of the working class and the absence of a revolutionary consciousness.[51] Nevertheless, it does capture an important aspect of Marcuse's response to what he took to be the trajectory of bourgeois society, an aspect enhanced by the blurred boundaries of class in the post-war world. He remained convinced that economic trends threatened to undermine bourgeois society and that a revival of fascist strategies was a possibility. Faced with this, his defence of the achievements of bourgeois society, which had always been present, grew in prominence. In his last book, *The Aesthetic Dimension*, he wrote that 'Today, the rejection of the individual as a "bourgeois" concept recalls and presages fascist undertakings.'[52] So strongly did he reject this dismissal of the fragile bourgeois individual that he sanctioned the 'flight into inwardness' of which Adorno had been so critical.[53] In the same vein he suggested that the increasing centralization of economic power and the 'subjection of the majority of the bourgeoisie to the hegemony of corporate capital' legitimated a new alliance of bourgeois and proletarian against the threat 'to cancel the achievements of the revolutions of the 18th and 19th centuries'.[54] This alliance, he hoped, could crystallize around an anti-capitalist, if not socialist politics. The centrality of the proletariat in Marxist theory was obsolete. Moreover, he implied that it had always been in one sense at least misguided. Marx had presented the interests of the proletariat as those of society as a whole, but now, Marcuse concluded, the 'identity between the proletariat and the universal interest has been superseded – if indeed it ever existed at all'.[55] Bourgeois society lived on in Marcuse's vision, despite all the profound socio-economic transformation of the mid-twentieth century, the demise of the free market, the concentration of capital, the creation of a manipulated consumer society, because its cultural traits still survived in the interstices of late capitalism.

Horkheimer and Adorno drew a similar conclusion, albeit a more pessimistic one. This was most evident in the case of Horkheimer, to whom Söllner's suggestion of a return to bourgeois conservatism applies better than to Marcuse. Horkheimer's return to bourgeois conservatism did not mean that he ever shared the neo-conservatism enthusiasm for a revival of free-market capitalism. That was excluded on the grounds that liberal capitalism had irredeemably failed and also that the material benefits of a managed capitalism were sufficient to make calls for any return to the discredited free market reprehensible. There was, however, a price to be paid for the increase in social justice, namely a decrease in freedom. Horkheimer's image of this new society was that of the 'administered world'.[56] As with his adoption of Pollock's model of state capitalism, this was not an image which accurately reflected the current condition of society but a telos to which it was, apparently irrevocably, committed.[57] Measured against this end state bourgeois man came to represent much that Horkheimer feared would disappear, above all the capacity for moral judgement and independence of thought. Horkheimer ended by elevating idealized bourgeois patterns of behaviour into models for how general concepts of freedom and morality were to be embedded in the concrete lives of individuals. With only slight exaggeration it could be said that Horkheimer's vision had shrunk to the model of bourgeois society and its antithesis – the administered world. These models were limited only by the postulation of a quasi-theological concept of the 'completely other'.[58]

Adorno had formulated the idea of the 'administered world' in conjunction with Horkheimer. Together they argued that fewer and fewer spheres of life allowed the individual room for decision. Whether in the economy, the free professions or education, the individual was being reduced to an 'administrative functionary'.[59] The growth and expansion of bureaucracy had, of course, been one of the prime themes of Max Weber's work. Adorno duly invoked Weber in support of the model of the administered world, but gave the process of bureaucratization a different twist. What was it, he asked, which accounted for the bureaucratization of spheres of life previously untouched by these administrative practices? The answer, he claimed, was the 'expansion of the exchange relationship'.[60] This process did not halt at the values of the bourgeoisie. High culture was no more immune than law or education.

Adorno followed Horkheimer in holding onto the abstract possibility of an alternative to this fateful development but refusing to give it a name, to even hint at what this alternative would be. In this he clearly differs from Marcuse. There are, however, traces of a greater confidence in the capacity of the individual than is the case of Horkheimer, traces which bring him a little closer to Marcuse, albeit not without reservations. For example, he protested that he did not want to sanction the 'division into a public professional and a private sphere' for this was characteristic of the 'divided society'. Again it is not difficult to see Adorno's earlier criticism of the cult of inwardness at work. Yet he claimed that precisely this division, which posed some limit to the 'administered world', should not be disavowed, for it alone provided the individual with the possibility of some critical distance.[61]

The weaknesses of the older generation's analysis of bourgeois society are not difficult to discern. From the more orthodox Marxist perspective of Grossmann there was a tendency to lose sight of the complex social structure when developing formal models of epochal transformation. This was not an inevitable consequence of their position, as Horkheimer's 'Egoism and the freedom movement' suggests. A more fundamental weakness is the under-lying assumption, strongest in Adorno, that all spheres or sub-systems of society move in the same direction and move according to the same logic,[62] whether this logic be that of the administered society or the exchange principle. The impact of the latter, as registered by Marx and reiterated in varying form by the growing literature on globalization, has, of course, been enormous. Yet to hold up that logic as the only prism can lead to significant distortions of historical development. That was evident in Horkheimer's 'The Jews and Europe'.

There is also much that is elusive in their general assessment of the decline of the liberal bourgeois order. The claim that this was fully in accordance with the dynamics identified by Marx yet brought an end to those dynamics; the claim that the divisions of (bourgeois) society identified by Marx per-sisted, even in sharper form, but had become opaque; the continued use of Marxist concepts, especially that of surplus value, despite the acknowl-edgment of their weakness; all reflected the faltering grasp of the older generation on the dynamics of twentieth-century society. There are, how-ever, some senses in which their analysis is quite prescient. Ironically the very attempt of governments in the 1980s, a decade after Adorno's death, to revive elements of the free market of the liberal order redeems some of Adorno's apparently more extravagant claims. For in some sectors at least the attempt ultimately failed. The outcome was the introduction of pseudo-markets in which not competition but chance, political linkage and ideological conformity were decisive. The commodification of spheres of life previously exempt, in part at least, from this logic, health and education for example, had the kinds of consequence which Adorno emphasized in his attempt to link the exchange relationship and the 'administered world'. Commodification served only to undermine the autonomy of these spheres and to prepare them for administration by standardized rules.

It is also arguable that their comments on the relationship between the public and private spheres, a relationship decisive for their understanding of bourgeois society, are still pertinent. The fragility of that relationship has recently been emphasized by Ulrich Beck, who argues that:

> The private sphere is not what it appears to be: a sphere separated from the environment. It is the *outside turned inside and made private, of conditions and decisions* made elsewhere, in the television network, the educational system, in firms or labour markets, or in the transportation system, with general disregard of their private biographical conse-quences.[63]

The private sphere is not immune from the wider environment. To the contrary, decisions as diverse as those about the portrayal of role models, educational opportunities, forms of employment and access to labour mar-kets, can all have profound effects upon individual biographies. From this perspective the cult of inwardness is as futile as Adorno said it was.

Adorno left the concept of the individual as a precarious point of refuge, couterposed to a society which, so to speak, pursued the individual into his own domain. The discrepancy between the two, individual and society, was so great that impotence of the individual was an inevitable consequence of the dyadic construct. Habermas's *Structural Transformation of the Public Sphere* offers a third term, the public sphere, which lifts the concept of the individual out of its monadic isolation without handing it over to the administered society. It is notable that in order to make this model plausible Habermas had to go back to the eighteenth century and earlier, to focus, as Horkheimer had initially done, on the rise of bourgeois society, rather than on its high point and decline around the turn of the nineteenth to the twentieth century.[64] The emergence of the public sphere in the earlier phase presupposed the development of the distinction between the private and the public but also that the former could be construed as 'publicly relevant'.[65] On this basis the bourgeois public sphere emerged. According to Habermas this sphere

> may be conceived above all as the sphere of private people come together as a public; they soon claimed the public sphere regulated from above [by the state] against the public authorities themselves, to engage them in a debate over the general rules governing relations in the basically privatized but publicly relevant sphere of commodity exchange and social labor.[66]

Within this public sphere considerations of status and wealth were, in principle, set aside. Only the 'authority of the better argument' was supposed to prevail.

Habermas was well aware of the limitations of the model. In reality both status and wealth counted. So far as the public sphere existed, it did so for a very small percentage of the population. Moreover, in the early stages this 'public' sphere had to be constituted in secret lodges and societies, free from the prying eyes of the public authorities.[67]

Indeed much of Habermas's book was devoted to the decline of the public sphere, a decline that followed through the trajectory of bourgeois society in a manner not dissimilar to the accounts of the older generation. In the first place, the status of the public sphere was challenged 'as soon as the mass of non owners made the general rules governing transactions in society into a topic of *their* critical public debate'.[68] The core of Habermas's argument, however, concerned developments in the last third of the nineteenth century and after, developments which undermined the access of the bourgeoisie to a public sphere as well as that of the working class. It was then that both governments and private associations intervened in what was in principle the apolitical, social realm. The role of private associations was crucial: 'That society was essentially a private sphere became questionable only when the powers of "society" themselves assumed functions of public authority.'[69] This applied to industrial organizations as well as to the weaker trade unions.

The same process of growing state intervention also stripped the family of its traditional functions, a process paralleled by the transformation of the family into a unit of consumers. Echoing Adorno's criticism of the cult of inwardness, Habermas complained of an 'illusion of an intensified privacy in an interior domain'.[70] The pattern of consumption, consumption that is of cultural products, was important also, for it was not the lower classes that were the prime consumers in this sense. The passive consumption of culture as a commodity, claimed Habermas, was characteristic of the higher social orders and only subsequently spread downwards.[71]

The attractions of Habermas's conception of the public sphere are simple. It provides a model which seems to reconcile the bourgeois distinction between private and public, without sacrificing the individual to the state or the 'administered world' while at the same time allowing the individual to escape from his isolation, to be something more than merely private. It appears to be a solution to the dilemma of the fragile bourgeois individual, which had so agitated the older generation. Yet the public sphere is, by Habermas's account, itself highly fragile. He presents it as the product of a class that can only maintain this fiction of a public sphere at the expense of suspending the pressure of interests, resisting the attempt to pursue its interests through the organization of political power. By his own account such self-restraint proved impossible:

> Although limited to a framework of interests common to private people insofar as they owned property, the public was nonetheless kept free from the competition between individual private interests to such an extent that the decisions falling within the domain of political compromise could be handled by the procedures of rational debate. However, as soon as private interests, collectively organized, were compelled to assume political form, the public sphere necessarily became an arena in which conflicts also had to be settled that transformed the structure of political compromise from the ground up.[72]

The theme of the deformation of the public sphere, in the sense of its depoliticization, was taken up again in *Legitimation Crisis*, with the intent of demonstrating that while the motivations supplied by bourgeois culture were becoming dysfunctional, the bourgeois project was in some senses still viable. The dysfunctional elements of bourgeois culture were defined as 'civil privatism' and 'familial-vocational privatism'. By the former, Habermas understood the limitation of participation in political processes as formulated by Almond and Veba. In their words 'the democratic citizen is called on to pursue contradictory goals; he must be active, yet passive; involved yet not too involved, influential yet deferential'.[73] By 'familial-vocational privatism' he understood orientation to family and vocation as formulated by Weber's model of the Protestant ethic. In order to substantiate these claims Habermas invoked a host of highly condensed arguments, which can be broken up into two groups. Typical of the first group, were the assertions that the 'achievement ideology', that is the conviction that rewards would be roughly proportionate to effort, and 'possessive individualism', that is the conviction that needs could be ranked within a stable preference system and could be met by the private acquisition of material goods, were no longer plausible. Habermas argued that the evident injustices of market mechanisms were sufficiently widespread to undermine the former. Possessive individualism was undermined by the inability to formulate stable preference systems and the increasing importance to individuals of needs – 'transportation, leisure, health care, education etc.' – which could only be supplied in the form of communal goods and hence were not amenable to 'forms of differential demand and private appropriation'.[74] These are ambitious and empirical claims for which Habermas provided limited evidence. There is some intuitive plausibility in the suggestion that the achievement ideology makes little sense to a social underclass permanently excluded from the labour force.[75] However, the obstacles to the strategy of possessive individualism are more problematic. Habermas conceded the possibility of commercial manipulation of needs counterbalanced by an 'opportunistic adaptation of consumers to market strategies of monopolistic competition'.[76] Moreover, the supposition that needs could increasingly be met only through the provision of communal goods, though not without plausibility, was vulnerable to government strategies of the privatization of such provision, albeit in the form of pseudo-markets. Typical of the second group was the claim that traditional values and orientations were being dismantled at an accelerating rate and that only a universalistic ethics had withstood this process. The discrepancy between the demands of this universalistic ethics and the reality of contemporary society increasingly issue in crises of personality formation at the stage of adolescent development. While the empirical referent in this claim, the increasing predominance of adolescent crisis, did not lack evidence, it is far from clear that it is rooted in the discrepancy Habermas identifies, as opposed to a discrepancy between ego ideals purveyed by the consumer society and the capacity of individuals to realize those ideals.[77]

Habermas's attempt to mobilize the remnants of bourgeois culture in order to predict the crisis of contemporary society were of limited success. Subsequent comments acknowledge the persistence of the achievement ideology, a revival of the cult of inwardness and the manipulation of traditional values in an attempt to gloss over the tensions and discrepancies of modern society.[78] As Habermas took stock in *The Theory of Communicative Action*, the dynamics and structure of bourgeois society appeared both less and more relevant. The decisive change came with renewed criticism of Marx. Like the older generation, but more consistently, he had expressed doubts about the labour theory of value central to Marx's model. Now, however, he decisively rejected it as a reductionist strategy.[79] Equally important was the conclusion that he drew at the end of this:

> Marx conceives of capitalist society so strongly as a totality that he fails to recognize the *intrinsic* evolutionary *value* that media-steered systems possess. He did not see that the differentiation of the state apparatus and the economy *also* represents a higher level of system differentiation, which simultaneously opens up new steering possibilities *and* forces a reorganization of the old, feudal, class relationship.[80]

Marx, Habermas claimed, had confounded the separation out of the economy as an independent sub-system of society, which Habermas took to be characteristic of modernity, with the 'class specific forms' which accompanied that differentiation.[81] Habermas had thus opened up a gap between the bourgeoisie and the economy that marked a radical break with the older generation.

Yet he could rightly invoke Marcuse and Adorno as two of the few Marxists who had sought to come to terms with the more complex and fragmented structure of late capitalism. The central problem according to Habermas was that 'The unequal distribution of social rewards reflects a structure of privilege that can no longer be traced back to class positions in any unqualified way.'[82] Of special importance to Habermas was the role of the 'client' of welfare state agencies alongside the enhanced role of the 'consumer'. Whereas Marx had selected the role of 'employee' as decisive, the roles of 'client', 'consumer' and 'citizen' deserved equal emphasis. This did not signify any diminution of critical intent. These roles were no less reified than that of the alienated labour of the employee. It was consistent with this broader overview that Habermas discerned a different pattern of protest movement. Now, he claimed, 'only the feminist movement stands in the tradition of bourgeois-socialist liberation movements'.[83] Other protest movements – anti-nuclear, environmentalist, alternative life movements – were not motivated by the assertion of universal rights, but were better characterized as defensive movements that sought to protect the lifeworld from the depredations of the economic system as well as from state intervention.[84] In drawing this distinction the concept of the 'lifeworld' played a major role. By 'lifeworld' he meant the 'more or less diffuse, always unproblematic, background convictions' which he saw as a precondition of processes of communications, socialization and cultural reproduction.[85] He insisted that the concept of the lifeworld should not be conflated with that of society as a whole. It forms, he claimed, only one mechanism of integration alongside the economic and political systems. In the latter two spheres 'social relations are regulated only via money and power. Norm-constitutive attitudes and identity-forming social memberships [both characteristic of the lifeworld] are neither necessary nor possible in these spheres'.[86] Where these

spheres intrude into the lifeworld in a disruptive manner, a process Habermas characterized as the 'colonization of the lifeworld', they could meet with
resistance. It is in this sense that the typical contemporary protest movements
count as 'defensive'.

The concept of the lifeworld is a systemic category within which bourgeois society appears as a historically specific form. Yet bourgeois society,
especially the ideals of that form as expressed in the French Revolution, has
remained of great importance to Habermas.[87] The postmodernist attack on
'modernity' and the ideals of the bourgeois era have prompted Habermas to
step into the defence of these values. Speaking of the scope for the formation
of identity, of autonomy and shaping of personal biography, he explicitly
invoked the bourgeois tradition: 'In this sense the life forms of the European
bourgeoisie are exemplary.'[88] He did not neglect to refer to the exclusion and
repression practised by that form of society but held to its ideals with greater
confidence than the older generation. Amongst those ideals was the distinction between private and public, which lay behind the concern with the
fragility of the bourgeois individual. Habermas did not defend the distinction
in terms of a difference between private and public spheres. Indeed he argued
that this difference threatened to set up a bogus dichotomy in which the
expansion of one was seen as the inevitable contraction of the other. In the
place of this zero sum game he argued that the private and public autonomy
of the individual were interdependent. Underlying this was the 'intuition
that, on the one hand, citizens can make adequate use of their public
autonomy only if, on the basis of their equally protected private autonomy,
they are sufficiently independent; but that, on the other hand, they can arrive
at a consensual regulation of their private autonomy only if they make
adequate use of their political autonomy as enfranchised citizens'.[89] The
proximity of this intuition to the one that motivated *The Structural Transformation of the Public Sphere* is quite clear. In both, private autonomy was
the presupposition of the public sphere and could, in turn, only be maintained against the depredations of power and money by means of the public
sphere. Nor had Habermas renounced his earlier criticism of the historical
degeneration of the bourgeois public sphere into one dominated by the mass
media.[90] His emphasis had changed, however. In the place of the chronicle of
that degeneration stepped a militant, normative defence of private autonomy
and public autonomy.

As the political dimension of the public sphere moved into the foreground,
again Habermas had made some significant changes which bring into question the continuing validity of the concept of bourgeois society for
Habermas's work:

> The expression 'civil society' ... has taken on a meaning different from
> that of the 'bourgeois society' of the liberal tradition, which Hegel
> conceptualized as a 'system of needs' ... What is meant by 'civil

society' today, in contrast to its usage in the Marxist tradition, no longer includes the economy as constituted by private law and steered through markets in labor, capital and commodities. Rather its institutional core comprises those nongovernmental and noneconomic connections and voluntary associations that anchor the communication structures of the public sphere in the society component of the lifeworld.[91]

Habermas drew this distinction to mark out a realm in which the fragile bourgeois ego could escape its isolation without falling prey to what Horkheimer and Adorno called the administered world, and without embarking upon strategies so ambitious that they would inevitably issue in, if anything at all, political catastrophe. From this position society could not, as Horkheimer had once hoped, be made intelligible to and be brought under the control of the members who sustained it. In some respect, society would continue to reproduce itself over their heads. In the light of the evaporation of revolutionary expectations and even more so the deformation of revolutionary processes in the twentieth century, such caution is not without its attractions. Yet it also rests upon some questionable assumptions, most notably that the realms of power and money operate in isolation from, or in relative immunity to, 'norm-constitutive attitudes and identity-forming social memberships'. The latter are also often heavily influenced by power and money. In this respect the older generation's adherence to a concept of bourgeois society in which Hegel's system of needs received its full due has not lost its attraction either.

CHAPTER 7

Paradoxes of Reason

That reason is a central category for understanding the critical theorists follows from their self-understanding as the heirs of Kant and Hegel, as being contemporaries of the Young Hegelians, and from their persistent attempts to grasp the epochal significance of bourgeois society or modernity. Its centrality was consolidated by their conduct of a dual defence of reason against what they saw as its positivistic truncation and its relegation in favour of either the new metaphysics or cultural relativism. The defence of reason was, however, problematic, not least because of the scale of the tasks that were bequeathed to it by the modern era. According to Habermas, Hegel was the first to grasp this, that is the 'first to raise to the level of a philosophical problem the process of detaching modernity from the suggestion of norms lying outside of itself in the past'.[1] Hegel was also the first to turn the history of philosophy into a central feature of his argument. The history of philosophy, or more broadly of consciousness, was central in the systematic sense that each stage was considered to be necessary in the emergence of modern consciousness. There were no avoidable detours, errors or regressions. Each stage exhibited a certain coherence and validity in its own right yet was a historical product and was doomed to go under.[2] As is well known, Hegel exempted his own time from this contingency. Since all the moves that consciousness might make had already been made, Hegel could offer his contemporaries the reassurance that all that remained was the recollection of the process leading up to the present. Once it became clear that Hegel's elaborate conceptual framework could not cope with the novelty of the modern world the reassurance evaporated, leaving behind it a sense of the contingency of Hegel's own efforts and the suspicion that subsequent efforts suffered from the same affliction. A second reassurance was no more enduring. Hegel had claimed to give full acknowledgement to the principle that each individual should be able to judge the world in the light of his own reason without the external constraint of past tradition. Indeed he rejected the possibility, whose attraction he recognized, of remaining 'in a state of unthinking inertia'.[3] Like it or not, the individual would be forced to recapitulate the journey leading up to the present, at the end of which he would be reassured both that the demands of his own reason were met and that his judgement was in accordance with that of his contemporaries. Again the reassurance quickly proved to be implausible.

Of the older generation Marcuse became and remained the most convinced of the virtues of Hegel's enterprise. Heidegger's influence induced sympathy for the construction of an ontology that, paradoxically, would incorporate history into its underlying structure. In place of the ontological search for permanence beneath the flux of history, the transience of life, and the uncertainty of knowledge, Marcuse followed Hegel in construing history as the source of the unity sought by the ontologist. In his early work the strain of holding together these two apparently incompatible approaches frequently showed through, with ontological permanence gaining the upper hand.[4] By the time of *Reason and Revolution* (1941) Marcuse was more consistent in giving priority to history but was still sympathetic to Hegel's idea of ontology. This is evident where he sought to explain what he claimed was 'the most fundamental of his propositions, namely, that, Being is, in its substance, a "subject"', where subject means 'not only the epistemological ego or consciousness, but a mode of existence' which in varying degrees characterizes everything that exists.[5] Thus inanimate objects like stones exhibit a certain permanence while undergoing change at the hands of external forces. But stones have no inherent principle of development. Animate objects, even plants do. A plant has an inherent pattern of development but no comprehension of its own potential. Man, however, does: 'Man alone has the power of self-realization, the power to be a self-determining subject in all processes of becoming, for he alone has an understanding of potentialities'. Similarly, 'Reason presupposes freedom, the power to act in accordance with knowledge of the truth, the power to shape reality in line with its potentialities.'[6] Marcuse had bundled together reason, self-determination and truth as the realization of potentiality in thorough idealist fashion. Leaving aside the plausibility of the expansive concept of subjectivity, the crucial question becomes how did Marcuse identify the relevant potential? In part the answer lay in his basic model: the potential was self-realization guided by reason. That, however, serves only to identify the problem of modernity as outlined by Hegel, ruling out reliance upon prescription by tradition, recourse to vague intuitions and the like. What Marcuse had in mind is indicated in another attempt to explain the problematical Hegelian concept of the subject:

> Subject denotes a universal that individualizes itself, and if we wish to think of a concrete example, we might point to the 'spirit' of a historical

epoch. If we have comprehended such an epoch, if we have grasped its notion, we shall see a universal principle that develops, through the self-conscious action of individuals, in all prevailing institutions, facts and relations.[7]

The first problem with this is that the 'notion' of bourgeois society contained much that Marcuse held to be deplorable. The reason reflected in the institutions and relations of this society was a 'reason distorted by the blind necessity of the economic process and perverted through competition of conflicting private interests'.[8] Marcuse was forced back upon a selective reading of the 'universal', picking out ideas of inalienable rights, the rule of law, the multiplication of human wants and desires. These, frustrated as they were by the same society that generated them, identified the potential which could be realized by another form of society.

Ironically, in the same year in which he published *Reason and Revolution* Marcuse offered a different version of reason in the shape of 'technological rationality'. According to this version 'Rationality is being transformed from a critical force into one of adjustment and compliance. Autonomy of reason loses its meaning in the same measure as the thoughts, feelings and actions of men are shaped by the technical requirements of the apparatus which they have themselves created.'[9] What especially bothered Marcuse was that this process was accompanied by the appropriation, as it were, of the rhetoric of the potentiality of the individual. Even the idea of the inalienable human rights of the individual had, Marcuse noted, served the interests of 'efficiency and concentration of power'.[10] It was this which inhibited him from taking what might appear to be the obvious course of action, that is arguing that the appropriation of this language was illegitimate. He did seek to identify trends even amidst the 'technological rationality' which might presage a move towards the kind of potential he had sought to unfold in *Reason and Revolution*, but he was clearly unnerved by the apparent ease with which the ideas that he himself upheld could be pressed into the service of oppressive regimes.[11]

Marcuse's Hegelianism gave him greater conviction in reason than either Horkheimer or Adorno, though it was a conviction tied to the viability of the Hegelian edifice and even then it was not immune from subversion. At the beginning of the 1930s Horkheimer professed that he saw no problem with the 'paradox of reason', that it was necessary to make judgements with firmness while conscious of the fact that each judgement was subject to subsequent revocation. He approvingly quoted Hegel's' assertion that '*mod esty* of thought ... is the worst of vices'.[12] He also concurred with the triumph of reason over tradition, again quoting Hegel to make the point.[13] This did not mean that he was convinced of the efficacy of reason. In fact he emphasized the limits to the motivational force of reason. Insight alone would not dispel 'even the darkest superstition if this sort of thinking performs an important function in the dynamics of a moderately stable social structure'.[14] Large strata of society could be quite indifferent about whether or not certain assertions were true or not. Where they were not indifferent they might well shun some insight or other which would make it more difficult to conduct their daily lives. Again this was not so different from Hegel's account of the emergence of a new spirit of the age.[15]

In one respect, however, Hegel exhibited traits common to the bourgeois conception as a whole, traits which Horkheimer used to demarcate his own version of critical theory's conception of reason. In Hegel's system,

> All relationships in the completed system are conceived as immutable. Thus morality ... appears together with abstract bourgeois law as an eternal moment of ethical life ... The abstract categories of all parts of the system – both those of pure logic (such as quantity and quality) and those of individual realms of culture (such as art and religion) – are to be put together in an enduring image of concrete Being.[16]

From Descartes to Husserl this had been the ideal of reason, to formulate a coherent, non-contradictory set of propositions, which would have universal validity. The facts supplied by the senses or empirical research are then to be subsumed under the relevant category. What slipped through this conceptual net, Horkheimer complained, was the historical process in which the significance of the categories, the relationship between them and the relationship between categories and facts were bound up. From this perspective forms of morality and law as well as the 'darkest superstitions' had to be set in the context of the functions which they fulfilled.[17]

If Horkheimer objected to reason as the source of eternally valid categories immune to the vicissitudes of history, to the elevation of reason above its earthly origins and applications, he was equally opposed to the reduction of reason to a purely instrumental tool. This 'confounding of calculatory with rational thinking as such solidifies the monadological isolation of the individual engendered by the present form of economy'.[18] Consider, he suggested, a prison in which a large number of men were inadequately provided for. The prisoners would have to be shrewd in order to maximize their share of the inadequate provisions. They would have to anticipate their respective moves and might employ psychological insights. Their characteristics would be 'shrewdness, empirical rationality and calculation'. Such a form of thought, however, was not the only one conceivable. It was the legitimate task of reason not merely to provide for the adaptation of the individual to a chaotic social order but also to redefine the social order. Horkheimer sought to pitch reason beneath the insight into eternal verities, to relate it to specific historical dilemmas and tasks, yet to pitch it above the mere instrumental pursuit of goals assigned from outside.

Although Horkheimer never completely lost sight of this goal, he found it increasingly difficult to articulate. The more pessimistic tone was evident even in the titles: 'The end of reason', 'Reason against itself' and *Eclipse of Reason*.[19] Though the title of his joint work with Adorno, *Dialectic of Enlightenment*, was less ominous it has come to symbolize the collapse of faith in reason as a concept and social force. That is hardly surprising given its authors' announcement that:

> The dilemma that faced us in our work proved to be the first phenomenon for investigation: the self-destruction of the Enlightenment. We are wholly convinced – and therein lies our *petitio principii* – that social freedom is inseparable from enlightened thought. Nevertheless, we believe that we have just as clearly recognized that the notion of this very way of thinking ... already contains the seed of the reversal universally apparent today.[20]

Written in 1944, these words questioned the contrast between enlightenment and reason on the one hand and the barbarism practiced by the Third Reich on the other. The abandonment of enlightenment was not, they claimed, due to the temporary triumph of pagan and nationalist myths but was rooted in the 'Enlightenment itself when paralyzed by fear of the truth'.[21] The equivocation entailed by the phrase 'when paralyzed by the fear of the truth', which suggests a redeemable condition, persisted throughout the text but was never fully explicated. That is one of the reasons for the difficulty in assessing the work, but only one. *Dialectic of Enlightenment*, like Horkheimer's related works, contains a series of overlapping but far from identical theses, some of which are systematically ambiguous. Even the teleological thrust whereby enlightenment, intended as an escape from myth, reverts to mythology, was, as Horkheimer recognized, potentially misleading. That is the implication of his comment

> on the observation that human anatomy is the key to that of the monkey. The meaning of that truth is that once we know man, we can discover his beginnings in earlier forms of life. Once Fascism had developed in European society, we now are able to find its hallmarks in earlier stages of history, but it would be an error to say that, because of those traces the development was a necessary one.[22]

Yet this discrimination was not incorporated into the text, save in the elusive and equivocal sense already indicated. Even from the perspective of the late 1960s, the authors of *Dialectic of Enlightenment* reaffirmed its teleology, conceding only that it had been 'interrupted, but not abrogated'.[23]

The teleological thrust was enhanced by a history of philosophy, often presented in what Horkheimer admitted was a dogmatic style,[24] whose tendency was turned into a judgement on the validity of the concept of reason. The same thrust was reinforced by what was really a sociological claim about the contemporary level of conviction in the idea of reason. It was the latter with which he opened 'The end of reason'. The new generation, he claimed, treated the ideas of freedom, justice and truth, behind which lay the concept of reason, with skepticism. From there he moved on to scour the history of philosophy for evidence of the seeds of the end of reason. The first he lighted upon was the trend towards the increasing formalism of reason. His conclusion was that as one guiding star after another had been revealed as an illusion, reason was bereft of any guidance at all: 'None of the categories of rationalism has survived. Modern science looks upon such of them as Mind, Will, Final Cause, Transcendental Creation, Innate Ideas, res extensa and res cogitans as spooks, despising them even more than Gallileo did the cobwebs of scholasticism.'[25] There was, however, one sense in which reason still found widespread acceptance: reason as the instrument of self-preservation. But this too, he claimed, was flawed. The sacrifice of the individual for the safety of the community had always been justified in terms of the dependence of the individual upon the protection of the community. The individual, at least the propertied individual, could take some comfort from the idea that his family and property would endure and hence a part of himself would endure after his sacrifice. For those without property, however, the men of the Enlightenment recommended not reason but religion and the courts. Now, however, the security of property had given way to the dictates of the command economies and the interests of the monopolies.[26] In summary, reason could offer no stable guideline, the promised preservation of the individual had been equivocal and partial, and the self which was to be preserved had lost its footing in society. The argument was consistent, heaping up one deficiency and betrayal upon another. It was also flawed. Much of its force rested upon the presumption of a generalized insecurity of property which, even for the Third Reich, was questionable, as Marcuse had argued. There was more plausibility in the catalogue of abandoned concepts, the debris of the history of philosophy, but the presumption that a formalized reason was the same as the calculatory reason of the hypothetical prison was too hasty, as Habermas was later to argue. Many of Horkheimer's arguments relied upon a short circuit that he could as easily have exposed as such. Thus he noted some of the arguments which had been used to 'bring men to reason', referring to Luther, Voltaire and Kant, all of whom allotted pain a role in stimulating men and teaching them prudence. Extrapolating from this he conceded that 'During the breathing spells of civilization, at least in the civilized mother countries, brute physical pain was inflicted only upon the abjectly poor; to others it loomed on the horizon only as the ultima ratio. Under Fascism society has invoked this ultima ratio.'[27] The notion that society keeps coercion in reserve is undeniable and the historical discrepancy in the practical resort to coercion, including brute physical pain, depending upon the wealth and status of the individual, is not difficult to illustrate. The short circuit lies in the casuistry that coercion 'brings men to reason', for what is glossed over therein is that, whatever this means, it is clear that men are not brought to this reason by reason. Horkheimer could, and should, have argued that the means undermined the goal.

Dialectic of Enlightenment rehearsed the general theme of 'The end of reason' but on a much extended scale and again with a set of overlapping motives. One motive was to counter the interpretation by the authoritarian Ludwig Klages of Greek myth as symbolic of an age untainted by enlightenment and reason. Where Klages found sheer myth, Adorno and Horkheimer discerned the shrewdness, cunning and deceit which was practiced by the bourgeois as a matter of daily affairs. That was a second reason for reaching back so far in history, to pick out the earliest indications of something like the bourgeois individual.[28] A third motive was to unravel the complicity of enlightenment in domination from the origins of myth at one end to Kant and de Sade and the culture industry at the other. In this account

> The myths which fell victim to the Enlightenment were its own products ... In the place of the local spirits and demons there appeared heaven and its hierarchy; in place of the invocations of the magician and the tribe the distinct gradation of sacrifice and the labour of the unfree mediated through the word of command ... The gods are distinguished from material elements as their quintessential concepts. From now on, being divides into the *logos* ... and into the mass of all things and creatures without.[29]

Domination over external nature was gained by distancing the self from the animistic world of magic. Whereas the magician had to adopt different masks, different persona, in order to placate the various demons which inhabited his world, his successors maintained a more consistent self-identity against a natural world increasingly ordered into a conceptual unity. Yet this was not merely the product of a change in conceptual perspective. Its plausibility was achieved by labour, the shaping and the management of the natural world carried out in stratified societies. The distance from nature, the imposition of order and unity, was real. In this Adorno and Horkheimer applied Marx to the origins of the Enlightenment and, arguably even more so, Hegel's dialectic of lordship and bondage.[30] The linkage of concept formation, self-identity and domination over nature and man evident in the latter was supplemented by recourse to Durkheim's attempt to identify the social origin of early concept formation. As Horkheimer later put it 'French sociology has taught that the hierarchical arrangement of primitive general concepts reflected the organization of the tribe and its power over the individual.'[31]

While Adorno and Horkheimer implicated enlightenment in domination they were far from idealizing an earlier more primitive condition of life. Indeed they drew a picture which was bleaker than Hobbes's state of nature: 'It is not the soul which is transposed to nature, as psychologism would have it; *mana*, the moving spirit, is no projection, but the echo of the real supremacy of nature in the weak souls of primitive men.'[32] This was the fear from which the Enlightenment promised escape. Supremacy over nature was, as it were, encoded into the concepts of the Enlightenment. Whatever stood outside the conceptual framework had to be stripped away as inessential or exposed as mere projection and fantasy, as myth. Yet Adorno and Horkheimer argued that this promise had not been fulfilled. The impotence of the individual which was central to their analysis of bourgeois society had to be linked to the perpetuation of fear. Only thus did it make sense to claim that the Enlightenment was 'paralyzed by fear of the truth'. It is possible to construe this as meaning that the Enlightenment was paralysed by neglect of its origins, of what had to be stripped away in order to impose the regularity and clarity sought by enlightenment. But the outcome of this would be a disenchanted world. Its vice would be indifference, but not fear.[33]

Indifference was construed not as a vice but as a virtue by Nietzsche and de Sade. The selection of these two authors as illustrative of the telos of enlightenment may seem strange. Their attraction for Horkheimer and Adorno was that they did not halt at the virtues of the bourgeoisie, but in doing so they merely radicalized the bourgeoisie's own principles. Their attitude towards this was ambivalent. They clearly held it to be reprehensible and inhuman yet they praised its proclamation. The paradox lies in the strategy of holding up Nietzsche and de Sade as mirrors of a society and form of reason which they saw as the end product of radical enlightenment. It is this which leads to the assertion that 'stoic indifference from which the bourgeois coldness, the antithesis of compassion, is descended kept wretched faith to the universal which it rejected than the participant communality which adapted itself to the world'.[34] The vice of indifference, they argued, had the virtue of avoiding the implicit confirmation of the unavoidability of suffering and injustice by making exceptions to the general rule rather than calling into question the prevalence of suffering and injustice. In this Kant, the archetypal moralist, was quoted alongside de Sade and Nietzsche, who threw morality overboard. According to Kant compassion easily turned into 'softheartedness' and lacked the 'dignity of virtue'.[35]

As they faithfully followed through the logic of the formalization of reason, the exposure of every goal and virtue as another piece of mythology, Adorno and Horkheimer were led to two conclusions, one inherently critical and the other resigned. The former goes some way to rescuing the central thesis of *Dialectic of Enlightenment*, that enlightenment, which promised escape from myth, reverts to it. According to this conclusion 'Since it exposes substantial goals as the power of nature over mind, as the erosion of its self-legislation, reason is – by virtue of its very formality – at the service of any natural interest. Thinking becomes an organic medium pure and simple, and reverts to nature.'[36] If reason is no more than the means for realizing individual preferences, over which it has no jurisdiction, then there is nothing other than natural inclination to determine which preference is to be pursued. Or, to use older terminology, if reason is the slave of passions then it cannot weigh one passion against another. From there it is a small step to the argument of Nietzsche that cruelty is as natural, and hence as unobjectionable, as its opposite, or to de Sade's chronicles of sadism. While the statement that in all this enlightenment 'reverts to nature' contains an inherent criticism, namely that it is a betrayal of enlightenment, the second conclusion loses touch with even this equivocal criticism. Here the judgement was that 'Not to have glossed over or suppressed but to have trumpeted far and wide the impossibility of any fundamental argument against murder fired the hatred which the progressives ... still direct against Sade and Nietzsche. They were significantly unlike the logical positivists in taking science at its word.'[37] There is, of course, no necessity to take science at its word in this sense. More importantly it is subject to a similar response to that which can be made to Hume's assertion that, once reason is construed as a slave to the passions, 'It is not contrary to reason to prefer the destruction of the whole world to the scratching of my little finger.'[38] Even from Hume's truncated view of reason the reply is that such a preference is self-destructive, exhibits a complete lack of proportion and discrimination.[39] Similarly, Horkheimer's conclusion in *Eclipse of Reason* can be marshalled against his logic in *Dialectic of Enlightenment*, without stepping outside his own pessimism: 'we are the heirs, for better or worse, of the Enlightenment and technological progress. To oppose these by regressing to more primitive stages does not alleviate the permanent crisis they have brought about. On the contrary, such expedients lead from historically reasonable to utterly barbaric forms of social domination.'[40]

This is not the only occasion on which the arguments of the authors of *Dialectic of Enlightenment* can be turned against the main thrust of that text, again without even having to repudiate the entwinement of domination in the origins of reason. For they noted that 'The instruments of domination, which would encompass all – language, weapons, and finally machines – must allow themselves to be encompassed by all ... The "objectivity" of the means, which makes it universally available, already implies the criticism of that domination as whose means thought arose.'[41] That they did not pursue such insights had less to do with the dialectic of the Enlightenment than with the fact that they were paralysed by the image of the Third Reich. That image acted as a filter through which specific features of the dialectic of the Enlightenment gained a higher profile. The error lay in not recognizing Horkheimer's own warning against such a procedure.

There were other, related, escape routes from the cul-de-sac into which they had driven themselves. Habermas has referred to comments linking reason and speech in a way that points to his own solution.[42] Indeed, the underlying intent of some of their comments on language is remarkably close to Habermas's programme. In a letter to Adorno in 1941 Horkheimer noted that both the invocation of bourgeois ideals and the critique of political economy no longer seemed to offer them a sure footing. He then asked Adorno for his opinion on some comments on the function of speech, namely that:

> To address someone ultimately means to recognize him as the future possible member of an association of free men. Speech posits a common relation to truth, therefore the innermost affirmation of the alien existence which is addressed ... The speech of an overseer in a concentration camp is in itself a fearful nonsense completely regardless of its content ... [43]

Despite Adorno's enthusiastic endorsement of this suggestion, neither man explored its full potential. They were acutely aware that the fragmentary nature of *Dialectic of Enlightenment* was unsatisfactory and discussed how they might proceed with their theme, which Horkheimer identified as the 'salvation of the Enlightenment'. At first Horkheimer suggested that they start with Schopenhauer, but Adorno rejected this. In response Horkheimer turned to the contemporary political agenda, but here Adorno feared that they would be able to offer nothing more than mere analogies. His own offer to begin with logic ran aground on Horkheimer's fear of the scale of the undertaking.[44] The conversation was prophetic, for having failed to agree to try to relink their theory more directly to the contemporary political agenda each went his own way: Horkheimer to a fragmentary philosophy of pity in which Schopenhauer played a prominent role, Adorno back to his efforts to expose the earthly origins of the concepts of idealism.

Adorno's strategy arguably provided the stronger defence of reason, but it was a static one in that his negative dialectic involved the meticulous refutation of any attempt to escape from the paradox of reason: that reason must assert the identity of concept and object and yet that this same reason must constantly acknowledge that something always slipped through the conceptual net.[45] Put another way, the paradox was that 'The subject has no way at all to grasp universals other than in the motion of individual human consciousness.'[46]

Behind this fixation lay not just the dialectic of reason or as Habermas would have it the insufficiency of the philosophy of consciousness. What also lay behind it was the deadening weight of Adorno's analysis of bourgeois society. It was this which explains his conclusion to his study of Husserl:

> That consciousness assumes a monadological shape, that the individual feels knowledge of himself is more immediate and certain than the same knowledge of all others – that is the correct appearance of a false world in which men are alien and uncertain to each other and every individual immediately relates only to his particular interest but in which, nevertheless, universal 'essential' laws are indeed realized ... [47]

By this account the individual is confined to his monadic isolation and must be wary of any bogus immediate community, which promised to relieve him from his isolation. Yet at the same time he should not take refuge in a cult of inwardness, which merely sanctions his isolation. He is then left with no alternative other than to try to pull himself out of his prison by his own conceptual hair. It was this paradox which induced Habermas to respond that Adorno's fixation was only tenable if 'one makes it at least minimally plausible that there is *no way out*'.[48] For Habermas there was a way out.

This was already evident quite early on in Habermas's work. Whereas Adorno dwelt on the notion that 'men are alien and uncertain to each other', Habermas referred to contexts of interaction which were normatively laden. These were investigated as valuable in their own right as well as forming an alternative to technocratic models of reason. The latter issued in an image that combined elements of Horkheimer's hypothetical prison and elements of the administered world. For Habermas it would be society divided between 'social engineers and the inmates of closed institutions'.[49] This image was less threatening to Habermas than it had been to Horkheimer for the former was more convinced of its inherent implausibility. The model of technical control over natural processes simply could not be transferred to the historical process. The contingency of the historical process condemned the technocratic vision to failure.[50] Furthermore, whereas Horkheimer emphasized the limited efficacy of reason, Habermas looked for arguments that would link reason with interest and action, building the latter into the very core of the former. This is the reason for his interest in Fichte. For Fichte, Habermas explained, 'Only the ego that apprehends itself in intellectual intuition as the self-positing subject obtains autonomy.'[51] What is central to this is that Fichte construes intuition on the model of self-determination; theoretical reason (reflection) is construed after the model of practical reason (self-determination). Habermas was not tempted to follow Fichte very far. His concentration of this self-determination in a single illuminating act was too implausible. Instead Habermas considered Hegel's alternative. What Fichte had concentrated into a single act Hegel stretched out in a historical recapitulation of the forms of self-determination and reflection of the entire species. This too Habermas rejected. Ultimately both Fichte and Hegel construed their respective models as self-enclosed processes that left no room for historical contingency and fused reflection and self-determination so completely that the difference between them evaporated. Habermas had to look elsewhere for linkages between reason and action. In *Knowledge and Human Interests* he found the answer, as the title suggests, in the idea of interests that 'aim not at the existence of objects but at successful instrumental actions and interactions as such'.[52] While instrumental action bears a clear resemblance to the instrumental reason into which Horkheimer believed reason had collapsed, it also included an element of a broader concept of interaction. For, as part of his criticism of positivism, Habermas had insisted that the instrumental action of science and technology was dependent upon theories whose validity was secured by consensus within the scientific community. Yet he had to maintain a distinction between instrumental action and interaction as such for that led him out of the cul-de-sac in which reason as a whole collapsed into instrumental reason. It was, as even sympathetic critics like Richard Bernstein pointed out, a difficult balancing act.[53]

By the time Habermas replied to Bernstein he had turned to the analysis of language in order to anchor the idea of reason and its relation to language. Inherent in speech, he claimed, are certain claims, namely that what we say is either true, legitimate, or veracious and that what we say is comprehensible. Claims to truth are made about the external world of nature, claims to legitimacy or rightfulness are made about claims relating to norms or values, claims to veracity are made about our expressed intentions.[54] It is important to Habermas that these various claims are not reducible to each other. In part, for example, this means the standard assertion that 'ought' cannot be derived from 'is', obligations from descriptions. He also insisted that 'comprehensibility has nothing to do with "truth"'. The claim to truth is, he explained, a claim about the relationship between our statements and the world, whereas 'comprehensibility is an internal relation between symbolic expressions and the associated system of rules according to which we can bring forward these expressions'.[55] Although Habermas sought to ground this idea that 'validity claims are embedded in the structure of language'[56] in great detail, the prima-facie plausibility of his approach can be appreciated by considering a case of the systematic violation of these claims. Thus communication with someone who was either systematically incomprehensible, or who, when comprehensible, tells us things which are factually wrong, or tells us to do things which we regard as morally reprehensible, or who systematically lies about his own intentions, would either be totally impossible or futile.[57]

As is well known, however, the devil lies in the detail. From the perspective of his *Theory of Communicative Action* Habermas recalled that 'The deeper I penetrated into the theories of action, meaning, speech acts, and other similar domains of analytic philosophy, the more I lost sight in the details of the aim of the whole endeavor.'[58] The purpose of the endeavour was to show how someone could 'rationally motivate' someone else to agree to do something.[59] In the *Theory of Communicative Action* he approached this aim more directly, beginning with some preliminary observations on the meaning of rationality. We call someone rational, Habermas argued, when someone can provide good reasons for his assertions that something is the case or that a particular course of action has good prospects of success. The rationality lies in the reasons which are, or could be, offered in response to criticism of his assertions. With these issues of truth and success we are in some sense still within the domain of what Horkheimer would have recognized as instrumental reason, even if his presentation and justification of it would have been substantially different. But, Habermas continued:

> There are obviously other types of expressions for which we have good reasons, even though not tied to truth or success claims. In contexts of communicative action, we call someone rational ... also if he is following an established norm and is able, when criticized, to justify his action by explicating the given situation in the light of legitimate expectations. We even call someone rational if he makes known a desire or an intention, expresses a feeling or a mood, shares a secret, confesses a deed etc., and is then able to reassure critics in regard to the revealed experience by drawing practical consequences from it and behaving consistently thereafter.[60]

There is here a discrepancy in the force of the argument. While the predicate rational would be applied in the first case, where issues of truth or success are at stake, it is not clear that it would be in the second case, where following norms is at stake. So strong is the hold of instrumental reason that it is more likely that in the second case we would select predicates like just, moral, fair or good. Ironically the third case, where desires and so on are at stake, is more likely to invoke the predicate rational, if only because 'drawing practical consequences and consistency of behaviour' are also characteristics of action orientated towards success. Nevertheless, someone who could not give good reasons for following a norm might well invite the predicate irrational where we disapprove of the norm and his action, and might even invite it where we approve of the norm and his action.

Tying normative behaviour to good reasons was only one part of Habermas's strategy. As with *Knowledge and Human Interests* he sought both to identify the underlying unity of reason across different domains of action and to demarcate them from each other. Only thus could he prevent the specific rationality of one domain from pre-empting that of another. In *The Theory of Communicative Action* he pursued this intent by starting out from different types of action and asking what ' "ontological" assumptions' are presupposed by those types of action. In the case of teleological action, intended to bring about some state of affairs in the world, or strategic action, with the same intent but where the world includes other actors, only the objective world is presupposed. The presence of other, human actors, in addition to other animals, inanimate objects and so on, makes no difference. Normative action, however, presupposes two worlds, the objective world common to it and teleological/strategic action, plus 'the social world to which the actor belongs as a role-playing subject, as do additional actors who can take up normatively regulated interactions among themselves'.[61] The assertion of a third form of action followed on from the tripartite division of reasons, though this third form, dramaturgical action, was evidently more problematic.[62]

Nevertheless the tripartite model of social action was important not only because of the tripartite model of good reasons, but also because Habermas wished to construct a tripartite model of societal rationalization. The complexity of Habermas's model, the symmetrical differentiation of types of reason, forms of action and forms of rationalization, was intended to avoid the analytic and normative inadequacies of earlier theories of rationalization, specifically those of Weber, Marx, Adorno and Horkheimer. Despite their substantial differences they all 'identify societal rationalization with expansion of the instrumental and strategic rationality of action contexts; on the other hand, they all have a vague notion of an *encompassing societal rationality* – whether in the concept of an association of free producers [Marx], in the historical model of an ethically rational conduct of life [Weber], or in the idea of fraternal relations with a resurrected nature [Adorno and Horkheimer]'.[63] Moreover, Habermas claimed that the 'action theoretic concepts that Marx, Weber, Horkheimer and Adorno take as basic are not complex enough to capture all those aspects of social action to which societal rationalization can attach' and that their theories suffered from 'the confusion of basic action-theoretic and systems-theoretic concepts. The rationalization of action orientations and lifeworld structures is not the same as the expansion of the "rationality", that is, complexity of action systems.'[64] In contrast to this Habermas maintained that it was possible to delimit fairly sharply three realms of rationalized action, a realm concerned with truth (science and technology), a realm concerned with rightfulness (law and morality) and a realm concerned with veracity or beauty (art). Within each realm tradition gave way to the development of increasingly formal standards of criticism and justification. The standards in each were autonomous and hence problems encountered within any one of them could not be solved by reference to arguments developed in the others. Weber had 'presupposed a differentiation of all three value spheres' but he had not followed through the process in all three. More importantly he had not grasped the full significance of this differentiation. Instead he had focused upon the rationalization of ethical systems in order to account for the development of a type of behaviour conducive to the emergence of capitalism.[65] For Habermas the significance was that it was an irreversible differentiation, yet one which allowed for the development of rationally motivated consensus on an increasingly universal basis within each sphere. Similarly, the differentiation of social sub-systems, that is of the economy and the state, was also irreversible and could not be brought back within the purview of an undifferentiated lifeworld. There was no single 'encompassing societal rationality' under which the complexity of the modern society or the differentiation of autonomous value spheres could be reversed. In different ways, Marx, Weber, Adorno and Horkheimer all erred, in the first place, by privileging instrumental and strategic action as the outcome of modernization, and in the second place, by construing modernization as necessarily pathological, issuing in a loss of meaning and freedom.[66]

Yet this did not commit Habermas to an apologetic stance towards the modernization process. He did not deny the pathologies of modernity but argued that these were remediable. There was an escape from the paradox of modernity, that is that modernization witnessed both increasing rationalization and complexity and a perspective, either utopian or tragic, from which this same process stood condemned. Modernization had not only led to the distortions and disorientation identified by Marx, Weber, Adorno and Horkheimer, it had also led to the formation of new potentialities for communicative action in which rationally motivated consensus was possible. It was possible insofar as the different cultural spheres, of science and technology, morality and law, and art, were developed and institutionalized in a balanced way, and were protected from incursions from each other and from subordination to the imperatives of the economy and the state.[67]

Compared with the Hegelian concept of reason, still evident in Marcuse, Habermas presented a more thin-blooded and dispersed notion. Even so, it was reliant upon a set of arguments which stretched from general reflections on the meaning of rationality, through concepts of social action, to a theory of modernization with the aim of interpreting and refining Weber's model of modernization. With such an ambitious scope it is not surprising that this complex edifice has offered numerous points for attack.[68] Yet its main attraction is simple. It offers a perspective from which the paradox of modernity can be escaped without recourse to anything outside the process of modernity itself. It requires neither the sacrifice and demonization of reason nor the invocation of a utopian vision, which can only form an impotent contrast to the complexity of the modern world. It is more successful than the concepts of the older generation of critical theorists in making plausible the primacy of practical reason to which they all subscribed. That plausibility has been purchased at a high price. It issues in no code, contains no standards other than those governing the structure of discourse as such and has an increasingly weak link with motivation. The transition from the concept which Horkheimer's bourgeoisie painted on their standard to the concept inherent in communicative action is the transition from noun, 'reason', to the adjective, 'rational'. It is this that marks the difference between Habermas's concept of communicative reason and the older ideal of practical reason. The latter was taken to refer to the capacity inherent in each individual (Kant) and was even inflated into the capacity of a supra-individual subject (Hegel). For Habermas 'Communicative rationality is expressed in a decentred complex of pervasive, transcendentally enabling structural conditions, but it is not a subjective capacity that would tell actors what they *ought* to do.'[69] Severing this link between the subject and reason aggravates, as Habermas acknowledged, the problem which bedeviled Kant's reflections: the connection between reason and motivation. Compared with his earlier formulations, Habermas's recent comments have compounded that problem. Habermas's communicative reason 'pertains only to insights – to criticizable utterances that are accessible in principle to argumentative clarification – and thus fall short of a practical reason aimed at motivation, at guiding the will'.[70] Thereby, of course, he avoided Horkheimer's and Adorno's problem. They had construed the link between reason and motive, in the shape of the imperative of self-preservation, so tightly that the motive threatened to swallow reason, leaving only the residual hope for a radically different social context in which another deployment of reason would be possible. Habermas's communicative reason stands between Kant's practical reason and the instrumental reason of the administered society. Whereas Kant sought to purge practical reason of its earthly origins, to define its autonomy by the absence of all interest and passion,[71] Adorno and Horkheimer rooted it so firmly that its autonomy was almost inevitably ephemeral.

CHAPTER 8

The Contours of Critical Theory

It has been common to treat critical theory primarily as a distinctive methodology. Yet when asked about the general characteristics of critical theory Löwenthal protested that he found such questions comical and never knew how to reply.[1] He conceded that something had been 'codified', especially in Horkheimer's essay on 'Traditional and critical theory' and in Marcuse's 'Philosophy and critical theory', but still refused to emphasize this. His hesitancy was in fact fully in accord with the declaration by Horkheimer that 'contemporary materialism', that is the theory which he later labelled critical theory, 'is not principally characterized by the formal traits which oppose it to idealist metaphysics. It is characterized rather by its content: the economic theory of society. Only when the formal traits are abstracted from this content do they emerge as distinguishing marks'.[2] It was the perceived need to distinguish critical theory from its competitors which pushed Horkheimer and his colleagues towards a more formal presentation of their position.

Of the older generation Adorno's position undeniably seems to be at odds with this methodological reserve. It has indeed been argued that 'Adorno's originality lay not in the material substance of his theoretical arguments, but in the way he put them together.'[3] The plausibility of this interpretation even seems to be reflected in the titles of many of his works, which suggest an acute concern with issues of methodology or style: *Zur Metakritik der Erkenntnistheorie, Negative Dialectics, Eingriffe. Neun kritische Modelle, Prisms, Stichworte. Kritische Modelle 2*. To elevate style above substance was, however, contrary to Adorno's intention. He held reflection upon methodological and stylistic considerations to be significant insofar as, and only insofar as, substantive issues underlay such considerations.[4] He even linked the contemporary 'inclination towards method' with Horkheimer's idea of instrumental reason.[5] The point of that comparison was that what mattered was not the logic, as it were, of instrumental reason but the social conditions

127

from which it had arisen, conditions which instrumental reason was blind to. This did not signify any indifference towards considerations of style and methodology. To the contrary it signified a conviction that method and substance were inseparable, a conviction which Adorno took from Hegel.[6] The extent to which it is true that Adorno's originality lay in his style rather than the substance of his argument would be the extent to which he had failed to live up to his own criteria.

Although Hegel had less attraction for Habermas, he too agreed that 'as we have known since Hegel and Marx, problems of presentation are not extrinsic to substantive problems'.[7] Despite agreement in principle on this point, the differences between Adorno and Habermas in matters of methodology are substantial. After *Knowledge and Human Interests* Habermas rejected the need for a methodological foundation of critical theory. To be sure, the imprint of methodological consideration was still evident in his work, but methodology did not have the same significance that it did for Adorno. There is, however, one sense in which there is a strong continuity between the older generation and Habermas. When Löwenthal was pressed about the general characteristics of critical theory and had denied the centrality of methodology, he emphasized instead a concern with the obstacles, which stood in the way of a 'revival of the unity of theory and practice'.[8] It was inevitable that, as Marxists, they were concerned with this. The presence of Lukacs and Korsch, two key figures in the Marxist debate over theory and practice, at the First Marxist Work Week which preceded the foundation of the Institute, was significant in this respect. Lukacs was also a central reference point, albeit a negative one, for Habermas's understanding of the relation between theory and practice.[9] Of the older generation Horkheimer and Adorno were also critical of Lukacs. Horkheimer implicitly grouped him amongst those guilty of a 'metaphysical transfiguration of the revolution'.[10] Nevertheless they continued to worry about the theory–practice relationship long after any hope of revolution had faded or, in the case of Marcuse, taken on ever more desperate forms.

Their initial hopes had been bolstered by the Marxist conviction that revolution was not a wilful or arbitrary act but was immanent in bourgeois society. Their own theory was indeed pervaded by the idea of an immanent critique, which was indebted not only to Marx but also to Hegel. Although Hegel generally avoided the term, the concept was central to his argument. Opposing positions were not to be criticized from arbitrary standpoints: 'the refutation must not come from outside, that is, it must not proceed from assumptions lying outside the system in question and inconsistent with it ... The genuine refutation must penetrate the opponent's stronghold and meet him on his own ground; no advantage is gained by attacking him somewhere and defeating him where he is not.'[11]

Underlying this strategy were several assumptions. The first was that the opponent was not merely irrational or misguided. His position was intelligible and even had a certain justification. Thus Horkheimer, who followed Hegel here, conceded that *Lebensphilosophie*, originally at least, was a legitimate protest against the soulless capitalism of the day and grasped a characteristic of cognition that was typically ignored.[12] The second assumption was that the opponent's own arguments could be turned against him to the point where they called into question his own standards and criteria. The third assumption was that thought could, by means of its inherent criteria in each form of consciousness, be driven forward until it formed a seamless whole.[13]

It was quite in accordance with Hegel's professed intent that Horkheimer construed this immanent critique not purely as conceptual process or merely a device for developing a history of ideas. It was characteristic of the relation between ideas and society and was the key to his attempt to find an alternative to the challenge of relativism. How central this was is evident from the fact that he held on to it despite his growing pessimism at the beginning of the 1940s. Thus in a brief attempt to set out the Institute's approach in 1941 Horkheimer suggested that 'Social theory may be able to circumvent a skeptical spurning of value judgements without succumbing to normative dogmatism. This may be accomplished by relating social institutions and activities to the values they themselves set forth as their own standards and ideals.' This was to be done, however, 'without accepting these as valid and evident'.[14] What Horkheimer had in mind can be discerned in his account of 'Egoism and freedom movements'. There he set out from the contrast between the egoism presumed and promoted by bourgeois society and the frequent condemnation of egoism by those he saw as bourgeois philosophers, including figures as diverse as Machiavelli, Luther and Rousseau.[15] The easy answer from an orthodox Marxist perspective would have been to dismiss the latter as mere ideology. Horkheimer did see them as fulfilling an ideological function but not as being reducible to that. He claimed that disparagement of egoism did enable the bourgeoisie to appeal to the lower orders, in the name of justice and equality, in order to mobilize them in support of the bourgeoisie's interest in the removal of restrictions upon its own development. Second, disparagement of egoism could be used to reject the claims of its allies, the lower orders, when these threatened private property and profit. All this is relatively orthodox. Horkheimer began to go further when he suggested that this was not merely a matter of the defence of sectional, bourgeois, interest. Bourgeois society itself needed a degree of self-restraint lest it be torn apart by the competition which was its own principle of organization. Moreover, he drew a wider conclusion from this: 'Thus, the moralistic view of man contains a rational principle, albeit in mystified, idealistic form ... Both themes, universal social interest and class interest, pervade the critique of egoism.'[16] He added one further twist to the argument. He did not argue that egoism should be supplanted by some higher communal interest. The problem was not with egoism itself but the form that it took in bourgeois society. The future society would preserve egoism in a different form, not reject it.[17] The latter claim, as Horkheimer realized, is the most tenuous stage in the argument, though such a wide-ranging survey, heavily reliant upon a unified concept of class over several centuries, provides other points of attack. There is, however, another problem that is directly related to Horkheimer's later pessimism. The privileging of immanent criticism, when tied to specific societies, only had critical purchase so long as those societies espoused principles which might plausibly be seen as having a certain justification and might plausibly be seen as having a more universal reference, beyond whatever sectional interests they might serve. This was precisely the problem for Horkheimer. He was faced with societies that no longer seemed to do this, but instead, at best, cynically manipulated the old bourgeois values. Hence his warning that the rhetoric of freedom had to be used with great care: 'Freedom in the abstract goes too well with the decrees of French police prefects and the redemption of our Austrian brothers.'[18] His concession was more than a little hasty,[19] but the general point can be made simply. If we take not just a society which has abandoned certain values that are deemed worthwhile, but a society which adopts values in which no intrinsic merit can be found, then where can an immanent critique gain its foothold? Nazi racial theory, for example, provides no such foothold. It was a barbaric assertion of a sectional interest totally devoid of any relation to a 'universal social interest'.

Although Horkheimer never stopped criticizing Hegel's assumption that immanent critique issued in a seamless whole, he conceded that even this had its limited truth. Its truth, however, lay not in the promise of conceptual reconciliation held out by Hegel, under the legend of 'absolute knowledge', but in Marx's critique of political economy. There,

> In a purely intellectual construction, the concept of value is derived from the basic general concept of the commodity. From it, Marx develops the categories of money and capital in a closed system; all the historical tendencies of this form of economy ... are posited with this concept and deduced in strict succession ... This attempt to carry theory through to the end in the enclosed form of an inherently necessary succession of ideas has an objective significance. The theoretical necessity mirrors the real compulsiveness with which the production and reproduction of human life goes on in this epoch, the autonomy which the economic forces have acquired in respect to mankind, the dependence of all social groups on the self-regulation of the economic apparatus.[20]

Of course Marx's intellectual construction was supposed to mirror as well the collapse of this economy, revolution and the emergence of new forms of society. That too was part of the immanent critique. As the predicted collapse failed to appear, at least in the form it was supposed to, Horkheimer held more tightly to the mirror of compulsion despite his own insight into its limitations. Referring to the development of bourgeois society, he had noted that 'there has never been a congruence between its critical representation and its historical development which could not be broken down'.[21] He did not take this as an indication that it was necessary to turn to the vagaries of history, despite the fact that different social strata 'await life or death depending upon whether reformism, bolshevism or fascism is victorious'.[22] He took it as the occasion for reaffirming the futility of all faith in the inevitability of revolution – something which he had never believed in anyway – and for asserting the possibility of a revolutionary transformation which would mark such a radical break with previous history that he lost all connection with the idea of an immanent critique. 'Such an outcome [the revolutionary transformation]', he wrote, 'is not a further acceleration of progress, but a qualitative leap out of the dimension of progress.'[23]

With the postulation of an indeterminate realm of progress, effectively equivalent to known history, and a transcendent realm to be introduced by the revolutionary act, Horkheimer's immanent critique ground to a halt.[24] The foreshortening of history involved in this was encouraged by Adorno's persistent efforts to discern the modern in the archaic and vice versa. This had a useful critical role to the extent that it deflated attempts to invoke some mythical golden age as a counterweight to the values of modernity. It can serve to buttress the principled suspicion that attempts to construe social arrangements as if they are in conformity with laws of nature amount to the degradation of men to the status of beings ruled by myth at best. As an approach to history it is too cavalier. Yet both, critical insight and indifference to the vagaries of history, are evident in Adorno's claim that 'To recognize in its fateful force the most recent injustice, which is laid down in just exchange itself, means nothing else than to identify it with the antiquity which it destroyed.'[25]

Ironically this foreshortening of history arose from the intention to do full justice to the historical origins of thought and to do so by means of an immanent critique. Thus, when Adorno wrote to Horkheimer that Marcuse's article on the 'Concept of essence' was too much a history of ideas, what he found wanting was a closer demonstration of the relation between intellectual and social trends. Marcuse, he complained, simply presented two parallel developments but had not demonstrated how the traits of society pressed into idealist philosophy, in this case Husserl's, despite all of Husserl's efforts to keep such traits out.[26] The aim once again was to use a purely immanent critique to make this clear.[27] Whereas Marcuse deployed an account of social trends, the trajectory of bourgeois society, and sought to illustrate the social significance of various doctrines by reference to that account, Adorno claimed to deduce the social trend from within the doctrine. The inherent difficulty of doing this with a doctrine which sought to strip away such contingency showed through in Adorno's own account. At the end of the day he had to bring in arguments which had no place in Husserl's edifice.[28] Moreover, his attempt to avoid doing precisely this meant that the earthly origins of Husserl's philosophy which he claimed to discern took on a vaguer form than Marcuse's more explicit social theory.

Despite these differences they agreed on the essential characteristics of immanent critique. As one moves from Adorno to Marcuse it is the emphasis which changes. Marcuse's greater sympathy for the history of ideas brings out more forcefully the idea of an immanent development from Kant through Marx to Hegel, though the same development is portrayed by Adorno as being no less stringent than Marcuse believed it was.[29] In both cases a central point is Marx's claim to have deciphered Hegel's *Phenomenology of Spirit* as the encoded history of man's self-creation through labour. Both quoted the same passage from Marx's early 'Economic and philosophical manuscripts': 'The outstanding achievement of Hegel's *Phenomenology* and of its final outcome ... is thus ... that Hegel grasps the essence of labour and compre-hends objective man – true, because real man – as the outcome of man's own labour.'[30] It is notable, though, that Adorno explicitly worried about whether or not Marx's interpretation constituted a violation of Hegel's principle of immanent critique.[31] Adorno's greater sensitivity to methodo-logical issues as well as his problems with his account of Husserl served as constant reminders of the difficulty of a strictly immanent critique. This applied to Heidegger no less than to Marx's interpretation of Hegel. As Adorno put it in *Negative Dialectics*: 'We have no power over the philosophy of Being if we reject it generally, from outside, instead of taking it on in its own structure – turning its own force against it, in line with Hegel's desideratum.'[32]

The third assumption of Hegel's idea of immanent critique, that the process would issue in a seamless conceptual web, was more problematic, not least because of the form in which Lukacs had put it on the political agenda. According to Lukacs:

It is not the primacy of economic motives in historical materialism that constitutes the decisive difference between Marxism and bourgeois thought, but the point of view of totality. The category of totality, the all-pervasive supremacy of the whole over the parts is the essence of the method which Marx took over from Hegel and brilliantly transformed into the foundations of a wholly new science ... The category of totality, however, determines not only the object of knowledge but also the subject. Bourgeois thought judges social phenomena ... from the standpoint of the individual. No path leads from the individual to the totality ... The totality of an object can only be posited if the subject itself is a totality ... In modern societies only the *classes* can represent this point of view.[33]

To be more precise, Lukacs identified one class that could constitute a subject in this sense, the proletariat, and since the proletariat's grasp of reality was distorted by capitalism, the party had to stand in for it as the privileged subject. This was part of the 'metaphysical transfiguration of revolution' of which Horkheimer had complained.[34]

Despite their antipathy to Lukacs's political strategy, they did make use of the concept of totality, largely in a negative form. It formed, as it were, the counterpart to the idea of the fragility and impotence of the individual. In Adorno's work it became constitutive of the idea of a form of experience which resolutely refused to take flight into the cult of inwardness. Experience rather was defined by recognizing the oppressive weight of society even in the apparently most private realm.[35] In methodological terms this meant that the concept of totality had to be both construed and denied. It had to be construed to ward off the delusion that individuals were masters of their own fate in advanced capitalist societies. It had to be denied in order to ward off the delusion that individuals could be reconciled with this form of society.[36]

Adorno had turned the conviction that capitalist society both maintained the lives of its members and frustrated their purposes, enhanced their abilities and crippled the opportunities for deploying those abilities, into a methodological virtue. That was a logical outcome, if not an inevitable one, of the stubborn survival of capitalism itself. Earlier, though committed to Marx's prognosis of the end of capitalism, the older generation had acknowledged that there was no metaphysical guarantee that it would come about. Ironically, Horkheimer's commitment to the revolutionary ambition of Marxist theory combined with his insistence on the integrity of Marx's deductive, closed system, to raise the stakes of failure. As noted above, he was well aware of the tension between Marx's conceptual system and the historical reality of capitalism, but the conclusion he drew from this was that 'From the fact that the representation of a unified object is true as a whole, it is possible to conclude only under special conditions the extent to which isolated parts of the representation can validly be applied, in their isolation, to isolated parts of the object.'[37] He did not take this as an excuse to immunize Marxism as a theory from the tests of reality. Critical theory was, after all, precisely the attempt to revise Marxism in a way which would take account of developments unanticipated by Marx. But there was a more severe test. The theory's ambition was not the creation of an accurate model but revolution: 'the critical theory of society is, in its totality, the unfolding of a single existential judgement'.[38] It was precisely because he meant this quite literally that the rapidly accumulating weight of the evidence of failure had such dramatic consequences. At first, he held on to this existential judgement as if it were frozen at the end of history, leaving only the possibility of a 'qualitative leap out of the dimension of progress'. In the post-war world even this faded, leaving only the 'Longing for the completely other' which no longer had any positive connection with Marx.[39]

Marcuse clung more tenaciously to the original vision but could not escape from the tension between the theoretical insight and the absence of any connection to political practice. As he complained at the beginning of the 1970s, the dilemma was compounded by the fact that the 'petrification of Marxian theory violates the very principle which the New Left proclaims: the *unity of theory and practice*'.[40] Although Adorno showed little of Marcuse's inclination to search the Marxist corpus for insights which might better account for late capitalist society, and open up the possibility for Horkheimer's now ethereal 'qualitative leap', he too held more tenaciously, if more subtly, to the original intuition. That had an effect upon his concept of practice. He held to the idea that, since Hegel, 'unpolitical reflection on praxis' was not persuasive. But Hegel's judgement on Kant had been suspended. Both Kant's conception of practical reason and Hegel's philosophy of law 'maintain their right against each other so long as reality does not reveal a possibly higher form of praxis'.[41] There was no indication that it was about to do this.

There was one distinction of methodological significance that Horkheimer held on to, namely the Marxist distinction between the logic of research and the logic of presentation.[42] According to Marx the historical order in which concepts had been discovered or been decisive in the structure of societies and economies was no guide to the order in which they had to be presented in an analysis of capitalism. Indeed, 'Their sequence is determined, rather, by their relation to one another in modern bourgeois society, which is precisely the opposite of that which seems to be their natural order, or which corresponds to historical development.'[43] Horkheimer took up this distinction as a general characteristic of critical theory, though he emphasized less the contrast between historical order and the order dictated by bourgeois society, than the extent to which concepts 'acquire new functions in the course of the presentation'.[44] Such considerations went back, as Marx acknowledged, at least to Hegel. For Horkheimer, Marcuse and Adorno, it issued in an antipathy to fixed definitions of key concepts.[45] There is, however, an important difference between the older generation and those whom they saw as the progenitors of this disposition, namely, Kant, Hegel and Marx. All of the latter sought to provide highly systematic expositions in which the meanings of key concepts were explicated. Hence Kant's assertion that 'the definition in all its precision and clarity ought, in philosophy, to come rather at the end than at the beginning of our enquiries'.[46] The older generation, however, were never able to repeat something analogous to these expositions. In part they had no desire to, being suspicious, at least in the case of Hegel, of their metaphysical ambition. But this was not the only obstacle. Horkheimer, had, after all, contemplated a 'dialectical logic' but had not been able to see how he could carry it through. The systematic intent of Marcuse's early work had foundered on the tension between its Hegelian–Heideggerian origins and a historically committed Marxism. Of the three, only Adorno showed an abiding antipathy to any such enterprise. So strong was this that when he was asked to put together a collection on norms and guidelines (*Leitbilder*) in aesthetics, he did so only on condition that he could publish it under the title 'without guidelines' (*Ohne Leitbilder*).[47] The motive underlying this obduracy is evident in another collection which he suggested be understood as something that, 'systemless and discontinuous, presents what crystallizes through the unity of experience into a constellation'.[48] Put more prosaically, neither the nature of contemporary society nor the individual's goals could be set out in a comprehensive or prescriptive form without underestimating the imperviousness of society to the goals of the individual and consequently overestimating the scope still left to the individual. The unity of experience was precisely awareness of that dilemma. There was then a symmetry between the incapacity of theory and the incapacity of practice.

When Habermas took up the relation of theory and practice he leant towards Hegel's option and looked back beyond Hegel to Aristotle. Here, Habermas defended a conception of practice as communal deliberation about the pursuit of the good life, where prudence, not technical skill or even theoretical knowledge, was to guide men. Yet, Habermas continued, 'Wherever we encounter the latter, it seems hopelessly old-fashioned to us.'[49] One of the reasons why it seemed old-fashioned was the predominance of a positivistic and technocratic understanding of theory.[50] Against that Habermas sought to mobilize the idea of a cognitive interest in emancipation. In doing so, however, critics, including his ally Karl-Otto Apel, argued that he tended to conflate theoretical insight into historically generated constraints on action and political action.[51] In reaction to this and other criticisms, Habermas drew a tripartite distinction, between theoretical debate, processes of enlightenment and tactical political decisions. Lukacs, he noted, had fused all three, in a theory that made each dependent upon organizational considerations, that is upon the primacy of the party. Habermas insisted that it was necessary to distinguish, in the first place, between theoretical debate subject to the normal scientific criteria, and processes of enlightenment which were only fully validated when all those subject to the process of enlightenment accepted the preferred explanation of their subordination to various constraints. There was some difficulty here, which was evident in his conclusion that the 'superiority of those who did the enlightening over those who are to be enlightened is theoretically unavoidable, but at the same time it is fictive and requires self-correction: in a process of enlightenment there can only be participants'.[52] Quite how it can be both is difficult to see. The most important distinction was that between processes of enlightenment and tactical political decisions. Here he noted that there could be no question of a privileged grasp of the truth. Underlying this was the conviction that the 'sole possible justification at this level is consensus ... among the participants, who ... are the only ones who can know what risks they are willing to undergo, and with what expectations'.[53]

In drawing these distinctions, Habermas was clearly limiting the claims of theory, and he was doing so with a heavy emphasis upon the specific characteristics of political practice. Parallel to this he also drew a methodological distinction that had an analogous effect. In *Knowledge and Human Interests* he had, he conceded, conflated the idea of reconstruction and the idea of self-reflection. In this he had implicitly followed Hegel, who had fused both ideas under the single term reflection. The difference was important, he continued, insofar as in reflection

> (a) Criticism is brought to bear on objects of experience whose pseudo objectivity is to be revealed, whereas reconstructions are based on 'objective' data like sentences, actions, cognitive insights, etc., which are conscious creations of the subject from the start.
> (b) Criticism is brought to bear on something particular – concretely speaking, on the particular self-formative process of an ego, or group, identity – whereas reconstructions try to understand anonymous systems of rules which can be followed by any subject at all provided it has the requisite competence.
> (c) Criticism is characterized by its ability to make unconscious elements conscious in a way that has practical consequences. Criticism changes the determinants of *false* consciousness, whereas reconstructions explicate correct know-how, i.e. the intuitive knowledge we acquire when we possess rule-competence, *without* involving *practical* consequences.[54]

Interestingly, Habermas defended both Marx and the older generation of critical theorists against the charge that they too had succumbed to this confusion.[55] Marx's error lay elsewhere, in the *'reduction of the self-generative act of the human species* to labor'.[56] Where the older generation quoted Marx's observation on the 'outstanding achievement' of Hegel's *Phenomenology* in complete agreement with Marx's verdict, Habermas quoted it as a prelude to the suggestion that Marx had discerned the link between labour and communicative interaction in Hegel, only to then privilege the role of labour in mankind's self-creation.[57] Subsequently, Habermas drew out the full methodological significance of this and, in the process, consolidated the distinction between the two types of reflection, reflection proper and reconstruction. A further consequence of this was that he strengthened the gap between his own position and that of the older generation, especially by distinguishing his own position from their orientation towards a 'qualitative leap out of progress'.

This emerged most clearly in 'Toward a reconstruction of historical materialism'. There Habermas noted that Marx employed his materialist theory of history 'in the role of historian, to interpret particular historical situations or development – unsurpassedly in *The Eighteenth Brumaire of Louis Bonaparte*'.[58] Habermas explained that this was not his main concern, which was, rather, with the adequacy of Marx's work as a theory of social evolution. In the course of elaborating upon the latter, Habermas did draw distinctions that do bear upon Marx 'in the role of historian'. He noted that there was no need within Marx's theory to posit a macro-subject that realized itself through history: the 'bearers of evolution are rather societies and the acting subjects integrated into them'.[59] He then suggested that it was desirable to 'separate the logic from the dynamics of development – that is, the rationally reconstructible *pattern* of a hierarchy of more and more comprehensive structures from the *processes* through which the empirical substrates develop'.[60] The purpose of this was to retain the idea of progress – marked here by the greater comprehensiveness of structures – without attracting the suspicion that such progress was in any way necessary and inevitable, to separate out the milestones on the road of progress from the historical contingency which afflicts the development of any given society. Thereby, Habermas also weakened the links of his own theory to the 'dynamics of development' and gave precedence to a reconstructive critique at the expense of reflection upon 'the particular self-formation process of an ego, or group identity'.[61]

There were, however, other aspects of his arguments that pushed theory back towards critique in the second sense. As noted earlier, Habermas had some difficulty convincing sympathetic critics that a firm line could be drawn between the natural and social sciences.[62] Once post-empiricist theories of science gained dominance, natural science seemed all too dependent upon theoretical frameworks legitimated through the scientific community. There was, however, Habermas argued, one fundamental difference. In the words of Anthony Giddens, 'sociology, unlike natural science, deals with a pre-interpreted world where the creation and reproduction of meaning frames is a very condition of that which it seeks to analyze, namely human social conduct: that is why there is a double hermeneutic in the social sciences'.[63] Habermas drew two further conclusions from the distinctiveness of the social sciences. First, he claimed that the social scientist, insofar as he is inevitably involved in collecting meaning-dependent data, is in the same position as anyone else who participates in communicative interaction. Both the social scientist and the layman must seek to understand the meaning expressed by some other person. He acknowledged that there are limits to this analogy. Typically the layman is seeking to reach an agreement in order to pursue some course of action. This does not apply, however, to the social scientist, who 'takes part in the observed action system, *subject to the withdrawal, as it were, of his qualities as an actor*'.[64] Second, and here Habermas relied heavily on the analogy between the layman and social scientist, he claimed that just as the layman assesses the claims of his interlocutor so too must the social scientist. According to Habermas 'if, in order to understand an expression, the interpreter must *bring to mind the reasons* with which a speaker would ... defend its validity, he is *himself* drawn into the process of assessing validity claims'.[65] It is far from clear, however, that this is the case.[66] To put it simply, an agnostic interpreter can surely understand an expression which a speaker would justify by reference to God's will, without abandoning his agnosticism. Whatever the plausibility of Habermas's argument, there is, despite the different contexts of the arguments and at a very general level, a certain similarity between these observations and his earlier comments on the relation of theory and practice. In both cases three motives are at work. First, Habermas seeks to strengthen the status of the layman. Second, he reduces the distance between the layman and theorist or social scientist. Third, he seeks to endow both with the capacity for giving good reasons for what they do.

In *The Theory of Communicative Action* Habermas sought to make this plausible by combining a dual-track history of theory and more systematic reflections upon social action and the concepts of systems and lifeworld. At the end he drew these together in the history of theory and the systematic intent in a way that also emphasized the dilemma of modernity which, he claimed, had first been identified by Hegel.[67] Central to this conclusion were Marx's reflections upon the method of political economy, from which Habermas quoted extensively. There Marx had sought to justify the key role which he ascribed to the abstract concept of labour, a concept which had appeared relatively recently but which had universal significance. According to Marx, 'the simplest abstraction which modern economics places at the head of the discussion and which expresses an immeasurably ancient relation valid in all forums of society, nevertheless achieves practical truth as an abstraction only as a category of the most modern society'.[68] Only in the capitalist economy had labour, irrespective of its particular form, been identified as the source of wealth. Marx's reflections upon the method of political economy might be said to have redeemed and justified his earlier conviction, derived from his criticism of Hegel, that labour was the means of man's self-creation. For Habermas, of course, communicative action has equal, and in some senses superior, status to the concept of labour. But he also saw a strong analogy between Marx's concept of labour and his own concept of communicative action. The latter was, like the abstract concept of labour, itself a historical product that nevertheless was supposed to have universal validity. For both Marx and Habermas, history had given their contemporaries 'privileged access' to these concepts. For Marx it was the theory of capital that explained how this privileged access arose. Habermas also had to account for the analogous privileged access to the centrality of communicative action. He did so by arguing that 'In modern societies there is such an expansion of the scope of contingency for interaction loosed from normative contexts that the inner logic of communicative action "becomes practically true" in the deinstitutionalized forms of intercourse of the familial private sphere as well as in a public sphere stamped by the mass media.'[69] The crumbling of tradition has inevitably exposed to his contemporaries the truth of communicative action, that is that communicative action has always been the precondition of social integration but could only be recognized as such, in its abstraction, from a perspective where there is no alternative to recourse to it. Thereby, Habermas claimed to have resolved a problem with which the older generation had struggled: to have accounted for the possibility of his own theoretical insight.

Talk of 'privileged access' to truth inevitably conjures up the spectre of élitism, be it in the shape of Lukacs's party or in other guises. Yet this is clearly far removed from Habermas's intent. The truth of communicative action is a privileged insight available to all. Despite the depredations of the mass media, it stands before his contemporaries as a daily reality. Ironically, this makes the status of Habermas's theory dependent upon the historical process; ironically because he turned to what became the theory of communicative action in order to provide a normative foundation for critical theory that was not tied to the contingency of the historical process. Yet the truth of the theory of communicative action is in some sense dependent upon the fact that it 'becomes practically true', that is, that it is recognized as the only basis upon which men can live in the disenchanted modern world without resort to deception and coercion.

Habermas was equally far removed from offering communicative action as a panacea. Although he has insisted upon the cognitive claims engendered in communicative action, he has also taken care to stress the limits of his theory of communicative action and the limits of the processes to which that theory refers. With respect to the latter, Habermas retained that sense of caution that was already evident in his early reflections on the risk involved in political action. As he moved away from conceiving of political action as a revolutionary type of action, the sense of caution grew rather than receded. Thus he wrote that, 'Unfettering normative contexts and releasing communicative action from traditionally based institutions – that is from obligations of consensus – loads (and overloads) the mechanism of reaching understanding with a growing need for coordination.'[70] The inherent threat of overload poses a firm, if indeterminate, limit to how much change can be managed.

In this process theory is of limited help. Although earlier formulation suggested that the rules of discourse themselves constituted moral norms, Habermas subsequently drew a distinction between the rule of discourse and the moral norms which might emerge from such discourse.[71] Similarly, he came to regret his earlier references to 'an ideal speech situation' and the more explicit speculation that this might be a central characteristic of a future form of society.[72] Communicative action, he continued to argue, does necessarily entail certain idealizing assumptions, but these assumptions must not be projected into the future as if they were the prefiguration of an alternative society. Indeed Habermas took increasing care in his choice of terminology to avoid even the implication that he subscribed to any such notion.[73] The implications of this caution are evident in his assertion that:

> Socialism too ought never to have been conceived as the concrete whole of a determinate, future form of life – this was the greatest *philosophical* error of this tradition. I've always said that 'socialism' is useful only if it serves as the idea of the epitome of the necessary conditions for emancipated forms of life, about which the participants *themselves* would have to reach understanding.[74]

It was no part of a philosophical theory to prescribe what those forms of life might be.

It was part of the role of philosophy, in conjunction with empirical sciences, to try to formulate what those necessary conditions are. Beyond that, philosophy is to put itself forward as an interpreter, translating the ever more specialized language of the sciences for the sake of a broader public.[75] With this Habermas returned to the themes of *The Structural Transformation of the Public Sphere* and his early criticism of technocratic models. Although he continued to note that technocratic social theories *per se* were still out of fashion, what he called the 'technocratic incapacitation of the public sphere' is an evident concern of his last major work.[76] Underlying this was the abiding conviction that 'In a democracy, there can be no political privilege based on expertise.'[77]

For both the older generation and Habermas, it was substantive issues, not methodology *per se*, that mattered. Yet the older generation were clearly much more tied to certain methodological principles, especially the idea of immanent critique and, in a more equivocal sense, the concept of totality. If anything, their understanding of the problems of the status and role of their own theories was aggravated by precisely those concepts. The idea of an immanent critique, not merely as a tool of the history of ideas or as a device in debate but as something inherent in the development of society, tied the fortunes of their theory so closely to the fate of mid-twentieth-century Euro-Atlantic culture, that the relation of theory to practice had to become strained. That tension was heightened by the fact that they never relinquished what Habermas has claimed is no longer attainable or even desirable, namely a philosophically justified form of life in which society no longer appeared as alien to its members but was, as it were, fully transparent. Habermas, by contrast, has ascribed theory a more modest role and has made neither the concept of immanent critique nor the concept of totality central to his project. The latter has been presented as either unattainable, in its positive form, or as unnecessary, in its negative form. The danger for Habermas lies not in the monolithic appearance of society *vis-à-vis* the individual, but in such a degree of cultural specialization and social complexity that the individual loses all sense of orientation.

The central, formative, concept of the older generation, immanent critique, fused together a favoured rhetorical device, critique of society and a conception of practice geared to revolution. For as long as revolution remained a possibility, that left them with the traditional Marxist problem of how to construe the relation between theory and practice, how to envisage the mechanisms by which large bodies of men would implement the supposed theoretical insight. It was a problem that they were temperamentally disinclined to solve by traditional means of organization and indoctrination. That was evident in Horkheimer's comments on the type of character which revolution seemed to require.[78] More importantly, when the immanent critique to which they subscribed was paralysed, so too was the relation between theory and practice. Habermas avoided this, not only because he never adhered to their initial revolutionary ambitions. He avoided it because the contours of his theory were radically different. It is arguable that his conduct of debate shows at least as much, if not more, commitment to the idea of immanent critique than the older generation.[79] But the idea of immanent critique did not have the structural significance that it did for the older generation. The central distinction between reflection and reconstruction allowed him to consolidate and justify an earlier political conviction, that the decision to act has to be taken by those who bear the risks of action. The unity of critical theory beyond the older generation does not lie in its methodology. It lies in its context, the persistence of its opponents and the concern for the fragility of the individual.

CHAPTER 9

The Authoritarian and the Democratic State

For Marxists it was axiomatic that economic crisis is accompanied by political crisis. By the time Horkheimer took over the directorship of the Institute economic crisis was firmly on the agenda, and the crisis of the democratic order was following hard on its heels. The rhetoric of crisis was not far behind. Historians, economists, political scientists and philosophers seem to have almost competed in their desire to convey the magnitude of the challenges which faced them as the accelerating economic and political crises pressed them towards ever greater rhetorical flourishes. The mood was captured by the historian Arnold Toynbee, according to whom 'The catastrophe ... which western minds were contemplating in 1931 was not the destructive impact of any external force but a spontaneous disintegration from within.'[1] The critical theorists joined in the competition. The first issue of the Institute's journal included a brief contribution by Horkheimer, 'Notes on science and the crisis', which was followed by an economic assessment written by Pollock. His article began with a quote on the economic crisis which, he said, 'reads like a military report on a lost war'.[2]

Although the early 1930s undoubtedly gave added force and immediacy to this sense of crisis, it had been prevalent since the end of the First World War, and indeed earlier. To use the language of a later historian, Karl-Dietrich Bracher, 'the forms of crisis thought' brought the disappointment of more progressive spirits into proximity to those who cultivated pessimism as an article of faith.[3] In the 1920s at least there had been some room for optimism, albeit cautious and guarded. As the historian Charles Maier has argued, the stabilization of the bourgeois order in the middle of that decade was precarious and was achieved only at the expense of the weakening of the traditional liberal elements of the political system.[4] Yet even self-avowed radicals could reconcile themselves, as Horkheimer complained, to the '"unfortunately" stabilized capitalism' with a measure of equanimity.[5]

142

Stabilization did not last long, least of all in Germany. The most detailed response to the emerging crisis came not from Horkheimer, but from two men who were not yet members of the Institute: Kirchheimer and Neumann. However, as the decision to prepare for emigration demonstrates, Horkheimer quickly drew his own conclusion from the question posed in the title of Kirchheimer's essay, 'Weimar – and what then?' Interpretation of the work of Kirchheimer and Neumann in this period, up until the end of the Weimar Republic, has been plagued by the question of their relationship to Carl Schmitt. Kirchheimer especially was attracted by the radicalism of Schmitt's conceptual distinctions and by the open acknowledgement of the conflictual nature of politics. In much the same way, Marcuse had been attracted to theorists of whom he was otherwise critical because they could be used to unfold an understanding of Marxism which offered an alternative to revisionism, on the one hand, and the 'transcendental-sociological' Marxism of Max Adler on the other. In place of these, Karl Mannheim's theory, with its emphasis upon the social roots of ideology, including Marxism, helped to point to Marxist theory as the 'concrete theory of proletarian praxis' which was 'oriented towards the revolutionary act'.[6] Similarly, if more thoroughly, Kirchheimer adopted some of Schmitt's distinctions. In his early work on 'The Socialist and the Bolshevik theory of state', for example, he mobilized Schmitt's distinction between sovereign and commisarial dictatorship in order to claim that the 'Bolshevik concept of dictatorship is a truer one, because it serves to designate a state of emergency.'[7] There were, however, substantive differences between Kirchheimer and Schmitt. Although both wrote very much with the contemporary political agenda in mind, Schmitt simplified the complexity of the historical context in order to give his polemical conceptual distinctions some purchase. Kirchheimer sought to bring historical complexity into view in order to exhibit the social function of conceptual distinctions. It was this that led Kirchheimer towards an increasingly critical stance towards Schmitt's arguments and to qualify his own earlier enthusiasm for the Bolshevik state. In both cases a crucial factor is his assessment of Schmitt's assertion of a strict link between social homogeneity and democracy. Kirchheimer had initially accepted this as a variation upon the Rousseauian vision of democracy and as a promissory note to be redeemed by a communist society. In doing so, he seems to have ignored the pronounced emphasis upon ethnic homogeneity which marks Schmitt's work.[8]

However, towards the end of the Weimar Republic Kirchheimer was emphasizing the dangers of the Bolshevik model as well as its virtues. He still acknowledged the tactical advantages of a centralized party, yet worried that lack of internal democracy not only led to intra-party conflict but also to a failure to integrate the mass of the proletariat, a failure which 'will be compensated by increasing emphasis on the repressive power of the state'.[9] In 'Remarks on Carl Schmitt's *Legality and Legitimacy*', written in 1932,

Kirchheimer turned directly to Schmitt's assertion of the indispensability of social homogeneity to democracy. With explicit reference to Rousseau, he still expressed sympathy for a reduction of social diversity. There was, however, a clear change of emphasis. Now he wrote that 'In accordance with Rousseau's *Social Contract*, we have to assume the inevitability of the emergence of special interests within every society.'[10] More striking still was his dismissal of unmitigated homogeneity as 'a utopian idea because it would imply the destruction of individuality itself.'[11] Schmitt's assertion was not only theoretically untenable, but it was also empirically bogus. Citing Britain, France and the United States, he argued that social heterogeneity and a democracy that might well be flawed, but was still worth the name, were evidently compatible. Moreover, whereas Schmitt saw social diversity as a threat to the sovereignty of the state, Kirchheimer invoked the existence of heterogeneity as a justification for state protection.[12] Kirchheimer also paused to criticize the conceptual reductionism to which Schmitt was prone. According to Kirchheimer, Schmitt reduced the concept of liberty to a pre-political sphere and effectively to the rights to property and freedom of conscience. Against this Kirchheimer argued that the concept of liberty 'constitutes the foundation both of citizenship rights necessary for democracy and private rights'.[13]

Neumann's answer to Kirchheimer's question: 'Weimar – and what then?' was simple: 'the answer can only be "First Weimar"!'[14] By this he meant that the socialist elements in the, albeit inconsistent, second half of the Weimar constitution should be realized first. In this Neumann, despite the increasingly precarious and polarized political climate, revealed his commitment to the reformist wing of German socialism and his faith in the law. So strong was this that as late as February 1933 he was still talking about his desire to 'awaken and strengthen in the working class an understanding of the importance of the law'.[15] It was, however, precisely this faith that had given him a certain immunity to the charms of Schmitt's valorization of conflict. Whereas Schmitt elevated the distinction between friend and foe into the existential nature of politics, Neumann saw the possibility for compromise.[16] This was a compromise based not on good will, but on a balance of power within the Weimar Republic. Neumann's strategy presupposed that the state could maintain a degree of independence *vis-à-vis* the major social actors and that parliamentary sovereignty could be liberated from restraint by judicial review, thereby opening up the possibility of legislation to extend the socialist dimension of the Weimar constitution.[17] There were numerous threats to this optimistic scenario, that the trade unions might be incorporated into an authoritarian state on the model of Italian fascism, that the state might lose its independence *vis-à-vis* the social actors, that the judiciary might assert a conservative veto over reform and so on. Above all there was the possibility that the balance of power might degenerate, leaving something close to Schmitt's conflictual model. Indeed on the eve of the collapse of the Republic Neumann conceded precisely this in a letter to Schmitt.[18]

Finally forced to face the collapse of his vision, Neumann responded with an orthodox Marxist explanation of the Nazi seizure of power which crudely underestimated the Nazi movement: 'German National Socialism is nothing but the dictatorship of monopolized industry and of big estate owners, the nakedness of which is covered by the mask of a corporative state.'[19] Even before the Nazi seizure of power, Kirchheimer had shown a greater grasp of the dynamics of the ailing Republic, though he too underestimated the Nazis. Both the insight and the underestimation were combined in his claim that alongside the threat of the Nazi party, 'of at least as much importance is the growing tendency towards the independence of the state and military apparatus. One would underestimate the action of 20 July [1932], if one saw in it only the desire to shake off the Social Democratic Party and not also the desire to build an independent bureaucratic power as security against the National Socialists.'[20] With this Kirchheimer grasped the demise of the Weimar Republic as a twin-track process, marked on the one hand by the growth of the Nazi movement and on the other hand by the search for an authoritarian alternative independent of political parties of any kind. He recognized the underlying weakness of that search: the impossibility of turning the political clock back to the era of Bismarck, but he missed the willingness of the authoritarian élites to compromise with the Nazis in the interest of destroying the democratic order.[21]

Accounting for the emergence of the Nazi state was only one of the tasks confronting those forced to flee from the new regime. Understanding what kind of entity it was, proved to be no less difficult. So radical was the Nazi revolt against the liberal state that it seemed to call into question the explanatory utility of the general concepts which had characterized not only the liberal state *per se* but also earlier forms of state. This applied not just to distinctions between the private and the public realm, but also to the very concepts of law and state. Within the Institute itself Marcuse was the first to point to some of these problems. In 'The struggle against liberalism in the totalitarian view of the state' he argued that even the regime's self-proclaimed ideologues were unable to make sense of what was happening. Their constructs foundered on the amorphous and arbitrary exercise of power, leaving them only with intellectual self-abasement as a strategy. His own former teacher, Heidegger, provided symbolic expression of this: 'Let not doctrines and "ideas" be the rules of your being. Today and in the future the *Führer* himself is German reality and law.'[22]

Both Kirchheimer and Neumann continued to reflect on the legal system from exile, both before and after joining the Institute. The basis for Neumann's assessment was laid in *The Rule of Law*. There he concluded that 'law does not exist in Germany, because law is now exclusively a technique of transforming the political will of the leader into constitutional reality. Law is nothing but an *arcanum dominationis*.'[23] This outcome was not an abrupt reversal of the previous form of law, but the culmination of a trend already evident in the Weimar Republic. Central to this was the undermining of the generality of the form of law. The introduction of 'general standards of conduct', of 'good faith' and the like – as specifically independent of any existing body of law, yet as superordinate to these laws – completely transformed the legal system. Neumann's defence of the generality of law was qualified. He was too well aware that conservative jurists, including Schmitt, had invoked the principle of the generality of law to set limits to the intervention of the state in the economy. According to Neumann there was an economic rationale to the limits of the general form of law. The latter was quite appropriate to the anonymous market of liberal capitalists with its numerous producers. It provided the predictable and calculable environment that they needed. In the age of monopoly capital, however, the concentration of economic power made it much more difficult to operate by means of purely general laws. To illustrate his argument he cited the presidential decree of 1931 prohibiting applications for bankruptcy against a specific bank and asked: 'Should he [the President] have been compelled to issue a law in abstract terms prohibiting such applications for all banks, if economically only the fate of this large bank was really decisive?'[24] In his first two essays in the Institute's journal, Neumann rehearsed these arguments but with a notable change in emphasis to the conclusions. This was most marked in the second, on 'Types of natural law'. There he noted that despite the possibility of the invocation of natural law theories to defend the existing property order, they were in principle rational constructs that left scope for argument. Even those intended to justify absolutists or conservative political systems were 'based on the view that man is a rational creature'.[25]

When Neumann turned to the question of the nature of the Third Reich, his answer echoed his judgement on law in the Nazi regime. To the extent that the concept of the state required some notion of the rule of law, then clearly the Third Reich was no state. He considered, but rejected, the suggestion that the Third Reich could be characterized as a 'dual state', consisting on the one hand of traditional, rule-bound bureaucracies, and on the other, a prerogative state in which arbitrary political measures predominated. Even this conceded too much reality to the existence of law in Germany.[26] Nor did he accept that it constituted a state in the more limited sense of a highly unified political structure. Rather 'Under National Socialism, the whole of society is organized in four solid, centralized groups, each operating under the leadership principle, each with a legislative, administrative, and judicial power of its own.'[27] Between these four blocs, the party, the army, the bureaucracy and industry, there was no need for a formal mechanism for securing agreement. A loose consensus sufficed.

Neumann was not the only one to struggle with the complexity of the political structure of the Third Reich. Horkheimer responded to this with a semi-developed theory of rackets. There were various motives for introducing this image. It embodied the privatization of public power that he discerned in the fascist states. Again this had a marked significance for the concept of the state: 'The concept of the state completely loses its contradiction to the concept of a dominant particularity, it is the apparatus of the ruling clique, a tool of private power, and this is more true the more it is idolized.'[28] This is in many ways a highly perceptive comment. It captures the ambiguity of many Nazi organizations and the extent to which they blurred the boundary between the public and the private. This was true of the party itself, the security apparatus and even economic enterprises like the *Reichswerke Hermann-Göring*. The same image of the Nazi state as a racket was suggestive in another sense, for the intense competition between rackets, especially protection rackets, reflected the intense rivalries within the Nazi state. Indeed, Horkheimer was so swayed by this image that he speculated that 'this tension is so great that Germany could dissolve overnight into a chaos of gangster battles'.[29] The imagery of rackets and gangsterism brought other features into focus, including the parasitic and criminal nature of the regime. It is notable that besides the obvious, broader sense in which the Nazi state was criminal, rumours of involvement of leading Nazis in more mundane criminal activities, of theft and fraud, were commonplace during the Third Reich. The semi-developed theory of rackets had two other major attractions. First, the idea that one of the functions of the state is to protect its citizens in return for compensation is an orthodox point, but the idea of the protection racket identified the racketeer or Nazi as both the source of the threat and as the source of protection.[30] Second, the image of several competing rackets, to any of which the individual might fall victim, captured the anarchic nature of the Nazi regime. The triumph of rackets signified the triumph of factions of society over the individual. In Horkheimer's Hegelian terminology, rackets were particularistic, not universal or individual. The triumph of the racket meant the triumph of the group over both the individual and society as a whole.

Horkheimer, typically, was not content to employ the idea of rackets as a heuristic tool in order to account for the peculiarities of the Third Reich. He inflated it into the archetypal form of domination, of which the Nazi regime provided only the most extreme example.[31] The danger of this was pointed out by Kirchheimer.[32] Horkheimer effectively dissolved the concept of the state into the concept of a racket and lost touch with the concept of the state as a *Rechtstaat* that Neumann, for example, clung to as a critical concept against which the Nazi non-state could be measured.[33] Nor does the image escape the suspicion which Adorno voiced, albeit without reference to Horkheimer, of trivializing the power of the Nazi state and the complicity of more overtly respectable power brokers.[34]

Despite Kirchheimer's reservations about Horkheimer's general model of the racket as the archetypal form of domination, he too drew heavily upon the idea of the predominance of groups and the fragmentation of the state.

147

This was evident in both 'Criminal law in national socialist Germany' and 'The legal order of national socialism'. In the former Kirchheimer noted the loss of independence of the judiciary and referred to those general standards of conduct that had worried Neumann. The latter, in this case the 'sound feelings of the people', were, he noted, to be discerned not by judicial intuition of the actual inclinations of the people, but by reference to the pronouncements of the Nazi leaders and to the judiciary's own corporate instincts.[35] More important than this, however, was the 'disappearance of a unified system of criminal law behind innumerable special competencies (departmentalization)'.[36] He identified the most obvious groups first, the Nazi Party, the SS, the Labour Service and the Army, but also referred more broadly to the blurring of the boundary between criminal law and commercial-administrative law. Central too was the idea that corporations of the Nazi regime frequently combined the power of coercion as well as functions of economic direction. This he concluded was fatal, for the 'separation of the functions between the entrepreneur and the coercive machinery of the state is one of the main guarantees of liberty in a state of affairs where few people control their own means of production'.[37] The consequence of this was elaborated in the second essay. There he argued that the individual was subject to two types of control: the command of the state and the command of the professional group to which he was ascribed. Appeal against either was limited and unlikely to succeed. Moreover the legal form of a contract became less and less relevant to the majority of the population. For the latter, 'contract has been replaced by the peculiar compound of private command and administrative order'.[38] There are limits to the persuasiveness of Kirchheimer's argument. Taking the labour contract as the most important which most people entered into, his argument entails the displacement of the labour contract by private command and administrative order. While the enhanced power of the factory director over his workers, now redesignated as 'followers', was marked, the regime asserted only patchy control over the labour market. Moreover, as it took more vigorous measures in this field the exigencies of rearmament and warfare, with the attendant shortage of labour, created some room for manoeuver. Despite such reservations, the Institute's members had identified the central ambiguities of the Nazi regime, ambiguities which still bedevil the efforts of historians, who now have access to a wealth of empirical research far in excess of that available to Neumann, Kirchheimer and Horkheimer. The kinds of distinctions they drew and concerns they had are arguably still central to the contemporary debate.[39]

The relative reticence of the Institute on the Soviet Union has often been noted. Even as the initial, qualified, sympathy for the developments in Russia faded, Horkheimer and Adorno were still fearful of being pressed into the service of an anti-Soviet front, despite their awareness that such sentiments were exploited by the Soviet regime.[40] Horkheimer also resisted pressure in

1946, from Löwenthal and Paul Massing, for more explicit criticism of the Soviet Union on the grounds that they should concentrate on 'the social development in industrialized society as a whole'.[41] Despite these reservations, Horkheimer had already identified the Soviet Union as 'the most consistent form of authoritarian state'.[42] The hostility of Horkheimer and Adorno to the Soviet Union was clear enough, but it was never developed in any systematic way. Only Marcuse devoted a book to the subject, and that has been regarded by even sympathetic critics as a very equivocal work. Again, reluctance to be drawn into the service of an ideological Cold War campaign against the regime was at work. It is also likely, as Douglas Kellner has argued, that Marcuse was influenced by the reforms introduced by Khrushchev in the mid-1950s.[43] The argument of Marcuse's *Soviet Marxism* was also influenced by the decision, in line with the older generation's principles, to approach its subject matter via an immanent critique. Given the vagaries of Soviet ideology this was problematic, as Marcuse recognized. He tried to get around the obvious qualms about the commitment of the Soviet leaders to Marxism by claiming that their commitment was not relevant, since 'once incorporated into the foundations of the new society, Marxism becomes subject to a historical dynamic which surpasses the intentions of the leadership and to which the manipulators themselves succumb'.[44] Though not without some merit, insofar as the decision to adopt a particular body of theory will have some constraining influence on the moves that can be made within it, Marcuse's claim amounts to little more than side-stepping the problem. There is a similar evasiveness in his attempt to deal with the status of the Soviet bureaucracy. This had long agitated Marxist critics of the regime. Marcuse referred to it as a 'separate class' but denied it had the unity and consistency necessary to assert its 'special interests' at the expense of society as a whole. Instead he claimed that it 'represents the social interest in hypostatized form, in which the individual interests are separated from the individuals and arrogated by the state'.[45] Compared with the outright rejection of ideology as insignificant in accounting for the regime, Marcuse's decision to take it at its word has its attractions. But there is little of the sensitivity to the ambiguities of ideology that he had shown in his wartime reports on the German mentality. Moreover, it is at least possible that he could have taken up Neumann's image of the anarchic state, or even Horkheimer's comments on rackets, as heuristic devices, without having to succumb to the flat identification of the Nazi and Soviet state which characterized the Cold War theories of totalitarianism.

While Marcuse's survey of the Soviet state remained an isolated effort, the nature of the democratic order in the West naturally received broader treatment by the older generation. Again it was Neumann and Kirchheimer who offered the more specific observations. Horkheimer's fragmentary comments exhibited at best an equivocal attitude. Called upon to address the Academy of Labour in 1962, he recalled the words uttered at a 1949 trades union conference, namely that there must never again be another 1933. His scepticism about such assurances was evident when he noted that many of those present in 1949 would have recalled another such promise: that there must not be a second 1914.[46] He also proclaimed that 'trade unions by their very essence are sworn enemies of totalitarian dictatorship', though a defensive attitude was marked. He noted that the German workers should have fought in 1933 and warned that an authoritarian tone was evident in French political debate.[47] Both references, to the past and the present, conjured up threats to the democratic order. Not that he was optimistic about the results of the democratic process. What hope was there, he wondered, when, in 1968, after all the upheaval in France and despite a significant communist constituency, the Gaullists could enjoy such electoral support.[48]

Kirchheimer and Neumann also worried about the vitality of the basic institutions of parliamentary democracy. Reflecting on the events which brought de Gaulle back to power and led to the constitution of the Fifth Republic, Kirchheimer noted the constitutional constraints on parliament. He then added,

> In spending part of its energy on keeping the National Assembly in a subordinate role, it largely fights against windmills, because in France, as everywhere else, the legislative – constitutional provisions notwithstanding – [parliament] has ceased to be a decisive factor in political life, having yielded many of its functions to the administration and the political parties.[49]

In arguing thus, he was reasserting his assessment of a political trend made in the Institute's journal before the war.[50] In the post-war world he emphasized the changing nature of political parties, the decline of the class- and denomination-based mass parties in favour of 'catch-all' parties and the related decline of the vigour of opposition displayed by those parties. He viewed this trend as a mixed blessing. The old mass-based parties clearly had their vices. Their adoption of an 'opposition of principle' lessened their prospects of attaining power as well as encouraged their opponents to resort to discriminatory or repressive measures. Further, they could give precedence to the integration of their members into the party and its subculture at the expense of integrating them into the broader political community.[51] Yet, he warned that we could come to regret the demise of those parties, for they offered the individual a closer relationship to the party than their contemporary successors. The mass parties, 'part channel of protest, part source of protection, part purveyor of visions of the future', precisely because of their scope facilitated more vigorous participation. The catch-all party provided 'more intermittent' opportunities and had to compete with administrative agencies and interest groups for the attention of the citizen.[52] Although he suggested that we could react to this trend with little more than regret, he did offer one clear-cut warning. The party risked what vitality it had if it indulged in 'premature identifications' with the state. With explicit reference to the fate of the German Social Democrats in the Weimar Republic, he wrote that this would consign parties to 'existing under the protection of the state's symbols, while yet lacking the strength and will to fashion this same state according to their own image'.[53]

The need to maintain some distance from the state was also emphasized by Neumann. The object of his concern was the trade unions. Like Horkheimer, but more pointedly, he referred to the acquiescence of the trade unions in 1933. Their passivity arose in part, he continued, because of the entwinement of union and state bureaucracy. Still haunted by this, he opposed the programme of co-determination, which recalled the 'economic democracy' favoured by socialist and Catholic trade unionists in Weimar. The essence of this was 'a kind of semicorporate system under which the trade unions per se should enter into public and private bodies on equal terms with the employer'.[54] Whereas the Weimar trade unionists had seen an opportunity to enhance their power *vis-à-vis* the employers, Neumann saw a threat to their independence in an untested post-war German democracy. Nor was this the only danger. Weimar and the Third Reich had also demonstrated the danger of delegating state power to interest groups. The conclusion that Neumann drew from this was that the responsibility of the government before the electorate was the 'sole criterion of democracy'.[55]

The relatively liberal tone of this criterion was echoed by Neumann's comments on rights and the generality of the law. Although he acknowledged the need for extensive state intervention, he argued against justifying this in the language of rights. The latter should be reserved for those personal and political rights that were essential for democracy. He did suggest that the difficulty of securing freedom against the depredations of the interventionist state 'may not appear so depressing if one considers political power not as an alien power (as expressed in the formula citizen versus state) but as one's own'.[56] That was very much in line with the general principle of the older generation, namely that society was the product of the activity of its members and yet appeared as an alien power. While in the 1930s the prospect of doing away with its alien quality seemed attractive, Neumann was now less sure. Without qualification it too readily pointed towards Rousseau's utopian vision of the identity of man and citizen.

As William Scheuerman has argued, Neumann's caution may be excessive. The supposition, mobilized by defenders of the free-market economy like Hayek and Leoni,[57] that state intervention necessarily undermines the generality of law, enhancing the scope for arbitrary government action, is not necessarily persuasive. In making this point, Scheuerman quotes Kirchheimer against Neumann's pessimism: 'it is not intelligible why social security rules cannot be as carefully framed and community burdens as well calculated, as rules concerning damage claims deriving from negligence actions'.[58]

Yet Kirchheimer was far from having a naïve faith in the efficacy of the rule of law. He argued, here in agreement with Hayek, that the rule of law was dependent not only upon proper legislation and judicial institutions, but also upon a wider willingness to initiate action. The record of the Federal Republic of Germany in dealing with Nazi war crimes was a stark reminder of the importance of these wider considerations.[59]

The impact of the Third Reich upon Neumann's and Kirchheimer's estimation of the post-war democratic state is evident, but not overwhelming. Their general concerns about changes in the party system, the status of the rule of law, the relative autonomy of both the state and interests groups, have become the stock in trade of post-war political science. At the same time their later works were in some respects closer to Horkheimer, Adorno and Marcuse than their earlier works. Kirchheimer, for example, in 'Private man and society', portrayed the impotence of the individual in the face of the consumer society with scarcely more optimism than Adorno. His reference to the 'industrial jungle-dwellers and one-dimensional privates in the consumers' army' foreshadowed Marcuse's better known title of *One-Dimensional Man*. His conclusion offered only the consolation that 'consciousness of his inability to control his job is at the same time the measure of mass man's distance from being irrevocably engulfed by mass society'.[60] What marked them out from their former colleagues was their cautious but positive affirmation of the virtue of the democratic state as the best that was on offer. Their focus on the institutions and practices of the democratic state provided a more nuanced picture than Adorno's resolute focus on the dichotomy of man and mass society. Moreover, their defence of democracy on the basis of the deficiencies of men protected them from Marcuse's more relativistic approach to democratic institutions.[61]

One of the conclusions which Neumann drew in his later works was the 'primacy of politics over economics', which, he claimed, had always been evident to reactionary political theorists.[62] As Habermas noted much later, in response to discussion of his *Between Facts and Norms*, Ulrich Preuss had brought out the specific characteristics of the concept of political power in the German legal tradition. In Habermas's words, the relation between law and political power in Germany had been seen as 'an irrevocable competition between two *mutually exclusive* forms of political integration, one through the law and the other through the executive power of the state'.[63] Elaborating on this point, Habermas accepted that his own project was an attempt to re-establish a link between law and political power, to deny the dichotomy which celebrated the power of the state (*Staatsgewalt*) as an independent force, unmediated by law.

That motive was also evident in his much earlier work, *The Structural Transformation of the Public Sphere*. That too sought to deal with the duality of will and reason in the idea of political authority. Habermas argued that constitutional restraint on the exercise of the sovereign's will was ultimately unacceptable to the bourgeoisie, since it did not guarantee that the sovereign would act in their interests:

> Only with the power to legislate did the public, constituted of private people, obtain this certainty. The constitutional state as a bourgeois state established the public sphere in the political realm as an organ of the state so as to ensure institutionally the connection between law and public opinion.[64]

This was an unstable achievement plagued by ambiguities about the nature of power and second thoughts about the social underpinning of the enterprise. It was ambiguous, claimed Habermas, because it was the product of an assertion of will in the constitutional struggles of the day, yet its advocates did not want to understand it as such an assertion. The idea was to 'transform voluntas into a ratio'.[65] Taken to its logical conclusion, this meant that 'The bourgeois idea of the law-based state, namely the binding of all state activities to a system of norms legitimated by public opinion ... already aimed at abolishing the state as an instrument of domination altogether.'[66] Second thoughts arose as the public sphere was expanded to incorporate the lower classes. The association of public opinion and reason now seemed tenuous, and those liberals who held to it could only preserve the idea of the rationality of debate at the expense of contemplating restrictions to public opinion. It is at this point that Habermas located the liberalism of de Tocqueville and Mill, for whom public opinion appeared as a pressure to conform. In order to salvage the rationality of public opinion, Mill argued for a representative democracy in which those represented 'would have to be satisfied that "their judgement would have to be exercised upon the character and talents of the person they appoint to decide these questions for them, than upon the questions themselves"'.[67]

Throughout the rest of *The Structural Transformation of the Public Sphere* Habermas traced the dissolution of this original vision, stressing the increasing power of organized private interests, spearheaded by the transformation of the press, over the institutions of the public sphere, changes in the concepts and function of parties and citizenship. Following Kirchheimer, he noted the decline of parliament in favour of extra-parliamentary bargaining as well as the effective delegation of the functions of the state to non-state agencies.[68] Economic and political trends combined to displace the public sphere as an arena of debate in favour of the manipulation of public opinion, now divested of all pretence to rationality and treated as socio-psychological residues, mere attitudes and opinions, whose 'public' character was supposedly rescued by identifying the dominant opinion of a group.[69] The presumption of the irrationality of the public was matched by the public appearance of political leaders as competitors for mass acclamation. Against this, Habermas could only invoke the demand to open up or create '*public spheres internal to parties and special-interest associations*.[70] Exactly how and by whom this was to be done, he did not specify.

In large part, Habermas's subsequent reflections on the democratic order can be seen as elaborations on themes introduced in *The Structural Transformation of the Public Sphere*. The first of these was the extent to which public spheres could be revitalized. The second was the extent to which the initial promise of the connection between law and reason could be plausibly restored. He sought to elaborate on these themes in response to the changing political agenda of the next two decades, but to do so against the background of a principled caution about the precise nature of the political institutions of the democratic order. The principled caution was evident when he considered Schumpeter's famous definition of democracy as the periodic selection, by means of elections, between competing élites. This, he acknowledged, might be quite appropriate depending upon wider circumstances. He did take exception to one thing, namely that Schumpeter 'defines democracy by procedures that have nothing to do with the procedures and presuppositions of free agreement and discursive will-formation'.[71] The latter was necessary because, according to his linkage of reason and communication, this was the only way of justifying whatever concrete institutional procedures might be adopted. Nevertheless, Habermas insisted that 'democratization cannot mean an a priori preference for a specific type of organization, for example, for so-called direct democracy'.[72] In fact the increasing emphasis placed upon the idea that the administrative and economic systems of modern society operate autonomously inevitably weakened the prospects of direct democracy in Habermas's theory. Whole realms of social action were, at the least, placed at arm's length from democratic processes: 'a *thoroughgoing internal* reorganization of the economy in accordance with the principles of self-administration is neither possible nor necessary'.[73] This marked a step back from his earlier willingness to consider the application of participatory democracy to planning processes within modern societies.[74]

The changed political climate of the late 1970s and even more so the early 1980s, with its mix of a swing to the right and the emergence of radical protest groups, gave Habermas both cause for concern and the basis for some optimism. His assessment of the role of political parties, though far from unequivocal, had not improved: 'the parties engage ... in the legitimation process almost exclusively from above – that is, from the perspective of an integral part of the state apparatus'.[75] The virtue of the new protest movements was that, being autonomous from the state, they were better suited to promoting 'free agreement and discursive will-formation'. The tension between the turn to the right and the new protest movements, especially calls for the effective criminalization of even peaceful protest, induced Habermas to stake out the scope of civil disobedience which a democratic state ought to tolerate. Drawing on the work of John Rawls, Habermas insisted first that civil disobedience had to be a 'morally *based* protest'. Personal interest or privately held convictions do not suffice. Second, the protest had to be a '*public* act'. Habermas even suggested that it ought typically to be announced beforehand in order to allow the authorities to take appropriate action. Third, it should involve only the '*provisional* violation' of specific laws and should not call into question the legal order as a whole. Fourth, perpetrators of civil disobedience must be prepared to bear the legal penalties that follow from their action. Finally, the disobedience must be of a purely '*symbolic character*', that is it must not involve any form of violence.[76]

In drawing up these fairly stringent criteria, Habermas was seeking to balance the need for protest, which was linked to the revitalization of the public sphere, against the need to maintain the status of the law as characteristic of the democratic state. Quite how central law was to his conception was evident in *The Theory of Communicative Action*. There he had not only argued for the centrality of law to the democratic state but also to the nature of the state in general. Thus he emphasized that '*Because judicial office is itself a source of legitimate power, political domination can first crystallize around this office.*'[77] The distinctiveness of the state as a form of social organization, divorced from the charisma of the individual or ties of kinship, arises where there is some legitimate body of rules which the 'ruler' implements. He also emphasized that though the power to enforce sanctions is essential to this office, power alone is insufficient. This argument clearly goes hand in hand with the attempt to break the dichotomy between power and law referred to earlier. It is, however, a questionable empirical claim. According to Günter Dux early forms of state arose as the product of military conquest and even once they had formed, justice for most remained a matter for the subordinate local communities.[78] Indeed far beyond the confines of early state formation it has been argued that:

> At least for European experience of the past few centuries, a portrait of war makers and state makers as coercive and self-seeking entrepreneurs bears a far greater resemblance to the facts than do its chief alternatives: the idea of a social contract, the idea of an open market in which operators of armies and states offer services to willing customers, the idea of a society whose shared norms and expectations call forth a certain kind of government.[79]

As the title, 'War making and state making as organized crime', in which the historian Charles Tilly made this claim, indicates, Horkheimer's analogy between the state and the protection racket is not without its plausibility. It does not follow from this, of course, that such states can claim legitimacy. Nor is it difficult to think of some states that do not fit the pattern of state-making as organized crime.

Law was not presented as an entirely unmixed blessing. Law is well suited, Habermas wrote, to serve '*as a means for organizing media-controlled subsystems* [the economy and public administrative system] that have, in any case, become autonomous in relation to the normative contexts of action oriented by mutual understanding'.[80] Indeed, precisely because these sub-systems have attained that autonomy, legal regulation is required. According to Habermas, this came in three broad waves, associated with the bourgeois state, that is the definition of the sovereign state and the formation of civil law, the bourgeois constitutional state, giving citizens 'actionable civil rights against a sovereign', and the democratic constitutional state, in which citizens acquired rights of political participation.[81] A fourth wave, the emergence of the welfare state, was intended to remedy some of the defi-ciencies bequeathed by the preceding waves, but had an inherently ambiguous effect. Habermas did not deny the need for this fourth wave, which in some respects also dealt with the autonomous sub-systems. He cited regulation of working hours, redundancy legislation and workers' bargain-ing rights as examples of this. But the fourth wave went beyond these spheres. In attempting to deal with poverty, illness and the like – in all of which the fourth wave marked a welcome progress – the 'juridification' of these issues threatened to disrupt a lifeworld based on 'normative contexts of action oriented by mutual understanding'. In their place stepped bureau-cracies whose 'clients' became the objects of administrative procedures. While Habermas continued to insist on this as a characteristic of the welfare state, he drew back from the stronger claim that it was an inherent character-istic: 'the criteria by which one can identify the point where empowerment is converted into supervision are, even if context-dependent and contested, not arbitrary'.[82]

Political and moral autonomy were at the heart of Habermas's *Between Facts and Norms* and the surrounding debate. His argument consisted of a highly elaborate attempt to set out the constitutional framework in which both political and private autonomy could be reconciled, while at the same time providing for the maximum revitalization of public spheres. It was the stress on political autonomy and the vitality of the public spheres which led to his criticism of Rawls. Habermas objected to Rawls's project, deriving a constitutional framework from a hypothetical 'original position', on the grounds that, in pre-empting so many decisions, it exhausted the scope for the experience of political autonomy. According to Habermas, Rawls's hypothetical citizens

> Cannot reignite the radical democratic embers of the original position in the civic life of their society, for from their perspective all of the *essential* discourses of legitimation have already taken place within the theory ... Because the citizens cannot conceive of the constitution as a *project*, the public use of reason does not actually have the significance of a present exercise of political autonomy but merely promotes the nonviolent *preservation of political stability*.[83]

It was consistent with this criticism that Habermas had explicitly sought to preserve the scope for conceiving of the constitution as a continuing project within his own model. It was also consistent with his understanding of the proper limits of the role of a normative political theory. The basic rights which form the core of this model are also clearly related to the waves of juridification which he had discussed earlier, though the latter cannot be mapped onto the former without qualification. The first category was 'basic rights that result from the politically autonomous elaboration of the *right to the greatest possible measure of equal individual liberties*'.[84] These are the traditional rights guaranteeing private autonomy. Second, 'Basic rights that result from the politically autonomous elaboration of the *status of a member* in a voluntary association of consociates under law.'[85] These are the rights governing citizenship, immigration and emigration. Third, 'Basic rights that result immediately from the *actionability* of rights and from the politically autonomous elaboration of individual *legal protection*.'[86] These are the rights of appeal for redress against the state, guaranteed by due process under an independent judiciary. Fourth, 'Basic rights to equal opportunities to participate in processes of opinion- and will-formation in which citizens exercise their *political autonomy* and through which they generate law.'[87] The first three categories are both constraining and enabling in relation to the fourth category, though Habermas gave firm emphasis to their enabling quality. They are constraining insofar as in exercising their rights as legislators, citizens cannot dispense with the rights in the first three categories. Indeed their legislation, giving precise form to the rights in the first three categories, constitutes part of the understanding of the constitution as a continuous project. They are enabling insofar as, in their absence, citizens cannot regulate their lives through the medium of law. The fifth category is derived from the first four. Habermas stated that they '*imply*', 'Basic rights to the provision of living conditions that are socially, technologically and ecologically safeguarded, insofar as the current circumstances make this necessary if citizens are to have equal opportunities to utilize the civil rights listed in (1) through (4).'[88] This category is context-dependent in a way in which the others are not.

The idea of the constitution as a continuing project is linked to the attempt to break through the dichotomy of law and power. Here Habermas referred to Hannah Arendt, contrasting her view with that of Max Weber. Whereas Weber construed power as the ability to assert one's will against that of others, Arendt construed it as the 'ability not just to act but to act in concert'.[89] It was, moreover, a quite specific ability. It was to be distinguished from the ability to pursue interests or collective goals and from the power exercised by an administrative machine. It was, rather, the '*authorizing* force expressed in "jurisgenesis" – the creation of legitimate law – and in the founding of institutions'.[90]

Habermas claimed that his model had another advantage. It provided an alternative to 'republican' conceptions which staked everything on the idea of the self-determination of political communities and which typically had to assume strong cohesive identities. The language in which Habermas couched his distance from the republican conception also marked his distance from the goal of the older generation: 'Discourse theory drops all those motifs employed by the *philosophy of consciousness* that lead one . . . to ascribe the citizen's practice of self determination to a macrosocial subject'.[91] It also provided an alternative to the liberal conception which typically downplayed the possibility of communicative power and self-determination in favour of an understanding of politics as the pursuit of interests and democracy as the preservation of rights against the power of the state.

The core of this model, the idea of communicative power, was deliberately restricted by Habermas. It was restricted in the first place by the existence of other forms of power, forms of power which it could not substitute for, short of overextending the precarious ability to act in concert without recourse to coercion. It was a keen awareness of the fragility and fallibility of communicative power that underlay the need to make provision for, yet to delimit, civil disobedience.[92] It was restricted in the second place by the fact that communicative power is supposed to be dispersed across a series of decentralized public spheres. Amongst these Habermas distinguished between '*episodic* publics', including street assemblies, '*occasional* or "arranged" publics', including party and church conferences, and '*abstract*' publics, including the audiences of television broadcasts.[93]

While the older generation provided an often acute analysis of the authoritarian state, a form which Habermas has largely neglected, their defence of the democratic state was equivocal, partly because of their revolutionary orientation, partly because of the difficulty they had in identifying the resources which a democratic order might mobilize against corrosive effects of organized socio-economic power blocs. Though highly conscious of the latter threat, Habermas focused on the resources that might support a radical democratic politics. It is arguable that in doing so he was tempted into overextending the role of law as opposed to that of state force (*Staatsgewalt*). Recognition of the historical prevalence of the latter, to the extent of questioning his account of the origins of states, does not entail a rejection of the virtues of his alternative to the reduction of the concept of power to that of sheer domination. Although Habermas has insisted that there can be no presumption that citizens are obliged to partake in the exercise of communicative power, there is an implicit warning of the consequences of a failure to do so. At the risk of trivialization, it may be put as follows: citizens either hang together, albeit in dispersed multiple publics and not as a collective citizenry, or they will be hung separately. Where communicative power evaporates, other forms of power will step into its place.

CHAPTER 10
Morality and Interests

When Kant defined practical reason in terms of the *'morally-practical'*, he set it apart from any notion of following 'technically-practical rules (i.e. those of art and skill generally, or even of prudence, as a skill in exercising an influence over men and their wills)'.[1] Exercising power over men's wills was merely a matter of applying the requisite knowledge of cause and effect to men, much as such knowledge could be applied to animals or inanimate nature. Man, however, was more than just another piece of the world subject to manipulation. Man had to be regarded as what Kant called an 'intelligible character' and as such 'must be considered to be free from all influence of sensibility and from all determination through appearance'. Of this intelligible character, he continued, 'nothing *happens* in it; there can be no changes requiring dynamical determination in time, and therefore no causal dependence upon appearances'.[2] Despite this radically dualistic conception of man, Kant was not content to leave the two halves completely unrelated. Indeed he devoted great effort to trying to show how developments in the world of appearance, where man was subject to the laws of cause and effect, need not frustrate man's moral purpose.[3]

Where Kant saw a compatibility between the two conceptions of man, a compatibility that permitted an optimistic view of history, Hegel saw only disemblance and duplicity. The moral act, if it was to be worthy of the name, had to embroil itself in the world from which it was, by Kant's very definition of practical reason, to be kept separate.[4] According to Hegel it was only possible to escape from the abstraction and impotence of Kant's moral absolutism within the context of a system of 'ethical life', which made explicit provision for what Kant wanted to exclude from the intelligible character on principle. Hence the incorporation of the concepts of family, civil society and state under the heading of 'ethical life' in Hegel's *Philosophy of Right*.

159

Within the sphere of ethical life, Hegel gave pride of place to the political community in the form of the state. For the young Marx this was quite in accordance with the historical development of both the modern state as an independent system and civil society as the depoliticized sphere of competing individuals. This in turn entailed the bifurcation of man. The modern world 'regards civil society, the world of needs, of labour, of private interests and of civil law, as the *foundation of its existence* ... man as he is a member of civil society is taken to be the *real* man ... whereas *political* man is simple abstract, artificial man, man as an *allegorical, moral* person'.[5] While Marx's goal was the reintegration of these two halves of man, his subsequent work focused on the activities of '*real* man', the world of interests.

From the perspective of Marx's critique of political economy, there was a certain irony in the fact that the language of political economy provided the terminology for a revival of moral discourse. As Schnädelbach explains, Nietzsche's critique of 'values' and the subsequent methodological debate about the value-neutrality of the social sciences were responsible for the popularity of the term. But it was Rudolf Lotze who had taken over the concept of value from political economy and made it into the centrepiece of philosophical debate.[6] The irony was not lost on Adorno: 'The economic concept of value, which served as a model both for Lotzes's philosophical concept, and that of the South West German School, and subsequently for the dispute on objectivity, is the original phenomenon of reification – namely the exchange value of the commodity.'[7] For Marx the concept of value arose from specific relations between men. Its reification consisted in it being seen as a property of a thing, the commodity. According to Adorno the hypostatization of a realm of values entailed an analogous confusion. Specific social problems were reflected in, but also obscured by, the postulation of values that were a 'poor and largely distorted copy' of those problems.[8] Adorno tried to explain this by reference to the value that all should be fed. He claimed that its significance varied depending on whether economic resources were insufficient to meet this demand or whether they were sufficient but the social structure prevented their deployment to meet this need. His point is that the abstract term 'value' glosses over the all-important difference between the two situations.

The relationship between the basic need for food and morality had attracted Horkheimer's attention much earlier. In one of the aphorisms published in 1934 he commented on the precept that 'Whoever doesn't want to work shouldn't eat.' The basis for his comment was the fact that socialists had adopted this principle as a moral condemnation of those who did not labour, that is the capitalists. Horkheimer was sceptical about a principle which made labour the central virtue of a future society, but he was also sensitive to the ambiguity of the principle in contemporary society where 'it justifies the capitalist. He works. But it damns the poor, for they don't. Everywhere, the bourgeois manages to reconcile an originally revolutionary thought of his own making, and which socialists retain as a general maxim, with the reactionary morality of the ruling class.'[9]

Socialists had in fact adopted quite diverse attitudes towards morality and especially towards Kant's moral doctrine. These issues had been put on the agenda by the broader revival of interest in Kant in the late nineteenth century and by socialists who turned to Kant in order to supplement or strengthen their Marxism. In this, Eduard Bernstein's invocation of Kant, made famous by the crystallization of the revisionist debate around his *Preconditions of Socialism*, was actually a rather muted revival of Kantian morality.[10] Karl Vorländer was much more thorough in his appropriation of Kant. Amongst those who opposed the importation of Kantian morality it was common to object, amongst other things, that Kant ignored the role of classes. Thus Heinrich Cunow complained that 'For Kant society is simply a collective composed of a number of individuals, a so-called aggregate.'[11] As a Marxist he opposed to this the image of a class-divided society. From this perspective, he argued that morality was merely a matter of collective solidarity and he quoted approvingly the defender of Marxist orthodoxy, Karl Kautsky, to the effect that truthfulness was only a duty towards one's class comrades.[12]

While Horkheimer would later show some sympathy for group solidarity as the sociological origin of morality, his main emphasis was upon the emergence of morality as a response to exactly the opposite: the lack of solidarity in bourgeois society. Morality, he argued, is a form of reflection appropriate to a society in which men have gained some distance from the force of habit and custom and are guided primarily by the pursuit of their own conflicting interests. The sphere of morality was defined by the gap between these private interests and the idea of a general interest. In bourgeois society the general interest could be nothing more than 'the various particular interests that falsely pretend to universality'.[13] By the same token, only the transformation of bourgeois society would bring about a condition in which private interests and general interests coincided and thereby put an end to morality as a specific form of reflection. In the existing society the impossibility of reconciling private interest with a general interest underlay the specific form of morality, that is the appearance of morality in the form of a duty which stood opposed to interest.[14]

Despite seeing morality as a hopefully transient form of thought, Horkheimer did not dismiss it as mere ideology. To the contrary, he wrote, 'it must be understood as a human phenomenon that cannot possibly be overcome for the duration of the bourgeois epoch'.[15] However, Horkheimer did reject the idea that universal moral rules could be justified in their own right. He took up four of Kant's examples to push home the point. According to Kant, someone intent on suicide ought to be persuaded not to kill himself by the fact that he could not wish that his action should become a universal law. Similarly Kant sought to mobilize the moral law in support of the payment of debts, the obligation to develop one's talents despite inclinations of indolence, and the obligation to be charitable. Horkheimer noted that the latter was not strictly supported by the moral law but by the calculation that the rich man might fall on hard times. But here, he argued, 'the rich person will quite justifiably prefer the secure present to the questionable future'.[16] Even the more appropriate examples were found deficient. For example, the talented man who stirred himself would hardly wish that all others followed his example, for thereby he would wish for even harsher competition that might frustrate the very purpose of his reluctant activity.

Horkheimer defended the moral sentiment, the 'human phenomenon', but not the moral form. He recognized that men 'are not content to rely on their feelings of indignation, compassion, love, solidarity and so on, but must relate their feelings to an absolute world order by calling them "moral"'.[17] But he explicitly rejected that justification. It was neither necessary nor plausible. There is no 'absolute world order' and the feelings of indignation and so on required no justification. Underlying the latter point was the eudemonism of Horkheimer's critical theory. The aspiration for happiness was, as he put it, 'a natural fact requiring no justification'.[18] Kant had both denied this by couterposing moral self-determination to interest and pleasure, which it was supposed to hold in check, and yet acknowledged it insofar as he allowed for the possibility that history might reward men with what his moral doctrine denied them.[19]

As Schnädelbach has argued, Horkheimer's eudemonism seems to bring him close to emotivism and decisionism. Yet, according to Schnädelbach, it would be misleading to ascribe either of these to Horkheimer's position. He was protected from the former by the fact that his eudemonism was constructed from the 'universal claim of *all* to happiness'.[20] Horkheimer sought to bolster this by reference to the concept of justice, which, he said, was older than that of morality. Common to all its manifestations, from the idea of equality of consumption (early Christianity), through the right to the product of one's own labour (Proudhon), to the right of the most sensitive to be the least burdened (Nietzsche), was a protest against arbitrary distribution. In the Enlightenment and the French Revolution, equality had finally been raised to an abstract and constitutional principle.[21] He was protected from decisionism by the fact that he linked the pursuit of happiness to an interest in the abolition of social injustice and 'Because of the cognitive and rational aspect of the interests, interest-governed decisions are never pure acts of will which occur where the force of argument cannot reach.'[22]

Both of these points were evident in Marcuse's article 'Towards a critique of hedonism'.[23] There Marcuse sought to identify the virtues and vices of hedonism, relating both to the condition of society. On the one hand he protested against the debasement of sensuousness to a 'lower, baser human faculty ... a region of undiscriminating instincts'.[24] Only in epistemology had the receptivity of sensuousness been preserved as relevant to truth and discrimination. On the other hand the critics of hedonism, including those hedonists who differentiated between indulgence and moderation, true and false or transient pleasures, were right insofar as they identified the distorted form of pleasure in existing societies. As Marcuse shuttled back and forth between these two perspectives, upholding even contingent pleasures against the blanket denigration of hedonism and defending the need to discriminate between pleasures against unbridled hedonism, a clearer strategy emerged. The 'moralization of pleasure' had been justified so long as this served a progressive function and it had a functional role in the 'existence of antagonistic society'.[25] The amoral assertion of hedonism was justified only insofar as it was linked to efforts to transcend this antagonistic society.[26] Underlying this was much the same point made by Horkheimer. Existing society swung from celebrating the private interest of the individual to disparaging this same interest in favour of the 'hypostatized general interest'.[27] The only escape from this dilemma would be the emergence of a society no longer based upon this contrast between the particular and the general interest.

The persuasiveness of this hedonism is reliant upon two main sets of arguments. First, it gains purchase to the extent that it exposes the supposed vice of hedonism as the product of a society which systematically disparages pleasure. As Marcuse put it, 'the unchained voluptuary who would abandon himself only to his sensual wants' was the product of a society that set up a dichotomy between work and pleasure, labour and consumption. Second, it gains purchase insofar as it seeks to get beyond the form of a morality divorced from motive and interest, a form of morality which was defined precisely by that opposition. Indeed, for Horkheimer and Marcuse, that opposition was definitive of morality *per se*. There are also corresponding weaknesses. Marcuse faced the first most directly. His critical appropriation of hedonism rests upon the distinction between true and false pleasures, true and false interests. The supposition that pleasures and interests might be different in a radically different society is quite conceivable, but what the new forms of pleasure and interest would look like, and how we might recognize the true from the false pleasures and interests, Marcuse could not tell us. The second weakness is more evident in Horkheimer. For all his criticism of morality as a form of reflection, he retained the idea of a set of feelings, of indignation and the like. Schnädelbach's defence that this was linked to a claim of all to happiness accurately reflects Horkheimer's intent, but Schnädelbach also readily concedes that this universalism requires a justification that Horkheimer did not provide.[28] Put at its simplest, it is not clear why indignation must generate a 'claim of all' to anything. There is a final risk inherent in Horkheimer's position. It is dependent upon an empirical phenomenon: the feeling of indignation, the psychic condition underlying the moral point of view. If this falls under systematic suspicion, then the whole edifice falls with it.

This is precisely what happened. As Horkheimer explained to his students, Kant relied upon the existence of a moral feeling, of conscience. But if someone denied that he had had any such experience, then how could we persuade him? For Horkheimer the answer was that we cannot.[29] If anything, Adorno pursued this argument with even greater resoluteness in *Negative Dialectics*. He noted 'Kant's stubborn endeavour to demonstrate' the prevalence of this moral feeling, and that there 'is no effort Kant will not make' to link a sense of one's personal worth to the moral law.[30] Much as Horkheimer had criticized Kant's attempt to illustrate the moral law, so Adorno questioned his attempts to illustrate the existence of conscience. Contrary to Kant's claim that the cheat must feel shame, Adorno objected that he might as likely take smug pleasure in his success. The basis of Adorno's criticism was put succinctly: 'When any thesis about the *mundus intelligibilis* seeks comfort from the empirical world, it must put up with empirical criteria. And these criteria speak against the comfort'.[31]

For all his scepticism about Kant's illustrations, Adorno sought to rescue two aspects of Kant's doctrine: its assertion of the efficacy of moral reasoning and its claim to universality. Efficacy, however, could only be rescued if Kant's insistence on the purity of moral reasoning, its separation from all impulse and interest, was abandoned: 'A will without physical impulses, impulses that survive, weakened, in imagination, would not be a will.'[32] Precisely because Adorno emphasized the spontaneity of moral volition he was suspicious of Kant's identification of freedom as self-determination according to a law or rule. In this he agreed with Horkheimer's aversion to the idea of the validity of universal moral laws. According to Adorno, 'Freedom can be defined in negation only, corresponding to the concrete form of a specific unfreedom.'[33] Thereby, he begs the question of how we are to recognize the 'unfreedom' in the first place. One partial answer to that was offered in his defence of Kant's formalism. This, he noted, had been a persistent criticism of Kant. Yet Kant's formalism contained 'something of substance: the egalitarian idea', which provided a defence against the elevation of communal identity into a moral criterion.[34] Adorno had additional reasons for favouring Kant's formalism, reasons that link his stance with Marx's criticism of the bifurcation of man in bourgeois society. It is this which lies behind his assertion that 'Encoded in the Kantian sentence that everyone's freedom need be curtailed only insofar as it impairs someone else's is a reconciled condition that would not only be above the bad universal, the coercive social mechanism, but above the obdurate individual who is a microcosmic copy of that mechanism.'[35] Thereby, he invoked the image of a society in which general and private interests were no longer opposed.

Adorno's attitude towards Kant's moral doctrines was notably more favourable, though still critical, in post-war works like *Negative Dialectics*. That was also true of Horkheimer and Marcuse. For Horkheimer too, Kant's formalism had its virtues. If nothing else, it stood in contrast to the rhetorical privileging of the collective, the communal, over the individual in the eastern bloc.[36] In the same spirit he wrote that Rousseau's concept of the general will had been 'superseded' in Kant's maxims, and defended his rejection of the 'pharisaic' argument that it was better to sacrifice the individual than to sacrifice an entire people.[37] Despite this, he did not relinquish his earlier criticisms. Instead, seeking a substitute, as it were, for Kant's moral doctrines, he took up with greater vigour a long-standing concern with the idea of pity. Pity had been identified in 'Materialism and morality' as one of the two forms in which the moral sentiment had contemporary significance, the other being politics.[38] The attraction of this is easy to see: pity, as an immediate sentiment, does not seem to call forth the formality of reason in a way that morality does, at least if morality is construed in its Kantian form. Yet Horkheimer's emphasis upon pity was not without philosophical justification. As became clearer in his post-war work, this justification was tied to his interest in the work of Schopenhauer. Schopenhauer's emphasis upon pity arose from a critique of Kant which issued in a metaphysical assertion of the unity of all life: 'it follows automatically that such a man, recognizing in all beings his own true and innermost self, must also take upon himself the pain of the whole world'.[39] Schopenhauer went further than this, linking this idea of the unity of all life with doctrines of reincarnation. Horkheimer did not believe in such notions, notions that also had unacceptable consequences for the idea of pity. If pity were founded on reincarnation it would amount to no more than mere calculation, the fear that one would also suffer in a future life if suffering were not relieved.[40] Yet Schopenhauer's metaphysics was not so easy to evade. This was evident when Horkheimer considered the case of someone who declared that he did not believe these doctrines and felt no pity. Schopenhauer, he conceded, could only reply, 'then you are stupid, you will be reborn many times and must suffer'.[41] Aside from the vagaries of Schopenhauer's metaphysics, there are other problems with the concept of pity. This became evident when Horkheimer tried to distinguish different 'forms of suffering':

> Only in its extreme is the suffering of every individual the same. Otherwise it differs, depending on his nature. Compassion must discover this. Where it is of the right kind, it is as differentiated as suffering itself. There is an affinity between the quality of a person's pain and the quality of his love and his longing. Mr. Franco does not suffer like a decent human being.[42]

It is far from clear that this is persuasive. Franco was not a 'decent human being' by any stretch of the imagination. His suffering, however, was no different from anybody else's. It is possible to argue that some men, more sensitive to the pain of others, might be more tormented on account of that. But the man indifferent to the suffering of others might be equally tormented by other things. There is no reliable affinity of the sort Horkheimer claimed.

Nor is this the only problem with pity. As the eighteenth-century English and Scottish philosophers of moral sentiment had recognized, pity or sympathy privileges those who are closest to us by virtue of kinship, physical proximity or culture. That restriction may be less severe in an age of global media, but it is not without some force. Horkheimer, moreover, recognizing the limited scope of pity, had recourse to Christian moral injunctions in order to claim a more expanded role for pity: 'The command to love one's neighbour included from the start love of the most distant.'[43]

Despite his acrimonious split from the Institute, Fromm retained many of the distinctions that had formed common ground within the Institute. Thus in *Man for Himself* he revisited the clash between the denunciation of egoism and the advocacy of egoism as the standard guide for behaviour in a competitive society.[44] Similarly, he upheld as a goal 'a society in which the interest of "society" has become identical with that of all its members'.[45] Until that goal was reached there would be a continual tension between 'universal' and 'socially immanent ethics'. It was in accordance with his strong emphasis upon the realization of human potentiality that Fromm defined 'universal' ethics in terms of potentiality rather than scope. Socially immanent ethics were those that were functional for the survival of a particular social order, and were subdivided into those functional for the society as a whole and those functional for the individual's survival within a specific class. While the latter still reflected the critical edge of Fromm's pre-war work, his treatment of the bourgeois ambivalence about egoism took on a more optimistic note. 'Self-love', he suggested, could be distinguished from 'selfishness'. The former was more expansive, including love of others, while the latter involved not only excluding others but issued in disparagement of oneself. The relentless pursuit of self-interest, typically construed in materialist terms, led to a neglect of those human capacities that mattered most. The vacuity of much of this is, however, evident in the indiscriminate way in which Fromm piled up the virtues of 'self-love': '*affirmation of one's own life, happiness, growth, freedom*', all of which are supposedly '*rooted in one's capacity to love, i.e. in care, respect, responsibility, and know*ledge'.[46]

Fromm's main critic in the dispute over revisionism in psychoanalytic theory, Marcuse, was not free from the inclination to pile virtue upon virtue, though he was more inclined to pile vice upon vice in his denunciation of one-dimensional man.[47] Yet Marcuse was also constrained by his attempt to build a utopian project on the basis of what he took to be the insights of Kant and German idealism. Thus, in *Eros and Civilization* Marcuse sought to revive his old criticism of the traditional disparagement of sensuousness as a lower, baser faculty and to break down the barrier which Kant had established between morality on the one hand, and desire and interest on the other hand. He found support for this in none other than Kant himself. Kant, he wrote, had titled paragraph 59 of his *Critique of Judgement*: 'Of Beauty as the Symbol of Morality'.[48] Since the aesthetic was bound up with the sensuous, and since Kant had linked beauty and morality, Marcuse believed that he had found an alternative to the opposition of morality and interest in the work of the prophet of that opposition. Yet Marcuse's argument gains its plausibility only if Kant's caution is ignored. In the very paragraph which Marcuse selected, Kant wrote that in aesthetic judgement the 'mind becomes conscious of a certain ennoblement and elevation above mere sensibility'. Lest the point had been missed he added shortly afterwards that the beautiful 'pleases *apart from all interest*'.[49] The link Kant saw was in fact almost the opposite of the one that Marcuse saw. Of course, Kant's own interpretation of the aesthetic is not sacrosanct. Adorno, for instance, was critical of Kant's assessment of pleasure and art, but he still noted reservations that make him closer to Kant than Marcuse.[50] Indeed Marcuse later effectively conceded the weakness of his position in *Eros and Civilization*.[51]

In *One-Dimensional Man* Marcuse turned to ancient Greek philosophy in order to try to break down the rigid distinction between is and ought. This was really another attempt to derive ought from potentiality. Summarizing, Marcuse wrote that 'True discourse, logic, reveals and expresses that which really *is* – as distinguished from that which *appears* to be [real].'[52] Leaving aside the blanket characterization of Greek thought, Marcuse's strategy can only get beyond Fromm's homilies if some kind of ontology is plausible. The inherent difficulties of that can be seen in his assessment of Plato's ideal state, which, he said, 'retains and reforms enslavement while organizing it in accordance with an eternal truth'.[53] As Marcuse and his colleagues had had frequent occasion to point out, the earthly origins of theories, ontologies included, are often all too evident. By definition an ontology would have to demonstrate at some level its exemption from that relativity. In fact he no longer even tried to do this, relying instead upon recollection of the aspirations of the metaphysical tradition.

Overt disavowal of the ambition of that metaphysical tradition was characteristic of Habermas's position. Instead he sought to define a basis for a cognitivist morality in his theory of communicative action. Yet he acknowledged that there were limits to what this theory could provide. The problem of motivation, which had in various forms concerned the older generation, was one to which his discourse ethics could not provide an answer. This is an important concession, for Habermas has been acutely conscious of the fragility of the motivation to be moral. As he put it in *Between Facts and Norms*, 'A principled morality ... depends on socialization processes that meet it halfway by engendering the corresponding agencies of conscience, namely, the correlative superego formations. Aside from the weak motivating force of good reasons, such a morality becomes effective for action only through the internalization of moral principles in the personality system.'[54] It was precisely because of the weakness and fragility of moral motivation that Habermas came to emphasize the virtues of law. Following Kant, Habermas argued that while law has to be compatible with morality, it has to be possible for people to obey the law for other reasons. The conformity of law-abiding citizens need not rely upon moral motivation or on the force of custom, 'but on the *artificially produced facticity* found in the threat of sanctions that are legally defined'.[55] The way in which Habermas phrases the relationship between law and morality is quite important here. The fact that law stabilizes expectations and does so by virtue of being enforceable is clearly central. Yet Habermas does not write solely from this perspective. Nor is this only a question of insisting upon the legitimacy of law being derived from its democratic origins, vital though that is. The nuance of his perspective emerges when he argued that law '*relieves* the judging and acting person of the considerable cognitive, motivational, and ... organizational demands of a morality centred on the individual's conscience. Law, as it were, compensates for the functional weaknesses of a morality that ... frequently delivers cognitively indeterminate and motivationally unstable results.'[56] In the light of some of the issues raised by the older generation, the attractions of this are clear. Law's virtue is that it allows for the fallibility and weakness of the individual will, which Adorno and Horkheimer especially had so often emphasized. Its ability to do so, however, is reliant upon the rejection of their claim that universal rules must founder on the complexity of modern society.

Earlier Habermas had appeared more combative in his assertion of the resources of the moral agent and had been more favourably disposed towards Hegel. The latter, he wrote, 'sees through the concept of autonomous will' that lay at the heart of Kant's philosophy. Whereas Kant had posited this will as a moral fact, and had sought to bolster it by dubious appeals to the conscience of even the most depraved, Hegel had construed autonomy as the result of a struggle for recognition. Kant's autonomous will was 'an abstraction from the moral relationships of communicating individuals'.[57] Habermas considered the consequences of this abstraction to be quite severe, for he complained that by cutting out the origins of the will in communication, Kant effectively reduced moral action to 'a special case of what we today call strategic action'.[58]

In this sense, Habermas repeated the reaction of the older generation against the formalism of Kant's philosophy. In the place of the abstract will and reason of Kant, he put a more full-blooded agent replete with interests, identities and, above all, linguistically mediated relationships. There are of course limits to the analogy between Habermas's trajectory and that of the older generation. As has often been noted earlier, the human actor in Habermas's theory lacked the revolutionary pathos found in the older generation. To that extent Habermas's later caution was there from the outset. It did, however, become more carefully circumscribed in the attempt to strengthen the claims of the individual where, that is, those claims could be asserted without overburdening the individual. Therein lies the apparent paradox of Habermas's theory: his caution has been driven forward by a radical intent.

One of the consequences of these reformulations was a more circumscribed account of the relationship between morality and interest on the one hand and morality and values on the other hand. In *Legitimation Crisis* these were to some extent still fused together. There, Habermas disputed the decisionistic reduction of morality which based morality upon some authoritative command. He argued that this reductionism was unnecessary as soon as it was recognized that moral validity claims could be redeemed through discourse. Decisionism, he wrote, could be dispensed with 'as soon as argumentation is expected to test the general*izability* of interests, instead of being resigned to an impenetrable pluralism of ultimate value orientations (or belief-acts or attitudes)'.[59] Here morality and interests, values and morality, are elided under the central criterion of the 'generalizability of interests'. That same criterion played a critical role not only in its own right, but in the form of what Habermas called the '*model of the suppression of generalizable interests*'.[60] With explicit reference to Marx, he insisted upon the need both to account for why generalizable interests had to be suppressed at a given time and how, nevertheless, the normative claims inherent in that suppression could be criticized. The latter, he argued, required that the critic 'hypothetically' project the generalizability of interests, that he put forward a 'simulated discourse' which might issue in some notion of a generalized interest. In each case, he immediately added that such hypotheses or simulations could have no more than provisional validity.[61] As noted earlier, Habermas insisted that only those affected by the supposition of the existence of an interest, or who would be affected by a particular course of action, could take the final decision.

Amongst the distinctions that Habermas subsequently drew, one of the most contentious was that between morality and ethics. According to Habermas, 'Questions of justice or *moral* questions admit of justifiable answers ... because they are concerned with what, from an ideally expanded perspective, is in the equal interest of all. *Ethical* questions, by contrast, do not admit of such impartial treatment because they refer to what ... is in the long run good for me or for us – even if this is not equally good for all.'[62] This distinction was intended to salvage a universalist morality against communitarian critics who claim that moral action is possible only within the framework of a specific community. It was also intended to avoid overburdening this universalist morality by asking it to provide answers about identities and conceptions of the good life. The pressure for this distinction also arose from Habermas's recognition of the pluralism of modern societies, especially the co-habitation of groups with different identities, religious beliefs and so on. Yet it was not merely the fact of this pluralism that made this distinction so important. It was bolstered by some more specific ideas about the nature of interests and identities. Thus Habermas claimed that:

> Moral judgement presupposes a hypothetical outlook, the possibility of considering norms as something to which we can grant or deny social validity. The analogous assumption that we can choose forms of life in the same way is a contrast without sense. No one can reflectively agree to the forms of life in which he has been socialized in the same way as he can to a norm of whose validity he has convinced himself.[63]

In other formulations he stressed the 'indissoluble element of arbitrariness' in the choice of the good life because someone 'cannot accept or reject his biography in the same way as he can a norm'. Somewhat weaker was the claim that the choice of the good life depends on 'standards of happiness and well-being that we intuitively use to judge forms of life'.[64] That someone cannot accept or reject his biography or socialization, in the sense that the human infant can no more decree the time and place of its birth than it can the attitudes of its family and society, is evidently true. So too is the fact that most people do not adopt a radically sceptical view of the form of life into which they have been socialized. The claim, however, that they cannot do the latter is more dubious. It is difficult to see why the long history of religious conversion, or of migrations involving the deliberate adoption of a new identity, do not qualify as examples of precisely such radical reflection. Contemporary examples of individuals who, despite prosperous urban backgrounds, adopt rural or quasi-rural lifestyles with a relative minimum of material goods, are also not difficult to find. The fact that they can practice such radical reflection does not mean that most do, and certainly does not mean that anyone should be compelled to. The fact that religious conversion and migration have been induced by either poverty or coercion is an argument against poverty and coercion, not against the fact that people are capable of radical reflection on the good life, though the absence of poverty and coercion would arguably reduce the incidence of such reflection.

The precise formulation of this distinction between morality and ethics induced differing responses. Thus when Habermas wrote that 'Moral-practical discourses . . . require a break with all of the unquestioned truths of an established, concrete ethical life, in addition to distancing oneself from the contexts of life with which one's identity is inextricable interwoven',[65] Richard Bernstein, a long-standing sympathetic critic, reacted with some exasperation.[66] On reflection, he offered a series of objections, including the claim that ethical life need not be a matter of unquestioned truths but was rather characterized by doubt, uncertainty and debate. In reply, Habermas conceded that ethical life and reflection were indeed compatible but re-emphasized the idea that we cannot distance ourselves from our ethical formation in the same way as from *individual norms*.[67] The contrast between the totality of ethical self-understanding and individual norms may not, however, be the best defence of this position. In reply to a slightly different objection, Habermas referred to the idea that discourse acts 'like a filter' allowing through only certain types of argument.[68] Applied in the context of Bernstein's objection, this could change the emphasis to the idea that what is required is the exclusion of arguments whose supposed validity is derived from ethical self-understanding. In other words, in moral discourse we are not allowed to invoke arguments whose defence entails reference to supposed truths, whether unquestioned or not, dependent on the ethical context. The implication of this is, for example, that God has told me or us that X is right, is not a permissible argument in moral discourse.

Whatever the precise formulation, the distinction between moral and ethical discourses is intended to deal with the plurality of identities and ethical self-understanding not only between states but also within states. Habermas's moral discourse is strongly universalist. That universalism was specified in a principle, namely, 'For a norm to be valid, the consequences and side effects that its *general* observance can be expected to have for the satisfaction of the particular interests of *each* person affected must be such that *all* affected can accept them freely.'[69] The inherently expansive reference to '*all* affected' has been reflected in Habermas's insistence upon 'the universalistic meaning of the classical liberties that include all persons as such and not only members of a legal community'.[70] Yet that expansive, universalistic meaning was not taken as the occasion for sweeping away the distinction between the legal and the moral and, least of all, for a call for the moralization of the international realm.[71] Habermas accepted, moreover, that citizens of states have special obligations towards each other, but he insisted that these obligations arise from membership of the same legal community. He denied that these obligations could be derived from the criterion of ethnic identity and that such a criterion could be used to restrict duties to persons beyond the realm of the legal community.[72] Behind this insistence was the conviction that the scope for consensus in modern pluralistic societies could only be preserved by the increasing abstractness of moral and legal argument.[73]

Reviewing his assessment of the position of Kant and Hegel from the standpoint of the mid-1980s, Habermas showed a greater sympathy for Kant.[74] He still maintained his rejection of Kant's radical distinction between the intelligible realm and the realm of appearance, as well as Kant's presumption that the moral law could be formulated within each individual consciousness as long as it followed the correct procedures. The latter is especially important in comparison with the views of the older generation of critical theorists. According to Habermas, 'The singularity of Kant's transcendental consciousness simply takes for granted a prior understanding among a plurality of empirical egos; their harmony is preestablished.'[75] Much the same point had been made by Horkheimer. Horkheimer and Adorno, however, took the isolation of empirical egos as an accurate description of actors in contemporary society and sought to account for the shared understanding amongst these actors by reference to social processes which occurred behind their backs.[76] By contrast, Habermas has stressed moral interaction as a continuing, if threatened, fact of modern society and his discourse ethics 'prefers to view shared understanding . . . as the *result* of an intersubjectively mounted *public discourse*'.[77] In brief, what Horkheimer and Adorno ascribe to processes that are at best obscure to the individual, Habermas wants to bring into the full glare of the public arena.

Yet Habermas also defended Kant against Hegel's accusation that his formalism and abstract universalism rendered his ethics inconsistent and impotent. Against the charge of formalism, Habermas rejected the attempt to convict Kant on the grounds of the difficulty of construing formal statements which would be immune to the vagaries of circumstance. He supplemented this by mobilizing his distinction between moral and ethical questions to avoid overburdening the moral viewpoint which he and Kant wished to defend.[78] Against the charge of abstract universalism, Habermas conceded that Hegel had a point, but introduced a new distinction to reconcile the abstractness of moral norms and the contingencies of life. Kantian moral theory, he argued, focused on the justification of norms at the expense of issues of the application of such norms. This distinction served several other related purposes as well. It helped to fend off neo-Aristotelian claims that, in the light of the abstractness of Kantian moral reasoning, it was necessary to have recourse to a capacity for judgement, prudence, embedded in a specific form of life.[79] It helped in dealing with the objections raised by Albrecht Wellmer, namely that the consequences of following abstract norms might prove to be unacceptable.[80] It also helped to deal with the problem of the judicial usurpation of the role of the legislature that Habermas encountered in his defence of the democratic rule of law.[81] Habermas conceded that the abstractness of justifiable norms was a problem and, more specifically, that the gap between the abstractness of norms and the contingencies of life seemed to conjure up the possibility of a conflict between two or more justified norms. He had to find a way around this possibility, for it was central to his distinction between values and norms that the latter were either justified or not. Norms differ from values 'in the binary versus graduated coding of their validity claims'.[82] In other words, the answer to a moral question can only be yes or no. Questions about values permit answers of the type: to a certain extent.[83] Habermas also needed to defend the universal and binding character of norms, to preserve the consistency of all possible norms against the presumption that they might conflict, and to 'undo', as he put it, the abstractness of norms.

He claimed that the distinction between processes of justification and application was the answer to these problems. In processes of application what is at stake, he claimed, is not the validity of norms *per se*, but rather the question of what, in this particular case, is the singular appropriate norm.[84] This interpretation had the advantage of circumscribing the role of courts, specifically the German Federal Constitutional Court. Habermas warned against construing norms as values, which would encourage the Court to engage in weighing the relative merits of such misconstrued norms, or rather, of the Court seeking to prescribe ethical values to the legislature under the guise of the adjudication of the applicability of specific norms. All this could be avoided, he continued, if the Court understood its role as that of the application of norms in specific cases. Precisely in this restriction lay the rationality of legal discourse.[85] The distinction between processes of justification, taking place in legislatures and the wider public sphere, and adjudication also found institutional support. According to Habermas, 'the role of the impartial third party that defines the structure of judicial discourse would be out of place in discourses of justification, in which there cannot be any nonparticipants'.[86]

While the distinction between justification and application may help resolve some of the embarrassments which Horkheimer sought to expose in Kant's examples of the moral law, another weakness of Kant's theory that Horkheimer attacked, namely the problem of motivation, proved more obdurate.[87] Here, Habermas simply insisted upon the limits of what a moral theory could plausibly achieve. It is also notable that in explicating these limits he referred, amongst other things, to 'hunger and poverty in the third world'. In relation to this, he insisted that moral philosophy had no privileged insights and he ended by quoting Horkheimer's statement that 'What is needed to get beyond the utopian character of Kant's idea of a perfect constitution for humankind, is a materialist theory of society.'[88]

There are clearly several respects in which Habermas could not follow Horkheimer's notion of a materialist theory of society, most evidently in the dissolution of the autonomy of the moral point of view in the latter. Habermas has also exhibited an ambiguity about the role of interests. Interests were integrated into his model in explicit contrast to Kant's attempt to excise them. Habermas still distinguished between generalizable and non-generalizable interests. Indeed, his argument presupposes the persistent clash of interests, albeit between actors capable in principle of attempting to deal with these conflicts from the moral point of view. Yet Habermas has also treated interests as something contingent, unstable and arbitrary. In *The Theory of Communicative Action*, for instance, he argued that utilitarian considerations alone were insufficient to account for social integration. In support, he cited Durkheim's assertion that 'There is nothing less constant than interests.'[89] Similarly he invoked Weber's idea of value rationality. Summarizing the distinctive role of interests and values in this context, Habermas wrote that 'Interest positions change, whereas generalizable values are always valid for more than one type of situation.'[90] It is true that he held some interests to be 'generalizable' and that possibility is clearly crucial. Interests which are not universal, however, are consigned to the realm of strategic action and the balance of power. Here the best that can be achieved is a compromise.[91] Compromise need not be purely a matter of the balance of power. Habermas distinguished 'fair' compromises as those which allowed the parties equal access to the negotiating table and equal opportunities to exert influence. Yet even here the process is tainted by threat and inducement. The compromise itself was distinguished from true consensus: 'Whereas a rationally motivated consensus [*Einverständnis*] rests on reasons that convince all parties *in the same way*, a compromise can be accepted by the different parties each for its own *different* reason.'[92]

Interests, then, so far as they are not generalizable, fall into a realm of contingency. Habermas associated the interest-orientated actor with arbitrary choice.[93] This was reinforced by the tripartite division of practical reason into the pragmatic, ethical and moral. Whereas the moral employment of practical reason refers to the '*free will (freien Willen)*, the ethical to the '*resoluteness (Entschlusskraft)*' of a person, the pragmatic employment is guided by the '*arbitrary choice (Willkür)*' of someone.[94] In this distinction between generalizable and contingent and arbitrary interests there is a faint echo of the contrast between general and particular interests as elaborated by the older generation. There is also a great difference. Initially at least, the older generation gambled everything on the future possibility of a reconciliation of particular and general interests. In this gamble, morality lost any independent status. Only as the gamble failed, did they seek to salvage something from morality, independent of a historical project culminating in a socialist society. As they did so, they addressed more directly than Habermas the problem of motivation. Yet it may be that their early emphasis on interest is of equal importance. It is possible to accept that interest alone is insufficient without seeing interests as divisible into the universal and the contingent, unstable and arbitrary. Both Marxists and non-Marxists alike have often looked to interest as something capable of bestowing a certain stability on human action. The pursuit of interests was long associated with enlightenment. Moreover, as Albert Hirschman has argued, the 'near-total privatization [of interests] occurs only under certain authoritarian governments'.[95] Interests which fall short of the generalizable or universal may nevertheless have a place in the public realm that is characterized by more than just compromise.

Holding the balance between interest and morality has not proved easy. The older generation followed a radicalized version of Hegel's criticism of Kant, to the extent that they subsumed morality into a dialectic of interests. Habermas, seeking to salvage the moral point of view from the relativism that the older generation also feared, has produced an internally differentiated account that seeks to defend the moral point of view without overburdening it. In the complex societies of the modern world, the combination of a strong defence of morality with a delimitation of its scope is attractive. The alternatives are either a slide into relativism or more ambitious schemes with consequently higher penalties should they fail.

CHAPTER 11

Individual and Collective Identity

The common concern of the older generation as identified by Löwenthal, 'the increasing fragility of the bourgeois individual', took on a radical quality for a variety of reasons. In the first place, that concern is understandable in the context of the inter-war years in which the mounting rhetorical, and not only rhetorical, denunciation of the claims of the individual became ever more oppressive. The triumph of National Socialism in Germany naturally confirmed and radicalized the fears that the older generation already had. Yet the revolt against individualism was far from a purely German phenomenon. The anti-individualist sentiment was well expressed by the bombastic Italian fascist Dino Grandi, according to whom:

> The European revolution of the last century was a revolution of the individual, of the *ego*, of *man*, Luther, Kant and Rousseau.
>
> The revolution of the twentieth century is the *organization*, the *group*, the *syndicate*. The syndicate is not, as many believe, a *method*, and instrument. The syndicate is a *person* that tends to replace the old single physical person, who is insufficient, impotent and no longer adequate ... [1]

The older generation did not react to the disparagement of the individual with a complacent reaffirmation of the persistence of the single, physical person, for that was not what was at stake. The issue was whether or not the individual was, as Grandi put it, adequate to the times, that is, whether it still made sense to talk of the autonomy, interests and even passions of individuals.

The answer given by the older generation was complicated by its belief that there was nothing of significance about the individual that was ontologically guaranteed. Individual autonomy, interests and passions were all historical products and, as such, subject to the fate of the forms of society

175

which shaped them. For Adorno, writing in *Negative Dialectics*, 'To the powerless, who find more and more narrowly prescribed what they can and cannot attain, passion becomes an anachronism.'[2] On the other hand, the individual's significance persisted 'because the principle of the exchange society was realized only through the individuation of several contracting parities, because, therefore, the *principium individuationis* was literally its [exchange society's] principle, its universal'.[3] The context of these comments was Hegel's view of the role of individuality and the 'popular spirit' or national identity. It is noticeable that Adorno was more sympathetic to Hegel's ambiguity about the role of the individual than of the nation. Adorno treated the latter as even more anachronistic than the passions of the powerless, though he conceded that there was some inkling of this in Hegel's philosophy of history. It was, Adorno wrote, as if Hegel 'had deemed it possible for the world spirit some day to do without popular spirit and to make room for cosmopolitanism'.[4]

Though Adorno's antipathy to nationalism was clear-cut, his attitude to the concept of the individual was more ambiguous. In this Hegel and Kant were responsible for more than the choice of terminology, the entwining of the universal and the individual. The ambiguity about the concept of the individual itself was of idealist provenance. That is the second reason why the older generation's concern for 'the increasing fragility of the bourgeois individual' took on such a radical dimension. Working as they did from within the framework of German idealism, even when they were highly critical of it, the concept of the individual could not be set against concepts of society or the universal as if it were some point of refuge. The individual as more commonly understood, as the empirical individual, the single physical person, stood in an often opaque relationship to the concept of the transcendental ego. Kant had introduced the latter for the sake of the coherence of his epistemology. The immediate difficulty was the relationship of this ego, devoid as it was of the individuating traits of the empirical ego, to the empirical individual. It was this, argued Adorno, which drove forward German idealism. Ultimately the attempt to drag the transcendental ego away from the contingency of its empirical counterpart failed. The concept of the ego, of subjectivity, could not be understood save by reflection upon empirical experience of subjectivity, reflection upon the experience of some empirical ego or another.[5] Yet he also insisted that 'dialectical transmission of the universal and the particular does not permit a theory that opts for the particular to overzealously treat the universal as a soap bubble'.[6] The universal could not be so simply dismissed because to do so would entail the naïve presumption of the self-sufficiency of the individual. For Adorno, moreover, the very idea of self-sufficiency was precisely what idealism had aimed at.[7] Marcuse concurred, claiming that for idealism 'Something is authentic when it is self-reliant, can preserve itself, and is not dependent on anything else.'[8]

The concept of the individual, then, was both suspect and yet to be defended. It was suspect if construed as self-sufficient, yet had to be defended against an idealism in which the empirical contingency of individual experience evaporated. The criticism of self-sufficiency was not meant only as a criticism of idealist philosophy. Indeed it was intended much more as a criticism of the form that individual identity had taken in capitalist society: 'Now as before, the social process of production preserves in the enduring exchange process the *principium individuationis*, private disposition, and thus all the evil instincts of a man imprisoned in his ego.'[9] The link between personal identity and property was a common theme of the older generation. As Marxists, of course, they did not follow Hegel in endowing this with metaphysical sanction. Horkheimer especially emphasized the contingency of the relationship between property ownership and social position, with all the assumptions this brought about the character of the individual. Throughout the aphorisms published under the title *Dämmerung* he returned time and again to this theme. Fortune, not merit, was decisive. Yet the fortunate were better placed to develop their characters. Or, as he emphasized on several occasions, the same behaviour, the same characteristics, were regarded quite differently depending upon the social status of the individual.[10] These observations were strengthened by the appropriation of Freudian psychology. That was evident in Horkheimer's assertion that 'the entire conscious ego of the individual is in itself a thin veil'.[11] Marcuse developed the same themes at a more abstract level in 'The affirmative character of culture' and Löwenthal dealt with them through, for example, a study of Ibsen.[12]

With *Dialectic of Enlightenment* these observations took on a different significance. The predominant emphasis in the 1930s had been upon the nature of individual identity in bourgeois society. When Adorno and Horkheimer adopted Homer's *Odyssey* as the earliest record of the bourgeois individual, that form of individuality became conflated with individuality *per se*. What they discerned there was that 'men had to do fearful things to themselves before the self, the identical, purposive, and virile nature of man was formed, and something of that recurs in every childhood. The strain of holding the I together adheres to the I in all stages; and the temptation to lose it has always been there with the blind determination to maintain it.'[13] Odysseus, they argued, survived the various perils of his journey by a blend of deceit and calculation, along with his ability to deny himself the pleasures whose temptation his men frequently failed to resist. Symbolic of the blend of cunning and denial was how Odysseus outwits the Cyclops Polyphemus, by telling him that Odysseus's name is 'nobody'. When later the giant, blinded by Odysseus, identifies his attacker as 'nobody' his fellow Cyclopes fail to come to his aid. The point Adorno and Horkheimer discerned was that Odysseus has to deny his own identity in order to survive: 'his self-assertion – as in all epics, as in civilization as a whole – is self denial'.[14] The contrast between Odysseus and the Cyclops was also used to emphasize the link between the consistency of thought and individual identity. Thus 'when Homer calls the Cyclops a "lawless-minded monster", this does not mean merely that in his mind he does not respect the laws of civilization, but also that his mind itself, his thinking, is lawless, unsystematic and rhapsodical'.[15]

The connection between the identifying logic of consistent thought and the personal identity of the individual became a prime characteristic of Adorno's theory. In this dual sense *Negative Dialectics* is a 'critique of identity'.[16] Typical of the approach was one of the observations on Kant's notion of the transcendental ego: 'That the I is an entity is implicit even in the sense of the logical "I think which should be able to accompany all my conceptions" ... The pronoun "my" points to a subject as an object among objects, and again, without this "my" there would be no "I think".'[17] Essential to this claim is criticism of the idea of self-sufficiency, which Adorno and Marcuse had identified as the ambition of idealism. 'Identitarian thinking', as Adorno called it, recognizes only what is not different from itself. Whatever, for example, is not calculable is stripped out as inessential since the calculating mind cannot grasp it. Similarly 'the self, the identical, purposive, and virile nature of man', is purchased at the price of stripping away whatever would be different from those characteristics. Yet Adorno did not believe that there was an easy escape from this form of identity. Flat assimilation to whatever was different would be an abnegation of ones' own identity.

While Adorno worked through these themes in the language of idealist epistemology, Horkheimer and Marcuse often expressed themselves more directly. Thus, Horkheimer wrote that 'Each subject not only has to take part in the subjugation of external nature, human and nonhuman, but in order to do so must subjugate nature in himself.'[18] Like Odysseus the individual must resist temptation, must deny himself, in order to survive. It was precisely this logic which led Marcuse to speculate upon the 'the concrete link between the liberation of man and that of nature', only to draw back from the idealist supposition that the tension between the two could be dissolved.[19] Set in the context of contemporary psychological theories, the association of the repression of natural inclinations, the disciplining of the body and so on, with the formation of a purposive self-identity is hardly strange. What marks out the older generation is the rigour with which they pursued this kind of intuition.

Psychological theories were also relevant to the theme of the decline of the individual. In Horkheimer and Adorno's work this took on the form of a lament for the bourgeois entrepreneur.[20] In Horkheimer's words:

The society of middle-class proprietors, particularly those who acted as middlemen in trade and certain types of manufacturing, had to encourage independent thinking, even though it might be at variance with their particular interests. The enterprise itself, which, it was assumed, would be handed down in the family, gave the businessman's deliberations a horizon that extended far beyond his own life span . . . His sense of adequacy to the challenges of an acquisitive world expressed itself in his strong yet sober ego, maintaining interests that transcended his immediate needs.[21]

At one level this can be seen as a continuation of the idea of the link between property and identity which he and his colleagues had asserted in the 1930s. What is missing, however, is the earlier claim that the link between property and character was fortuitous, that character traits were assessed more in terms of the status of the person than in their own right. Adorno too is less than wholly consistent in dealing with the idea of the decline of the individual. At one level it involved him in claims which he otherwise held to be dubious. Thus he wrote that 'psychological processes, though they still persist in each individual, have ceased to appear as the determining force of the social process'.[22] Yet Adorno had frequently argued that psychological processes never had been the 'determining force of the social process'. To argue to the contrary was to succumb to an untenable psychological approach to history. Adorno's attempt to clarify his position involved him in postulating a position that he had decried. Underlying his claim was a more tenable position, namely, that it was becoming increasingly difficult to integrate one's various activities and beliefs into a more or less coherent role. It was precisely this coherence which was essential to his view of the individual: 'What is more than appearance in the individual hangs together with the moment of centralization, of the enduring unity of the manifold of experience.'[23] Marcuse also invoked the model of the economically induced decline of the family with its consequent effect upon the formation of individual identity.[24] Yet Marcuse's greater radicalism made him more immune to Horkheimer's nostalgia. Where they all agreed was in the threat to individual identity that came from the ever-greater pressure to adapt to changing circumstances over which the individual had no control.[25] The discrepancy between the exigencies of the modern world and the resources of the individual had grown so large that to Horkheimer it seemed as if the 'individual no longer has a personal history'.[26] Almost forty years later Löwenthal, who had undertaken several studies of popular biographies, used similar language. The heroes of these works had, he wrote, 'no individual destinies'.[27] Neither meant this literally. The point was, rather, that personal history or individual destiny was not the product of some project devised by the individual himself, but was rather the product of the pressure to adapt.

Shrinking space for the individual was matched by the manipulation of collective identity. The emphasis upon the manipulation of collective identity is hardly surprising. The propaganda of Nazi Germany, from which they were in exile, and the prevalence even in their American refuge of anti-Semitic agitation, pointed in the same direction. Employment by the United States government and the various projects on anti-Semitism offered the opportunity for extensive consideration of the techniques of such manipulation. Löwenthal noted that the apparent absurdity of the typical American agitator offered no comfort. The success of the demagogue had little to do with reason or interest. Indeed he argued that whereas the democratic leader claimed to share the interests of his followers and to have 'special talents for representing those interests', the agitator side-stepped the issue of interests. Instead 'he depicts himself as one of the plain folk, who thinks, lives and feels like them. In agitation this suggestion of proximity and intimacy takes the place of identification of interests.'[28] The cosmopolitan focus on interests was not merely a product of dealing with the manipulative ambitions of demagogues. It also reflected a more deep-seated antipathy to nationalism, which with little exaggeration can be described as an inclination to see the whole business as a swindle. That was evident in Adorno's protest against the 'unity trick' in the rhetoric of the agitator which was, he claimed, 'one of the innermost features of fascism, namely, the establishment of something utterly limited and particularistic as the totality, the whole, the community'.[29]

In part the older generation accounted for the intensity of the nationalism with which they were confronted in terms of the ideas they had developed to account for the formation of individual identity. Thus Horkheimer dealt with it in terms of the 'revolt of nature', that is the outbreak of what had to be suppressed in order to form and maintain the individual. He found confirmation for this in the frequency with which Nazi orators received the most rapturous applause when they imitated Jews.[30] Similarly, veneration of the nation was seen in correlation with the denial of the rights of the individual. The more the individual was supposed to suppress his interests, the more the nation was supposed to assert its interests. The most striking feature of their account of nationalism, however, is the recurrent suggestion that there was something not quite genuine about the national fervour.[31] At one level this is simply a product of the focus upon the manipulative strategies of fascist demagogues, the instrumentalist interpretation of Nazi ideology, and the focus on broader epochal trends. Horkheimer, for example, wrote of the 'Nazi blood community' as a 'racial racket', while Neumann held that the Jews were too useful a scapegoat for the Nazi regime to consider genocide.[32] At another level it was a response to the cynicism that Marcuse emphasized so heavily in his reports for the American Office of War Information. The 'new German mentality' was characterized, he claimed, by a 'pragmatic layer' as well as a 'mythological layer'.[33]

In those reports Marcuse had placed his hopes for post-war re-education in Germany on precisely that pragmatism. For Horkheimer, however, that same cynicism and pragmatism proved to be a major obstacle to the process of coming to terms with the German past. Indeed he regarded official gestures of regret and reconciliation as little more than excuses for the rehabilitation of the 'right kind of patriotism'. His own judgement was that 'Patriotism in Germany is so fearful because it is so groundless.'[34] His distrust was undoubtedly strengthened by the Institute's work on popular attitudes soon after its re-establishment in Germany. Summarizing the results of interviews, Adorno proceeded much as he and Löwenthal had in analysing the rhetoric of American demagogues, identifying defensive strategies just as they had identified manipulative rhetorical strategies. He noted anything from flat denial of the crimes of the regime and the rehashing of Nazi ideology through to more evasive responses.[35] Adorno recalled these interviews in an influential lecture on the meaning of coming to terms with the past (*Aufarbeitung der Vergangenheit*) at the end of the 1950s. There he dealt with the rhetoric of the guilt complex, from which it was claimed that the Germans suffered. But this too he claimed was deceptive. The very idea of a 'guilt complex' was suspect, for the psychological term, 'guilt complex', suggested that the guilt was disproportionate to what happened. The implication was that 'the murdered should be cheated out of the only thing which our impotence can give them: remembrance'.[36]

Suspicion of collective identity in the form of the nation took an especially sharp focus in the context of German identity. But the older generation had a wider fear of nationalism. Horkheimer did say that there was a 'moment of truth' in nationalism, but added that it was precisely this that facilitated the manipulation of men in the interests of the collective.[37] He also showed an equivocal sympathy for the idea of a Jewish state, but it was highly equivocal, tinged with regret that 'Zionism has proved a true prophet.'[38] He found a more attractive, if undeveloped, image in a late note listing ideas for future research, one of which read 'the community of the Jewish people in the diaspora, dispersal without power'.[39]

Set against the concerns of the older generation, Habermas's formulation of individual and collective identity exhibits both continuity and discontinuity. Continuity is evident in the desire to defend the idea of a form of individual identity characterized by what Adorno called 'the moment of centralization, of the enduring unity of the manifold of experience'. Fear of nationalism, especially in the context of Germany, is also marked, though as Habermas pointed out, the difference in biographical experience between himself and the older generation has coloured how that fear has been expressed. At the level of individual identity, one difference is that whereas the older generation emphasized the repression of 'inner nature', the realm of desires, the somatic and so on, in the formation of individual identity, Habermas, without denying this as a fact of individual development, sought to build access to 'inner nature' into his model of individual identity. Thus, he claimed that the 'model of unconstrained ego identity is richer and more ambitious than a model of autonomy developed exclusively from perspectives of autonomy'. 'Inner nature', he continued, 'is rendered communicatively fluid and transparent to the extent that needs can, through aesthetic forms of expression, be kept articulable.'[40] It might be objected that something like this was the ambition of the older generation, and this would be true. Yet their model of individual identity militated against this same ambition. Even Marcuse, who placed far greater emphasis upon the liberation of inner nature than Habermas, did so only from the utopian perspective of a radical break with existing forms of individuation.

This difference is related to the contrast between the model of identity formation in *Dialectic of Enlightenment* and Habermas's model in *The Theory of Communicative Action*. The latter, too, offers an account of identity formation at an early historical stage, much further back indeed than Homer's *Odyssey*. It does so through conjectures about the transition from a stage of 'gesture-mediated to symbolically mediated interaction' in the context of a conceptual refinement of the ideas of George Herbert Mead.[41] Although Habermas expresses several reservations about the empirical status of these conjectures, they do have a structurally analogous role to the analysis of the *Odyssey* in *Dialectic of Enlightenment*. More importantly, the basic features of the accounts differ systematically. In *Dialectic of Enlightenment* the story of the encounter between Odysseus and the Cyclops Polythemus involves the use of language in order to deceive. Odysseus intentionally creates a misunderstanding about his own identity in order to survive and this misunderstanding entails a denial of his own identity. By contrast, Habermas sought to make plausible how first gestures, then simple symbols, and subsequently differentiated language, could be used to reach understanding and co-ordinate action. The same process was said to account for the emergence of personal identity. In Mead's words, 'A person is a personality because he belongs to a community, because he takes over the institutions of that community into his own conduct. He takes its language as a medium by which he gets his personality, and then through a process of taking the different roles that all the others furnish he comes to get the attitude of the members of the community.'[42] Personality, then, is formed through a process of role-taking mediated by language. Role-playing involves 'taking the attitude of the other towards oneself'.[43] Habermas also took up Mead's distinction between the 'me' – that is the set of normative roles constitutive of personality – and the 'I'. According to Habermas, 'At the same time as this superego – the "me" – there takes shape an "I", a subjective world of experience to which one has privileged access.'[44] Habermas offered several other reasons, besides the idea of the expression of private experience, or, to use the earlier terminology, of inner nature, for why this distinction should be drawn. Amongst them was the idea that construing identity in terms of social roles was insufficient, for it failed to take account of the possibility that an individual might refuse to adopt a given role, fail to fulfil it adequately or simply misunderstand it. Whatever the cause of the discrepancy, the 'I' marks out this gap between role and individual.[45] The spontaneity associated with the 'I' provided the platform for an elaboration of this form of individuation, which culminated in the idea of individual identity defined in terms of personal biography and aspirations. Habermas placed the emphasis upon the latter in order to strengthen the symmetry between the distinction between the normative role-playing 'me' and the 'I' on the one hand, and the distinction between moral and ethical questions on the other hand.[46] In terms of the contrast with the model in the *Dialectic of Enlightenment*, however, the key point is that Habermas sought to extrapolate a tripartite definition of identity from contexts of understanding, role-playing and self-formation: 'numerical identification of an individual person, generic identification of a person as a speaking and acting subject, and qualitative identification of a specific person with an individual life history, particular character, and so on'.[47] The context in *Dialectic of Enlightenment* is characterized by deception and self-denial, both in terms of denial of 'inner nature' and denial of identity, all of which take place in a moral vacuum. Leaving aside the relative plausibility of the two sets of contexts, Habermas's model is better suited to provide an account of individual identity which dispenses with the idea of the self-sufficiency of the individual without conceding anything to the prophets of the insignificance of the individual. *Dialectic of Enlightenment* proceeded rather by making the idealist model its own in order to indict it for the price it exacted. Thereby Adorno and Horkheimer already conceded too much to the idealist model.

Though Dino Grandi set the syndicate against the individual, endowing it with personality, the more common candidate for supra-individual personality has been the nation or race. The extreme form this took in Germany does much to explain Habermas's reaction to the nation as a form of collective identity. The shadow of Auschwitz was explicitly invoked in his assertion that 'The only patriotism that does not alienate us from the West, is a constitutional patriotism. Unfortunately, in the cultural nation of the Germans, adhesion to universal constitutional principles anchored in convictions could be formed only after – and through – Auschwitz.'[48] According to Habermas, German identity must be built on the perception of the democratic *Rechtsstaat* as an 'achievement' and upon the end of the Second World War as a liberation from the dictatorship of the Third Reich.[49] The notion of constitutional patriotism to which he appealed has a long pedigree, but had a peculiar relevance to the Federal Republic of Germany. Not only was nationalism discredited, but Germany was divided. In this context constitutional patriotism had a distinct attraction as an alternative to ethnic patriotism and as a form of identity marked by loyalty to the Federal Republic. For Habermas, however, it was the broader principle that mattered. Hence when reunification heightened calls for Germans to see themselves once again as a 'normal' nation, he reacted by dismissing this as the 'second lie' (*zweite Lebenslüge*) which had been offered in the service of the Republic.[50]

While the specifically German context is essential to understanding the sharpness with which Habermas expressed his defence of constitutional patriotism, not least because of often vituperative advocacy of the return to normality, he clearly held it to have broader significance.[51] On occasion he suggested that this was because Auschwitz itself had a broader significance, though other arguments were more common.[52] Amongst them was the claim that constructing unified images of historical traditions was becoming increasingly problematic. Again this was set in the context of the traditional role of German historians as purveyors of meaning and guardians of national identity, a role which some were trying to revive, but this was not in principle limited to the German experience.[53] A second argument was that there was empirical evidence for the decline in the appeal of national symbols amongst younger age groups. Again the implications for the German context were sharply emphasized – 'if they are not misleading, they reveal only one thing: that we have not completely wasted the opportunity that the moral catastrophe could also represent' – but also again, the argument is not restricted to the German case.[54]

A more wide-ranging argument was also invoked, an argument which drew upon Habermas's concept of the democratic *Rechtsstaat* and especially upon his understanding of the role of the public sphere. He noted that the emergence of national identity had been instrumental in securing the internal social integration of European states that had been threatened by processes of modernization. Alongside cultural and ethnic identity, there emerged 'a new level of a *legally mediated solidarity* among citizens' in the shape of increasingly democratic forms of government.[55] He acknowledged that these two processes had been fused together historically, not least in the form of military service and conscription: ever since 'the French Revolution general conscription has gone with civil rights'.[56] Nevertheless he insisted on the gap between a culturally understood national identity and the idea of a nation of citizens. More precisely he insisted on the need to 'give priority to a cosmopolitan understanding of the nation as nation of citizens over and against an ethnocentric interpretation of the nation as a prepolitical entity'.[57] The latter 'naturalistic' interpretation had been encouraged, he suggested, by the sheer contingency of the boundaries of nation-states, that is their demarcation by the vicissitudes of war. The supposition of a common pre-political identity provided an apparent normative gloss for this contingency. Second, 'naturalistic' identities had been more or less consciously fabricated by intellectuals and had frequently been manipulated by governments. Again the echoes of the German experience can be heard, for a pre-political understanding of national identity is far from the only one. Habermas himself invoked the United States as one of the 'few counter-examples' to the prevalence of a 'culturally defined community'.[58] Yet France, though being a culturally defined community in many ways, especially in terms of the French language with its extensive cultural connotations, did not, in principle at least, subscribe to the idea of a pre-political nation. Germany, however, did subscribe to such a pre-political understanding of national identity.

The key issue, however, can be elaborated from the perspective of another of Habermas's claims, one which is difficult to dispute: 'today all of us live in pluralist societies that move further away from the format of a nation-state based on a culturally more or less homogenous population' and 'except for policies of ethnic cleansing there is no alternative' to this.[59] Strictly, policies of homogenization short of ethnic cleansing are far from excluded in practice, but the general point is that the trend is towards ethnic and cultural diversity. Pre-political conceptions of national identity are clearly incompatible with this trend. But even political conceptions of identity with cultural connotations will be strained by the trend towards diversity, unless those cultural connotations become more abstract. At that point the gap between such conceptions and Habermas's model of constitutional patriotism easily becomes a matter of nuance.

The German context was in the forefront in another sense. Here the issue was the judgement of the Federal Constitutional Court on the Maastricht Treaty of the European Union. Though sanctioning the treaty, the Court recorded several reservations, amongst which was the need to preserve the right of the nation to 'give legal expression to what spiritually, socially and politically binds it relatively homogenously'.[60] Such notions were not far removed, Habermas noted, from the idea that the development of the European Union would inevitably be limited by the absence of a European Nation. He protested that invoking the 'homogenous people' of the nation-state as a model for the European Union was simply the wrong analogy. Further progress in integration was not dependent for its legitimacy upon the creation of a European nation 'but rather on a communication network of a Europe-wide political public sphere'.[61] In this he included a 'common political culture', interest groups, non-state organizations, grass-roots movements and a European party system. This was a more extensive list than was included in the concept of 'civil society' in *Between Facts and Norms*, in some respects significantly more extensive. But the link is still clear enough. A form of collective identity transcending the nation-state has no need of a homogenous national identity, a form of identity that is problematic in any case. It is reliant only upon the existence of an extended version of the kind of public sphere that he had advocated in *The Structural Transformation of the Public Sphere*.

Interestingly, Habermas sought to cut off nationalist claims in another direction. There was, he claimed, no unequivocal right to secession from a state on the basis of self-determination. In the absence of discrimination, and as long as there are equal rights, there could be 'no talk' of a right to secession. Even where discrimination does exist, this need not entail secession: 'A demand for secession is only justified if the central state power is reserved to a part of the population which is concentrated on a territory.'[62]

Behind these restrictions lay the record of a Europe of nation-states whose boundaries were contingent, a Europe in which the formation of new nation-states had 'almost always been accompanied by bloody rituals of purification' and in which those who had been persecuted frequently themselves turned into the new persecutors.[63]

Habermas's cosmopolitanism was a limited one. Collective identity in a strong sense, that is in the sense of an answer to the question 'Who do we want to be?', is still a question that has to be answered. Typically, however, given the assumption that contemporary states are multicultural, that question will have to be answered at a sub-national level. At the national and trans-national levels, a more abstract form of identity will have to suffice. In principle the plausibility of this distinction is not difficult to see. Especially in states with distinct and strong subcultures the alternative has frequently been confrontation, advocacy of secession, and violence. Yet the distinction is also problematic. When Habermas insisted that Germans ought to have a specific commitment to constitutional patriotism, this obligation was grounded in a specific historical experience which includes Auschwitz, in a way in which the Danish historical experience, though still touched by Auschwitz, does not: 'With the life forms into which we were born and which have stamped our identity we take on very different forms of historical liability.'[64] But how does this relate to immigrants, born into different forms of life? Habermas has been a strong opponent of restrictive immigration and asylum laws and one of the virtues of his distinction between strong forms of collective identity and the weaker common political culture of a multicultural state is that it makes strong assimilationist strategies unnecessary. That still leaves the question of whether or not, or at what point, immigrants too take on the German 'historical liability'. At one level they take it on immediately, insofar as the German state and its representatives formulate policies or make symbolic gestures in the light of that liability, and are expected to do so by others. Since the state is also the state of the immigrant, he is bound to a 'historical liability' into which he was not born. The same argument applies to the heirs of those who were part of the state and nation at the time of Auschwitz. Leaving aside the fact that the sons are evidently not personally responsible for the sins of the fathers, the fathers themselves were not all personally responsible. Habermas rightly does not allow such considerations to distract from the 'historical liability' that must be borne by the Federal Republic.[65] The point is indeed that it has to be borne by the Federal Republic, by the state, and by the public spheres that act in this context as the conscience of the state. There is then an institutionally anchored link between historical identity and state, which in some respects overrides the distinction Habermas wants to draw, and that is not peculiar to the Federal Republic of Germany. There is, however, no need to take this as a substantial, let alone a fatal, objection. To apply one of Habermas's favourite devices, much depends on what question one is asking. His distinction is an eminently liberal one that prevents some people imposing their answers on others when there is no need to. That the hypothetical immigrant will have to watch his representatives act in the light of events to which he has no biographical connection, however distant, is a small price to pay.

The impact of the German experience of collective identity is evident in both the older generation and in Habermas. It is notable that recent attempts to shake off or lighten the weight of that 'historical liability' induced Habermas to defend the older generation, especially Adorno. It is equally notable that the biographical difference to which Habermas referred facilitated the formulation of conceptions of collective identity which, while clearly stamped by German history, have a much wider relevance.

Conclusion

The persistent attraction of the ideas of the critical theorists is evident from the ever-increasing volume of literature, the commemorative conferences, the publication of collected works, and the efforts to re-evaluate the contribution of those seen as comparatively neglected. Although the reasons are highly diverse it is possible to pick out a few general reasons for this enduring interest. First, there is the sheer range of their work. That was initially the product of Horkheimer's interdisciplinary programme, as well as the somewhat more contingent factor of the membership of the Institute for Social Research which brought together people with overlapping but far from identical interests. Habermas's work has also had a remarkably interdisciplinary range. Second, they have been very much critics in the public sphere, albeit with varying degrees of willingness. Ironically the years of greatest coherence, the exile of the Institute in the United States, were also the years of relative isolation, of enforced distance from their native public realm. The return of the Institute to Germany and its role in the intellectual reconstruction of that country marked the beginning of an increasingly prominent public profile. The radicalism of the 1960s, to which Marcuse made his own contribution, and what amounted almost to the rediscovery of the Institute's own radicalism of the 1930s, further extended their renown. There was some irony in the fact that revival of interest in their work was greatly assisted by American intellectuals. The land of exile and relative isolation became the land of public fame. It was an American, Martin Jay, who produced the first systematic history of the Institute. Habermas too has enjoyed a transatlantic reputation, albeit one which has been understandably less attentive to his role as a critic in the German public sphere.

Given the level of interest, it is not surprising that there has been a trend towards emphasizing the diversity of these people. The unity presupposed in the term 'Frankfurt School' seemed forced. Even the second systematic history of *The Frankfurt School* concluded with reservations about that unity. That unity gives way to diversity under intensified scrutiny is common-place in the history of ideas, so too is the periodic reassertion of unity, though usually in more guarded form. This book is no exception to that caution. It has been guided by the question of whether or not the idea of the unity of critical theory helps us to understand the ideas put forward, even where those ideas are in some respects evidently different. The claim in this book is, of course, that it does help us to understand. At the relatively abstract level of the preliminary definition of critical theory there is a common core of themes, the 'embedding of theoretical accomplishments in the practical contexts of their genesis and employment', the image of self-determination, and the concern with the fragmentation of consciousness, both as a characteristic of academic reflection and as a characteristic of the experience of modernity more generally. To press the idea of a definition of critical theory beyond this point, is probably not very helpful. This is not because of the absence of other definitional candidates, the most obvious of which is the idea of immanent critique. It is because it risks turning the unity of critical theory primarily into a matter of methodology. There is nothing intrinsically objectionable in this and despite their own reservations something like methodological unity can be discerned amongst at least core members of the older generation. Yet, it is not methodology but context which brings out the unity and which illumin-ates what otherwise seems puzzling. Context means in the first place that the 'dual confrontation of the old Frankfurt School, against positivism on the one side and *Lebensphilosophie* and general metaphysical obscuranticism on the other side, has sadly become contemporary again'.[1] It is this context which accounts for Horkheimer's attack upon the positivists, an attack whose ferocity baffled Otto Neurath.[2] It is this context which accounts for the ferocity of Habermas's attack upon the postmodernists. Context means in the second place the context of German history and thought. Even in exile, the public realm which the older generation addressed was still German, even down to the language. Often all that is required to see the significance of context is to take statements literally. For example, Habermas's idea of constitutional patriotism takes on distinctive force in the context of his claim that 'Unfortunately, in the cultural nation of the Germans, adhesion to universal constitutional principles anchored in convictions could be formed only after – and through – Auschwitz.'[3] There is, of course, a risk in emphasizing context, especially in the second sense. Context can serve to relativize. Yet it need not do so. The validity of Habermas's claims about the nature of collective identity is no more reducible to German historical experience than is the validity of Hobbes's theory to the experience of the English Civil War.

The issue of the validity of critical theory, its wider significance beyond the contexts of its emergence and reformulation, has been marked by recurrent attempts to take stock of its claims and to work out where critical theory is leading. While earlier these tended to set critical theory within the Marxist tradition, and to be motivated by concern for the possibility of some non-authoritarian form of socialism, more recent ones have been heavily influenced by Habermas's work.[4] Another notable change has been worry that with the incorporation of the Institute for Social Research into the history of ideas, the contemporary relevance of its ideas might drop from view.[5] Habermas, however, has been taken as a point of reference in an extremely diverse range of settings. According to Ricardo Blaug, it is advisable to classify the potential uses of Habermas's critical theory into three broad categories: critical theory 'as an interpretive tool' in the shape of cultural criticism of anything from economics to health care, critical theory as a programme of empirical research and critical theory 'as a test for legitimacy'.[6] Given the sheer diversity of uses to which his theory is being put, the question 'Whither critical theory?' seems to admit of all kinds of answers. That is a testament to its vitality.

There are some focuses that stand out from the perspective of an account that tries to balance the tension between the unity and diversity of critical theory, especially in relation to the contrast between the older generation and Habermas. The first of these concerns language. As noted earlier, Habermas has argued that there are glimpses of the potential inherent in language in Horkheimer's later work, but that 'Horkheimer remains too much a negative philosopher of history, too much a radical critic of reason, to have been able to see a spark of reason in the communicative practice of everyday life'.[7] Habermas went on to quote Horkheimer's suspicion that contemporary speech had become 'vapid'. It was not only that it had become vapid, incapable of expressing what really mattered, but also that speech was a tool of manipulation and of deceit. In part that is quite compatible with Habermas, insofar as alongside the 'spark of reason' there is also a dull fog of misunderstanding and deceit. The former, the validity redeeming discourse, is the island of light amidst this fog. The difference of course is that Horkheimer barley glimpsed the light at all. Habermas has concentrated on the 'spark of reason', but has also touched on the existence of 'systematically distorted communication'. He has, moreover, noted the need to pursue the latter more systematically.[8] Systematically distorted communication is, then, the first focus to emerge from consideration of the development of critical theory across the generations.

The second and third are linked. A common concern was the problem that Kant encountered in trying to endow practical reason with some plausible motivation, that is, to explain how moral intuitions gained some motivational force. Horkheimer especially took this as a central weakness in Kant's argument. Habermas recognized the problem but denied that it was one which moral theory could solve. Moral theory 'depends on socialization processes that meet it halfway by engendering the corresponding agencies of conscience, namely, the correlative superego formations'.[9] Motivation is also at the heart of the third possible focus. In one sense Habermas has presented a harsher account of the conflict of interests than the older generation. The image of a reconciliation of universal and particular interests which they upheld, albeit as a future, utopian, achievement, has given way to an image of the obduracy of interests. Only some interests are generalizable and which these are is dependent upon the unknown outcomes of discourse amongst those concerned. Yet alongside the greater obduracy of interests Habermas has also emphasized the contingent, unstable and arbitrary character of interests. This has in no way led to the old antipathy to interests, not in the Kantian form and certainly not in the form which calls for the sacrifice of interests in the service of some higher cause. To the contrary, the conflict of interests is central to Habermas's account and can be dealt with either by reaching agreement on what constitutes a generalizable interest, or, where this is not possible, through fair compromise. The plausibility of both, however, is strengthened to the extent to which interests can be seen as more permanent and reliable. What might be called the motivational deficit of Habermas's critical theory has frequently been noted, and has been openly acknowledged by Habermas. Motivational supplement has been sought, for example, in notions of 'needs and solidarity' and 'trust'.[10] It may be that interests have a certain advantage, for trust and solidarity point towards communal forms of life in a way that interests need not do. There is also a weakness here. Where the old Marxist hope that interests would override the claims of collective identity was put to the test, it was cruelly disappointed.

Notes

Introduction

1 Theodor Adorno, *Philosophische Terminologie* [1962–1963], vol. 1 (Frankfurt am Main, 1973), p. 62.

2 Max Horkheimer, 'Traditional and critical theory' [1937], in *Critical Theory* (New York, 1972), pp. 188–243; Herbert Marcuse, 'Philosophy and critical theory' [1937], in *Negations* (Harmondsworth, 1968), pp. 134–58.

3 The Gestapo's announcement can be found in Horkheimer, *GS*, vol. 15, pp. 111–12.

4 Ulrich von Aleman, *Grundlagen der Politikwissenschaft* (Opladen, 1995), p. 82.

5 Peter Uwe Hohendahl, *Reappraisals. Shifting Alignments in Postwar Critical Theory* (Ithaca, 1991), p. 4.

6 Martin Jay, *The Dialectical Imagination. A History of the Frankfurt School and the Institute of Social Research, 1923–1950* (Boston, 1973).

7 For an early example see Susan Buck-Morss, *The Origin of Negative Dialectics. Theodor W. Adorno, Walter Benjamin and the Frankfurt Institute* (Hassocks, 1977).

8 Again by way of illustration, see William E. Scheuerman, *Between the Norm and the Exception* (Cambridge, Mass., 1994) for a recent reappraisal of Franz Neumann and Otto Kirchheimer.

9 Leo Löwenthal, *Critical Theory and Frankfurt Theorists* (New Brunswick, 1989), p. 240.

10 This is the subtitle of Detlev Peukert's *The Weimar Republic. The Crisis of Classical Modernity* (London, 1991).

11 *Ibid.*, p. 83.

12 The *Habilitationsschrift* was required, in addition to a doctorate, in order to obtain permission to give lectures. Adorno's unsuccessful *Habilitationsschrift* is in his *GS*, vol. 1, pp. 79–322.

13 Rolf Wiggershaus, *The Frankfurt School* (Cambridge, 1994), pp. 75–6.

14 Jürgen Habermas, Silvia Bovenschen *et al.*, *Gespräche mit Herbert Marcuse* (Frankfurt am Main, 1978), p. 10.

15 Wiggershaus notes that Wolfgang Abendroth, Professor of Politics at Marburg from 1951, was an exception here. *The Frankfurt School*, p. 430.

16 Peter Dews (ed.), *Autonomy and Solidarity* (London, 1986), p. 149.

17 For the general significance of this see Hohendahl, *Reappraisals*, p. 5.

18 'Universalism and the situated critic', in Stephen K. White (ed.), *The Cambridge Companion to Habermas* (Cambridge, 1995), pp. 68–9.

19 See Wolfgang Bonss, 'The program of interdisciplinary research and the beginnings of critical theory', in Seyla Benhabib *et al.* (eds), *On Max Horkheimer* (Cambridge, Mass., 1993), pp. 99–125.

20 See Raymond A. Morrow, *Critical Theory and Methodology* (London, 1994), p. 158.

21 Anthony Giddens, *Modernity and Self-Identity* (Cambridge, 1991), p. 86.

22 Rene Görtzen, 'Theodor W. Adorno. Vorläufige Bibliographie seiner Schriften und der Sekundärliteratur', in Ludwig von Friedeburg and Jürgen Habermas (eds), *Adorno-Konferenz* (Frankfurt am Main, 1983), pp. 402–71 and 'Kommentierte Bibliographie der Schriften über Herbert Marcuse', in Institut für Sozialforschung (ed.), *Kritik und Utopie im Werk von Herbert Marcuse* (Frankfurt am Main, 1992), pp. 312–95.

23 Jay, *Dialectical Imagination*; David Held, *Introduction to Critical Theory* (London, 1980); Rolf Wiggershaus, *The Frankfurt School* (Cambridge, 1994); Jürgen Habermas, *Between Facts and Norms. Contributions to a Discourse Theory of Law and Democracy* (Cambridge, 1996).

24 For a helpful survey of the meaning of critical theory in different national contexts see Hohendahl, *Reappraisals*, especially pp. 1–20 and 198–228.

25 These two omissions are linked in that Benjamin's work was heavily influenced by, though not reducible to, aesthetic considerations. On Benjamin see Richard Wolin, *Walter Benjamin. An Aesthetic of Redemption* (New York, 1982). Benjamin was a friend of Adorno since 1923. He committed suicide in 1940.

26 Karl August Wittfogel (1896–1988) did not belong to the core of the Institute. Despite wide-ranging interests, he was valued within the Institute primarily for his work on China.

27 See for example Herbert Marcuse, 'The left under the counterrevolution' [1972], in *Counterrevolution and Revolt* (London, 1972), pp. 1–57.

28 Habermas, 'Themes in postmetaphysical thinking' [1992], in *Postmetaphysical Thinking* (Cambridge, 1992), p. 34.

29 Karl Marx, 'Critique of Hegel's Philosophy of Right. Introduction', in Karl Marx, *Early Writings* (Harmondsworth, 1975), p. 250.

30 Max Horkheimer and Theodor Adorno, *Dialectic of Enlightenment* [1944/47] (London, 1973).

31 Jürgen Habermas, 'Kritische Theorie und Frankfurter Universität' [1985], in *Eine Art Schadensabwicklung* (Frankfurt am Main, 1987), p. 58.

32 Löwenthal, *Critical Theory and the Frankfurt Theorists*, p. 232.

33 Habermas in Jürgen Habermas (ed.), *Observation on 'The Spiritual Situation of the Age'* (Cambridge, Mass., 1985), p. 15.

34 Löwenthal, *Mitmachen wollte ich nie* (Frankfurt am Main, 1980), p. 79.

Chapter 1: The Frankfurt School

1   The foundation of the Institute is described by Jay, *Dialectical Imagination*, pp. 3–9; Wiggershaus, *The Frankfurt School*, pp. 9–24; and Ulrike Migdal, *Die Frühgeschichte des Frankfurter Instituts für Sozialforschung* (Frankfurt am Main, 1981). For the intellectual climate in Frankfurt see also Wolfgang Schivelbusch, *Intellektuellendämmerung* (Frankfurt am Main, 1982).

2   Wiggershaus, *The Frankfurt School*, p. 25.

3   Henryk Grossmann, *Das Akkumulations- und Zusammenbruchgesetz des kapitalistischen Systems* (Leipzig, 1929) and Friedrich Pollock, *Die planwirtschaftliche Versuche in der Sowjetunion 1917–1927* (Leipzig, 1929).

4   Quoted in Migdal, *Frühgeschichte des Frankfurter Institututs*, p. 98.

5   Paul Kluke, *Die Stiftungsuniversität Frankfurt am Main* (Frankfurt am Main, 1972), p. 504.

6   The phrase 'critics in the public sphere' is taken from a book by Robert C. Holub, *Jürgen Habermas. Critic in the Public Sphere* (London, 1991). It can usefully be applied to the original members of the Institute, though there are important differences in the experience of this role between the original members and Habermas.

7   Schivelbusch, *Intellektuellendämmerung*, p. 20.

8   *Ibid.*, p. 72.

9   'The present situation of social philosophy and the tasks of an Institute for Social Research' [1931] in Max Horkheimer, *Between Philosophy and Social Science* (Cambridge, Mass., 1993), p. 13.

10 For the expectation of military intervention see his letter to Löwenthal of 6 July 1934, in Leo Löwenthal, *Mitmachen wollte ich nie* (Frankfurt am Main, 1980), p. 256. For the closing down of opportunities – 'I could only teach music to "non-Aryans" ' – see his letter to Ernst Krenek of 7 October 1934, in Theodor W. Adorno and Ernst Krenek, *Briefwechsel* (Frankfurt am Main, 1974), p. 43.

11 *Zeitschrift für Sozialforshung* [hereafter *ZfS*], vol. 1 (1932), p. i.

12 Institut für Sozialforschung, *Studien über Autorität und Familie* (Paris, 1936).

13 Otto Kirchheimer and Georg Rusche, *Punishment and Social Structure* (New York, 1939).

14 Alfons Söllner, 'Leftist students of the conservative revolution: Neumann, Kirchheimer and Marcuse', *Telos*, **61** (1984), pp. 60–1.

15 Franz Neumann, *The Rule of Law* [1936] (Leamington Spa, 1986).

16 Rainer Erd (ed.), *Reform oder Resignation. Gespräche über Franz Neumann* (Frankfurt am Main, 1985), pp. 86–9.

17 Letter of 25 July 1938, in Max Horkheimer, *GS*, vol. 16, pp. 450–1.

18 *Ibid.*, pp. 110, 654–7, 660–2, 666–7, 689–90.

19 The connection was drawn in a letter of 18 March 1935, Horkheimer, *GS*, vol. 15, pp. 334–5. For a survey of the project see *ibid.*, pp. 179–85 and Wiggershaus, *The Frankfurt School*, pp. 177–9.

20 The words were Adorno's. See Horkheimer, *GS*, vol. 16, p. 742. See also Horkheimer, *GS*, vol. 15, p. 725.

21 Franz Neumann, *Behemoth. The Structure and Practice of National Socialism* (London, 1941).

22 Friedrich Pollock, 'State Capitalism', *ZfS*, vol. 9 (1941), pp. 200–25.

23 *ZfS*, vol. 9 (1941), pp. 124–43.

24 See, for example, Löwenthal, *Critical Theory and Frankfurt Theorists*, pp. 247–8.
25 Theodor W. Adorno *et al.*, *The Authoritarian Personality* [1950] (New York, 1969).
26 Barry Katz, 'The criticism of arms: the Frankfurt School goes to war', *Journal of Modern History*, 59 (1987), pp. 439–78.
27 Douglas Kellner, 'Introduction', in Douglas Kellner (ed.), *Technology, War and Fascism* (London, 1998), pp. 22–3.
28 Franz Neumann, 'The labor movement in Germany', in Hans J. Morgenthau (ed.), *Germany and the Future of Europe* (Chicago, 1951), p. 103. His letter to Horkheimer is in Erd (ed.), *Reform oder Resignation*, pp. 149–50.
29 Franz Neumann, 'Anxiety and politics' [1954], in Franz Neumann, *The Democratic and the Authoritarian State* (New York, 1957), pp. 270–300.
30 Otto Kirchheimer, 'Private man and society' [1966], in Frederic S. Burin and Kurt L. Shell (eds), *Politics, Law and Social Change. Selected Essays of Otto Kirchheimer* (New York, 1969), pp. 458–9. On Neumann's and Kirchheimer's post-war views, see Alfons Söllner, 'Politische Dialektik der Aufklärung', in Wolfgang Bonns and Axel Honneth (eds), *Sozialforschung als Kritik* (Frankfurt am Main, 1982), pp. 281–326.
31 On militant democracy see Karl Loewenstein, 'Militant democracy and fundamental rights', *American Political Science Review*, 31 (1937), pp. 417–32, 638–58.
32 Otto Kirchheimer, *Political Justice* (Princeton, 1961).
33 Theodor Adorno and Max Horkheimer, *Dialectic of Enlightenment* [1944] (London, 1973), p. xi. The edition published in Horkheimer, *GS*, vol. 5 indicates the variations in the different editions described below.
34 Horkheimer, *GS*, vol. 12, pp. 594–605.
35 'Critical Theory and Frankfurt University' [1985] in Peter Dews (ed.), *Autonomy and Solidarity* (London), p. 218.
36 Quoted in 'Work and Weltanschauung: The Heidegger controversy from a German perspective' [1989], in Jürgen Habermas, *The New Conservatism* (Cambridge, 1989), p. 155. See also Dews (ed.), *Autonomy and Solidarity*, pp. 80, 190–2.
37 Theodor Adorno, *The Jargon of Authenticity* [1964] (London, 1973).
38 Herbert Marcuse, *Soviet Marxism* [1958] (Harmondsworth, 1971).
39 Jürgen Habermas, 'Psychic Thermidor and the rebirth of rebellious subjectivity' [1980], in Richard J. Bernstein (ed.), *Habermas and Modernity* (Cambridge, Polity, 1985), p. 68. See also Dews (ed.), *Autonomy and Solidarity*, pp. 206–7 and the comments quoted in Wiggershaus, *The Frankfurt School*, pp. 544–5.
40 Herbert Marcuse, *Eros and Civilization* [1955] (London, 1969).
41 For an account emphasizing the importance of the bourgeois era to Horkheimer see Peter M.R. Stirk, *Max Horkheimer: A New Interpretation* (Hemel Hempstead, 1992).
42 Theodor Adorno, *Against Epistemology* [1956] (Oxford, 1982).
43 Quoted in Wiggershaus, *The Frankfurt School*, p. 554.
44 Jürgen Habermas, *Structural Transformation of the Public Sphere* [1962] (Cambridge, 1989), p. 232.
45 Herbert Marcuse, *One Dimensional Man* [1964] (London, 1968) and 'Repressive tolerance', in Herbert Marcuse *et al.*, *A Critique of Pure Tolerance* [1965] (Boston, 1968).
46 Theodor Adorno, *Aesthetic Theory* (London, 1984).

47 The point is clearer in the German original 'Gewaltloser Widerstand *ist* Gewalt', Jürgen Habermas, 'Ziviler Ungehorsam – Testfall für den demokratischen Rechtstaat' [1983], in *Die neue Unübersichtlichkeit* (Frankfurt am Main, 1985), p. 79.
48 Jürgen Habermas, *Knowledge and Human Interests* [1968] (London, 1972).
49 Jürgen Habermas, *The Theory of Communicative Action* [1981], vol. 1 (London, 1984), vol. 2 (Cambridge, 1987).
50 Jürgen Habermas, *Zur Rekonstruktion des historischen Materialismus* (Frankfurt am Main, 1976). See the translations included in *Communication and the Evolution of Society* (London, 1979).
51 Jürgen Habermas, *The Philosophical Discourse of Modernity* [1985] (Cambridge, 1987).
52 'Critical Theory and Frankfurt University' [1985].
53 *Ibid.*, p. 214.
54 See Richard Wolin, 'Introduction' to Jürgen Habermas, *The New Conservatism*, p. xiv. For surveys see Richard J. Evans, *In Hitler's Shadow* (London, 1989) and Charles S. Maier, *The Unmasterable Past* (London, 1997).
55 Quoted in Wolin, 'Introduction' to Habermas, *The New Conservatism*, p. xvii.
56 Jürgen Habermas, *The Philosophical Discourse of Modernity* [1985] (Cambridge, 1987), pp. 365–6.
57 Theodor Adorno, *Negative Dialectics* [1966] (London, 1973), p. xxi.
58 Löwenthal, *Critical Theory and Frankfurt Theorists*, p. 250.
59 *Die Zeit* quoted in editors' Preface to Jürgen Habermas, 'Die postnationale Konstellation und die Zukunft der Demokratie', *Blätter für Deutsche Internationale Politik*, 7 (1998), p. 804.

Chapter 2: A Preliminary Outline of Critical Theory

1 Habermas, *The Philosophical Discourse of Modernity* [1985], p. 53. The same point is made in 'Themes in postmetaphysical thinking' [1992], *Postmetaphysical Thinking* (Cambridge, 1992), p. 29. See also his claim that 'A systematic appropriation of the history of (sociological) theory helped me to find the level of integration on which the philosophical intentions unfolded from Kant through Marx can be made scientifically fruitful today.' Habermas, *The Theory of Communicative Action* [1981], vol. 1, p. xl.
2 Adorno, *Negative Dialectics* [1966], p. 3.
3 Habermas, 'Themes in postmetaphysical thinking', p. 33.
4 *Ibid.*, p. 34.
5 Karl Marx, 'Critique of Hegel's Philosophy of Right. Introduction', in Karl Marx, *Early Writings* (Harmondsworth, 1975), p. 250.
6 Habermas, 'Themes in postmetaphysical thinking', p. 51. For the stance of the older generation see Horkheimer's letter of 17 December 1937, *GS*, vol. 16, p. 336.
7 Quoted in Thomas A. Spragens, *The Irony of Liberal Reason* (Chicago, 1981), p. 347.
8 G.W.F. Hegel, *Phenomenology of Spirit* (Oxford, 1977), p. 403.
9 Theodor Adorno, *Stichworte* (Frankfurt am Main, 1969), p. 174.
10 Letter of 30 November 1937, in Horkheimer, *GS*, vol. 16, p. 303.
11 *Ibid.*

12 Adorno, *Negative Dialectics*, p. 244.
13 Habermas, 'Toward a reconstruction of historical materialism' [1976], in *Communication and the Evolution of Society* (London, 1979), p. 136. Comments a few paragraphs later are more equivocal, pp. 137–8.
14 *Ibid.*, p. 146.
15 Adorno, *Negative Dialectics*, p. 244.
16 Habermas, 'Remarks on Hegel's Jena *Philosophy of Mind*' [1967], in *Theory and Practice* (London, 1974), p. 169.
17 Max Horkheimer, 'Traditional and critical theory', in Max Horkheimer, *Critical Theory* (New York, 1972), p. 207.
18 Quoted by Jürgen Habermas, *Towards a Rational Society* (London, 1971), p. 59.
19 Jürgen Habermas, *Legitimation Crisis* [1973] (London, 1976), p. 143.
20 See Theodor Adorno, 'Individuum und Organisation' [1953], in *Soziologische Schriften I* (Frankfurt am Main, 1972), pp. 440–56.
21 Max Horkheimer, 'History and psychology' [1932], in *Between Philosophy and Social Science*, p. 121.
22 For Adorno see 'The stars down to earth' [1957], *GS*, vol. 9.2, pp. 11–120; for Neumann, 'Anxiety and politics' [1954], in *The Democratic and the Authoritarian State* (New York, 1957), pp. 270–300. See also Adorno's caution in 'Bemerkungen über Politik und Neurose' [1954], *Soziologische Schriften I*, pp. 434–9.
23 Karl Marx, *Capital*, vol. 1 (Harmondsworth, 1976), pp. 169–70.
24 *Ibid.*, p. 169.
25 Herbert Marcuse, *Reason and Revolution* [1941] (London, 1955), p. 410.
26 Franz Neumann, 'Economics and politics in the twentieth century' [1951], in *The Democratic and the Authoritarian State*, p. 268. See also. p. 264.
27 Habermas, *The Structural Transformation of the Public Sphere* [1962], p. 200.
28 Jürgen Habermas, 'The classical doctrine of politics in relation to social theory' [1963], in *Theory and Practice*, p. 74. On the scientization of politics see Thomas McCarthy, *The Critical Theory of Jürgen Habermas* (London, 1978), pp. 1–16 . There is an interesting distinction between the *decisionistic model*, which Habermas associates with Hobbes, Weber and Schmitt, and the strictly *technocratic model*. See Habermas, 'The scientization of politics and public opinion', in *Toward a Rational Society*, pp. 62–80.
29 Schelsky, quoted in ibid., p. 59.
30 Habermas, *The Theory of Communicative Action*, vol. 2, p. 321. For similar concerns see Spragens, *The Irony of Liberal Reason*.
31 In *The Theory of Communicative Action* Habermas wrote that it 'is only with this that the conditions for a *colonization of the lifeworld* are met'; vol. 2, p. 355.
32 Habermas, 'Themes in postmetaphysical thinking', p. 51. For the stance of the older generation see Horkheimer's letter of 17 December 1937, *GS*, vol. 16, p. 336.
33 Habermas, *The Philosophical Discourse of Modernity*, p. 67. Under praxis philosophy Habermas includes not only Lukacs and the older generation of critical theorists but also radical democrats, *ibid.*, p. 394.
34 Horkheimer, 'Traditional and critical theory', p. 208.
35 Theodor Adorno, *Vorlesung zur Einleitung in die Soziologie* (Frankfurt am Main, 1973), p. 143. See also 'Spätkapitalismus oder Industriegesellschaft?' [1968], in *Soziologische Schriften I*, p. 369.

36 Horkheimer, 'Traditional and critical theory', p. 233. Translation amended. See *GS*, vol. 4, p. 207.
37 See Ulrich Wegerich, *Dialektische Theorie und historische Erfahrung* (Würzburg, 1994), pp. 33–4.
38 See Jürgen Habermas, 'Eine Diskussionsbemerkung (1972): Das Subjekt der Geschichte', in *Zur Logik der Sozialwissenschaften* (Frankfurt am Main, 1985), especially pp. 536–7 and 'History and evolution' [1976], *Telos*, **39** (1979), pp. 5–44.
39 Theodor Adorno, *Philosophische Terminologie* [1962–1963] (Frankfurt am Main, 1973), vol. 1, pp. 71–2.
40 Max Horkheimer, 'Über Kants *Kritik der Urteilskraft*' [1925], in *GS*, vol. 2, p. 146.
41 Horkheimer, 'Traditional and critical theory', p. 209.
42 Max Horkheimer, 'The present situation of social philosophy and the tasks of an institute for social research' [1931], in *Between Philosophy and Social Science*, p. 11. Culture in the narrower sense was quite broad, ranging from science to law and leisure activities.
43 *Ibid.*, p. 9.
44 Max Horkheimer, 'Materialism and metaphysics' [1933], in *Critical Theory*, pp. 33–4. This gave way in his increasing criticism of positivism.
45 Max Horkheimer, 'Zu Bergsons Metaphysik der Zeit' [1934], in *GS*, vol. 3, p. 226.
46 Theodor Adorno, 'Zum gegenwärtigen Stand der deutschen Soziologie' [1959] , in *Soziologische Schriften I*, p. 502.
47 *Ibid.*, p. 504.
48 *Ibid.*, p. 515.
49 Horkheimer, *GS*, vol. 12, p. 144.
50 Habermas, *The Theory of Communicative Action*, vol. 1, p. 5. The contrast with Adorno is not as dramatic as might appear, for Adorno's complaints related to the condition of German sociology in the 1950s while Habermas focuses on Weber in the light of his concern with 'the problematic of societal rationalization, which was largely ousted from professional sociological discussion after Weber'; *ibid.*, p. 7.
51 Habermas, *Between Facts and Norms* [1992], p. x.
52 Jürgen Habermas, 'Philosophy as stand-in and interpreter' [1983], in *Moral Consciousness and Communicative Action* (Cambridge, 1990), p. 16.
53 *Ibid.*, p. 20.
54 Jürgen Habermas, 'Toward a reconstruction of historical materialism' [1976], in *Communication and the Evolution of Society*, p. 140.
55 Habermas, 'History and evolution', especially pp. 41–2.
56 As noted by Charles S. Maier, *The Unmasterable Past*, p. 39.
57 Habermas, *The Theory of Communicative Action*, vol. 2, p. 309.
58 Strictly there are four concepts of action. The triadic structure reappears in the claims they make, to be true, right, truthful; *ibid.*, vol. 1, pp. 84–101.

Chapter 3: The Failure of Metaphysics

1 Herbert Schnädelbach, *Philosophy in Germany 1831–1933* (Cambridge, 1984), p. 5.
2 Jürgen Habermas, 'To seek to salvage an unconditional meaning without God is a

futile undertaking: reflections on a remark of Max Horkheimer' [1991], in *Justifica-tion and Application* (Cambridge, 1993), pp. 140–1.

3 Quoted by Schnädelbach, *Philosophy in Germany*, p. 142.

4 There have been attempts to claim that Adorno and Horkheimer were influenced by Klages. See Georg Stauth and Bryan S. Turner, 'Ludwig Klages (1872–1956) and the origins of critical theory', *Theory, Culture and Society*, 9 (1992), pp. 45–63. The argument never gets beyond analogies. For Horkheimer's reference to the new metaphysics see 'Materialism and metaphysics' [1933], in *Critical Theory*, p. 13.

5 Martin Heidegger, *Being and Time* (Oxford, 1978), p. 21.

6 *Ibid.*, p. 35.

7 The defence of Heidegger was not always unequivocal. See the critical assessment by Richard Wolin, 'French Heidegger wars', in *The Heidegger Controversy* (Cambridge, Mass., 1993), pp. 272–300.

8 Quoted in Calvin O. Schrag, *The Resources of Rationality. A Response to the Postmodern Challenge* (Bloomington, 1992), pp. 19–20. Note the qualification on the use of 'opinion' in footnote 14 on p. 20. For an assessment of Heidegger's defenders see Tom Rockmore, *On Heidegger's Nazism and Philosophy* (London, 1992), pp. 244–81.

9 Herbert Marcuse, 'Das Problem der geschichtlichen Wirklichkeit' [1931], in *Schrif-ten*, vol. 1 (Frankfurt am Main, Suhrkamp, 1978), p. 485.

10 Herbert Marcuse, 'Zur Auseinandersetzung mit Hans Freyers *Soziologie als Wirklich-keitswissenschaft*' [1931], in *Schriften*, vol. 1, p. 488. Freyer was one of numerous advocates of a 'conservative revolution' and author of *Revolution von rechts* (Jena, 1931).

11 Herbert Marcuse, 'Contributions to a phenomenology of historical materialism' [1928], *Telos*, 4 (Fall 1969), p. 15. Translation modified. See *Schriften*, vol. 1, p. 361.

12 Heidegger, *Being and Time*, p. 435. For Marcuse's quotation see 'Contributions to a phenomenology of historical materialism', p. 15.

13 For the 'philosophy of the revolutionary deed' see Söllner, 'Leftist students of the conservative revolution', p. 66. Söllner emphasizes the importance of Marcuse's interpretation of Marx's Paris Manuscripts in marking the break as did Marcuse himself in retrospect; 'Theory and politics', *Telos*, 38 (1978), pp. 125–6.

14 Herbert Marcuse, 'The struggle against liberalism in the totalitarian view of the state' [1934], in *Negations* (Harmondsworth, 1968), p. 33.

15 Horkheimer, *GS*, vol. 2, p. 354. See also pp. 430–2.

16 Quoted in Horkheimer, 'Remarks on philosophical anthropology' [1935], in *Between Philosophy and Social Science*, p. 153.

17 *Ibid.*, pp. 154 and 157.

18 Horkheimer, 'Materialism and metaphysics' [1933], p. 18. Translation modified, see *GS*, vol. 3, p. 78.

19 Horkheimer, 'Materialism and metaphysics', p. 19.

20 Horkheimer, 'Zur Emanzipation der Philosophie von der Wissenschaft' [*circa* 1928], in *GS*, vol. 10, p. 361.

21 *Ibid.*, p. 347. The terms used by Horkheimr are *Bild* and *Hypothese*. The translation of the former as 'model' better conveys Horkheimer's intent, though it glosses over differences between Mach and others. See Alan Janik and Stephen Toulmin, *Wittgen-stein's Vienna* (New York, 1973), pp. 133–44.

22 Schnädelbach, *Philosophy in Germany*, p. 186. Hence Hartmann, who followed Scheler, had to explain the historical variability of moral codes by claiming that each moral code entailed only a partial view of the realm of values. Nicolai Harmann, *Ethics* (London, 1932), vol. 2, p. 65.

23 Quoted in Marcuse, 'The Concept of Essence' [1936], in *Negations*, p. 63.

24 Hartmann, *Ethics*, vol. 1, pp. 90–1.

25 Horkheimer, 'The rationalism debate in contemporary philosophy' [1934], in *Between Philosophy and Social Science*, pp. 226–7.

26 For the relevance of this to contemporary disputes about postmodernism see McCarthy in David C. Hoy and Thomas McCarthy, *Critical Theory* (Oxford, 1994), p. 37.

27 Löwenthal, 'Knut Hamsun. Zur Vorgeschichte der autoritären Ideologie', *ZfS*, vol. 6 (1937), p. 302. Löwenthal was proud that his prediction of Hamsun's fascist sympathies was later corroborated. Löwenthal, *Critical Theory and Frankfurt Theorists*, p. 227.

28 Theodor Adorno, *In Search of Wagner* (London, 1981), especially pp. 143–7. These pages were first published in 1938.

29 Quoted in Horkheimer, 'The rationalism debate in contemporary philosophy', p. 231.

30 For an example of the similarities see J. Orr, 'German social theory and the hidden face of technology', *Archiv européene sociologie*, 15 (1974), pp. 321-36. See also Michael E. Zimmerman, *Heidegger's Confrontation with Modernity* (Bloomington, 1990).

31 Marcuse, *One Dimensional Man* [1964], p. 113.

32 See *ibid.*, pp. 117–18. See also his summary of Husserl on p. 133.

33 For his interpretation of Hegel see Marcuse, *Reason and Revolution* [1941], especially pp. 141–8. The emphasis on interests is evident in all of the essays published in the *ZfS* in the 1930s.

34 Horkheimer, 'Materialism and morality' [1933], in *Between Philosophy and Social Science*, p. 40.

35 Fred R. Dallmayr, 'Phenomenology and critical theory', *Cultural Hermeneutics*, 3 (1976), p. 372. The relevant text is *Der Begriff des Unbewusstsein in der transzendentalen Seelenlehre* [1927], in Adorno, *GS*, vol. 1, pp. 79–377. There have been attempts to argue for the proximity of Adorno and Heidegger, especially Hermann Mörchen, *Macht und Herrschaft im Denken von Heidegger und Adorno* (Stuttgart, 1980).

36 Adorno, *Philosophische Terminologie* [1962–3], vol. 1, p. 153. I have used the translation of Heidegger reproduced in Zimmerman, *Heidegger's Confrontation with Modernity*, p. 71.

37 Adorno, *Jargon of Authenticity* [1964], pp. 124–5 and *Negative Dialectics* [1966], pp. 112–15.

38 Adorno, *Jargon of Authenticity*, pp. 137–8.

39 *Ibid.*, p. 120. The translation is not sound. See Adorno, *GS*, vol. 6, p. 493. An amphiboly is 'a confounding of an object of pure understanding with appearance'. Immanuel Kant, *Critique of Pure Reason* (London, 1933), p. 282. Hegel provides a clear, if broad, definition of paralogisms: 'Paralogisms are a species of unsound syllogism, the especial vice of which consists in employing one and the same word in the two premises with a different meaning.' *Hegel's Logic* (Oxford, 1975), para. 47, p. 76.

40 Adorno, *Philosophische Terminologie*, vol. 1, pp. 84–5.
41 Theodor Adorno, *Eingriffe* (Frankfurt am Main, 1963), p. 17.
42 Adorno, *Jargon of Authenticity*, pp. 5–12, 63–5.
43 Adorno, *Negative Dialectics*, p. 121. This was put somewhat more simply by Josef Maier: 'Hegel does not start with experience at all. For that would have implied the realization that the categories employed are purely relational and have no inherent content. In his argument the admittedly given is not accounted for and explained but explained *away*. Hegel's dialectic remains paradoxically a pure *Gedankendialektitk* [conceptual dialectic].' *On Hegel's Critique of Kant* (New York, 1966: first published 1939) pp. 78–9.
44 Habermas, 'Work and Weltanschauung: the Heidegger controversy from a German perspective' [1989], in *The New Conservatism*, p. 143.
45 Marcuse, 'Das Problem der geschichtlichen Wirklichkeit', p. 485.
46 Habermas, *The Philosophical Discourse of Modernity* [1985], p. 149.
47 *Ibid.*, p. 152.
48 *Ibid.*, p. 141.
49 *Ibid.*, p. 338. See also 'The mindfulness of nature (*Eingedenken*) [Adorno's phrase] comes shockingly close to the recollection (*Andenken*) of being [Heidegger's phrase].' *Theory of Communicative Action* [1981], vol. 1, p. 385.
50 Jürgen Habermas, 'Französische Blicke, französische Befürchtungen' [1993], *Die normalität einer Berliner Republik* (Frankfurt am Main, 1995), p. 65.
51 Jürgen Habermas, 'Kritische Theorie und Frankfurter Universität' [1985], in *Eine Art Schadensabwicklung* (Frankfurt am Main, 1987), p. 58.
52 Habermas, 'Das Falsche im Eigenen' [1994], in *Die Normalitat einer Berliner Republik*, p. 129.
53 Habermas, 'The new intimacy between culture and politics' [1988], in *The New Conservatism*, pp. 201–2.
54 Jürgen Habermas, 'Modernity: an unfinished project', in M.P. D'Entreves and S. Benhabib (eds), *Habermas and the Unfinished Project of Modernity* (Cambridge, 1996), p. 53.
55 *Ibid.*
56 *Ibid.*, p. 54.
57 Quoted in Habermas, 'Neoconservative cultural criticism in the United States and Germany' [1982], in *The New Conservatism*, p. 26.
58 *Ibid.*, p. 32.
59 Habermas, 'Das Falsche im Eigenen', p. 130.
60 Habermas, *The Philosophical Discourse of Modernity*, p. 96.
61 *Ibid.*, p. 102.
62 *Ibid.*, p. 120.
63 *Ibid.*, p. 166.
64 *Ibid.*, p. 181.
65 *Ibid.*, p. 182.
66 Göran Dahl, 'Will "the other God" fail again? On the possible return of the conservative revolution', *Theory, Culture and Society*, 13 (1996), p. 36.
67 Habermas, 'Taking aim at the heart of the present: on Foucault's lecture on Kant's *What is Enlightenment?*' [1984], in *The New Conservatism*, pp. 173–9.
68 Habermas, *The Philosophical Discourse of Modernity*, p. 282.
69 *Ibid.*, p. 296.

CRITICAL THEORY, POLITICS AND SOCIETY

70 James Schmidt, 'Habermas and Foucault', in D'Entreves and Benhabib (eds), *Habermas and the Unfinished Project of Modernity*, p. 165.

71 *Ibid.*, p. 166.

72 Quoted in Richard J. Bernstein, *The New Constellation* (Cambridge, Mass., 1992), p. 214. Even Derrida's enthusiasts concede that there is a problem here. See Simon Critchley, *The Ethics of Deconstruction* (Oxford, 1992), p. 200.

73 Habermas, *The Philosophical Discourse of Modernity*, p. 181; Critchley, *The Ethics of Deconstruction*, p. 200.

74 Habermas's judgement of Horkheimer is harsher: see Jürgen Habermas, 'To seek to salvage an unconditional meaning without God is a futile undertaking', pp. 133–46.

75 Hence the final sentence of Adorno's *Negative Dialectics*: 'There is solidarity between such thinking [his own] and metaphysics at the time of its fall', p. 408. For a defence of Adorno's position see Jarvis, *Adorno*, especially pp. 207–11.

76 Peter Dews, *The Limits of Disenchantment* (London, 1995), pp. 13–14.

77 Habermas, 'Themes in postmetaphysical thinking' [1988], *Postmetaphysical Thinking*, p. 29.

78 *Ibid.*, pp. 29–34.

79 *Ibid.*, p. 35.

80 *Ibid.*, p. 51. See also Habermas, 'Metaphysics after Kant' [1987] in *Postmetaphysical Thinking*, p. 15 and 'Popular sovereignty as procedure' [1988] in *Between Facts and Norms*, p. 490.

81 Jürgen Habermas, 'Exkurs: Transzendenz von innen, Transzendenz ins Diesseits' [1988], in *Texte und Kontexte* (Frankfurt am Main, 1991), pp. 136–40.

82 For criticism of this see Dews, *The Limits of Disenchantment*, pp. 169, 190.

Chapter 4: The Critique of Positivism

1 Marcuse, *Reason and Revolution* [1941], p. 326.

2 *Ibid.*, p. 327.

3 A.J. Ayer, *Part of My Life* (London, 1977), p. 128. See also Russell Keat, *The Politics of Social Theory* (Oxford, 1981), pp. 29–30. Ironic confirmation is provided by the manner of their misunderstanding of Wittgenstein: Janik and Toulmin, *Wittgenstein's Vienna*, pp. 218–20.

4 *ZfS*, 6 (1937), pp. 140–51.

5 Horkheimer, *GS*, vol. 16, letters of 21 June 1937 and 29 June 1937, pp. 178–9 and 185. Neurath had already held discussions in the Institute in October and November 1936.

6 Horkheimer, *GS*, vol. 15, letter of 22 October 1936, pp. 688–9 and *GS*, vol. 16, letter of 30 January 1938, p. 374.

7 Horkheimer, *GS*, vol. 15, letter of 27 November 1936, p. 750.

8 Horkheimer, 'The latest attack on metaphysics' [1937], p. 139. See also *GS*, vol. 16, letter of 8 December 1936, p. 777.

9 Horkheimer, 'The latest attack on metaphysics', p. 183.

10 Horkheimer, 'Zur Emanzipation der Philosophie von der Wissenschaft' [circa 1928], *GS*, vol. 10, pp. 334–419, especially pp. 338–40 and pp. 418–19.

11 Thus Ernest Gellner, 'It [the Frankfurt School] thought that apart from facts, which

any old fool can gather and which do not mean anything, we have a thing called the critical method, which underneath the facts tells us the deeper facts and, incidentally, tells us the value direction.' 'Enlightenment – yes or no?', in Jozef Niznik and John T. Sanders (eds), *Debating the State of Philosophy* (Westport, 1996), p. 79.

12 Horkheimer's account is not as clear as it might have been because he does not pay much attention to the development of their ideas. His general point here is, however, supported by later commentators. See chapter 5, 'The elimination of experience', in O. Hanfling, *Logical Positivism* (Oxford, 1981).

13 For Marx's comments see Karl Marx and Frederick Engels, *The German Ideology* (London, 1974), p. 63. For Horkheimer's reference see 'Traditional and critical theory' [1937], p. 200. See also the comments of Alfred Schmidt, *The Concept of Nature in Marx* (London, 1971), p. 200.

14 Horkheimer, 'The latest attack on metaphysics', p. 183.

15 *Ibid.*, p. 178.

16 Moritz Schlick, *Problem of Ethics* (New York, 1962), p. 78. Horkheimer did not quote this passage but it illustrates clearly the attitude he criticized.

17 For the importance of formal logic to them, see Horkheimer, 'The latest attack on metaphysics', p.167 and Hanfling, *Logical Positivism*, p. 134.

18 Horkheimer, 'The latest attack on metaphysics', p.161 and 'Traditional and critical theory', pp. 209–11.

19 Moritz Schlick quoted in Marcuse, 'Concept of essence' [1936], p. 65.

20 *Ibid.*, p. 74.

21 Marcuse, *Reason and Revolution*, p. 321.

22 See James Bohman, *New Philosophy of Social Science* (Cambridge, Mass., 1990).

23 *ZfS*, 8 (1939–40), p. 228.

24 Horkheimer, *GS*, vol. 12, pp. 473–4. For the importance of this 'tension' for Horkheimer see 'On the problem of truth' [1935], in A. Arato and E. Gebhardt (eds) The *Essential Frankfurt School Reader* (Oxford, 1978), p. 421. This 'tension' was even more important for Adorno.

25 Horkheimer, 'On the problem of truth', p. 425.

26 *Ibid.*, pp. 410–11.

27 *Ibid.*, p. 425.

28 *Ibid.*, p. 429. For Adorno's use of similar language see 'Veblen's attack on culture', *ZfS*, 9 (1941), p. 413.

29 At a very general level this is not so different from the position adopted by Alan Sokal and Jean Bricament, *Intellectual Impostures* (London, 1998), pp.61–5.

30 Horkheimer, 'The end of reason' *ZfS*, 9 (1941), p. 366.

31 Horkheimer, *Eclipse of Reason* [1947] (New York, 1974), p. 43.

32 *Ibid.*, p. 174.

33 *Ibid.*, p. 168.

34 See Horkheimer, *GS*, vol. 14, pp. 139, 229–30, 267–8, 327, 329, 348, 443.

35 Horkheimer, 'Soziologie und Philosophie' [1959], *GS*, vol. 7, p. 113. One consequence of this is that the natural scientist would inevitably keep his theory in one pocket and any political commitment in another. The natural scientist must therefore appear as a positivist and must fall victim to Horkheimer's strictures in 'Traditional and critical theory' [1937], pp. 209–10.

36 *Ibid.*, p. 117.

37 *Ibid.*, p. 119.

38 See Wiggershaus, *The Frankfurt School*, p. 567.
39 See also Horkheimer's response in 'Zur Zukunft der Kritischen Theorie' [1971], in *GS*, vol. 7, p. 423.
40 Karl Popper, 'Reason or revolution?', in Theodor W. Adorno *et al.*, *The Positivist Dispute in German Sociology* (London, 1976), pp. 289, 292, 296–7.
41 Thus Habermas, 'A positivistically bisected rationalism' [1964], in Adorno *et al.*, *The Positivist Dispute in German Sociology*, p. 224.
42 Adorno, 'Introduction' [1969], in Adorno *et al.*, *The Positivist Dispute in German Sociology*, p. 53. Despite equating Wittgenstein with the 'positivists' in these sentences Adorno went on to distinguish him from the Vienna Circle, pp. 53–4.
43 Habermas, 'A positivistically bisected rationalism', pp. 213–15.
44 Adorno, 'Wissenschaftliche Erfahrungen' [1968], *GS*, vol. 10(2), p. 738.
45 See for example Adorno, *Negative Dialectics* [1966], pp. 152–3. In an extreme form this kind of experience is debilitating. Adorno's own life is illustrative of this.
46 Adorno, 'Introduction', p. 37.
47 *Ibid.*
48 It is interesting that Popper's attempt to rephrase some of Adorno's formulations in what he regards as clear but trivial formulations completely ignores the Marxism without which they are indeed trivial. Adorno, 'Reason or revolution?', in Adorno *et al.*, *The Positivist Dispute in German Sociology*, pp. 296–7. For a reassertion of Adorno's Marxism see Frederic Jameson, *Late Marxism* (London, 1996).
49 *Adorno, Against Epistemology* [1956], p. 51. The strategy pervades the book in various forms, e.g. that unless some unwanted presupposition or reference is made the argument is meaningless. For this variation see pp. 81–2. For the debt to Hegel see Theodor Adorno, *Drei Studien zu Hegel* (Frankfurt am Main, 1963), especially p. 77.
50 Habermas, 'Analytical theory of science and dialectics' [1963], in Adorno *et al.*, *The Positivist Dispute in German Sociology*, pp. 136, 133, 144–9.
51 Habermas, 'A positivistically bisected rationalism', p. 213.
52 Habermas, *Knowledge and Human Interests* [1968], p. 5.
53 Marcuse, *One Dimensional Man* [1964], p. 126. For the review of Husserl see *ZfS*, 6 (1937), pp. 414–15.
54 Marcuse, *One Dimensional Man*, p. 131.
55 *Ibid.*, p. 135.
56 *Ibid.*, chapter 9, and *An Essay on Liberation* (Boston, 1969), p. 19.
57 Even on the same page. See Marcuse, 'Nature and revolution', in *Counterrevolution and Revolt* [1972], p. 68.
58 Habermas, 'Technology and science as "ideology"' [1968], in *Toward a Rational Society*, p. 87.
59 Quoted in Habermas, 'Technical progress and social life-world' [1968], in *Toward a Rational Society*, p. 59. The same passage is also quoted in 'Von sozialen Wandel akademischer Bldung' [1963], in *Kleine Politische Schriften I–IV* (Frankfurt am Main, 1981), p. 113.
60 It does come close to Adorno's comments on interpretation referred to above. However, Adorno always held that this state of affairs was remediable, in principle at least. That is clear in his dispute with Gehlen who held similar views to Schelsky. See Christian Thies, *Die Krise des Individuums. Zur Kritik der Moderne bei Adorno und Gehlen* (Reinbek bei Hamburg, 1997), pp. 149–54.

61 Habermas, 'Arnold Gehlen: imitation, substantiality' [1970], in *Philosophical-Political Profiles* (London, 1983), pp. 121–2, 127. For their influence see Wiggershaus, *The Frankfurt School*, pp. 582–8.

62 Habermas, 'The scientization of politics and public opinion' [1968], in *Toward a Rational Society*, p. 75.

63 Habermas, 'Von sozialen Wandel akademischer Bildung', pp. 114–16.

64 Jürgen Habermas, *On the Logic of the Social Sciences* [1967] (Cambridge, 1988) , pp. 17–18, 22.

65 *Ibid.*, p. 3. The anti-positivist thrust is glossed over in William Outhwaite's characterization of the work as 'a positive critique of interpretative sociological methodologies'. William Outhwaite, *Habermas* (Cambridge, 1994), p. 23.

66 Habermas, *On the Logic of the Social Sciences*, pp. 33–5, 72–3, 82–3.

67 *Ibid.*, pp. 35–6.

68 Habermas, *Knowledge and Human Interests* [1968], p. vii.

69 *Ibid.*, p. 81.

70 *Ibid.*, p. 94.

71 *Ibid.*, p. 97.

72 See Jürgen Habermas, 'Wahrheitstheorien' [1973], in *Vorstudien und Ergänzungen zur Theorie des kommunikativen Handelns* (Frankfurt am Main, 1984), pp. 127–83 and 'A postscript to *Knowledge and Human Interests*', *Philosophy of Social Sciences*, 3 (1973), pp. 157–89.

73 Habermas, *Knowledge and Human Interests*, p. 303.

74 *Ibid.*, p. 178. One could say that whereas Horkheimer insisted that this practical relation was a characteristic of a specific theory, namely critical theory, Habermas sought to locate that relation in a theoretical tradition, the cultural sciences, and secure the validity of the latter by showing how they, at least once shorn of their positivistic self-misunderstanding, gained their plausibility by making transparent characteristics of social life without which self-identities and non-coercive co-ordinated action were impossible.

75 *Ibid.*, p. 135.

76 Habermas, 'The classical doctrine of politics in relation to social philosophy' [1963], in *Theory and Practice*, p. 43. Translation modified, see *Theorie und Praxis* (Neuwied, 1963), p. 15.

77 Habermas, 'A philosophico-political profile' [1985], in Dews (ed.), *Autonomy and Society*, p. 177.

78 Habermas, *The Theory of Communicative Action*, vol. 1, pp. 108-9-, 376–7.

79 Habermas, 'Life-forms, morality and the task of the philosopher' [1984], in Dews (ed.), *Autonomy and Society*, p. 192. See also 'Vorwort zur Neuausgabe' [1982], *Zur Logik der Sozialwissenschaften*, pp. 10–11.

80 *Ibid.*, p. 9.

Chapter 5: The Attractions and Limits of Psychology

1 Löwenthal, *Mitmachen wollte ich nie* [1980], p. 61. Horkheimer later told Martin Jay that Freud had written expressing his thanks for the Institute's assistance with the Psychoanalytic Institute. Jay, *Dialectical Imagination*, p. 88. See also Horkheimer's letter of 11 January 1971 to Sydney Lipshires, *GS*, vol. 18, p. 771.

2   Horkheimer, 'Vorrede [zu *Freud in der Gegenwart*]' [1957], *GS*, vol. 19, p. 17.
3   Horkheimer, 'Zur Zukunft der Kritischen Theorie' [1971], *GS*, vol. 7, p. 427.
4   Habermas, 'Philosophy as stand-in and interpreter' [1983] and 'Moral consciousness and communicative action' [1983], in *Moral Consciousness and Communicative Action*, pp. 14 and 117. It is also argued that psychoanalytic theory can contribute to the rejuvenation of critical theory. See Joel Whitebook, *Perversion and Utopia. A Study in Psychoanalysis and Critical Theory* (Cambridge, Mass., 1995).
5   The review was by Franz Borkenau, *ZfS*, 1 (1932), pp. 174–5.
6   Erich Fromm, 'The method and function of an analytic social psychology' [1932], in *The Crisis of Psychoanalysis* (Harmondsworth, 1973), p. 136. Wolfgang Bonss points out that Marx and Freud elaborate this basic point quite differently, through the concept of labour and instincts respectively. 'Psychoanalyse als Wissenschaft und Kritik', in Wolfgang Bonss and Axel Honneth (eds), *Sozialforschung als Kritik* (Frankfurt am Main, 1982), p. 382.
7   Fromm, 'The method and function of an analytic social psychology', p. 164.
8   *Ibid.*, p. 164.
9   Fromm, 'Psychoanalytic characterology and its relevance for social psychology' [1932], in *The Crisis of Psychoanalysis*, p. 207.
10 See Axel Honneth, 'Sociological deficit of critical theory', in Seyla Benhabib *et al.* (eds), *On Max Horkheimer* (Cambridge, Mass., 1993), p. 205. His claim that 'Fromm lets the basic concepts of a psychoanalytic personality theory mesh directly with the basic concepts of an economic theory of society; the dimension of *social action*, the concrete reality of which gradually forms individual instinctual potential, is, so to speak, crushed between these two conceptual frameworks' glosses over those points at which Fromm points to the role of broader cultural processes, but it is, nevertheless, a succinct analysis of the underlying problem.
11 Horkheimer, 'The present situation of social philosophy' [1931], in *Between Philosophy and Social Science*, p. 11.
12 Horkheimer, 'History and psychology' [1932], in *Between Philosophy and Social Science*, p. 119.
13 Horkheimer, 'History and psychology', pp. 120–1.
14 Horkheimer, 'Vorurteil und Charakter' [1952], *GS*, vol. 8, p. 65.
15 *Ibid.*, p. 76.
16 The importance of Fromm's contribution has been re-emphasized in recent years and his position has been defended against the accusations levelled at him by his former colleagues. See John Rickert, 'The Fromm–Marcuse debate revisited', *Theory and Society*, 15 (1986), pp. 351–400; Internationale Erich Fromm-Gesellschaft (ed.), *Erich Fromm und die kritische Theorie* (Münster, 1991); Stephen Eric Bronner, 'Fromm in America', in *Of Critical Theory and Critical Theorists* (Oxford, 1994).
17 Erich Fromm, 'Die gesellschaftliche Bedingtheit der psychoanalytischen Therapie', *ZfS*, 4 (1935), pp. 365–97.
18 Horkheimer, Letter of 21 March 1936, *GS*, vol. 15, p. 498.
19 Theodor Adorno, *Minima Moralia* [1951] (London, 1974) quoted in Helmut Johach, 'Erich Fromm und die Kritische Theorie des Subjekts', in Internationale Erich Fromm-Gesellschaft (ed.), *Erich Fromm und die Kritische Theorie*, p. 43.
20 Adorno, *Minima Moralia*, p. 61.
21 Johach, 'Erich Fromm und die Kritische Theorie des Subjekts', p. 43.
22 Horkheimer, Letter of 6 April 1937, *GS*, vol. 16, p. 110.

23 Letter from Landauer, 7 November 1937, in Horkheimer, *GS*, vol. 16, pp. 272–3.
24 Horkheimer, 'Egoism and freedom movements' [1936], *Between Philosophy and Social Science*, p. 105.
25 *Ibid.*, pp. 104–5.
26 Horkheimer, 'The relation between psychology and sociology in the world of Wilhelm Dilthey', *ZfS*, 8 (1939–40), p. 437.
27 *Ibid.*, pp. 441–2.
28 Ludwig Marcuse (1894–1971) was a writer and cultural historian who was periodically supported by the Institute. Horkheimer, *GS*, vol. 18, p. 975.
29 Horkheimer, Letter of 5 August 1936, *GS*, vol. 16, p. 604. Marcuse replied that he had been misunderstood and that his position was no different from the one defended by Horkheimer and Pollock, *ibid.*, pp. 615–18. The kind of explanation favoured by Horkheimer and Pollock is evident in Ian Kershaw, *Hitler 1889–1936* (London, 1998).
30 See especially Leo Löwenthal, 'Prophets of Deceit' [1949], in *False Prophets* (New Brunswick, 1987).
31 Horkheimer, 'Sociological background to the psychoanalytic approach', in Ernst Simmel (ed.), *Anti-Semitism: A Social Disease* (New York, 1946), p. 6.
32 Adorno, *The Authoritarian Personality* [1950], p. 749.
33 Adorno, 'Anti-semitism and fascist propaganda' [1946], in *Soziologische Schriften I*, p. 400.
34 Herbert Marcuse, 'The new German mentality' [1942], in *Technology, War and Fascism* (London, 1998), pp. 141–73.
35 Adorno, 'Anti-semitism and fascist propaganda', p. 403.
36 Theodor Adorno, 'Freudian theory and the pattern of fascist propaganda', in Geza Roheim (ed.), *Psychoanalysis and the Social Sciences*, vol. 3 (New York, 1951), p. 299. See also his comment, in response to criticism of *The Authoritarian Personality*, 'Nothing was further from my intention than to psychologically deduce a phenomenon like fascism.' 'Starrheit und Integration' [1959], in Adorno, *GS*, vol. 9(2), pp. 375–6.
37 Max Horkheimer, 'The lessons of fascism', in Hadley Cantril (ed.), *Tensions that Cause Wars* (Urbana, 1950), p. 230.
38 Adorno, 'Die revidierte Psychoanalyse' [1952], in *Soziologische Schriften I*, pp. 20–41. Fromm is mentioned directly on pp. 31–2 and his *Escape from Freedom* is credited with greater insight than Horney. The English edition had a slightly different title: *The Fear of Freedom* (London, 1942). Horkheimer and Adorno were more critical of his later book *Man for Himself* (New York, 1947). See Horkheimer, *GS*, vol. 18, pp. 22–4.
39 Max Horkheimer, 'Ernst Simmel and Freudian philosophy', *International Journal of Psychoanalysis*, 29 (1948), pp. 110–11. See also Adorno, 'Die revidierte Psychoanalyse', p. 40.
40 Adorno, 'Die revidierte Psychoanalyse', p. 36; 'Sociology and psychology II' [1955], *New Left Review*, 47 (1968), p. 81.
41 Horkheimer, Letter of 17 July 1943, *GS*, vol. 17, p. 463. See also letter of 31 October 1942, *ibid.*, p. 367.
42 Max Horkheimer, 'The soul' [1967], in *Critique of Instrumental Reason* (New York, 1974), pp. 51–62, especially pp. 57–9; Horkheimer, 'Die Psychoanalyse aus der Sicht der Soziologie' [1968], *GS*, vol. 8, pp. 294–305, especially pp. 294–5.

43 Adorno, *Philosophische Terminologie I* [1962–1963], pp. 180–1.

44 Erich Fromm, *The Sane Society* (London, 1963), p. 72.

45 Thus the healthy society 'furthers man's capacity to love his fellow men, to work creatively, to develop his reason and objectivity, to have a sense of self which is based on the experience of his own productive powers.' *Ibid.* David Burston provides a defence of Fromm against his critics but concedes that Fromm could be 'naive and dogmatic'. *The Legacy of Erich Fromm* (Cambridge, Mass., 1991), pp. 84–97, especially p. 87.

46 Marcuse, *Eros and Civilization* [1955], p. 23.

47 *Ibid.*, p. 46.

48 *Ibid.*, pp. 24, 95–6.

49 *Ibid.*, p. 124. See Sigmund Freud, *Civilization and its Discontents* (London, 1975), p. 2. and Bernard Görlich, 'Sublimierung als kulturelles Triebschicksal', in Institut für Sozialforschung (ed.), *Kritik und Utopie im Werk von Herbert Marcuse*, pp. 180–1. For other examples of Marcuse's neglect of the more obdurate aspects of Freud see Peter M.R. Stirk, '*Eros and Civilization* revisited', *History of the Human Sciences*, **12** (1999), pp. 73–90.

50 G. Flego, 'Erotisieren statt sublimieren', in Institut für Sozialforshcung (ed.), *Kritik und Utopie im Werk von Herbert Marcuse*, pp. 190–4 and H. Hyman, 'Eros and freedom: the critical psychology of Herbert Marcuse', in Robert Pippin et al., *Marcuse. Critical Theory and the promise of Utopia* (South Hadley, Mass., 1988), pp. 159–64.

51 Marcuse, *Eros and Civilization*, p. 16.

52 *Ibid.*, p. 25. Thereby, Marcuse sidesteps the question: are Freud's theories true? See J. Rickert, 'The Fromm–Marcuse debate revisited', p. 362.

53 Fromm, *The Crisis of Psychoanalysis*, p. 31. Equally damning is the point that Marcuse 'fails to grasp the essentially *traumatic* nature of their genesis'. Whitebook, *Perversion and Utopia*, p. 41.

54 Marcuse, *Eros and Civilization*, p. 125.

55 His interpretation of Kant and Schiller is equally flawed because it will not bear the strain of trying to reconcile their arguments with Freud's. See Stirk, '*Eros and Civilization* revisited', pp. 83–5.

56 Habermas, *Knowledge and Human Interests* [1968], p. 287.

57 The ambiguity is that 'The primary process, on the one hand, is "motivated" by defense, is due to the impact of repression on standard rational, secondary-process thinking. On the other hand, primary process is assumed to be the original form or mode of mentation according to the pleasure principle, which secondarily becomes changed by the exigencies of life, by "reality", resulting in a secondary-process mentation guided by the reality principle.' Whitebook, *Perversion and Utopia*, p. 179. My account of Habermas's approach to the concept of the unconscious follows Whitebook.

58 Habermas, *Knowledge and Human Interests*, p. 224. See also, '"id" is then the name for the part of the self that is externalized through defense ... ', *ibid.*, p. 242.

59 *Ibid.*, pp. 239, 285.

60 *Ibid.*, pp. 224, 226.

61 *Ibid.*, p. 241. For the criticism see Whitebook, *Perversion and Utopia*, pp. 182–8, especially p. 186 where he writes that 'Habermas ignores "the most general and most striking psychological characteristic" of a dream ... namely, that "a thought of

something that a wish is represented" not as a statement but, pictorially, "as a scene"'.

62　Habermas, *Knowledge and Human Interests*, p. 230.

63　*Ibid.*, p. 282.

64　*Ibid.*, p. 234.

65　*Ibid.*, p. 288.

66　McCarthy, *The Critical Theory of Jürgen Habermas*, pp. 211–12.

67　Thus Christopher Nichols, 'Science or reflection: Habermas on Freud', *Philosophy of the Social Sciences*, 2 (1972), pp. 266–7. The objection is similar to that made by Whitebook above.

68　'Habermas talking: an interview', *Theory and Society*, 1 (1974), p. 52.

69　Nichols, 'Science or reflection', p. 268.

70　Habermas, *Knowledge and Human Interests*, pp. 259–61. See especially p. 261 where the comparison of the validity of such hypotheses with those of the empirical analytic sciences is said to be 'correct in its way'.

71　Habermas, 'Some difficulties in the attempt to link theory and practice' [1971], in *Theory and Practice*, pp. 29–32. For summaries of the objections and Habermas's clarification see McCarthy, *The Critical Theory of Jürgen Habermas*, pp. 205–13; Fred R. Dallmayr, 'Critical theory criticized: Habermas's *Knowledge and Human Interests* and its aftermath', *Philosophy of the Social Sciences*, 2 (1972), pp. 222–4.

72　Dews (ed.), *Autonomy and Solidarity*, p. 162; 'Habermas talking', pp. 52–3.

73　See for example Habermas, 'Moral development and ego-identity' [1976], in *Communication and the Evolution of Society*, pp. 73–5.

74　Habermas, 'Alexander Mitscherlichs Sozialpsychologie' [1983], *Texte und Kontexte*, p. 170.

75　Habermas, 'Moral development and ego-identity', pp. 70–2.

76　Habermas, 'Überlegungen zur Kommunikationspathologie' [1974], in *Vorstudien und Ergänzungen zur Theorie des kommunikativen Handelns*, pp. 250–1.

77　*Ibid.*, p. 267.

78　*Ibid.*, p. 269.

79　Habermas, *The Theory of Communicative Action* [1981], vol. 2, p. 389.

80　*Ibid.*, p. 174.

81　Habermas, 'Historical materialism and the development of normative structures' [1976], in *Communication and the Evolution of Society*, pp.102, 110.

82　For a survey see Piet Strydom, 'The ontogenetic fallacy: the immanent critique of Habermas's developmental logical theory of evolution', *Theory, Culture and Society*, 9 (1992), pp. 65–93. See also Michael Schmid, 'Habermas's theory of social evolution', in John B. Thompson and David Held (eds), *Habermas. Critical Debates* (London, 1982), pp. 162–80; David Ingram, *Habermas and the Dialectic of Reason* (New Haven, 1987), pp. 132–4.

83　Gertrud Nunner-Winkkler, 'Knowing and wanting: on moral development in early childhood', in Axel Honneth *et al.* (eds), *Cultural-Political Interventions in the Unfinished Project of Enlightenment* (Cambridge, Mass., 1992), pp. 240–1.

84　Quoted in Strydom, 'The ontogenetic fallacy', pp. 84–5. Translation amended *Nachmetaphysisches Denken* (Frankfurt am Main, 1988), pp. 101–3.

85　Habermas, 'Reconstruction and interpretation in the social sciences' [1983], in *Moral Consciousness and Communicative Action*, p. 38.

86　*Ibid.*, pp. 38–9. This 'complementarity' thesis as Habermas called it had also been espoused by Kohlberg, *ibid.* See also Habermas, 'Lawrence Kohlberg and neo-Aristotelianism' [1991], in *Justification and Application*, pp. 114–15.

87 Habermas, see 'Moral development and ego identity', p. 91.

88 Habermas, 'Moral consciousness and communicative action' [1983], in *Moral Consciousness and Communicative Action*, pp. 187–8.

Chapter 6: The Analysis of Bourgeois Society

1   Theodor Adorno, 'Is Marx obsolete?', *Diogenes*, **64** (1968), p. 7. The use of italics follows the German text, whose different title sets out the contrast with which Adorno was concerned: 'Spätkapitalismus oder Industriegesellschaft', in *Soziologische Schriften I*, p. 361.

2   Adorno, 'Is Marx obsolete?', p. 11.

3   Karl Marx, 'Manifesto of the Communist Party', in *The Revolutions of 1848* (Harmondsworth, 1973), p. 70.

4   Jürgen Kocka, 'The European pattern and the German case', in Jürgen Kocka and Allen Mitchell (eds), *Bourgeois Society in Nineteenth-Century Europe* (Oxford, 1993), pp. 20–1.

5   Löwenthal, *Critical Theory and the Frankfurt Theorists*, p. 232.

6   Habermas in Jürgen Habermas (ed.), *Observation on 'The Spiritual Situation of the Age'* (Cambridge, Mass., 1985), p. 15.

7   Walter Struve, *Elites Against Democracy. Leadership Ideals in Bourgeois Political Thought in Germany, 1890–1933* (Princeton, 1973), p. 9.

8   See Wolfgang Mommsen: 'Weber's conception of a democratic mass leader who wins over the masses for his policies with the help of his charismatic capacities can be traced back to aristocratic individualism in which liberal assumptions are combined with the Nietzschian idea of the value setting personality.' *Max Weber and German Politics* (Chicago, 1984), p. 420. See also p. 402.

9   Leo Löwenthal, 'Conrad Ferdinand Meyers heröische Geschichtsauffasssung', *ZfS*, 1 (1932), pp. 34–62. Meyer's heroes were not, however, particularly 'responsive' to the needs of the lower orders, *ibid.*, p. 57.

10 Horkheimer, 'Egoism and the freedom movement' [1936], p. 62.

11 'Karl Kraus', in Walter Benjamin, *One Way Street* (London, 1979), p. 258.

12 Horkheimer, 'Authority and the family' [1936], in *Critical Theory*, p. 72.

13 Herbert Marcuse, 'A study on authority' [1936], in *Studies in Critical Philosophy* (London, 1972), p. 124.

14 Typical is Adorno's comment: 'Over it rules an ascetic spiritualism.' Theodor Adorno, *Kierkegaard* [1933] (Frankfurt am Main, 1962), p. 94.

15 Marcuse, 'Affirmative culture' [1937], in *Negations*, p. 95.

16 *Ibid.*, p. 122.

17 *Ibid.*, pp. 123–4. Although the critical theorists do not appear to have been aware of it, the life of Ludwig Wittgenstein is a good, indeed extreme, example of this. See Ray Monk, *Ludwig Wittgenstein. The Duty of Genius* (London, 1991).

18 Horkheimer, 'Traditional and critical theory' [1937], p. 203.

19 *Ibid.*, p. 200. See also Marcuse, 'Society, however, is not a conscious subject', *Reason and Revolution* [1941], p. 300.

20 Horkheimer, 'The latest attack on metaphysics' [1937], p. 181.

21 Henryk Grossmann, Letter to Horkheimer, 1 August 1937, in Horkheimer, *GS*, vol. 16, p. 205.

22 Such neglect was arguably inherent in the focus on bourgeois society and its cultural products, but it was far from inevitable as Horkheimer's 'Egoism and the freedom movement' demonstrates. Indeed he was an acute observer of the nuances of social divisions. See Max Horkheimer, *Dawn and Decline* (New York, 1978).

23 Marcuse, '33 Theses' [1947], in *Technology, War and Fascism*, p. 217.

24 Marcuse, 'Struggle against liberalism in the totalitarian view of the state' [1932], in *Negations*, pp. 9–11.

25 Marcuse, 'State and individual under national socialism' [1942], in *Technology, War and Fascism*, pp. 80–1.

26 Horkheimer, 'The Jews and Europe' [1939], in Stephen Eric Bronner and Douglas MacKay Kelner (eds), *Critical Theory and Society* (London, 1989), p. 78. Compare Wittgenstein's 'What we cannot speak about we must pass over in silence', *Tractatus Logico-Philosophicus* (London, 1974), p. 74.

27 Friedrich Pollock, 'State capitalism', *ZfS*, 9 (1941), p. 223.

28 Horkheimer, Letter to Neumann, 2 August 1941, *GS*, vol. 17, p. 116. Neumann claimed that Pollock's ideal type 'implies a leap from one reality [capitalism] into another reality' which he held to be an improper use of an ideal type. Letter to Horkheimer, 23 July 1941, *ibid.*, p. 104.

29 Horkheimer, 'The Jews and Europe', p. 80. Translation amended, 'Die Juden und Europa', *GS*, vol. 4, p. 312.

30 Horkheimer, 'The Jews and Europe', pp. 89–90.

31 Gershom Scholem, *Walter Benjamin* (London, 1982), pp. 222–3. On Horkheimer's treatment of anti-Semitism see Dan Diner, 'Reason and the "other": Horkheimer's reflections on anti-semitism and mass annihilation', in S. Benhabib *et al.* (eds), *On Max Horkheimer* (Cambridge, Mass., 1993), pp. 335–63. Steven Beller, 'Germans and Jews as central European and Mitteleuropäisch elites', in Peter Stirk, *Mitteleuropa* (Edinburgh, 1994), pp. 61–85, throws light on the latter of Scholem's questions.

32 For the hesitation see Adorno's letter to Horkheimer of 2 July 1941, in Horkheimer, *GS*, vol. 17, p. 96; for his adoption of Pollock's thesis see 'Spengler today', *ZfS*, 9 (1941), p. 310.

33 See A. Schweitzer, 'Plans and markets, Nazi style', *Kyklos*, 30 (1977), pp. 88–115; P. Temin, 'Soviet and Nazi economic planning in the 1930s', *Economic History Review*, 44 (1991), pp. 573–93; Ludolf Herbst, 'Die nationalsozialistische Wirtschaftspolitik im internationalen Vergleich', in W. Benz *et al.* (eds), *Der Nationalsozialismus* (Frankfurt am Main, 1993), pp. 153–76.

34 Horkheimer, 'The Jews and Europe', p. 81.

35 This afflicts all efforts to construe the Nazi experience and above all the Holocaust as products of modernity rather than as products of the development of specific, European, societies. For the modernist interpretation see, for example, Götz Aly, 'The planning intelligentsia and the "final solution" ', in Michael Burleigh (ed.), *Confronting the Nazi Past* (London, 1996), pp. 140–53 and Zygmunt Baumann, *Modernity and the Holocuast* (Ithaca, 1989). For criticism of this thesis see Nobert Frei, 'Wie modern war der Nationalsozialismus', *Geschichte und Gesellschaft*, 19 (1993), pp. 367–87.

36 Horkheimer, 'The Jews and Europe', p. 78.

37 Horkheimer, *GS*, vol. 12, pp. 398–416. See also a related discussion in 1937, *ibid.*, pp. 417–30.
38 Adorno, 'Reflexionen zur Klassentheorie' [1942], in *Soziologische Schriften I*, p. 379.
39 *Ibid.*, p. 378.
40 Adorno, 'Anmerkungen zum sozialen Konflikt heute' [1968], in *Soziologische Schriften I*, p. 182.
41 Adorno, 'Is Marx obsolete?', p. 5.
42 Arkadij Gurland, 'Technological trends and economic structure under national socialism', *ZfS*, 9 (1941), p. 262. Gurland's account of the relationship between industry and the Nazis was much more accurate than Horkheimer's and Adorno's, (see pp. 240–4), though his grip occasionally slipped (see p. 263).
43 For Marcuse's concession see *One Dimensional Man* [1964], p. 36. For his continued usage see 'Re-examination of the concept of revolution', *New Left Review*, 56 (1969), pp. 30–1; 'Obsolescence of marxism', in Nikolaus Lobkowicz (ed.), *Marx and the Western World* (Notre Dame, 1967), p. 412; *Counterrevolution and Revolt* [1972], p. 9.
44 *Ibid.*, pp. 33–4.
45 Horkheimer, 'Montaigne and the function of skepticism' [1938], in *Between Philosophy and Social Sciences*, p. 268.
46 See Horkheimer, 'Die Philosophie der absoluten Konzentration' [1938], *GS*, vol. 4, pp. 295–307.
47 Horkheimer, 'Montaigne and the function of skepticism', p. 281.
48 *Ibid.*, p. 290. Translation modified, 'Montaigne und die Funktion der Skepsis', *GS*, vol. 4, p. 268.
49 Neumann, 'Intellectual and political freedom' [1954], in *The Democratic and the Authoritarian State*, p. 215.
50 Alfons Söllner, 'Marcuse's political theory in the 1940s and 1950s', *Telos*, 74 (1987–8), p. 78.
51 See, for example Marcuse, '33 theses', p. 227 and Helmut Dubiel, 'Demokratie und Kapitalismus bei Herbert Marcuse', in Institut für Sozialforschung (ed.), *Kritik und Utopie im Werk von Herbert Marcuse*, pp. 655–70. Marcuse's sympathy for some kind of educational dictatorship is still evident in 'Protosocialism and late capitalism' [1979], in Ulf Wolter (ed.), *Rudolf Bahro: Critical Responses* (White Plains, New York, 1980), pp. 30–2.
52 Herbert Marcuse, *The Aesthetic Dimension* (New York, 1978), pp. 38–9.
53 *Ibid.*, pp. 4, 38.
54 Herbert Marcuse, 'The reification of the proletariat', *Canadian Journal of Political and Social Theory*, 3 (1979), p. 22.
55 Marcuse, 'Protosocialism and late capitalism', p. 33.
56 See the interview 'Verwaltete Welt' [1970], in Horkheimer, *GS*, vol. 7, pp. 363–84.
57 Horkheimer, 'Was wir "Sinn" nennen wird verschwinden' [1970], *ibid.*, p. 348.
58 Horkheimer, 'Die Sehnsucht nach dem ganz Anderen' [1970], *ibid.*, pp. 385–404.
59 Die verwaltete Welt oder: Die Krisis des Individuums' [1950], in Horkheimer, *GS*, vol. 13, pp. 121–42, here p. 124. This debate, with Eugen Kogon, was broadcast by radio in 1950. On the relationship between Kogon and his friend Walter Dirks and Horkheimer and Adorno see Rudolf Siebert, 'Horkheimer's sociology of religion', *Telos*, 30 (1976), pp. 128–30.

60 Adorno, 'Kultur und Verwaltung' [1960], in *Soziologisches Schriften I*, p. 125.

61 Adorno, 'Individuum und Organisation' [1953], *ibid.*, p. 456.

62 For criticism of this approach in the context of interpretations of the origins of Nazism see George Steinmetz, 'German exceptionalism and the origins of Nazism', in Ian Kershaw and Moshe Lewin (eds), *Stalinism and Nazism. Dictatorships in Comparison* (Cambridge, 1997), pp. 268–70.

63 Ulrich Beck, *Risk Society* (London, 1992), p. 133.

64 On the importance of the eighteenth century for Habermas's model see Keith Michael Baker, 'Defining the public sphere in eighteenth century France', in Craig Calhoun (ed.), *Habermas and the Public Sphere* (Cambridge, Mass., 1992), pp. 187–9.

65 Habermas took the latter point from Hannah Arendt. Habermas, *Structural Transformation of the Public Sphere* [1962], p. 19.

66 *Ibid.*, p. 27. Habermas's examples are drawn predominantly from eighteenth-century Europe, and include coffee houses, salons, theatres and so on, *ibid.*, pp. 31–43 and 57–73.

67 *Ibid.*, pp. 35–6.

68 *Ibid.*, p. 127.

69 *Ibid.*, p. 142.

70 *Ibid.*, p. 156.

71 *Ibid.*, pp. 173–4.

72 *Ibid.*, p. 198.

73 Quoted in Habermas, *Legitimation Crisis* [1973], p. 77.

74 *Ibid.*, p. 83.

75 See again Beck, *Risk Society*, pp. 133–4. Stephen K. White points to a 'renewed emphasis' upon possessive individualism in the era of Thatcher and Reagan, *The Recent Work of Jürgen Habermas* (Cambridge, 1988), p. 122.

76 Habermas, *Legitimation Crisis*, p. 83.

77 See Hans-Dieter König, 'Autoritarismus und Konsumsteuerung', in Institut für Sozialforschung (ed.), *Kritik und Utopie im Werk von Herbert Marcuse*, pp. 217–46.

78 Dews (ed.), *Autonomy and Solidarity*, pp. 68, 141; 'Modernity and postmodernity', *New German Critique*, 22 (1981), p. 13.

79 For earlier reservations see Habermas, *Legitimation Crisis*, pp. 55–7. For assessments see Ingram, *Habermas and the Dialectic of Reason*, pp. 151–6 and 230–1 and Tom Rockmore, *Habermas on Historical Materialism* (Bloomington, 1989), pp. 128–46 especially the conclusion on p. 144 that Habermas sidesteps Marx's arguments about the theory of value.

80 Habermas, *The Theory of Communicative Action* [1981], vol. 2, p. 339.

81 Hence the claim that Marx failed to see 'that *every* modern society, whatever its class structure, has to exhibit a high degree of structural differentiation', *ibid.*, p. 340. If by this he meant the kind of structural differentiation characteristic of capitalist economies Habermas's claim is palpably false, unless he could plausibly dismiss Soviet style economies from the category of modern economies. The case of Nazi Germany is more ambivalent but it is also a potential obstacle to the claim.

82 *Ibid.*, p. 348.

83 *Ibid.*, p. 393. Habermas added some qualifications to the general assertion but feminist critics still discern a specific skew in his interpretation of feminism. See, for example, Marie Fleming, 'Women and the "public use of reason"', in Johanna Meehan (ed.) *Feminists Reading Habermas* (New York, 1995), pp. 117–19.

84 Habermas, *The Theory of Communicative Action*, vol. 2, p. 393. See also 'A Philo-sophico-Political Profile' [1985] in Dews (ed.), *Autonomy and Solidarity*, pp. 177–8.
85 Habermas, *The Theory of Communicative Action*, vol. 1, p. 70. There he character-izes it as a 'conservative counterweight' but it is important to emphasize that it should not be construed as a realm of prejudice, though it can be that. See White's statement that 'The real distinctiveness of Habermas's account of the lifeworld enters with the introduction of the concept of a "rationalized lifeworld."' *The Recent Work of Jürgen Habermas*, p. 97. For the claim that the lifeworld is the source of irrationalist doctrines see Jeffrey Alexander, 'Habermas and critical theory', in Axel Honneth and Hans Joas (eds), *Communicative Action* (Cambridge, 1991), pp. 61–2.
86 Habermas, *The Theory of Communicative Action*, vol. 2, p. 154. The screening out of issues of norms and identities from these spheres is highly questionable. In response to such criticism Habermas stepped back a little: 'my thesis amounts merely to the assertion that the integration of action systems is *in the final instance*' not based on such issues. 'A Reply' in Honneth and Joas (eds), *Communicative Action*, p. 257.
87 For the importance of the French Revolution see 'Interview mit Robert Maggiori' [1988], in *Die nachholende Revolution*, p. 34.
88 Habermas, 'Die Postnationale Konstellation und die Zukunft der Demokratie' [1998], p. 812.
89 Jürgen Habermas, 'On the internal relation between the rule of law and democracy', *European Journal of Philosophy*, 3 (1995), p. 18. For the criticism of 'spheres' of the private and the public see *Between Facts and Norms* [1992], pp. 400–9.
90 Jürgen Habermas, 'Kants Idee des ewigen Friedens' [1995], in *Die Einbeziehung des Anderen* (Frankfurt am Main, 1997), p. 204.
91 Habermas, *Between Facts and Norms*, pp. 366–7.

Chapter 7: Paradoxes of Reason

1   Habermas, *The Philosophical Discourse of Modernity* [1985], p. 16. From the perspective of one of the Young Hegelians, Feuerbach, this meant that 'One who understands the language in which the spirit of world history speaks, cannot fail to recognize that our present is the copestone of a whole period in the history of humanity and is precisely thereby the starting point of a new life.' Quoted in Karl Löwith, *Martin Heidegger and European Nihilism* (New York, 1995), p. 184.
2   Hegel, *Phenomenology of Spirit*, p. 17.
3   *Ibid.*, p. 51.
4   As for example in Herbert Marcuse, 'Zur Wahrheitsproblematik der soziologischen Methode', *Die Gesellschaft*, 6 (1929), p. 369.
5   Marcuse, *Reason and Revolution* [1941], p. 8.
6   *Ibid.*, p. 9. Marcuse's position could be classified under the category of 'expressivism' used by Charles Taylor, *Hegel* (Cambridge, 1975), pp. 13–50.
7   Marcuse, *Reason and Revolution*, p. 155.
8   *Ibid.*, p. 215.
9   Marcuse, 'Some social implications of modern technology' *ZfS* 9 (1941), p. 422.
10 *Ibid.*, p. 423. A similar point was made by Bertrand de Jouvenal, *Power* (London, 1947), p. 52, in relation to the replacement of the monarch by the 'nation' as the source of power.

11   Marcuse, 'Some social implications of modern technology', pp. 423–4. One of the supposed redeeming features was the extent to which technical justification for social hierarchy was fading, *ibid.*, pp. 429–30.

12   Horkheimer, 'Beginnings of the bourgeois philosophy of history' [1930], in *Between Philosphy and Social Science*, p. 362.

13   Horkheimer, 'The rationalism debate in contemporary philosophy' [1934], *ibid.*, pp. 220–1.

14   *Ibid.*, p. 238.

15   'Spirit in its formation matures slowly and quietly into its new shape, dissolving bit by bit the structure of its previous world, whose tottering state is only hinted at by isolated symptoms.' Hegel, *Phenomenology of Spirit*, p. 5.

16   Horkheimer, 'The rationalism debate in contemporary philosophy', p. 239.

17   Horkheimer, 'Traditional and critical theory' [1937], pp. 224–5; 'Beginnings of the bourgeois philosophy of history', pp. 357–60; 'On the problem of truth' [1935], pp. 435–7.

18   Horkheimer, 'The latest attack on metaphysics' [1937], p. 180.

19   Max Horkheimer, 'The end of reason', *ZfS*, 9 (1941), pp. 366–88; Horkheimer, 'Die Vernunft im Widerstreit mit sich selbet' [1946], in *GS*, 12, pp. 105–18; Horkheimer, *Eclipse of Reason* [1947].

20   Adorno and Horkheimer, *Dialectic of Enlightenment* [1944], p. xiii.

21   *Ibid.*, *Dialectic of Enlightenment*, p. xiv.

22   Letter to Weil, 13 January 1943, Horkheimer, *GS*, vol. 17, p. 397.

23   Adorno and Horkheimer, *Dialectic of Enlightenment*, p. x.

24   This criticism was raised by Paul Tillich. Horkheimer acknowledged that Tillich was right but defended his neglect of qualifications to his arguments on the grounds that they would distract from the horror of what was being perpetrated. Horkheimer, *GS*, vol. 17, p. 315. What he had in mind is indicated by the claim that 'Subordinate clauses belong to the juristic, discursive phase of thought. Primitive and totalitarian [phases] speak in main sentences. "The Jew will be burned." In more differentiated social systems it would at least have run: "If the Jew does not convert … "'; 'Haupt- und Nebensatz' [1942], Horkheimer, *GS*, vol. 12, p. 279.

25   Horkheimer, 'The end of reason' [1941], p. 367.

26   *Ibid.*, p. 377.

27   *Ibid.*, p. 386.

28   Adorno and Horkheimer, *Dialectic of Enlightenment*, pp. 43–7.

29   *Ibid.*, p. 8.

30   For the latter see Hegel, *Phenomenology of Spirit*, pp. 111–19 and the quotation from that section in Adorno and Horkheimer, *Dialectic of Enlightenment*, p. 35.

31   Horkheimer, *Eclipse of Reason* [1947], p. 106. See also Adorno and Horkheimer, *Dialectic of Enlightenment*, p. 21.

32   *Ibid.*, p. 15. See also Adorno's later assertion, 'The undifferentiated state before the subject's formation was the dread of the blind web of nature, of myth; it was in protest against it that the great religions had their truth content.' 'Subject and object' [1969], in Andrew Arato and Eike Gebhardt (eds), *The Essential Frankfurt School Reader* (Oxford, 1978), p. 499.

33   Hence 'In the self-cognition of the spirit as nature in disunion with itself, as in prehistory, nature calls itself to account; no longer as *mana* – that is, with the alias that

signifies omnipotence – but as blind and lame.' Adorno and Horkheimer, *Dialectic of Enlightenment*, p. 39.

34 *Ibid.*, p. 103. Translation amended, Horkheimer, *GS*, vol. 5, p. 126.

35 Adorno and Horkheimer, *Dialectic of Enlightenment*, p. 102.

36 *Ibid.*, p. 87.

37 *Ibid.*, p. 118.

38 David Hume, *A Treatise of Human Nature, Books Two and Three* (London, 1972), pp. 156–7.

39 On this see A.C. Baier, *A Progress of Sentiments: Reflections on Hume's Treatise* (Cambridge, Mass., 1991).

40 Horkheimer, *Eclipse of Reason*, p. 127.

41 Adorno and Horkheimer, *Dialectic of Enlightenment*, p. 37.

42 Jürgen Habermas, 'Notes on the developmental history of Horkheimer's work' [1986], *Theory, Culture and Society*, 10 (1993), p. 73.

43 Letter of 14 September 1941, Horkheimer, *GS*, vol. 17, p. 172.

44 Horkheimer, *GS*, vol. 12, pp. 593–605. Anson Rabinbach stresses Horkheimer's admiration of Schopenhauer as the main obstacle; *In the Shadow of Catastrophe. German Intellectuals between Apocalypse and Enlightenment* (Berkeley, 1997), p. 197. But this is only half the point. It was the failure to agree on a turn to the political agenda which pushed Horkheimer towards making Schopenhauer central in his own later work.

45 Adorno, *Negative Dialectics* [1966], p. 85.

46 *Ibid.*, p. 46.

47 Theodor Adorno, *Against Epistemology* [1956] (Oxford, 1982), p. 234.

48 Habermas, *The Philosophical Discourse of Modernity* [1985], p. 128.

49 Habermas, 'Dogmatism, reason and decision: on theory and praxis in our scientific civilization' [1963], in *Theory and Practice*, p. 282.

50 *Ibid.*, p. 275. There was still an echo of the ambitions of critical theory in the early 1930s in Habermas's comment that 'The root of the irrationality of history is that we "make" it, without, however, having been able until now to make it consciously.' *Ibid.*, pp. 275–6.

51 Habermas, *Knowledge and Human Interests* [1968], p. 208.

52 *Ibid.*, p. 211.

53 See Richard J. Bernstein, *The Restructuring of Social and Political Theory* (Oxford, 1976), pp. 221–2.

54 Jürgen Habermas, 'Some distinctions in universal pragmatics', *Theory and Society*, 33 (1976), p. 160. See also 'Vorlesungen zu einer sprachtheoretischen Grundlegung der Soziologie' [1970–1971], in *Vorstudien und Ergänzungen zur Theorie des kommunikativen Handelns*, p. 110.

55 *Ibid.*, p. 111.

56 Habermas, 'Some distinctions in universal pragmatics', p. 160.

57 Strictly we might continue to talk to the liar or the criminal for strategic reasons, for example, long enough for the police to arrive and arrest him, but we would not be trying to reach an understanding with him in any meaningful sense. Habermas has repeatedly emphasized that most situations fall into a grey area. See for example, 'What is universal pragmatics?' [1976], in *Communication and the Evolution of Society*, p. 3.

58 Habermas, *Theory of Communicative Action* [1981], vol. 1, p. xxxix. For criticism of

some of the detail see John B. Thompson, 'Universal pragmatics', in Thompson and Held (eds), *Habermas*, pp. 116–33. Habermas's reply is in *ibid.*, pp. 269–74.

59 *Ibid.*, p. 270 where Habermas also felt that this focus was being underplayed by his critics.

60 Habermas, *Theory of Communicative Action*, vol. 1, p. 15.

61 *Ibid.*, p. 88.

62 *Ibid.*, pp. 85–94.

63 *Ibid.*, p. 144.

64 *Ibid.*, p. 145. For an objection to the use of 'system rationality' see Herbert Schnä-delbach, 'Remarks about rationality and language', in Seyla Benhabib and Fred Dallmayr (eds), *The Communicative Ethics Controversy* (Cambridge, Mass., 1991), p. 274.

65 Habermas, *Theory of Communicative Action*, vol. 1, pp. 197–8.

66 *Ibid.*, vol. 2, p. 330.

67 *Ibid.*, vol. 1, p. 240.

68 See the sympathetic assessments in Ingram, *Habermas and the Dialectic of Reason* and White, *The Recent Work of Jürgen Habermas*.

69 Habermas, *Between Facts and Norms* [1992], p. 4. Hence the complaint of Seyla Benhabib, that 'Any number of universalistic ethical theories are compatible with these rules of argumentation'; *Critique, Norm and Utopia* (New York, 1986), p. 325.

70 Habermas, *Between Facts and Norms*, p. 5.

71 Habermas, 'Remarks on discourse ethics' [1991], in *Justification and Application*, p. 34.

Chapter 8: The Contours of Critical Theory

1 He added facetiously, 'Now I can ask you [the interviewer Helmut Dubiel], you have even written a book about it.' Löwenthal, *Mitmachen wollte ich nie* [1980], p. 77. For an example of survey stressing methodology, see Raymond A. Morrow, *Critical Theory and Methodology* (London, 1994).

2 Horkheimer, 'Materialism and metaphysics' [1933], p. 45.

3 Susan Buck-Morss, *The Origin of Negative Dialectics* (Hassocks, 1977), p. 186. See also Gillian Rose, *The Melancholy Science* (London, 1978), pp. 11–26.

4 Adorno, *Vorlesung zur Einleitung in die Soziologie* [1968], p. 90.

5 *Ibid.*, p. 84.

6 See the comment in Theodor Adorno, *Prisms* [1967], (Cambridge, Mass., 1981), pp. 7–8.

7 Habermas, *The Theory of Communicative Action* [1981], vol. 1, p. xxxix.

8 Löwenthal, *Mitmachen wollte ich nie*, p. 79.

9 Habermas, 'Some difficulties in the attempt to link theory and practice' [1971], pp. 34–6; *The Theory of Communicative Action*, vol. 1, pp. 355–65, especially p. 364.

10 Horkheimer, *GS*, vol. 11 [1926–31], pp. 264–6. For more explicit criticsm see *ibid.*, p. 223. For a contrasting view see Helmut Dubiel, *Wissenschaftsorganisation und politische Erfahrung* (Frankfurt am Main, 1978), pp. 39–40, who argues that Hor-kheimer intially accepted Lukacs's thesis and only abandoned it later. Adorno's

position is well summarized by Simon Jarvis, *Adorno* (Cambridge, 1998), p. 54. Marcuse's attitude was equivocal, see Barry Katz, *Herbert Marcuse. Art of Liberation* (London, 1982), pp. 62–3, but was not far from a 'metaphysical transfiguration of revolution' himself.

11 *Hegel's Science of Logic* (London, 1969), pp. 580–1. Partially quoted in Adorno, *Against Epistemology* [1956], p. 5.

12 See Chapter 3.

13 The second assumption distinguishes metacritique from critique according to Garbis Kortian, *Metacritiqure* (Cambridge, 1980), who also points to Adorno's *Metakritik der Erkenntnistheorie* (Frankfurt am Main, 1956) and much earlier titles by Herder and Hamman, pp. 28–9. The connection is lost in the misleading translation of Adorno's title as *Against Epistemology*. This brief enumeration of three assumptions inevitably glosses over a great deal. For a more detailed overview see Karl Röttgers, *Kritik und Praxis* (Berlin, 1975), pp. 139–64.

14 Horkheimer, 'Notes on institute activities', *ZfS*, 9 (1941), p. 122. See also *Eclipse of Reason* [1947], especially the claim that 'Philosophy takes existing values seriously but insists that they become parts of a theoretical whole that reveals their relativity', p. 183.

15 Horkheimer, 'Egoism and the freedom movement' [1936], pp. 52–3.

16 *Ibid.*, pp. 54–5.

17 *Ibid.*, pp. 107–8.

18 Horkheimer, 'Die Philosophie der absoluten Konzentration' [1938], *GS*, vol. 4, p. 297.

19 But not entirely implausible if the term self-determination is used in place of freedom. Thus the redemption of our Austrian brothers, that is the unification of Austria and Nazi Germany, was presented as an act of self-determination by Austrian Germans. One could, rightly, respond that this was no act of self-determination but the product of manipulation and the threat of the use of force. However, to stop at this point would be to ignore the popularity of Hitler within Austria and the complicity of many Austrians in the subsequent policies of the Third Reich.

20 Horkheimer, 'On the problem of truth' [1935], pp. 433–4.

21 Horkheimer, 'The authoritarian state' [1940], in Arato and Gebhardt (eds), *The Essential Frankfurt School Reader*, pp. 108–9.

22 *Ibid.*, p. 101.

23 *Ibid.*, p. 107.

24 As Horkheimer's language suggests, this amounts to smuggling Kant's realm of freedom into Marx's theory of history; *ibid.*, p. 96. Confronted with the same contrast between the compulsivenss of the present and the corresponding elevation of the revolutionary act, Marcuse could only conclude that 'freedom has shrunk to the possibility of recognizing and seizing the necessity for liberation.' Marcuse, 'Sartre's existentialism' [1948], in *Studies in Critical Philosophy*, p. 183. See also Herbert Marcuse, 'Zum Begriff der Negation in der Dialektik', *Ideen zu einer Kritischen Theorie der Gesellschaft* (Frankfurt am Main, 1978), p. 186; Herbert Marcuse, 'The end of utopia' [1967], in *Five Lectures* (London, 1970), pp. 62–3.

25 Adorno, 'Reflexionen zur Klassentheorie' [1942], *Soziologische Schriften I*, p. 373.

26 Letter of 28 October 1937, in Horkheimer, *GS*, vol. 16, p. 256. For what Adorno had in mind see *Against Epistemology*, for example pp. 51–4 and 76–7.

27 Letter of 23 October 1937, in Horkheimer, *GS*, vol. 16, p. 255.

28 See the reference to Durkheim, *Against Epistemology*, p. 76.

29 For Marcuse see *Reason and Revolution* [1941]. For Adorno see *Drei Studien zu Hegel* [1963], pp. 10–26.

30 Marcuse, 'The foundations of historical materialism' [1932], in *Studies in Critical Philosophy*, pp. 21–2. Marcuse's was one of the earliest extensive reviews of this text. For Adorno, with a slightly more extensive quotation, see *Drei Studien zu Hegel*, p. 23.

31 *Ibid.*, pp. 24–5.

32 Adorno, *Negative Dialectics* [1966], p. 97.

33 Georg Lukacs, *History and Class Consciousness* (London, 1971), pp. 27–8.

34 See also Adorno's rejection of this 'metpahysics of history' and his assertion that compared to Lukacs's dialectic he preferred positivism. Horkheimer, *GS*, vol. 12, pp. 364, 527–8. Further see Adorno, *Negative Dialectics*, pp. 190–1 and Rose, *Melancholy Science*, pp. 40–1.

35 Adorno, *Negative Dialectics*, pp. 314–16.

36 'It is only because, to survive, they have to make an alien cause their own that there arises that appearance of reconcilement – an appearance which Hegelian philosophy, incorruptible in its recognition of the predominance of the universal, corruptibly transfigures into an idea.' *Ibid.*, p. 311.

37 Horkheimer, 'Traditional and critical theory' [1937], p. 227.

38 *Ibid.*

39 Thus the title of an interview in 1970, 'Die Sehnsucht nach dem ganz Anderen', Horkheimer, *GS*, vol. 7, pp. 385–404.

40 Marcuse, *Counterrevolution and Revolt* [1972], p. 34. For the initial tenacity see *Reason and Revolution*, p. 322.

41 Marcuse, 'Marginalien zu Theorie und Praxis' [1969], *Stichworte* (Frankfurt am Main, 1969), p. 175.

42 Horkheimer, 'Zur Zukunft der Kritischen Theorie' [1971], *GS*, vol. 7, p. 423.

43 Karl Marx, *Grundrisse* (Harmondsworth, 1973), p. 107.

44 Horkheimer, 'On the problem of truth', p. 437. An example of this would be the concept of enlightenment in *Dialectic of Enlightenment* [1944]. See Chapter 7.

45 Adorno traced it back to Kant, *Philosophische Terminologie* [1962–3], vol. 1, pp. 10–12.

46 Kant, *Critique of Pure Reason* (London, 1933), p. 588. Kant exempted only mathematics from this injunction, *ibid.*, p. 586.

47 Theodor Adorno, *Ohne Leitbild. Parva Aesthetica* (Frankfurt am Main, 1967), p. 7.

48 Adorno, *Stichworte*, p. 10.

49 Habermas, 'The classical doctrine of politics in relation to social philosophy' [1963], in *Theory and Practice*, p. 41.

50 See Chapter 4.

51 According to Apel he succumbed to a 'simple identification of reflection and practical engagement'. Quoted in McCarthy, *The Critical Theory of Jürgen Habermas*, p. 96. See also Matthias Kettner, 'Karl-Otto Apel's contribution to critical theory', in David M. Rasmussen (ed.), *Handbook of Critical Theory* (Oxford, 1996), p. 269.

52 Habermas, 'Some difficulties in the attempt to link theory and practice' [1971], p. 40.

53 *Ibid.*, p. 33.

54 Jürgen Habermas, 'A Postscript to *Knowledge and Human Interests*', *Philosophy of the Social Sciences*, 3 (1973), p. 182. See also Habermas, 'Some difficulties in the attempt to link theory and practice', pp. 22–3.

55 Habermas, 'A reply to my critics' [1982], in Thompson and Held (eds), *Habermas*, pp. 230–2.

56 Habermas, *Knowledge and Human Interests* [1968], p. 42.

57 Habermas, 'Labor and interaction: remarks on Hegel's Jena *Philosophy of Mind*' [1967], in *Theory and Practice*, pp. 168–9.

58 Habermas, 'Toward a reconstruction of historical materialism' [1976], p. 130.

59 *Ibid.*, p. 140.

60 *Ibid.*

61 See also Habermas, 'History and evolution', *Telos*, 39 (1979), pp. 5–44. But in an interview he suggested that this precedence was not a logical consequence of the distinction. 'A Philosophico-political profile' [1985], in Dews (ed.), *Autonomy and Solidarity*, p. 164.

62 See Chapter 4.

63 Quoted in Habermas, *The Theory of Communicative Action* [1981], vol. 1, p. 110.

64 *Ibid.*, p. 114.

65 *Ibid.*, p. 115.

66 See Herbert Schnädelbach, 'The transformation of critical theory', in Honneth and Joas (eds), *Communicative Action*, pp. 15–16. Schnädelbach focuses on Habermas's attempt to justify the link between understanding and assessing validity at a more formal level, later on in *The Theory of Communicative Action*.

67 For the importance of this see Chapter 7, pp. 124–5.

68 Quoted in Habermas, *The Theory of Communicative Action*, vol. 2, p. 402.

69 *Ibid.*, p. 403. See also Habermas, 'The dialectics of rationalization' [1981], in Dews (ed.), *Autonomy and Solidarity*, p. 100.

70 Habermas, *The Theory of Communicative Action*, vol. 1, p. 341.

71 Jürgen Habermas, 'Eine genealogische Betrachtung zum kognitiven Gehalt der Moral' [1996], pp. 62–3; *Erläuterungen zur Diskursethik* (Frankfurt am Main, 1991), p. 134; 'Discourse ethics: Notes on a program of philosophical justification' [1983], in *Moral Consciosness and Communicative Action*, pp. 93–4.

72 See, for example, Jürgen Habermas, 'Towards a theory of communicative competence', *Inquiry*, 13 (1970), pp. 372–4. There is already a question mark in the comment 'as form of life to be realised in the future?' in 'Wahrheitstheorien' [1973], in *Vorstudien und Ergänzungen zur Theorie des kommunikativen Handelns*, p. 181.

73 See Habermas, 'A reply to my critics', pp. 261–2; 'Morality, society and ethics' [1990], in *Justification and Application*, pp. 163–5; 'The unity of reason in the diversity of its voices', [1992] in *Postmetaphysical Thinking*, pp. 142–6.

74 Jürgen Habermas, 'What theories can accomplish – and what they can't', in *The Past as Future* (London, 1994), p. 113.

75 'Interview mit Barbara Freitag' [1989], in Habermas, *Die nachholende Revolution*, pp. 109–10.

76 Habermas, *Between Facts and Norms* [1992], p. 373.

77 'An interview with Jürgen Habermas', *Theory, Culture and Society*, 13(3) (1996), p. 6.

78 'The capitalist process of production has thus driven a wedge between the interest in

socialism and the human qualities necessary to its implementation.' Horkheimer, *Dawn and Decline* [1926–31], p. 62.

79 For a very clear statement see Habermas 'Coping with contingencies – the return of historicism', in Jozef Niznik and John T. Sanders (ed.), *Debating the State of Philosophy* (Westport, 1996), pp. 23–4.

Chapter 9: The Authoritarian and the Democratic State

1 Royal Institute of International Affairs, *Survey of International Affairs 1931* (Oxford, 1932), p. 5. For an economist's view see Wilhelm Röpke, 'Die säkulare Bedeutung der Weltkrisis', *Weltwirtschaftliches Archive*, 37 (1933), pp. 1–27. For a philosopher's view see Edmund Husserl, *The Crisis of the European Sciences and Transcendental Phenomenology* (Evanston, 1970).

2 Pollock 'Die gegenwärtige Lage des Kapitalismus und die Aussichten einer plan-wirtschaftlichen Neuordnung', *ZfS*, 1 (1932), p. 8.

3 Karl Dietrich Bracher, *The Age of Ideologies* (London, 1984), pp. 130–46, especially p. 133.

4 According to Maier, this stabilization 'involved the displacement of power from elected representatives or a career bureaucracy to the major organized forces of European society and government, sometimes bargaining directly amongst them-selves, sometimes exerting influence through a weakened parliament, and occasionally seeking advantages through new executive authority'. Charles Maier, *Recasting Bourgeois Europe* (Princeton, 1975), p. 9.

5 Under this heading Horkheimer recalled that 'Whenever during the years 1927 and 1928 "literary radicals" told me that capitalism had once again stabilized for the foreseeable future, they were never as downcast as when they related some personal misfortune.' *Dawn and Decline*, p. 78.

6 Marcuse, 'Zur Warheitsproblematik der soziologischen Methode' [1929], p. 358. See also his praise of Hans Freyer for grasping 'not the logical, not the ethical, not the pure epistemological, but rather the activist-decisive attitude as the basic character of the science of sociology'. 'Zur Auseinandersetzung mit Hans Freyers "Soziologie als Wirklichkeitswissenschaft"' [1931], in Marcuse, *Schriften*, vol. 1, p. 488.

7 Otto Kirchheimer, 'The Socialist and the Bolshevik theory of state' [1928], in Frederic S. Burin and Kurt L. Shell (eds), *Politics, Law and Social Change. Selected Essays of Otto Kirchheimer* (New York, 1969), p. 15. Translation modified, Otto Kirchheimer, *Von der Weimarer Republik zum Faschismus* (Frankfurt am Main, 1976), p. 45.

8 William E. Scheuerman, *Between the Norm and the Exception* (Cambridge, Mass., 1994), pp. 27–30. Alfons Söllner, 'Jenseits von Carl Schmitt', *Geschichte und Gesell-schaft*, 12 (1986), pp. 509–10, tries to mitigate Kirchheimer's agreement on the principle of homogeneity.

9 Kirchheimer, 'Marxism, dictatorship and the organization of the proletariat' [1933], in Burin and Shell (eds), *Politics, Law and Social Change*, p. 32.

10 Otto Kirchheimer, 'Remarks on Carl Schmitt's *Legality and Legitimacy*' [1933], in William E. Scheuerman (ed.), *The Rule of Law under Siege* (Berkeley, 1996), p. 66.

11 *Ibid.*

12 *Ibid.*, p. 74.

13 *Ibid.*, p. 66.

14 Franz Neumann, 'The social significance of the basic laws in the Weimar constitution' [1930], in *Economy and Society*, **10** (1981), p. 342.

15 Quoted in Volker Neumann, 'Kompromiss oder Entscheidung', in Joachim Perels (ed.), *Recht, Demokratie und Kapitalismus* (Baden-Baden, 1984), p. 77.

16 *Ibid.*, pp. 67–8. See also Söllner's contribution in Erd (ed.), *Gespräche über Franz Neumann*, pp. 47–8.

17 On the origins of this strategy in the ideas of Hugo Sinzheimer, Otto Bauer and Karl Renner see *ibid.*, pp. 34–5.

18 The letter is reproduced in *ibid.*, pp. 79–80. Scheuerman sees stronger links to Schmitt, *Between the Norm and the Exception*, pp. 55–61, but acknowledges that the constraints of the political situation were severe, *ibid.*, p. 59.

19 Neumann, 'The decay of German democracy' [1933], in Scheuerman (ed.), *The Rule of Law under Siege*, p. 43.

20 'Verfassungsreform und Sozialdemokratie' [1932], in Otto Kirchheimer, *Funktionen des Staats und der Verfassung* (Frankfurt am Main, 1972), pp. 94–5. The action of 20 July 1932 was the dismissal of the socialist–centre coaltion government in Prussia by Chancellor Fritz von Papen.

21 For the weakness see his observation that 'even the ideologists of the new regime ought to see that the contrasting of parties and people is nothing but a catchword of the presidential party [*Präsidialpartei*], not a sociological reality.' Kirchheimer, 'Constitutional reaction in 1932' [1932], in Burin and Shell (eds), *Politics, Law and Social Change*, p. 86.

22 Quoted in Marcuse, 'The struggle against liberalism in the totalitarian view of the state', [1934], p. 41. Part of the problem was that all offers, and there were several, to draft a new constitution for the Third Reich were rebuffed by Hitler.

23 Franz Neumann, *The Rule of Law* [1936] (Leamington Spa, 1986), p. 298.

24 *Ibid.*, p. 275.

25 Neumann, 'Types of natural law' [1940], in *The Democratic and the Authoritarian State*, p. 90.

26 Neumann, *Behemoth* [1942], p. 382. The dual state thesis was advanced by Ernst Fraenkel, *The Dual State* (Oxford, 1941). The thesis has been criticized more recently for neglecting the activist role of even the 'traditional' bureaucracies. See Jane Caplan: 'the ultimate clash was not between the adminstrative rationality of the state and the dynamic parasitism of the party, but between two political concepts that were equally dynammic and irrational'. *Government and Adminstration* (Oxford, 1988), p. 337.

27 Neumann, *Behemoth*, pp. 382–3.

28 Horkheimer, 'The Jews and Europe' [1939], p. 85.

29 *Ibid.*

30 Horkheimer, 'Zur Soziologie der Klassenverhältnisse' [1943], *GS*, vol. 12, p. 102.

31 Horkheimer, 'Die Racket und der Geist' [1939–42], *ibid.*, p. 288; 'The end of reason' [1941], p. 379.

32 Letter to Horkheimer, 20 September 1943, *GS*, vol. 17, pp. 474–5. Despite which Kirchheimer too used it in an overtly more expansive manner than its quasi-legalistic origins suggested. See Kirchheimer, 'In quest of sovereignty'' (1944), in Burin and Shell (eds), *Politics, Law and Social Change*, pp. 178–80.

33 The broader difficulties of the concept of rackets are discussed in Stirk, *Max Horkheimer*, pp. 209–11.

34 Adorno's criticism was directed at Brecht's play, *The Resistable Rise of Arturi Ui*. See

Theodor Adorno, 'Engagement' [1962], *Noten zur Literatur* (Frankfurt am Main, 1974), pp. 417–18.

35 Otto Kirchheimer, 'Criminal law in National Socialist Germany', *ZfS*, **8** (1940), p. 448.

36 *Ibid.*, p. 453.

37 *Ibid.*, pp. 453–4.

38 Otto Kirchheimer, 'The legal order of national socialism', *ZfS*, **9** (1941), p. 461.

39 As is noted by Caplan, *Government and Adminstration*, p. 330. See Michael Geyer, 'The state in National Socialist Germany', in C. Bright and S. Harding (eds), *State Making and Social Movements* (New York, 1984), pp. 193–232, especially his reference to the various agencies which he characterizes as 'producers of domination ... entering and occupying the political arena as autonomus political actors', p. 204.

40 See the draft '[Die UdSSR und der Frieden]' [1950], in Horkheimer, *GS*, vol. 19, pp. 29–31 and the editorial note on p. 28.

41 In correspondence in September and October 1946, Horkheimer, *GS*, vol. 17, p. 761.

42 Horkheimer, 'The authoritarian state' [1940], p. 101. See also p. 115. On this see Dubiel, *Wissenschaftsorganisation*, pp. 91–4.

43 Douglas Kellner, *Herbert Marcuse and the Crisis of Marxism* (Basingstoke, 1984), p. 224–5. See also Kellner's observation on Marcuse's blend of criticism and 'apologetic overtones', p. 227.

44 Marcuse, *Soviet Marxism* [1958], p. 15.

45 *Ibid.*, pp. 99–100. See also Kellner, *Herbert Marcuse*, pp. 206–12.

46 Horkheimer, 'Die Bildungsauftrag der Gewerkschaften' (1962), in *GS*, vol. 8, p. 201.

47 *Ibid.*, pp. 215–16.

48 Horkheimer, 'Der Wahlsieg de Gaulles', *GS*, vol. 14, pp. 488–9. The Gaullists won 385 out of 485 seats.

49 Kirchheimer, 'France from the Fourth to the Fifth Republic' (1958), in Burin and Shell (eds), *Politics, Law and Social Change*, p. 243.

50 Otto Kirchheimer, 'Changes in the structure of political compromise', *ZfS*, **9** (1941), pp. 264–89, especially the conclusion on p. 288.

51 Kirchheimer, 'The waning of opposition in parliamentary regimes' (1957) and 'The transformation of the western European party system' (1966), in Burin and Shell (eds), *Politics, Law and Social Change*, pp. 299 and 351–4.

52 *Ibid.*, pp. 369–70.

53 Kirchheimer, 'Party structure and mass democarcy in Europe' [1954], *ibid.*, p. 267.

54 Neumann, 'The labor movement in Germany', in Hans J. Morgenthau (ed.), *Germany and the Future of Europe* (Chicago, 1951), p. 102.

55 Neumann, 'The concept of political freedom' [1953], p. 192.

56 *Ibid.*, p. 189.

57 F. A. Hayek, *The Constitution of Liberty* (London, 1960) and Bruno Leoni, *Freedom and the Law* (Indianapolis, 1991).

58 Kirchheimer, 'The *Rechtsstaat* as magic wall' [1967], in Burin and Shell (eds), *Politics, Law and Social Change*, p. 434, quoted in Scheuerman, *Between Norm and Exception*, p. 223. For Scheuerman's own examples of United States' legislation see *ibid.*, p. 212.

59 Kirchheimer, '*Rechtsstaat* as magic wall', pp. 441–4.

60 Kirchheimer, 'Private man and mass society' (1966), in Burin and Shell (eds), *Politics, Law and Social Change*, pp. 458–9 and 477.

61 Kirchheimer, 'Party structure and mass democracy in Europe', in *ibid.*, p. 268. On Marcuse see Helmut Dubiel, 'Demokratie und Kapitalismus bei Herbert Marcuse' in Institut für Sozialforschung (ed.), *Kritik und Utopie im Werk von Herbert Marcuse*, pp. 61–73. His claim that 'For Marcuse liberal-democratic institutions have no normative value per se', p. 69, goes too far.

62 Neumann, 'Economics and politics in the twentieth centuries' [1951], in *The Democratic and the Authoritarian State*, pp. 268 and 264.

63 Jürgen Habermas, 'Reply to symposium participants', in Michael Rosenfield and Andrew Arato (eds), *Habermas on Law and Democracy* (Berkeley, 1998), p. 437.

64 Habermas, *The Structural Transformation of the Public Sphere* [1962], p. 81.

65 *Ibid.*, p. 83.

66 *Ibid.*, p. 82.

67 *Ibid.*, p. 137, quoting Mill.

68 *Ibid.*, p. 198.

69 *Ibid.*, pp. 241–2.

70 *Ibid.*, p. 232.

71 Habermas, 'Legitimation problems in the modern state' [1976], in *Communication and the Evolution of Society*, p. 187.

72 *Ibid.*, p. 186. Compare Marcuse's affirmation of direct democracy in *Counterrevolution and Revolt* [1972], pp. 44–5.

73 Habermas, 'Ideologies and society in the post-war world' [1979] in Dews (ed.), *Autonomy and Solidarity*, pp. 52–3.

74 Habermas, 'Die Utopie des guten Herrschers' (1972), in *Kleine Politische Schriften I–IV*, pp. 325–6; *Legitimation Crisis* [1973], pp. 136–8.

75 Habermas, 'A philosophico-political profile' [1985], in Dews (ed.), *Autonomy and Solidarity*, p. 179. He did express some optimism about the Greens and even noted 'salutory effects . . . on the internal life of the SPD.' *Ibid.*

76 Habermas, 'Zivil Ungehorsam-Testfall für den demokratischen Rechtsstaat' [1983], in *Die Neue Unübersichtlichkeit*, pp. 83–4.

77 Habermas, *The Theory of Communicative Action* [1981], vol. 2, p. 177.

78 Günter Dux, 'Communicative reason and interest', in Honneth and Joas (eds), *Communicative Action*, pp. 92–3.

79 Charles Tilly, 'War making and state making as organized crime', in Peter B. Evans *et al.* (eds), *Bringing the State Back In* (Cambridge, 1985), p. 169.

80 Habermas, *The Theory of Communicative Action*, vol. 2, p. 365. Habermas took the idea of media-steered systems from Parson's attempt to find analogies for the role of money within the economy, *ibid.*, pp. 256–76.

81 *Ibid.*, pp. 358–61.

82 Habermas, *Between Facts and Norms* [1992], p. 416. See also 'An interview with Jürgen Habermas' [1996], p. 14.

83 Jürgen Habermas, 'Reconciliation through the use of reason: remarks on John Rawls's political liberalism', *Journal of Philosophy*, 92 (1995), p. 128. Rawls responded by expressing some surprise at this, 'Reply to Habermas', *ibid.*, pp. 154–6.

84 Habermas, *Between Facts and Norms*, p. 122.

85 *Ibid.*

86 *Ibid.*
87 *Ibid.*, p. 123.
88 *Ibid.*
89 Quoted in *ibid.*, p. 148.
90 *Ibid.*
91 *Ibid.*, pp. 298–9. The elision of the republican conception and the idea of a macro-social subject – where the latter carries the overtones of German idealism – is somewhat strained.
92 For some general observations on the threats to communicative power see Klaus Günther, 'Communicative freedom, communicative power and jurisgenesis', in Rosenfield and Arato (eds), *Habermas on Law and Democracy*, pp. 248–50.
93 Habermas, *Between Facts and Norms*, p. 374.

Chapter 10: Morality and Interests

1 Immanuel Kant, *Critique of Judgement* (Oxford, 1952), p. 9.
2 Kant, *Critique of Pure Reason*, p. 469.
3 On this see Howard Williams, *Kant's Political Philosophy* (Oxford, 1983).
4 Hegel, *Phenomenology of Spirit*, pp. 374–83, especially p. 377.
5 Marx, 'On the Jewish question', in *Early Writings*, p. 234.
6 Schnädelbach, *Philosophy in Germany*, p. 161.
7 Adorno, 'Introduction' [1969], *The Positivist Dispute*, pp. 61–2. The South West German School was founded by Heinrich Rickert and Wilhelm Windelband.
8 *Ibid.*, p. 62.
9 Horkheimer, *Dawn and Decline* [1926–31], p. 84. It is 'of his own making' in the sense that what Weber called the Protestant ethic was a bourgeois creed. It is still reflected in Veblen's criticism of the leisure class. See Adorno, 'Veblen's attack on culture' [1941], p. 400.
10 Muted insofar as he denied that it was possible to construct a socialist ethics on the basis of Kant. See Manfred B. Steger, *The Quest for Evolutionary Socialism* (Cambridge, 1997), pp. 113–19.
11 Heinrich Cunow, *Die Marxsche Geschichts-, Gesellschafts- und Staatstheorie* (Berlin, 1923), vol. 2, p. 301.
12 *Ibid.*, p. 302.
13 Horkheimer, 'Materialism and morality' [1933], p. 25.
14 '[M]orality rests upon the distinction between interest and duty'; *Ibid.*
15 *Ibid.*, p. 22.
16 *Ibid.*, p. 23.
17 Horkheimer, 'Materialism and metaphysics' [1933], p. 23.
18 *Ibid.*, p. 44.
19 Horkheimer, 'Materialism and morality', p. 27.
20 Herbert Schnädelbach, 'Max Horkheimer and the moral philosophy of German idealism', *Telos*, **66** (1985–6), p. 92.
21 Horkheimer, 'Materialism and morality', pp. 38–40.
22 Schnädelbach, 'Max Horkheimer and the moral philosophy of German idealism', p. 94.

23 Herbert Marcuse, 'Zur Kritik des Hedonismus', *ZfS*, 7 (1938), pp. 55–89 is translated as 'On hedonism', *Negations*, pp. 159–200.

24 *Ibid.*, p. 170. Marcuse's link between hedonism and the epistemological respect for sense-experience is strengthened by the ambiguity of the German term *Sinnlichkeit*. He drew this out explicitly in *Eros and Civilization* [1955]: 'In German, *sensuousness* and *sensuality* are still rendered by one and the same terms: *Sinnlichkeit*. It connotes instinctual (especially sexual) gratification as well as cognitive sense-perceptiveness and representation (sensation)', p. 133.

25 Marcuse, 'On hedonism', p. 178.

26 What Marcuse meant may be better clarified by Karl Kraus's ambiguous accounts of prostitution and sexual scandal in the Habsburg Empire. Although lacking the direct link to any political struggle suggested by Marcuse, Kraus counterposed an exaggerated amoral sexuality to the prevalent, and hypocritical, demonization of sexuality. The point, as Edward Timms puts it, was to reject 'a double standard of morality, denying to women sexual freedoms readily conceded to men.' Edward Timms, *Karl Kraus* (New Haven, 1986), p. 63.

27 Marcuse, 'On hedonism', p. 194.

28 Schnädelbach, 'Max Horkheimer and the moral philosophy of German idealism', p. 97.

29 Horkheimer, 'Der Begriff der Seele seit Leibniz' [Lectures 1958], in *GS*, vol. 13, pp. 548–50.

30 Adorno, *Negative Dialectics* [1966], pp. 218, 220.

31 *Ibid.*, p. 225.

32 *Ibid.*, p. 241.

33 *Ibid.*, p. 231.

34 Ibid., p. 236. More precisely, against 'the fascist practice of making blind phenomena, men's membership or nonmembership in a designated race, the criteria of who was to be killed'. This was foreshadowed by the linguistic distortion of the concept of humanity, that is by the Nazi restriction of the concept in the term 'Aryan humanity'. For the latter see John Wesley Young, *Totalitarian Language* (Charlottesville, 1991), p. 107.

35 Adorno, *Negative Dialectics*, p. 283.

36 Horkheimer, 'Macht und Gewissen' [1962], in *GS*, vol. 7, p. 157.

37 Horkheimer, 'Kants Philosophie und die Aufklärung' [1962], in *ibid.*, p. 170.

38 Horkheimer, 'Materialism and morality', pp. 36–7.

39 Arthur Schopenhauer, *The World as Will and Representation* (New York, 1969), vol. 2, p. 600.

40 Horkheimer, 'Schopenhauer today' [1961], in *Critique of Instrumental Reason*, p. 88.

41 Horkheimer, *GS*, vol. 14, p. 301.

42 Horkheimer, *Dawn and Decline* [1961–2], pp. 207–8.

43 Horkheimer, 'Der Planet – unsere Heimat' [1968], in *GS*, vol. 8, p. 322.

44 Erich Fromm, *Man for Himself. An Enquiry into the Psychology of Ethics* (London, 1949), p. 127.

45 *Ibid.*, p. 243.

46 *Ibid.*, p. 130.

47 For an example of the former see Herbert Marcuse, *An Essay on Liberation* [1969], pp. 87–9.

48 Marcuse, *Eros and Civilization*, p. 129.

49 Kant, *Critique of Judgement*, paragraph 59, p. 224.

50 Adorno, 'Whoever enjoys art concretely is banausic', *Ästhetische Theorie* [1970], *GS*, vol. 7, pp. 26–7.

51 ' ... the Beautiful seems to be "neutral" ... One can speak of the beauty of a fascist feat (Leni Riefenstahl has filmed it!)'; Marcuse, *The Aesthetic Dimension* [1978], p. 63.

52 Marcuse, *One Dimensional Man* [1964], p. 105.

53 *Ibid.*, p. 112.

54 Habermas, *Between Facts and Norms* [1992], pp. 113–14. See also 'Morality and ethical life: does Hegel's critique of Kant apply to discourse ethics?' [1986], in *Moral Consciousness and Communicative Action*, pp. 207–8.

55 Habermas, *Between Facts and Norms*, p. 30. The contrast between facticity and validity can be summed up as the distinction between the law prevailing and the law being valid, in the sense of legitimate.

56 Habermas, 'Postscript (1994)', in *ibid.*, pp. 452–3.

57 Habermas, 'Labor and interaction: remarks on Hegel's Jena *Philosophy of Mind*' [1967], in *Theory and Practice*, p. 150.

58 *Ibid.*, p. 151.

59 Habermas, *Legitimation Crisis* [1973], p. 108.

60 *Ibid.*, p. 113.

61 *Ibid.*, pp. 114, 117.

62 Habermas, 'Reconciliation through the use of reason: Remarks on John Rawls's political liberalism', *Journal of Philosophy*, 92 (1995), p. 125. See also 'Moral questions can in principle be decided ... in terms of *justice* or the generalizability of interests. Evaluative questions present themselves ... as issues of the *good life* (or of self-realization)'; 'Discourse ethics' [1983], in *Moral Consciousness and Communicative Action*, p. 108.

63 Habermas, *The Theory of Communicative Action* [1981], vol. 2, p. 109.

64 *Ibid.*, pp. 109–10.

65 Habermas, 'On the pragmatic, the ethical and the moral employments of practical reason' [1991], in *Justification and Application*, p. 12.

66 'My first response to the claims made in this passage is that they are simply false!'; Richard Bernstein, 'The revival of the democratic ethos', in Rosenfeld and Arato (eds), *Habermas on Law and Democracy*, p. 302.

67 Habermas, 'Reply to symposium participants' [1998], in *ibid.*, p. 387.

68 *Ibid.*, p. 385.

69 Habermas, 'Moral consciousness and communicative action' [1983], p. 120.

70 Habermas, 'Postscript' [1994], in *Between Facts and Norms*, p. 456.

71 Against the latter see Habermas, 'Kants Idee des ewigen Friedens – aus dem historischen Abstand von 200 Jahren' [1995], in *Die Einbeziehung des Anderen*, pp. 192–236.

72 Habermas, 'Citizenship and national identity' [1990], in *Between Facts and Norms*, pp. 511–12. He did allow that proximity justifies special obligations within families and neighbourhoods, *ibid*.

73 In an interesting argument Thomas McCarthy suggested that this brings Habermas close to Rawls; 'Kantian constructivism and reconstructivism: Rawls and Habermas in dialogue', *Ethics*, 105 (1994), pp. 44–63, especially pp. 56–7.

74 This is even more marked in *Between Facts and Norms*. See especially the comment in the Preface: 'If I scarcely mention the name of Hegel and rely more on the Kantian theory of law, this also expresses my desire to avoid a model that sets unattainable standards for us', p. x.

75 Habermas, 'Morality and ethical life' [1986], p. 203.

76 Horkheimer, 'Traditional and critical theory' [1937], pp. 199–205.

77 Habermas, 'Morality and ethical life', p. 203.

78 There are interesting echoes of Adorno and Horkheimer in Habermas's approval of moral standpoints which 'heed the prohibition of graven images, refrain from positive description, and . . . refer negatively to the damaged life instead of pointing affirmatively to the good life; *ibid.*, p. 205. For example, the subtitle of Adorno's *Minima Moralia* was *Reflections from Damaged Life*.

79 Habermas, 'Morality and ethical life', p. 206.

80 In this respect Wellmer's argument is similar to Horkheimer's. As Wellmer put it, unbending truthfulness 'would be harsher for the victims than for their persecutors'; Albert Wellmer, *The Persistence of Modernity* (Cambridge, 1991), p. 155. The figures of the dissident and the secret policeman in an authoritarian state clarify the point.

81 Habermas, *Between Facts and Norms*, pp. 253–86.

82 *Ibid.*, p. 255.

83 For example, if asked about commitment to career, public life and family, someone can respond by ranking each, by specifying amounts of time, money and so on to be devoted to each. It is not necessary, and would be regarded as perverse, to select one and dismiss the others. Responses to questions about commitment to something like equality before the law do not admit of such graduation.

84 Habermas, *Between Facts and Norms*, p. 260.

85 *Ibid.*, p. 266.

86 Habermas, 'Reply to symposium participants', p. 430. This follows in part from the principle of discourse ethics: 'Every valid norm would meet with the approval of all concerned if they could take part in a practical discourse'; 'Moral consciousness and communicative action', p. 121.

87 In the case of the repayment of debt, for example, one norm, that debts must be repaid, might appear to clash with another, that one should not abet criminal enterprise, assuming, that is, that there is some reason for supposing the repayment would have this effect. From Habermas's standpoint it would presumably be a question of deciding which norm was appropriate in the specific circumstances.

88 Quoted in Habermas, 'Morality and ethical life', p. 211.

89 Quoted in Habermas, *The Theory of Communicative Action*, vol. 2, p. 116.

90 *Ibid.*, vol. 1, p. 172.

91 *Ibid.*, p. 35.

92 Habermas, *Between Facts and Norms*, p. 166.

93 *Ibid.*, p. 121. This is clearer in the German edition where he referred to the attitude of a 'nutzenkalkulierenden und willkürlich entscheidenden Aktors'; Jürgen Habermas, *Faktizität und Geltung* (Frankfurt am Main, 1992), p. 154.

94 Habermas, 'On the pragmatic, the ethical and the moral employments of practical reason' [1991], p. 9.

95 Albert O. Hirschman, 'The concept of interest', in *Rival Views of the Market and Other Recent Essays* (New York, 1988), p. 53.

Chapter 11: Individual and Collective Identity

1   Quoted by David Roberts, *The Syndicalist Tradition and Italian Fascism* (Manchester, 1979), p. 201.
2   Adorno, *Negative Dialectics* [1966], p. 343.
3   *Ibid.* Translation modified, Adorno, *GS*, vol. 6, p. 336. The translation refers to 'barter society' where the original has *Tauschgesellschaft* and thereby glosses over the Marxist framework of Adorno's comments.
4   Adorno, *Negative Dialectics*, p. 341.
5   As Adorno put it in *Against Epistemology* [1956]: 'The idealists may call the conditions of the possibility of the life of consciousness, which have been abstracted out of it, transcendental. They still remain allotted to a determined and somehow "factual" life of consciousness', p. 226. For the centrality of the problem to German idealism see *Philosophische Terminologie II* [1962–3], p. 21.
6   Adorno, *Negative Dialectics*, p. 199.
7   As so often, Adorno effectively credited Hegel with this insight only to accuse him of having covered it up again. For the insight see *ibid.*, p. 161.
8   Marcuse, 'Philosophy and critical theory' [1937], p. 138.
9   Adorno, *Negative Dialectics*, p. 343. Translation amended, Adorno, *GS*, vol. 6, p. 337. See also Marcuse, 'Philosophy and critical theory', p. 139.
10 See for example, Horkheimer, 'Either–Or', in *Dawn and Decline* [1926–31], pp. 43-4 and 'Das Ansehen der person', in Horkheimer, *GS*, vol. 2, pp. 398–400. This is not included in *Dawn and Decline*, which is a partial translation of *Dämmerung*.
11 Horkheimer, 'Das Ansehen der Person', p. 399.
12 Marcuse, 'The affirmative character of culture' [1937], especially pp. 123–4; Löwenthal, 'Das Individuum in der individualistischen Gesellschaft. Bemerkungen über Ibsen', *ZfS*, 5 (1936), pp. 321–61.
13 Adorno and Horkheimer, *Dialectic of Enlightenment* [1944], p. 33.
14 *Ibid.*, p. 68. Odysseus, however, cannot resist blurting out his cunning and hence his reassertion of his identity brings him into danger.
15 *Ibid.*, p. 65.
16 Adorno, *Negative Dialectics*, p. 183.
17 *Ibid.*
18 Horkheimer, *Eclipse of Reason* [1947], p. 93.
19 Marcuse, *Counterrevolution and Revolt* [1972], pp. 61 and 68–9.
20 Similar laments can still be found, for example in a leading German newspaper: 'For the middle-class entrepreneur of the 1950s, who wanted to bequeath his concern to his children, it could seem quite natural to link business and family values. They still exist, but at the forefront of its development capitalism shows a different face. The holder of a share portfolio, in which the share certificates can be reshuffled like lightening according to the state of the market, no longer has "property" in any enduring sense.' *Die Zeit*, 5 November 1998.
21 Horkheimer, *Eclipse of Reason*, p. 140.
22 Adorno, 'Freudian theory and the pattern of fascist propaganda' [1951], p. 299.
23 Horkheimer, *GS*, vol. 12, pp. 452–3. The clarification offered by Christian Thies is extremely useful here; *Die Krise des Individuums*, pp. 111–12. This is consistent with Habermas's claim that the contemporary problem is one of a fragmentation of consciousness; *Theory of Communicative Action* [1981], vol. 2, p. 355.

24 Marcuse, *Eros and Civilization* [1955], pp. 78–9.

25 See, for example, Marcuse, 'Some social implications of modern technology', pp. 139–47; Adorno, *Erziehung zur Mündigkeit* (Frankfurt am Main, 1970), p. 144; Horkheimer, *Eclipse of Reason*, pp. 128–61.

26 Horkheimer, *Eclipse of Reason*, p.159.

27 Löwenthal, 'Sociology of literature in retrospect' [1981], in *Critical Theory and Frankfurt Theorists*, p. 121.

28 Löwenthal, 'Prophets of Deceit' [1949], in *False Prophets*, p. 129.

29 Adorno, 'The psychological techniques of Martin Luther Thomas' radio addresses' [1943], *GS*, vol. 9(1), p. 58.

30 Horkheimer, *Eclipse of Reason*, p. 117.

31 *Ibid.*, pp. 121–2.

32 Horkheimer, draft letter, *GS*, vol. 17, p. 295; Neumann, *Behemoth* [1942], p. 107. The draft letter was highly critical of Neumann, especially of his account of the ideological roots of National Socialism.

33 Marcuse, 'The new German mentality' [1942], in *Technology, War and Fascism*, pp. 141–90.

34 Horkheimer, 'Hinter der Fassade' [1959–60], *GS*, vol. 6, p. 303.

35 Adorno, 'Schuld und Abwehr' [1955], *GS*, vol. 9(2), pp. 121–324, here pp. 167–8, 201.

36 Adorno, 'Was bedeutet: Aufarbeitung der Vergangenheit' [1959], in *Erziehung zur Mündigkeit*, p. 12.

37 Horkheimer, 'Die Wahrheit des Nationalismus' [1957–1967], *GS*, vol. 14, p. 337. See also pp. 374–6.

38 Horkheimer, 'The German Jews' [1961], in *Critique of Instrumental Reason*, p. 110. On the nuances of this equivocation see Diner, 'Reason and the "other"', p. 359.

39 This was dated March 1969; Horkheimer, *GS*, vol. 14, p. 140. The strength of the nationalist NPD at the time is evidently significant. See letter of 5 May 1969, *GS*, vol. 18, pp. 722–4.

40 Habermas, 'Moral development and ego identity' [1976], p. 93.

41 Habermas, *The Theory of Communicative Action* [1981], vol. 2, p. 9.

42 Quoted in *ibid.*, p. 24.

43 *Ibid.*, p. 32.

44 *Ibid.*, p. 41.

45 *Ibid.*, p. 59.

46 *Ibid.*, p. 106.

47 *Ibid.*, p. 102.

48 Habermas, 'Apologetic tendencies' [1986], in *The New Conservatism*, p. 227. Translation modified, 'Apologetische Tendenzen', in *Eine Art Schadensabwicklung*, p. 135. See also Jürgen Habermas, 'Grenzen des Neohistorismus' (1989), in *Die nachholende Revolution* (Frankfurt am Main, 1990), p. 152.

49 Habermas, 'Die Hypotheken der Adenauerschen Restauration', [1994], in *Die Normalität einer Berliner Republik*, p. 95.

50 The first was the slogan in the Adenauer years that 'we are *all* democrats'; Habermas, 'Die zweite Lebenslüge der Bundesrepublik: Wir sind wieder "normal" geworden', in Siegfried Unseld (ed.), *Politik ohne Projekt?* (Frankfurt am Main, 1993), pp. 291–2.

51 The mood is well conveyed by Max Pensky, 'Universalism and the situated critic', in

Stephen K. White (ed.) *The Cambridge Companion to Habermas* (Cambridge, 1995), pp. 67–94.

52 For the broader significance of Auschwitz see Habermas, 'Historical consciousness and post-traditional identity' [1987], in *The New Conservatism*, pp. 251–2.

53 Habermas, 'Apologetic tendencies', pp. 226–7.

54 *Ibid.*, p. 227.

55 Jürgen Habermas, 'The European nation-state – its achievements and its limits', in G. Balakrishan (ed.), *Mapping the Nation* (London, 1996), p. 285.

56 *Ibid.*, p. 287. For some tensions in this see April Carter, 'Liberalism and the obligation to military service', *Political Studies*, 46 (1998), pp. 68–81.

57 Habermas, 'The European nation-state – its achievements and its limits', p. 285.

58 *Ibid.*, p. 286.

59 *Ibid.*, p. 289.

60 Quoted in Habermas, 'Inklusion – Einbeziehen oder Einschliessen?' [1997], in *Die Einbeziehung des Anderen*, p. 181.

61 *Ibid.*, p. 184.

62 *Ibid.*, p. 170.

63 *Ibid.*

64 Habermas, 'Historical consciousness and post-traditional identity', p. 251.

65 *Ibid.*

Conclusion

1   *Eine Art Schadensabwicklung*, p. 58.

2   Though this still did not suffice for Hans-Joachim Dahms, *Positivismusstreit* (Frankfurt am Main, 1994), pp. 402–3.

3   Habermas, 'Apologetic tendencies' [1986], in *The New Conservatism*, p. 227. Translation modified, 'Apologetische Tendenzen', in *Eine Art Schadensabwicklung*, p. 135.

4   For an earlier example, see William Leiss, 'Critical theory and its future', *Political Theory*, 2 (1974), pp. 330–49. For one firmly focused on Habermas, see Ricardo Blaug, 'Between fear and disappointment: critical, empirical and political uses of Habermas', *Political Studies*, 45 (1997), pp. 100–17.

5   Thus Wolfgang Bonss and Azel Honneth, 'Einleitung: Zur Reaktualisierung der Kritischen Theorie', in Bonss and Honneth (eds), *Sozialforschung als Kritik*, pp. 7–27.

6   Blaug, 'Between fear and disappointment', p. 102. See also John S. Dryzek, 'Critical theory as a research programme', in White (ed.), *The Cambridge Companion to Habermas*, pp. 97–119.

7   Habermas, 'Notes on the developmental history of Horkheimer's work' [1986], p. 73.

8   James Bohman, *Public Deliberation* (Cambridge, Mass., 1996) has taken this up through a consideration of the '*capacities* . . . citizens need to participate effectively as equals in public dialogue', p. 110.

9   Habermas, *Between Facts and Norms*, p. 113.

10 See, for example, Benhabib, *Critique Norm and Utopia* and William Rehg, *Insight and Solidarity* (Berkeley, 1997).

Select Bibliography

This bibliography lists the major works referred to in the text. For each author, items are listed in chronological order of the works cited and not in order of first publication.

Adorno, Theodor W., *Metakritik der Erkenntnistheorie*, Frankfurt am Main, 1956.

Adorno, Theodor W., *Kierkegaard*, Frankfurt am Main, 1962.

Adorno, Theodor W., *Drei Studien zu Hegel*, Frankfurt am Main, 1963.

Adorno, Theodor W., *Eingriffe*, Frankfurt am Main, 1963.

Adorno, Theodor W., *Ohne Leitbild. Parva Aesthetica*, Frankfurt am Main, 1967.

Adorno, Theodor W., 'Sociology and psychology II', *New Left Review*, **47** (1968), pp. 79–97.

Adorno, Theodor W., 'Is Marx obsolete?', *Diogenes*, **64** (1968), pp. 1–16.

Adorno, Theodor W. *et al.*, *The Authoritarian Personality*, New York, 1969.

Adorno, Theodor W., *Stichworte*, Frankfurt am Main, 1969.

Adorno, Theodor W., *Gesammelte Schriften*, Frankfurt am Main, 1970–.

Adorno, Theodor W., *Erziehung zur Mündigkeit*, Frankfurt am Main, 1970.

Adorno, Theodor W., *Soziologische Schriften I*, Frankfurt am Main, 1972.

Adorno, Theodor W. and Horkheimer, Max, *Dialectic of Enlightenment*, London, 1973.

Adorno, Theodor W., *Philosophische Terminologie*, 2 vols, Frankfurt am Main, 1973.

Adorno, Theodor W., *The Jargon of Authenticity*, London, 1973.

Adorno, Theodor W., *Negative Dialectics*, London, 1973.

Adorno, Theodor W., *Vorlesung zur Einleitung in die Soziologie*, Frankfurt am Main, 1973.

Adorno, Theodor W., *Minima Moralia*, London, 1974.

Adorno, Theodor W., *Noten zur Literatur*, Frankfurt am Main, 1974.

Adorno, Theodor W. and Krenek, Ernst, *Briefwechsel*, Frankfurt am Main, 1974.

Adorno, Theodor W., 'Subject and object', in Andrew Arato and Eike Gebhardt (eds), *The Essential Frankfurt School Reader*, Oxford, 1978, pp. 497–511.

Adorno, Theodor W., *In Search of Wagner*, London, 1981.

Adorno, Theodor W., *Prisms*, Cambridge, Mass., 1981.

Adorno, Theodor W., *Against Epistemology*, Oxford, 1982.

Alexander, Jeffrey, 'Habermas and critical theory', in Axel Honneth and Hans Joas (eds), *Communicative Action*, Cambridge, 1991, pp. 49–73.

Arato, Andrew and Gebhardt, Eike (eds), *The Essential Frankfurt School Reader*, Oxford, 1978.

Aly, Götz, 'The planning intelligentsia and the "final solution" ', in Michael Burleigh (ed.), *Confronting the Nazi Past*, London, 1996, pp. 140–53.

Ayer, A.J., *Part of My Life*, London, 1977.

Baier, A.C., *A Progress of Sentiments: Reflections on Hume's Treatise*, Cambridge, Mass., 1991.

Baker, Keith Michael, 'Defining the public sphere in eighteenth century France', in Craig Calhoun (ed.), *Habermas and the Public Sphere*, Cambridge, Mass., 1992, pp. 181–211.

Baumann, Zygmunt, *Modernity and the Holocaust*, Ithaca, 1989.

Beck, Ulrich, *Risk Society*, London, 1992.

Beller, Steven, 'Germans and Jews as central European and Mitteleuropäisch elites', in Peter Stirk, *Mitteleuropa*, Edinburgh, 1994, pp. 61–85.

Benhabib, Seyla, *Critique, Norm and Utopia*, New York, 1986.

Benjamin, Walter, *One Way Street*, London, 1979.

Bernstein, Richard J., *The Restructuring of Social and Political Theory*, Oxford, 1976.

Bernstein, Richard J., *The New Constellation*, Cambridge, Mass., 1992.

Bernstein, Richard J., 'The revival of the democratic ethos', in Michel Rosenfeld and Andrew Arato (eds), *Habermas on Law and Democracy*, Berkeley, 1998, pp. 287–305.

Blaug, Ricardo, 'Between fear and disappointment: critical, empirical and political uses of Habermas', *Political Studies*, 45 (1997), pp. 100–17.

Bohman, James, *New Philosophy of Social Science*, Cambridge, Mass., 1990.

Bohman, James, *Public Deliberation*, Cambridge, Mass., 1996.

Bonss, Wolfgang, 'Psychoanalyse als Wissenschaft und Kritik', in Wolfgang Bonss and Axel Honneth (eds), *Sozialforschung als Kritik*, Frankfurt am Main, 1982, pp. 367–425.

Bonss, Wolfgang and Honneth, Axel, 'Einleitung: Zur Reaktualisierung der Kritischen Theorie', in Wolfgang Bonss and Axel Honneth (eds), *Sozialforschung als Kritik*, Frankfurt am Main, 1982, pp. 7–27.

Bracher, Karl Dietrich, *The Age of Ideologies*, London, 1984.

Bronner, Stephen Eric, *Of Critical Theory and Critical Theorists*, Oxford, 1994.

Buck-Morss, Susan, *The Origin of Negative Dialectics*, Hassocks, 1977.

Burin, Frederic S. and Shell, Kurt L. (eds), *Politics, Law and Social Change. Selected Essays of Otto Kirchheimer*, New York, 1969.

Burston, David, *The Legacy of Erich Fromm*, Cambridge, Mass., 1991.

Caplan, Jane, *Government and Adminstration*, Oxford, 1988.

Carter, April, 'Liberalism and the obligation to military service', *Political Studies*, 46 (1998), pp. 68–81.

Critchley, Simon, *The Ethics of Deconstruction*, Oxford, 1992.

Cunow, Heinrich, *Die Marxsche Geschichts-, Gesellschafts- und Staatstheorie*, Berlin, 1923.

Dahl, Göran, 'Will "the other God" fail again? On the possible return of the conservative revolution', *Theory, Culture and Society*, 13 (1996), pp. 25–50.

Dahms, Hans-Joachim, *Positivismusstreit*, Frankfurt am Main, 1994.

233

Dallmayr, Fred R., 'Critical theory criticized: Habermas's *Knowledge and Human Interests* and its aftermath', *Philosophy of the Social Sciences*, 2 (1972), pp. 211–29.

Dallmayr, Fred R., 'Phenomenology and critical theory', *Cultural Hermeneutics*, 3 (1976), pp. 367–405.

Dews, Peter (ed.), *Autonomy and Solidarity*, London, 1992.

Dews, Peter, *The Limits of Disenchantment*, London, 1995.

Diner, Dan, 'Reason and the "other": Horkheimer's reflections on anti-semitism and mass annihilation', in S. Benhabib *et al.* (eds), *On Max Horkheimer*, Cambridge, Mass., 1993, pp. 335–63.

Dryzek, John S., 'Critical theory as a research programme', in Stephen K. White (ed.), *The Cambridge Companion to Habermas*, Cambridge, 1995, pp. 97–119.

Dubiel, Helmut, *Wissenschaftsorganisation und politische Erfahrung*, Frankfurt am Main, 1978.

Dubiel, Helmut, 'Demokratie und Kapitalismus bei Herbert Marcuse', in Institut für Sozialforschung (ed.), *Kritik und Utopie im Werk von Herbert Marcuse*, Frankfurt am Main, 1992, pp. 61–73.

Dux, Günter, 'Communicative reason and interest', in Axel Honneth and H. Joas (eds), *Communicative Action*, Cambridge, 1991, pp. 74–91.

Erd, Rainer (ed.), *Reform oder Resignation. Gespräche über Franz Neumann*, Frankfurt am Main, 1985.

Evans, Richard J., *In Hitler's Shadow*, London, 1989.

Flego, G., 'Erotisieren statt sublimieren', in Institut für Sozialforschung (ed.), *Kritik und Utopie im Werk von Herbert Marcuse*, Frankfurt am Main, 1992, pp. 187–200.

Fleming, Marie, 'Women and the "public use of reason"', in Johanna Meehan (ed.) *Feminists Reading Habermas*, New York, 1995, pp. 117–37.

Fraenkel, Ernst, *The Dual State*, Oxford, 1941.

Frei, Nobert, 'Wie modern war der Nationalsozialismus', *Geschichte und Gesellschaft*, 19 (1993), pp. 367–87.

Freud, Sigmund, *Civilization and its Discontents*, London, 1975.

von Friedeburg, Ludwig and Habermas, Jürgen (eds), *Adorno-Konferenz*, Frankfurt am Main, 1983.

Fromm, Erich, *The Fear of Freedom*, London, 1942.

Fromm, Erich, *Man for Himself*, New York, 1947.

Fromm, Erich, *Man for Himself. An Enquiry into the Psychology of Ethics*, London, 1949.

Fromm, Erich, *The Sane Society*, London, 1963.

Fromm, Erich, *The Crisis of Psychoanalysis*, Harmondsworth, 1973.

Gellner, Ernest, 'Enlightenment – yes or no?', in Jozef Niznik and John T. Sanders (eds), *Debating the State of Philosophy*, Westport, 1996, pp. 77–84.

Geyer, Michael, 'The state in National Socialist Germany', in C. Bright and S. Harding (eds), *State Making and Social Movements*, New York, 1984, pp. 193–232.

Giddens, Anthony, *Modernity and Self-Identity*, Cambridge, 1991.

Görlich, Bernard, 'Sublimierung als kulturelles Triebschicksal', in Institut für Sozialforschung (ed.), *Kritik und Utopie im Werk von Herbert Marcuse*, Frankfurt am Main, 1992, pp. 171–86.

Grossmann, Henryk, *Das Akkumulations- und Zusammenbruchgesetz des kapitalistischen Systems*, Leipzig, 1929.

Günther, Klaus, 'Communicative freedom, communicative power and jurisgenesis', in

Michel Rosenfield and Andrew Arato (eds), *Habermas on Law and Democracy*, Berkeley, 1998, pp. 234–54.

Habermas, Jürgen, *Theorie und Praxis*, Neuwied, 1963.

Habermas, Jürgen, 'Towards a theory of communicative competence', *Inquiry*, **13** (1970), pp. 360–75.

Habermas, Jürgen, *Towards a Rational Society*, London, 1971.

Habermas, Jürgen, *Knowledge and Human Interests*, London, 1972.

Habermas, Jürgen, 'A postscript to *Knowledge and Human Interests*', *Philosophy of Social Sciences*, **3** (1973), pp. 157–89.

Habermas, Jürgen, *Theory and Practice*, London, 1974.

Habermas, Jürgen, 'Habermas talking: an interview', *Theory and Society*, **1** (1974), pp. 37–58.

Habermas, Jürgen, 'A positivistically bisected rationalism', in Theodor W. Adorno *et al.*, *The Positivist Dispute in German Sociology*, London, 1976, pp. 198–225.

Habermas, Jürgen, 'Some distinctions in universal pragmatics', *Theory and Society*, **33** (1976), pp. 155–67.

Habermas, Jürgen, *Zur Rekonstruktion des historischen Materialismus*, Frankfurt am Main, 1976.

Habermas, Jürgen, *Legitimation Crisis*, London, 1976.

Habermas, Jürgen, 'History and evolution', *Telos*, **39** (1979), pp. 5–44.

Habermas, Jürgen, *Communication and the Evolution of Society*, London, 1979.

Habermas, Jürgen, *Kleine Politische Schriften I-IV*, Frankfurt am Main, 1981.

Habermas, Jürgen, 'Modernity and postmodernity', *New German Critique*, **22** (1981), pp. 3–14.

Habermas, Jürgen, 'A reply to my critics', in John B. Thompson and David Held (eds), *Habermas. Critical Debates*, London, 1982, pp. 219–83.

Habermas, Jürgen, *Philosophical-Political Profiles*, London, 1983.

Habermas, Jürgen, *Vorstudien und Ergänzungen zur Theorie des kommunikativen Handelns*, Frankfurt am Main, 1984.

Habermas, Jürgen, *Observation on 'The Spiritual Situation of the Age'*, Cambridge, Mass., 1985.

Habermas, Jürgen, *The Theory of Communicative Action*, vol. 1, London, 1984; vol. 2, Cambridge, 1987.

Habermas, Jürgen, *Zur Logik der Sozialwissenschaften*, Frankfurt am Main, 1985.

Habermas, Jürgen, *Die neue Unübersichtlichkeit*, Frankfurt am Main, 1985.

Habermas, Jürgen, 'Psychic Thermidor and the rebirth of rebellious subjectivity', in Richard J. Bernstein (ed.), *Habermas and Modernity*, Cambridge, 1985, pp. 67–77.

Habermas, Jürgen, *The Philosophical Discourse of Modernity*, Cambridge, 1987.

Habermas, Jürgen, *Eine Art Schadensabwicklung*, Frankfurt am Main, 1987.

Habermas, Jürgen, *Nachmetaphysisches Denken*, Frankfurt am Main, 1988.

Habermas, Jürgen, *On the Logic of the Social Sciences*, Cambridge, 1988.

Habermas, Jürgen, *Structural Transformation of the Public Sphere*, Cambridge, 1989.

Habermas, Jürgen, *Moral Consciousness and Communicative Action*, Cambridge, 1990.

Habermas, Jürgen, *Die nachholende Revolution*, Frankfurt am Main, 1990.

Habermas, Jürgen, *Texte und Kontexte*, Frankfurt am Main, 1991.

Habermas, Jürgen, *Erläuterungen zur Diskursethik*, Frankfurt am Main, 1991.

Habermas, Jürgen, 'A reply', in Axel Honneth and H. Joas (eds), *Communicative Action*, Cambridge, 1991, pp. 214–64.

Habermas, Jürgen, *Faktizität und Geltung*, Frankfurt am Main, 1992.

Habermas, Jürgen, *Postmetaphysical Thinking*, Cambridge, 1992.

Habermas, Jürgen, *Justification and Application*, Cambridge, 1993.

Habermas, Jürgen, 'Notes on the developmental history of Horkheimer's work', *Theory, Culture and Society*, 10 (1993), pp. 61–77.

Habermas, Jürgen, 'Die zweite Lebenslüge der Bundesrepublik: Wir sind wieder "normal" geworden', in Siegfried Unseld (ed.), *Politik ohne Projekt?*, Frankfurt am Main, 1993, pp. 283–97.

Habermas, Jürgen, *The Past as Future*, London, 1994.

Habermas, Jürgen, *Die normalität einer Berliner Republik*, Frankfurt am Main, 1995.

Habermas, Jürgen, 'On the internal relation between the rule of law and democracy', *European Journal of Philosophy*, 3 (1995), pp. 12–20.

Habermas, Jürgen, 'Reconciliation through the public use of reason: remarks on John Rawls's political liberalism', *Journal of Philosophy*, 92 (1995), pp. 109–31.

Habermas, Jürgen, *Between Facts and Norms. Contributions to a Discourse Theory of Law and Democracy*, Cambridge, 1996.

Habermas, Jürgen, 'Modernity: an unfinished project', in M.P. D'Entreves and S. Benhabib (eds), *Habermas and the Unfinished Project of Modernity*, Cambridge, 1996, pp. 38–55.

Habermas, Jürgen, 'An interview with Jürgen Habermas', *Theory, Culture and Society*, 13(3) (1996), pp. 1–17.

Habermas, Jürgen, 'Coping with contingencies – the return of historicism', in Jozef Niznik and John T. Sanders (ed.), *Debating the State of Philosophy*, Westport, 1996, pp. 1–24.

Habermas, Jürgen, 'The European nation-state – its achievements and its limits', in G. Balakrishan (ed.), *Mapping the Nation*, London, 1996, pp. 281–94.

Habermas, Jürgen, *Die Einbeziehung des Anderen*, Frankfurt am Main, 1997.

Habermas, Jürgen, 'Reply to symposium participants', in Michel Rosenfeld and Andrew Arato (eds), *Habermas on Law and Democracy*, Berkeley, 1998, pp. 381–452.

Habermas, Jürgen, 'Die postnationale Konstellation und die Zukunft der Demokratie', in *Blätter für Deutsche Internationale Politik*, 7 (1998), pp. 804–17.

Hanfling, O., *Logical Positivism*, Oxford, 1981.

Hartmann, Nicolai, *Ethics*, vol. 2, London, 1932.

Hayek, F.A., *The Constitution of Liberty*, London, 1960.

Hegel, G.W.F., *Hegel's Science of Logic*, London, 1969.

Hegel, G.W.F., *Hegel's Logic*, Oxford, 1975.

Hegel, G.W.F., *Phenomenology of Spirit*, Oxford, 1977.

Heidegger, Martin, *Being and Time*, Oxford, 1978.

Herbst, Ludolf, 'Die nationalsozialistische Wirtschaftspolitik im internationalen Vergleich', in W. Benz *et al.* (eds), *Der Nationalsozialismus*, Frankfurt am Main, 1993, pp. 153–76.

Hirschman, Albert O., *Rival Views of the Market and Other Recent Essays*, New York, 1988.

Hohendahl, Peter Uwe, *Reappraisals. Shifting Alignments in Postwar Critical Theory*, Ithaca, 1991.

Holub, Robert C., *Jürgen Habermas. Critic in the Public Sphere*, London, 1991.

Honneth, Axel, 'Sociological deficit of critical theory', in Seyla Benhabib *et al.* (eds), *On Max Horkheimer*, Cambridge, Mass., 1993, pp. 187–214.

Horkheimer, Max, 'Sociological background to the psychoanalytic approach', in Ernst Simmel (ed.), *Anti-Semitism: A Social Disease*, New York, 1946, pp. 1–10.

Horkheimer, Max, 'Ernst Simmel and Freudian philosophy', *International Journal of Psychoanalysis*, 29 (1948), pp. 110–13.

Horkheimer, Max, 'The lessons of fascism', in Hadley Cantril (ed.), *Tensions that Cause Wars*, Urbana, 1950, pp. 209–42.

Horkheimer, Max, *Critical Theory*, New York, 1972.

Horkheimer, Max, *Critique of Instrumental Reason*, New York, 1974.

Horkheimer, Max, *Dawn and Decline*, New York, 1978.

Horkheimer, Max, 'The authoritarian state', in Andrew Arato and Eike Gebhardt (eds), *The Essential Frankfurt School Reader*, Oxford, 1978, pp. 95–117.

Horkheimer, Max, *Gesammelte Schriften*, Frankfurt am Main, 1985–96.

Horkheimer, Max, 'The Jews and Europe', in Stephen Eric Bronner and Douglas MacKay Kellner (eds), *Critical Theory and Society*, London, 1989, pp. 77–94.

Horkheimer, Max, *Between Philosophy and Social Science*, Cambridge, Mass., 1993.

Hoy, David C. and McCarthy, Thomas, *Critical Theory*, Oxford, 1994.

Hume, David, *A Treatise of Human Nature, Books Two and Three*, London, 1972.

Husserl, Edmund, *The Crisis of the European Sciences and Transcendental Phenomenology*, Evanston, 1970.

Hyman, H., 'Eros and freedom: the critical psychology of Herbert Marcuse', in Robert Pippin *et al.*, *Marcuse. Critical Theory and the Promise of Utopia*, South Hadley, Mass., 1988, pp. 143–66.

Institut für Sozialforschung, *Zeitschrift für Sozialforschung*, Leipzig/Paris/New York, 1932–41.

Institut für Sozialforschung, *Studien über Autorität und Familie*, Paris, 1936.

Institut für Sozialforschung (ed.), *Kritik und Utopie im Werk von Herbert Marcuse*, Frankfurt am Main, 1992.

Internationale Erich Fromm-Gesellschaft (ed.), *Erich Fromm und die kritische Theorie*, Münster, 1991.

Jameson, Frederic, *Late Marxism*, London, 1996.

Janik, Alan and Toulmin, Stephen, *Wittgenstein's Vienna*, New York, 1973.

Jarvis, Simon, *Adorno*, Cambridge, 1998.

Jay, Martin, *Dialectical Imagination. A History of the Frankfurt School and the Institute of Social Research, 1923–1950*, Boston, 1973.

Johach, Helmut, 'Erich Fromm und die Kritische Theorie des Subjekts', in Internationale Erich Fromm-Gesellschaft (ed.), *Erich Fromm und die Kritische Theorie*, 1991, pp. 33–53.

Jouvenal, Bertrand de, *Power*, London 1947.

Ingram, David, *Habermas and the Dialectic of Reason*, New Haven, 1987.

Kant, Immanuel, *Critique of Pure Reason*, London, 1933.

Kant, Immanuel, *Critique of Judgement*, Oxford, 1952.

Katz, Barry, *Herbert Marcuse. Art of Liberation*, London, 1982.

Katz, Barry, 'The criticism of arms: the Frankfurt School goes to war', *Journal of Modern History*, 59 (1987), pp. 439–78.

Keat, Russell, *The Politics of Social Theory*, Oxford, 1981.

Kellner, Douglas, *Herbert Marcuse and the Crisis of Marxism*, Basingstoke, 1984.

237

Kellner, Douglas (ed.), *Technology, War and Fascism*, London, 1998.

Kershaw, Ian, *Hitler 1889–1936*, London, 1998.

Kettner, Matthias, 'Karl-Otto Apel's contribution to critical theory', in David M. Rasmussen (ed.), *Handbook of Critical Theory*, Oxford, 1996, pp. 258–86.

Kirchheimer, Otto and Rusche, Georg, *Punishment and Social Structure*, New York, 1939.

Kirchheimer, Otto, *Political Justice*, Princeton, 1961.

Kirchheimer, Otto, *Funktionen des Staats und der Verfassung*, Frankfurt am Main, 1972.

Kirchheimer, Otto, *Von der Weimarer Republik zum Faschismus*, Frankfurt am Main, 1976.

Kluke, Paul, *Die Stiftungsuniversität Frankfurt am Main*, Frankfurt am Main, 1972.

Kocka, Jürgen, 'The European pattern and the German case', in Jürgen Kocka and Allen Mitchell (eds), *Bourgeois Society in Nineteenth-Century Europe*, Oxford, 1993, pp. 3–39.

König, Hans-Dieter, 'Autoritarismus und Konsumsteuerung', in Institut für Sozialforschung (ed.), *Kritik und Utopie im Werk von Herbert Marcuse*, Frankfurt am Main, 1992, pp. 217–46.

Kortian, Garbis, *Metacritique*, Cambridge, 1980.

Leiss, William, 'Critical theory and its future', *Political Theory*, 2 (1974), pp. 330–49.

Leoni, Bruno, *Freedom and the Law*, Indianapolis, 1991.

Loewenstein, Karl, 'Militant democracy and fundamental rights', *Amercan Political Science Review*, 31 (1937), pp. 417–32, 638–58.

Löwenthal, Leo, *Mitmachen wollte ich nie*, Frankfurt am Main, 1980.

Löwenthal, Leo, *False Prophets*, New Brunswick, 1987.

Löwenthal, Leo, *Critical Theory and Frankfurt Theorists*, New Brunswick, 1989.

Löwith, Karl, *Martin Heidegger and European Nihilism*, New York, 1995.

Lukacs, Georg, *History and Class Consciousness*, London, 1971.

McCarthy, Thomas, *The Critical Theory of Jürgen Habermas*, London, 1978.

McCarthy, Thomas, 'Kantian constructivism and reconstructivism: Rawls and Habermas in dialogue', *Ethics*, 105 (1994), pp. 44–63.

Maier, Charles S., *Recasting Bourgeois Europe*, Princeton, 1975.

Maier, Charles S., *The Unmasterable Past*, London, 1997.

Maier, Josef, *On Hegel's Critique of Kant*, New York, 1966.

Marcuse, Herbert, 'Zur Wahrheitsproblematik der soziologischen Methode', *Die Gesellschaft*, 6 (1929), pp. 356–69.

Marcuse, Herbert, *Reason and Revolution*, London, 1955.

Marcuse, Herbert, 'Obsolescence of Marxism', in Nikolaus Lobkowicz (ed.), *Marx and the Western World*, Notre Dame, 1967, pp. 409–17.

Marcuse, Herbert, *One Dimensional Man*, London, 1968.

Marcuse, Herbert, 'Repressive tolerance', in Herbart Marcuse *et al.*, *A Critique of Pure Tolerance*, Boston, 1968, pp. 81–117.

Marcuse, Herbert, *Negations*, Harmondsworth, 1968.

Marcuse, Herbert, *An Essay on Liberation*, Boston, 1969.

Marcuse, Herbert, *Eros and Civilization*, London, 1969.

Marcuse, Herbert, 'Contributions to a phenomenology of historical materialism' [1928], *Telos*, 4 (Fall 1969), pp. 3–34.

Marcuse, Herbert, 'Re-examination of the concept of revolution', *New Left Review*, 56 (1969), pp. 27–34.

Marcuse, Herbert, *Five Lectures*, London, 1970.

Marcuse, Herbert, *Soviet Marxism*, Harmondsworth, 1971.

Marcuse, Herbert, *Studies in Critical Philosophy*, London, 1972.

Marcuse, Herbert, *The Aesthetic Dimension*, New York, 1978.

Marcuse, Herbert, *Schriften*, vol. 1, Frankfurt am Main, 1978.

Marcuse, Herbert, *Ideen zu einer Kritischen Theorie der Gesellschaft*, Frankfurt am Main, 1978.

Marcuse, Herbert, 'Theory and politics', *Telos*, 38 (1978–9), pp. 124–53.

Marcuse, Herbert, 'The reification of the proletariat', *Canadian Journal of Political and Social Theory*, 3 (1979), pp. 20–3.

Marcuse, Herbert, 'Protosocialism and late capitalism', in Ulf Wolter (ed.), *Rudolf Bahro: Critical Responses*, White Plains, New York, 1980, pp. 24–48.

Marcuse, Herbert, *Technology, War and Fascism*, London, 1998.

Marx, Karl, *The Revolutions of 1848*, Harmondsworth, 1973.

Marx, Karl, *Grundrisse*, Harmondsworth, 1973.

Marx, Karl, *Early Writings*, Harmondsworth, 1975.

Marx, Karl, *Capital*, vol. 1, Harmondsworth, 1976.

Marx, Karl, and Engels, Frederick, *The German Ideology*, London, 1974.

Migdal, Ulrike, *Die Frühgeschichte des Frankfurter Instituts für Sozialforschung*, Frankfurt am Main, 1981.

Mommsen, Wolfgang, *Max Weber and German Politics*, Chicago, 1984.

Monk, Ray, *Ludwig Wittgenstein. The Duty of Genius*, London, 1991.

Mörchen, Hermann, *Macht und Herrschaft im Denken von Heidegger und Adorno*, Stuttgart, 1980.

Morrow, Raymond A., *Critical Theory and Methodology*, London, 1994.

Neumann, Franz, *Behemoth. The Structure and Practice of National Socialism*, London, 1942.

Neumann, Franz, 'The labor movement in Germany', in Hans J. Morgenthau (ed.), *Germany and the Future of Europe*, Chicago, 1951, pp. 100–7.

Neumann, Franz, *The Democratic and the Authoritarian State*, New York, 1957.

Neumann, Franz, 'The social significance of the basic laws in the Weimar constitution', *Economy and Society*, 10 (1981), pp. 329–47.

Neumann, Franz, *The Rule of Law*, Leamington Spa, 1986.

Neumann, Volker, 'Kompromiss oder Entscheidung', in Joachim Perels (ed.), *Recht, Pemokratie und Kapitalismus*, Baden-Baden, 1984, pp. 65–78.

Nichols, Christopher, 'Science or reflection: Habermas on Freud', *Philosophy of the Social Sciences*, 2 (1972), pp. 261–70.

Nunner-Winkkler, Gertrud, 'Knowing and wanting: on moral development in early childhood', in Axel Honneth *et al.* (eds), *Cultural-Political Interventions in the Unfinished Project of Enlightenment*, Cambridge, Mass., 1992, pp. 219–43.

Orr, J., 'German social theory and the hidden face of technology', *Archiv européene sociologie*, 15 (1974), pp. 321–36.

Outhwaite, William, *Habermas*, Cambridge, 1994.

Pensky, Max, 'Universalism and the situated critic', in Stephen K. White (ed.), *The Cambridge Companion to Habermas*, Cambridge, 1995, pp. 67–94.

Pollock, Friedrich, *Die planwirtschaftliche Versuche in der Sowjetunion 1917–1927*, Leipzig, 1929.

Popper, Karl, 'Reason or revolution?', in Theodor W. Adorno *et al.*, *The Positivist Dispute in German Sociology*, London, 1976, pp. 288–96.

Rabinbach, Anson, *In the Shadow of Catastrophe. German Intellectuals between Apocalypse and Enlightenment*, Berkeley, 1997.

Rawls, John, 'Reply to Habermas', *The Journal of Philosophy*, **92** (1995), pp. 132–80.

Rehg, William, *Insight and Solidarity*, Berkeley, 1997.

Rickert, John, 'The Fromm–Marcuse debate revisited', *Theory and Society*, **15** (1986), pp. 351–400.

Roberts, David, *The Syndicalist Tradition and Italian Fascism*, Manchester, 1979.

Rockmore, Tom, *Habermas on Historical Materialism*, Bloomington, 1989.

Rockmore, Tom, *On Heidegger's Nazism and Philosophy*, London, 1992.

Röpke, Wilhelm, 'Die säkulare Bedeutung der Weltkrisis', *Weltwirtschaftliches Archive*, **37** (1933), pp. 1–27.

Röttgers, Karl, *Kritik und Praxis*, Berlin, 1975.

Rose, Gillian, *The Melancholy Science*, London, 1978.

Royal Institute of International Affairs, *Survey of International Affairs 1931*, Oxford, 1932.

Scheuerman, William E., *Between the Norm and the Exception*, Cambridge, Mass., 1994.

Scheuerman, William E. (ed.), *The Rule of Law under Siege*, Berkeley, 1996.

Schivelbusch, Wolfgang, *Intellektuellendämmerung*, Frankfurt am Main, 1982.

Schlick, Moritz, *Problem of Ethics*, New York, 1962.

Schmid, Michael, 'Habermas's theory of social evolution', in John B. Thompson and David Held (eds), *Habermas. Critical Debates*, London, 1982, pp. 162–80.

Schmidt, Alfred, *The Concept of Nature in Marx*, London, 1971.

Schmidt, James, 'Habermas and Foucault', in Maurizio Passerin D'Entreves and Seyla Benhabib (eds), *Habermas and the Unfinished Project of Modernity*, Cambridge, 1996, pp. 147–71.

Schnädelbach, Herbert, *Philosophy in Germany 1831–1933*, Cambridge, 1984.

Schnädelbach, Herbert, 'Max Horkheimer and the moral philosophy of German idealism', *Telos*, **66** (1985–6), pp. 81–101.

Schnädelbach, Herbert, 'The transformation of critical theory', in Axel Honneth and Hans Joas (eds), *Communicative Action*, Cambridge, 1991, pp. 7–22.

Schnädelbach, Herbert, 'Remarks about rationality and language', in Seyla Benhabib and Fred Dallmayr (eds), *The Communicative Ethics Controversy*, Cambridge, Mass., 1991, pp. 270–92.

Scholem, Gershom, *Walter Benjamin*, London, 1982.

Schopenhauer, Arthur, *The World as Will and Representation*, New York, 1969.

Schrag, Calvin O., *The Resources of Rationality. A Response to the Postmodern Challenge*, Bloomington, 1992.

Schweitzer, A., 'Plans and markets, Nazi style', *Kyklos*, **30** (1977), pp. 88–115.

Siebert, Rudolf, 'Horkheimer's sociology of religion', *Telos*, **30** (1976), pp. 127–44.

Sokal, Alan and Bricament, Jean, *Intellectual Impostures*, London, 1998.

Söllner, Alfons, 'Politische Dialektik der Aufklärung', in Wolfgang Bonns and Axel Honneth (eds), *Sozialforschung als Kritik*, Frankfurt am Main, 1982, pp. 281–326.

Söllner, Alfons, 'Leftist students of the conservative revolution: Neumann, Kirchheimer and Marcuse', *Telos*, **61** (1984), pp. 55–70.

Söllner, Alfons, 'Jenseits von Carl Schmitt', *Geschichte und Gesellschaft*, **12** (1986), pp. 502–29.

Söllner, Alfons, 'Marcuse's political theory in the 1940s and 1950s', *Telos*, **74** (1987–8), pp. 65–78.

Spragens, Thomas A., *The Irony of Liberal Reason*, Chicago, 1981.

Stauth, Georg and Turner, Bryan S., 'Ludwig Klages (1872–1956) and the origins of critical theory', *Theory, Culture and Society*, **9** (1992), pp. 45–63.

Steger, Manfred B., *The Quest for Evolutionary Socialism*, Cambridge, 1997.

Steinmetz, George, 'German exceptionalism and the origins of Nazism', in Ian Kershaw and Moshe Lewin (eds), *Stalinism and Nazism. Dictatorships in Comparison*, Cambridge, 1997, pp. 251–84.

Stirk, Peter M.R., *Max Horkheimer: A New Interpretation*, Hemel Hempstead, 1992.

Stirk, Peter M.R., '*Eros and Civilization* revisited', *History of the Human Sciences*, **12** (1999), pp. 73–90.

Struve, Walter, *Elites Against Democracy. Leadership Ideals in Bourgeois Political Thought in Germany, 1890–1933*, Princeton, 1973.

Strydom, Piet, 'The ontogenetic fallacy: the immanent critique of Habermas's developmental logical theory of evolution', *Theory, Culture and Society*, **9** (1992), pp. 65–93.

Taylor, Charles, *Hegel*, Cambridge, 1975.

Temin, P., 'Soviet and Nazi economic planning in the 1930s', *Economic History Review*, **44** (1991), pp. 573–93.

Thies, Christian, *Die Krise des Individuums. Zur Kritik der Moderne bei Adorno und Gehlen*, Reinbek bei Hamburg, 1997.

Thompson, John B., 'Universal pragmatics', in John B. Thompson and David Held (eds), *Habermas. Critical Debates*, London, 1982, pp. 116–33.

Thompson, John B. and Held, David (eds), *Habermas. Critical Debates*, London, 1982.

Tilly, Charles, 'War making and state making as organized crime', in Peter B. Evans *et al.* (eds), *Bringing the State Back In*, Cambridge, 1985, pp. 169–91.

Timms, Edward, *Karl Kraus*, New Haven, 1986.

Wegerich, Ulrich, *Dialektische Theorie und historische Erfahrung*, Würzburg, 1994.

Wellmer, Albrecht, *The Persistence of Modernity*, Cambridge, 1991.

White, Stephen K., *The Recent Work of Jürgen Habermas*, Cambridge, 1988.

Whitebook, Joel, *Perversion and Utopia. A Study in Psychoanalysis and Critical Theory*, Cambridge, Mass., 1995.

Wiggershaus, Rolf, *The Frankfurt School*, Cambridge, 1994.

Williams, Howard, *Kant's Political Philosophy*, Oxford, 1983.

Wittgenstein, Ludwig, *Tractatus Logico-Philosophicus*, London, 1974.

Wolin, Richard, 'French Heidegger wars', in *The Heidegger Controversy*, Cambridge, Mass., 1993, pp. 272–300.

Young, John Wesley, *Totalitarian Language*, Charlottesville, 1991.

Zimmerman, Michael, *Heidegger's Confrontation with Modernity*, Bloomington, 1990.

Index

Abendroth, Wolfgang x, 26
Adler, Max 143
Adorno, Theodor W. ix, 1–5, 7, 8–11,
    18–19, 24–5, 27, 30–6, 41–2, 44, 51,
    57, 61, 91, 93, 96–7, 99–101, 103–4,
    110, 113, 115–21, 124–6, 127–9,
    134–5, 147, 152, 167, 171–2, 180,
    187
  concept of immanent critique 131–3
  concept of individuality 176–9, 181–3
  criticism of Heidegger 53–5, 55–6
  hostility to positivism 65–6, 68–70, 74
  on morality 160, 164, 167
  psychology and 79–80, 82–4, 86
amphiboly of reason 54, 200
anti-semitism 21–2, 81–3, 99, 180
Apel, Karl-Otto 135
Arendt, Hannah 157
Ayer, A.J. 62

Bataille, Georges 56, 58
Benjamin, Walter 7, 96, 193
Beck, Ulrich 104
Becker, Carl Heinrich 14–15
Bergson, Henri 41, 51
Bernstein, Eduard 161
Bernstein, Richard 122, 170
Bloch, Ernst 4
bourgeois society 3, 10–11, 93–110, 113,
    153, 156

communication 119–26, 135, 137–9, 158,
    190
  distorted 86–7, 89, 190, 216
Comte, Auguste 62, 74
Cornelius, Hans 18
cosmopolitanism 176, 180, 184, 186
critical theory 1, 5–8, 31–45, 205
  and methodology 11, 69–70, 127–8
  collective identity and 180–7
  and constitutional patriotism 183–4,
    189
  concept of identity and 6, 13, 89–91,
    94
  concept of individual and 6, 53, 101–5,
    107, 175–9, 181–3
  interdisciplinary character 5–6, 9, 17,
    40–2
  Marxism and 4, 5, 14–16, 28, 48–9,
    66–7, 69, 77–9, 93–4, 97, 100–2,
    107–10, 132–4, 142–3, 190–1
  ontology and 52
  see also metaphysics
critique 136–8, 218
  immanent critique 12, 33, 128–33,
    140–1, 149
Cunow, Heinrich 161

Dacqué, Edgar 51–2
democracy 22–4, 27, 143–4, 152–8,
    184–5

and civil disobedience 24, 154–5
Derrida, Jacques 47, 56, 58–60
Descartes, René 114
Dewey, John 66
Dews, Peter 60
Dilthey, Wilhelm 46, 48, 73, 81
Dregger, Alfred 27
Driesch, Hans 66–7
Durkheim, Émile 117, 173
Dux, Günter 155

Eder, Klaus 90
enlightenment 9, 56, 59
    Dialectic of Enlightenment 23–5, 28,
        93, 115–17, 177–8, 182–3
essence, concept of 65, 72, 131

Fichte, Johann Gottlieb 121
Foucault, Michel x, 56, 58–60
Frankfurt School
    and the public sphere 8, 16–17, 19, 20,
        29–30, 33–4
    generational gap 3, 28, 34, 39, 42,
        44–5, 60–1, 140–1
    Nazis and 64–5
    unity of 1–3, 27–8, 31–2, 59–61, 74–5,
        92, 141, 188–9, 216
Freud, Sigmund 3, 4, 25, 76–88, 91–2
Freyer, Hans 71
Fromm, Erich ix, 2, 3, 18, 20, 31, 36,
    166, 206, 208
    criticism of Marcuse 85
    ethics of 166
    social psychology of 76–8, 83–4

Gadamer, Hans-Georg 28
Gehlen, Arnold 24, 71, 204
Gerlach, Kurt Albert 15
Giddens, Anthony 6, 137
Grandi, Dino 175, 183
Grossmann, Henryk 15, 63, 98
Grünberg, Carl 15–16
Gumperz, Julian 20, 100
Gurland, Arkadij R.L. 101

Habermas, Jürgen ix–x, 2–6, 7, 8, 9, 10,
    11, 13, 24–31, 35, 40–4, 62, 94,
    105–11, 120–6, 128, 189–91
    Adorno and 57–60, 119, 124, 201

collective identity and 183–7
concept of individuality 181–3
concept of the lifeworld 38, 108–9,
    124, 214
criticism of Heidegger 24–5, 55–6
distinction between ethics and morality
    170–1
Horkheimer and x, 26, 59–60, 119,
    124, 202
neo-conservatism and 56–7
on law and power 12, 152–3, 158
on morality 167–74
on public sphere 37–8, 105–10, 140,
    152–8
on relation between theory and practice
    135–41
on scientization of politics 26, 38,
    71–2, 121, 140
positivism and 70–5, 121–2
psychology and 76, 85–92, 208
student radicals and 26–7
Hartmann, Nicolai 49–51, 199–200
Hayek, Friedrich A. 151
Hegel, Georg W.F. 31, 33–5, 42–3, 46–7,
    52, 54–5, 69–70, 110–13, 117, 125,
    128–30, 132, 134–6, 159–60, 171–2,
    174, 176–7, 201
Heidegger, Martin ix–xi, 4, 18, 24–5,
    47–9, 53–6, 58–9, 145, 200
Held, David 7
Hamsen, Knut x, 51
historians' dispute 28–9
Hobbes, Thomas 83, 189, 197
Horkheimer, Max x–xi, 1, 2, 3, 4, 5, 8, 9,
    17, 18–24, 32, 34–7, 39, 44, 61, 95,
    97–100, 110, 114–19, 124–6, 134,
    149–52, 171–2, 187, 189–90
    becomes Director of the Institute for
        Social Research 16
    concept of immanent critique 129–31,
        140–1
    concept of individual 177–9, 181–3
    criticism of new metaphysics 49–52
    differences with Habermas x, 26,
        59–60, 119, 124
    friendship with Pollock 16
    intended dialectical logic 21
    materialism 50, 127, 173

on morality 160–6
on the Soviet Union 149
on will and reason 40
positivism and 63–9, 74
psychological theories and 76–82
theory of rackets 146–8
Horney, Karen 80, 83
Hume, David 63, 119
Husserl, Edmund 8, 70, 114, 120, 131–2

idealism 31–2, 34, 39, 46, 49, 52–3, 112, 120, 131, 176–8, 183, 191
Institute for Social Research 188
closure by Nazis 1–2, 18
empirical studies 18–19, 21–2, 24, 69, 202–3
interpretation of the Nazi state 21, 99–102, 222
origins of 14–15
interests 12–13, 79, 87, 95, 98, 101, 106, 121, 149, 129–30, 160–2, 166–9, 173–4
inwardness, cult of 6, 72, 96, 102–6

James, William 66–7
Jay, Martin ix, 2, 7, 188
Jonas, Hans 56
Jünger, Ernst 51–2, 55

Kant, Immanuel 31, 33, 40–1, 44, 50, 53–4, 64, 67, 70, 85, 117, 118, 125–6, 128, 134, 159, 161–8, 171–5, 176–8, 190–1
Kierkegaard, Søren 8, 96
Kirchheimer, Otto x, 2, 3, 4, 19–20, 22–3, 31, 145, 149, 153
relationship with Carl Schmitt 143–4
criticism of Horkheimer's theory of rackets 147
on law in the Third Reich 148
on postwar democracy 150–2
Klages, Ludwig 46–7, 55, 117
Kocka, Jürgen 93–4
Kohlberg, Lawrence 88, 90–1
Korsch, Karl 4, 14, 128
Kraus, Karl 96

labour, concept of 35, 107–8, 117, 132, 136–8, 160

Landauer, Karl 76, 80
Laski, Harold xi, 20
Lebensphilosophie 10, 50, 56, 129, 189
Leoni, Bruno 151
Locke, John 63
Löwenthal, Leo x, 2, 3, 4, 10–11, 15, 17–18, 27, 30, 76, 94–5, 127–8, 149, 177
studies of demagogues 82, 179–80
Lotze, Rudolf 160
Luhmann, Niklas 28
Lukacs, Georg 4, 14, 37, 128, 132–3, 135, 197, 219
Lyotard, Jean François 47

Maier, Charles 142
Mannheim, Karl 16–17, 60, 143
Marcuse, Herbert xi, 2, 3, 4, 6, 8, 10, 11, 18, 22, 25, 34, 37, 44, 50, 96–8, 102, 131–2, 142, 145, 152, 176–7, 179, 182, 188
appropriation of Freud 84–7, 90, 92
criticism of positivism 62, 65, 70–1, 74
Hegelian concept of reason 11, 112–14, 134
influenced by Heidegger 47–9, 112, 134
on morality 163, 166–7, 226
on the Soviet Union 149
student radicals and 27
Marcuse, Ludwig 81
Marx, Karl 8, 32, 34–7, 62, 64, 69, 93–4, 117, 124, 130–2, 136–8, 160
Massing, Paul 149
Mayer, Hans 34
Marxism see critical theory, Marxism and
Mead, George Herbert 88, 182
metaphysics 46–62, 72, 83–4, 111, 165, 167
of history 39
Mill, John Stuart 153
modernity 4, 6, 43–4, 57, 111, 124–5, 211, 213
Montaigne, Michel E. 101
morality 12–13, 33, 64, 74, 91–2, 129–30, 159–74

neo-Aristotelianism 56, 172
neo-Kantianism 4–5, 31, 48

Neumann, Franz Leopold xi, 2, 3, 4,
    20–1, 22–3, 31, 36
  on primacy of politics 37
  on the rule of law 144–8
  on the nature of the Third Reich 146
  on postwar democracy 149–50
Neurath, Otto 62–5, 189
Nietzsche, Friedrich 57–8, 118, 160, 162,
    210
Nolte, Ernst 29
Nunner-Winkler, Gertrud 91

paralogism 54, 200
Peirce, Charles Sanders 72–3
Pensky, Max 5, 10
Peukert, Detlev 4
Piaget, Jean 88, 90
Pollock, Friedrich xi, 2, 3, 15–17, 21, 81,
    99–101, 142
Popper, Karl 26, 68–9, 204
positivism 10, 62–75, 111, 189, 203
  logical positivism 62–6, 72, 74, 98
positivist dispute 26, 68–70
post-modernism 9, 28, 58–60, 109
practice, concept of 32–4, 48, 64–5, 128,
    135–8, 143
pragmatism 66–7, 180–1
psychology 10, 36, 42, 76–92, 178–9

rackets 37, 180
  see also Horkheimer
Rawls, John 154–6
reason 11, 111–28
  motivation and 11, 121–2, 125–6,
    167–8, 190–1
relativism 8, 34, 111, 129
Riezler, Kurt 16, 18
Rousseau, Jean-Jacques 143–4, 151, 165,
    175
Rusche, George x, 19

Sade, Donatien A.F. de 83, 117–19
Schmidt, Fritz 16
Scheler, Max 49–50, 199

Schelsky, Helmut 35–6, 38, 71, 204
Scheuerman, William 151
Schiller, Johann C. F. 85
Schlick, Moritz 64, 72
Schmidt, Helmut 27
Schmitt, Carl x, 4, 12, 20, 55, 143–6,
    160, 197
Schnädelbach, Herbert 46, 50, 160, 162
Scholem, Gershom 99
Schopenhauer, Arthur 120, 165
Schumpeter, Joseph 154
Söllner, Alfons 102
Sombart, Werner 77
Spaeman, Robert 56
Spengler, Oswald 51
Steinfels, Peter 57
Stürmer, Michael 28–9
subject, concept of 39, 97–8, 112–13,
    158, 215

Tillich, Paul 16–17, 215
Tocqueville, Alexis de 153
totality, concept of 132–3, 140
Toulmin, Stephen 32
Toynbee, Arnold 142

utopianism 4, 9–10, 25, 151, 182

Vorländer, Karl 161

Wagner, Richard 51
Weber, Max 28, 95, 103, 107, 124–5,
    157, 173, 197–8, 210
Weil, Felix 14–16
Wellmer, Albrecht 57
Wiggershaus, Rolf 7
Wittfogel, Karl 7, 18, 193
Wittgenstein, Ludwig 68, 98–9

Young Hegelians 31, 43–5, 62, 111, 214

Zeitschrift für Sozialforschung 19–20, 25,
    63